Additional Praise for
Retire Secure!

"*Retire Secure!* is a very practical investment guide on how to defer taxes and efficiently plan for retirement and your estate."

> — Roger G. Ibbotson
> Professor, Yale School of Management
> Chairman, Ibbotson Associates

"In *Retire Secure!*, CPA and tax attorney James Lange provides clear guidance for understanding the process of making your money last during distribution. The author is an experienced advisor and it shows."

> — Phyllis Bernstein, CPA/PFS
> Former Director, AICPA Personal Financial Planning
> and Author of *Financial Planning for CPAs*

"Jim Lange's book is a must in the retirement library of anyone with a large IRA. Not only does it provide thorough coverage of a difficult topic, but it does so with crisp writing, surrounded with charts and tables to help you understand your options. I wholeheartedly recommend *Retire Secure!*

> — Robert S. Keebler
> CPA, MST, Author, Educator

"Everyone planning for retirement should read this book."

> — Dr. Allan Meltzer
> Political Economy Professor, Carnegie Mellon University

"Written for the sophisticated and successful lay person (and a great guide for professionals working in this field), *Retire Secure!* is like a master class in the subject with the instructor taking the student by the hand through each step of the process. Jim Lange, a practicing CPA and attorney, provides both key real-world questions and answers—as well as numerous examples, illustrations, and practical side-bar comments."

> — Stephan R. Leimberg
> CEO, Leimberg Information Services, Inc. (LISI)

"*Retire Secure!* shows how to maximize retirement income while explaining IRA and retirement plan rules in language you can understand (and that is no easy task). Every retiree should read James Lange's chapter on *Optimal Spending Strategies for Retirees*."

> — Gregory Kolojeski
> President, Brentmark Software

"There are few areas of financial planning more complex than making decisions about retirement plans. *Retire Secure!* not only explains many of these issues in plain English but Jim provides the reader with common sense guidance in making choices. As advocates of the important role that philanthropy plays in raising financially responsible children, we especially appreciate the inclusion of a chapter on charitable estate planning with IRA and retirement assets."

> — Eileen Gallo, Ph.D and Jon Gallo, J.D.
> Authors, *Silver Spoon Kids* and
> *The Financially Intelligent Parent*

"IRA and other retirement plan assets comprise a huge and growing component of so many people's wealth, yet the growth in these important assets requires sound, practical, and most important, understandable advice. All had been lacking until this excellent book, *Retire Secure!*, by James Lange. James brings to the fore practical tact usable by both attorney and accountant on how to deal with these critical assets. Topics that he delves into, including using trusts to protect beneficiaries are topics that few lay people are aware of and most professionals don't address. Protect yourself and your family with the insightful comments of *Retire Secure!*"

> — Martin M. Shenkman, Attorney
> Author, *Inherit More*

"Jim Lange has updated and improved his material in this fine book. We have always said that the planning comes before the doing. He tells you how to plan your retirement, to maximize your wealth and to minimize your taxes."

> — Garry D. Kinder, CLU, RFC
> Author, Lecturer and Financial Industry Consultant
> The KBI Group

"This new version of **Retire Secure!** shows you more great ideas to help you achieve the most important financial goal of your life. Make your money last and go further than you ever thought possible."

> — Brian Tracy, Speaker, Sales Trainer
> Author, *Getting Rich Your Own Way*

"Advisor James Lange has written the definitive up-to-the-minute guide for retirement planning. **Retire Secure!** is absolutely "essential" reading for all practitioners in the estate and retirement planning field, as well as for those brave souls who take this task on as a do-it-yourself project."

> — Jack Gargan, Founder
> International Association of Registered Financial Consultants
> Author, *The Complete Estate Planning Guide*

"The flexible *Lange's Cascading Beneficiary Plan* offers a practical solution to the bewildering array of qualified retirement options – many of which are improperly used. Jim's book makes a valuable contribution to the field of personal finance – for both the consumers and the professional advisors who serve them!"

> — Edwin P. Morrow, CLU, ChFC, CFP, CEP, RFC
> Chairman & CEO, International Association. of
> Registered Financial Consultants

"**Retire Secure!** should be in everyone's home who has money to invest. It is well written and in language that anyone can understand. I plan to make this book available for my children and grandchildren to read."

> — Frank Thomas
> Former Pittsburgh Pirate (286 home runs)

"If taxes were the only consideration in financial planning, I'd give James Lange, JD, CPA a one hundred percent grade! Every financial advisor ought to have a copy of *Retire Secure!* at his or her fingertips, plus copies to give more serious clients. After clients have been taught how to save and where to place their investments, James Lange's book is the definitive answer to the very important tax considerations."

> — Vernon D. Gwynne, CFP, RFC
> Chairman Emeritus & Former Director of Financial
> Planning Association

"*Retire Secure!* does a fine job of explaining why, when and how folks should move money into, out of, and between the myriad tax-advantaged employer-sponsored retirement savings plans and IRAs. The key points are summarized clearly, but a more thorough, equally clear explanation is also offered for those who want it. The book is well-organized, with plenty of practical examples. It will be a valuable resource to people in both the accumulation and distribution of their retirement assets—and to their advisors, as well."

> — Michael T. Palermo, Attorney, CFP
> Author, *AARP Crash Course in Estate Planning*

"Read this book before you meet with any tax or financial advisor about how to get the most out of your IRA, 401(k) or other retirement plans. *Retire Secure!* will help you ask the right questions and find out if your advisors really know what they're talking about."

> — Paul Merriman, Financial Educator
> Author, *Live It Up Without Outliving Your Money:*
> *Getting the Most from your Investments in Retirement*

"You've worked hard to build-up your retirement funds – now, finish the job and read the new edition of Lange's *Retire Secure!* You should carefully examine each of his main points, and take full advantage of his suggestions to stretch your money as long as possible before paying taxes. In these troubled times, Lange's ideas are particularly relevant."

> — John A. Tracy, Ph.D., CPA, Author
> *How to Read a Financial Report and Accounting For Dummies*

"Jim created the most flexible and effective estate guide for IRA and retirement plan owners."

> — Charles "Tremendous" Jones, RFC
> Author, *Life Is Tremendous*

"Jim has done a brilliant job making a complicated topic easy to understand. His "Case Studies" and "Key Ideas" in **Retire Secure!** are smart and spot on."

> — Bill Losey, CFP, Author
> *Retire in a Weekend! The Baby Boomer's Guide to Making Work Optional*

"James Lange is a genius at making the most difficult subject of estate/retirement planning easy to understand. His book is an absolute must for anyone who wants the peace of mind that comes from knowing they will retire secure."

> — Eleanor Schano
> Former TV News Anchor, Host *LifeQuest*
> (WQED Multimedia)

"Nice girls eventually become old women who want to retire. Let this book help you to ensure you have all the money you need to live your life the way you want in retirement."

> — Lois P. Frankel, Ph.D.
> Author, *Nice Girls Don't Get the Corner Office: Unconscious Mistakes Women Make That Sabotage Their Careers*

"A clear, concise, and well-written book that explains where and how to save for retirement so that you don't outlive your assets, pay too much in taxes, or have too little to pass on to your heirs. In non-technical terms, *James Lange* compares and contrasts various strategies for the accumulation, preservation, and the distribution of wealth. No one should invest in a retirement plan, or take a distribution from one, until he or she has first read **Retire Secure!**"

> — Gary S. Lesser, JD
> Author, *Roth IRA Answer Book*

"Jim Lange is a clear and concise communicator. He takes the complicated and makes it simple. *Retire Secure!* is a must read for anyone wanting a secure financial future."

> — Diane L. McCurdy, CFP
> Author, *How Much is Enough?*

"*Retire Secure!* is the most well-written explanation of why maximizing the use of your retirement accounts, both tax-deferred and tax-free, will help you to retire with as much financial security as possible. Every serious individual investor should read this book!"

> — James M. Dahle, MD
> Author, *The White Coat Investor: A Doctor's Guide to Personal Finance and Investing*

"Whether you are an individual planning for, or in, retirement, or a financial advisor, Jim Lange's *Retire Secure!* is a must read. The book, while addressing complex issues, is written in plain, simple language.

It also provides many concrete examples of how the recommendations can be implemented. This book belongs in everyone's library to be referred to over and over again."

> — Larry Swedroe,
> Director of Research of the BAM ALLIANCE
> Author, *The Incredible Shrinking Alpha and Reducing the Risk of Black Swans*

RETIRE SECURE!

THIRD EDITION

RETIRE SECURE!

A GUIDE TO GETTING THE MOST OUT OF WHAT YOU'VE GOT

JAMES LANGE
CPA / ATTORNEY

Cartoons by Michael McParlane.

Contents

Part One
The Accumulation Years: The Best Way to Save for Retirement

Part Two

The Distribution Years: Spend the Right Funds First and Other Critical Decisions You Face in Retirement   79

4.   Optimal Spending Strategies for Retirees   81

5.   Required Minimum Distribution Rules   95

6. **Should You Transfer Your 401(k) to an IRA at Retirement?**   **109**

7. Roth Conversions   137

Part Four

Foreword

I can't remember a time when people were more worried about their economic future. The potholes on Wall Street and Main Street are big enough to swallow a car, and people are anxiously looking for a safe route to protect what they have. If you are looking for a guidance system that will help you take control of your financial future and protect your family, this book is it. Think of *Retire Secure!* as a GPS for your money. You may know where you are and where you want to go, but you don't know how to get there. Jim offers the best routes.

Jim's work has been time tested and vetted by the best in the business. He doesn't just speculate, he "runs the numbers," and all of his recommendations are backed up by real world results.

If you follow Jim's strategies, you are sure to get the most out of your IRAs and retirement plans. Whether you are still working, preparing to retire, or have already retired, this book will point you in the right direction. Jim also helps you chart a course for your family after you are gone, with an estate plan that offers great flexibility. The advice and recommendations in *Retire Secure!* will be particularly beneficial for those approaching retirement or already retired. Those individuals have the least amount of time to make up market losses, and strategic planning is critical. If you are among that constituency, this book is definitely for you.

What about short-term planning? Wouldn't you like to save taxes and keep more money for yourself? What about taking advantage of Roth IRA conversions now or in 2015? A Roth IRA conversion could save you tens of thousands of dollars and could provide an additional million dollars or more to your children and grandchildren. If this piques your curiosity, the answers are inside this book.

Read *Retire Secure!* and learn how Jim's strategies can work for you. Then get additional advice if you think you need it. As Jim points out, too many people go it alone and miss out on many opportunities. The information in this book will help you recognize a good advisor, and you will definitely bring great ideas to the table.

So don't just try to avoid the potholes. Take control, and find a really good route to follow. Use Jim's advice to minimize wrong turns and detours as you travel the road to a comfortable and secure retirement.

— Larry King

Acknowledgments

Though my name is listed as author, the genuine truth is that this book is really a monumental team effort. I and the readers that find value in these pages are indebted to a team of the best CPAs, attorneys, financial planners, writers and other professionals that I could possibly hope to work with.

Steven T. Kohman, Certified Public Accountant, Certified Specialist in Retirement Planning, Certified Specialist in Estate Planning, has worked with me for over 19 years and has co-authored many articles with me. Steve is a skilled number cruncher and combines his extensive tax background with his superb quantitative and computer skills. Steve's quantitative analysis, evidenced in the graphs and charts throughout the book, presents compelling proof of the fundamental concepts that make up the backbone of *Retire Secure!* His extensive writing and analysis in the area of IRAs, Roth IRA conversions, and life insurance make the third edition of this book even more valuable than the first two editions. He also has mentored two former "junior number crunchers" who have reached senior number cruncher status, Carol Palmer and Shirl Trefelner, CPA, both of whom have made major contributions to the book.

Matt Schwartz, Esq., is an exceptionally bright and gifted IRA and estate attorney who has worked with me for 12 years. I am proud to have him as a colleague. While most readers and clients don't really care where someone went to school and what they majored in, the fact that Matt went to Northwestern and graduated with a Math degree is actually quite significant to the work he does now. It is rare to get a quantitative attorney working to help readers and clients have a better and richer life by developing retirement and estate planning strategies by understanding the numbers. But that is only part of what Matt does. The other part is to implement the strategies we come up with by drafting and implementing our recommended planning solutions.

Carol Palmer has made major contributions to the third edition. She possesses a rare combination of talents that make her perfect for her role in updating and improving the book. She is a skilled tax preparer and after Steve's mentoring, a skilled "numbers runner," and a fine writer and editor. Finally, she is a joy to work with and possesses a wicked sense of humor. Like the time she found a mistake in Steve's analysis and boldly proclaimed "Kohman is going down."

Shirl Trefelner, CPA also had a major hand in the quantitative analysis of this edition of *Retire Secure!* Shirl is seasoned tax preparer and now a valued "number cruncher." Shirl also loves to find mistakes that Steve made, but unfortunately for her, the mistakes almost always turn out to be differences in the assumptions made rather than a mistake in the analysis.

Cynthia Nelson has been working with me for over 17 years. During this period, she has had full editing and writing responsibilities for virtually all my published works. She is a rare find. She cuts through some of the technical and legal jargon that I sometimes fall into and expresses complex thoughts in a way the lay reader can understand. She also allows me to express my humanity, and she adds touches of her own that make reading the book a better experience.

Special thanks to Larry King. Your Foreword adds sizzle.

I also want to thank all the readers and reviewers of *Retire Secure!* Special thanks go to Charles Schwab and Ed Slott, both of whom provided insight and suggestions for the original manuscript. Many more of my colleagues and peers offered thoughtful testimonials. I have included as many as I could. Your support means more to me than I can adequately express.

I also want to thank Ed Slott for writing such a thoughtful Introduction.

I must also convey my gratitude to my full-time coworkers (in addition to Steve and Matt) who provide so much help in my practice that without them the book could never have been written: Glenn Venturino, CPA (how can I properly thank you for 27 years of superb service to our clients); Sandy Proto, our office manager (without Sandy the office would cease to function); Karen Mathias, Esq., a true utility player with multiple roles in our company (tax return preparation, drafting of wills and trusts and our resident Social Security expert); Alice Davis, who is so wonderful and personable with our clients; Donna Master, who keeps my books, which would certainly be a shambles without her dedicated precision; and Daryl Ross, our legal administrative assistant/master tax return compiler who rolls up her sleeves and gets it done year after year. Special thanks to my marketing director, Amanda Cassady-Schweinsberg, who has helped with the legwork needed to get this book in your hands. My internet marketing director, Eric Emerson, has made monumental efforts in spreading the word through Amazon, social media and the internet.

There is also a special subcontractor who works on my behalf whom I want to thank. Steve May, my webmaster for 19 years! How can I properly thank you?

And closest to my heart I want to thank my beloved wife, Cindy Lange, who surely is one of the few women alive who could put up with me. Her imprint is on every page of the book. This book would never have happened without her help, support, and love. Finally, thank you to my 20-year-old daughter, Erica, whom I love dearly. Thank you for not complaining when I went back to the office after dinner to work on the first two editions. Now that you are thriving as a Computer Engineering student at the University of Pittsburgh, I could not be more proud.

Thank you all.

How to Read This Book

I recommend that you start with "The Big Retirement Question" and "A Summary of Tax Reduction Strategies" so you can begin to think about the underlying theme of "pay taxes later" with respect to your personal situation. Then, please look at the detailed table of contents and pick out the chapters that grab your attention. We have spent many hours on the detailed table of contents and feel for this book, it is a far superior starting point to searching for any topic than any index that we could have but chose not to create.

Virtually every chapter contains proof that my recommendations have been tested and proven worthy. You may want to skip over portions of the proof and just read the advice. Sometimes, when I am looking for information or advice, I want to scream, "Don't tell me *why*, just tell me *what* to do." If you feel similarly, or you find yourself moving in that direction after realizing there is enormous support for virtually every recommendation I make, the book's sidebars and summaries at the end of the chapters will serve you well.

Obviously, you would benefit greatly if you read the book cover to cover, and then took action on the recommendations appropriate for you and your family. I do, however, live in the real world and recognize that you may only read or even skim portions you know are personally relevant. But, no matter how you read the book, the important point is: Take action to make your retirement and estate planning the best it can be for you and your family.

I have tried to spice up the content by including some true stories (modified for confidentiality), an occasional sarcastic comment, at least one witty quote per chapter, and perhaps the most fun, the cartoons. I hope you enjoy them.

What *Retire Secure!* Doesn't Cover

Retire Secure! does not provide direct investment advice nor do I recommend any specific stocks, bonds, mutual funds, or even asset allocation models. Obviously choosing appropriate investments is critical, but this book is not the place for direct investment advice.

The Big Retirement Plan Question

"Will my money last as long as I do and how can I get the most from what I've got?

That's the $64,000 question.

While you can never answer that question with 100% certainty, you can take action on two fronts which will dramatically improve your odds.

1. *Develop an appropriate portfolio.* With the exception of several observations interspersed throughout, I leave the discussion of building a portfolio to another day.

2. *Make the optimal decisions regarding Social Security,* another important issue that we leave to another day.

3. *Take action to drastically reduce your taxes.* This is easier than you may think. With this book in hand, you have the tools to significantly reduce your and your family's tax burden. Reducing your taxes will dramatically increase your chances of financial success.

The U.S. tax structure rewards certain actions and punishes others. The difference can mean, literally, millions of dollars.

Retire Secure! explains how you can use IRAs, retirement plans, and other tax-favored investments to let Uncle Sam subsidize your life style and increase the odds that you will have sufficient income for the rest of your and your spouse's life.

Retire Secure! is a summation of my best advice garnered from 36 years as a practicing CPA and 31 years as an estate attorney. Though the optimal treatment of IRAs and retirement plans is the focus of this book, even readers with IRAs and retirement plans as their primary assets, have other concerns besides planning for their retirement assets. Therefore, this book isn't limited to IRA and retirement plan advice but contains my best advice in many related areas as well. *Retire Secure!* provides critical advice for all stages of IRA and retirement plan saving and spending. We cover the best strategies for accumulating wealth while you are working, and distributing IRAs and retirement plans when you are retired.

In addition, ***Retire Secure!*** gives you a *uniquely flexible* solution for disbursing the IRA or retirement plan after the death of the IRA owner. The inherent flexibility of Lange's Cascading Beneficiary Plan provides the maximum flexibility for your survivors. We think it is highly likely you will prefer this plan to the more traditional, fixed-in-stone type of estate planning. Flexibility is important because we can't predict the future; changes in investments and in the tax environment are likely to affect the best plans. If we provide flexibility in our estate planning, we will often get a better result for the family.

Retire Secure! is supported with peer-reviewed mathematical proof that these strategies result in more dollars—sometimes millions of additional dollars—to you and your family.

A Summary of Tax Reduction Strategies

For the reader who wants to take what I have to say on faith, and wants the most important information in the book condensed in to two pages or less, here you go.

The Clear Advantage of IRA and Retirement Plan Savings during the Accumulation Stage

Mr. Pay Taxes Later and Mr. Pay Taxes Now had identical salaries and spending habits, and made the same investment choices. There was one big difference though – Mr. Pay Taxes Later invested his money in his tax-deferred retirement plans – even though his employer did not match his contributions. Mr. Pay Taxes Now contributed nothing to his retirement plan at work, and instead put his money in a taxable investment account.

On the graph below, Mr. Pay Taxes Later's investment is represented by the light gray curve, and Mr. Pay Taxes Now's, by the dark gray curve. Look at the dramatic difference in their wealth over time. Which individual would you rather be?

Figure 1.1
Retirement Plans and Tax-Deferred Savings vs. After-Tax Savings Accounts

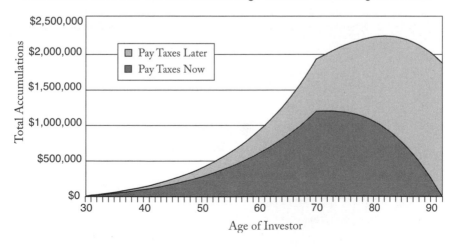

If you have access to a retirement plan at work, you should contribute the maximum amount your employer is willing to match or even partially match. If you can afford to, make additional non-matched contributions. If you don't have a retirement plan available where you work, contribute the maximum you can to your personal retirement plans.

Contributing to a Roth IRA is always preferable to contributing to a non-deductible IRA and is usually preferable to contributing to a deductible IRA. High-income individuals who are not eligible to contribute to a Roth IRA can still participate in a Roth environment by contributing to a Roth 401(k)/403(b) plan at work, or by converting a Traditional retirement account to a Roth.

After You Retire, Spend Your After-Tax (Nonretirement or Non-IRA) Money First

Mr. Tax-Efficient and Mr. Tax-Inefficient, both aged 65, retire with the exactly the same amount of money and the same investments inside and outside of their retirement plans. Mr. Tax-Inefficient refuses to spend any of his after-tax money because he wants to spend his retirement plan money first. Each withdrawal from his retirement plan triggers income tax, so he is paying taxes now.

Mr. Tax-Efficient does the opposite. He spends none of his retirement money until he spends every last dime from his non-retirement investments, or until he is required to begin minimum distributions at age 70½. On the chart below, Mr. Tax Efficient's wealth is represented by the light gray line, and Mr. Tax Inefficient's wealth is represented by the dark gray line.

Figure 4.1
Benefits of Spending After-Tax Savings Before Traditional Retirement Plans

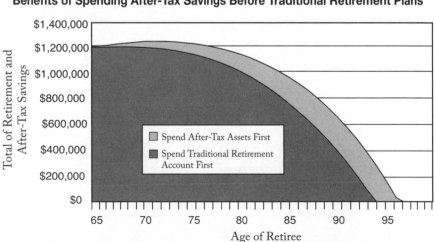

When spending your savings during retirement, you should spend your after-tax money first. Changes to the capital gains tax rules in 2012 have made capital gains on after-tax savings an issue for far fewer people than in previous years. Then spend your Traditional and Roth retirement accounts strategically, depending on your specific tax situation. Leaving money in the tax-deferred and tax-free environments for as long as possible confers advantages that almost always outweigh concerns over paying capital gains on your after-tax assets. This strategy is also important for your heirs as well.

My Best Advice – Read This Book

To learn the most tax-efficient strategies for planning your retirement, you should read this book and then act on my suggestions. Whether you do it on your own or hire a professional advisor, pay attention to your investments and change your portfolio to reflect changing times. I have presented ideas that will help you reap the rewards of a richer life. Under most circumstances, you and your family will be better off for doing so, potentially by millions of dollars.

An Outline Overview of the Whole Process

While you are still working:

- Contribute the maximum amount to your retirement plan or plans (Chapter 1)

- If you have a choice, choose the right plan (Roth or traditional savings), or even non-deductible IRAs. Allow the tax favored accounts to build wealth for you while continuing to make new contributions (Chapter 1)

After you retire:

- First, spend the money on which you have already paid income tax (Chapter 4)

- Take advantages of windows of opportunity to make Roth conversions with the lowest possible tax impact (Chapter 7)

- After that money is spent, spend your traditional and Roth accounts strategically, depending on your personal tax situation (Chapter 4)

- When you turn 70½, you will have to begin taking Required Minimum Distributions. If you can afford to, limit your annual distribution to the minimum you are required to take, and allow the rest of the account to continue to grow (Chapter 5)

When you are planning for your heirs:

- Develop an estate plan that continues the tax-deferred status of your retirement plan for as long as possible (Chapter 15)

- Understand that estate taxes are no longer a threat for most people and revise outdated documents if necessary (Chapter 11)

What's New!

Introduction

Legislative changes enacted since the publication of the second edition of this book (2009) have challenged us to revamp the advice we give to retirees on many topics. Major changes in the tax laws mean that IRA and retirement plan owners need to shift their focus from worrying about estate taxes to worrying about income taxes. Married taxpayers can now pass more than $10 million federal estate-tax free to their heirs with very little or no planning. Therefore, the emphasis for most IRA owners is to minimize income taxes, both while you are alive and for your heirs. The classic principals of *Retire Secure!*, however, endure and our core recommendations remain unchanged. We still believe that saving in retirement plans beats saving in the after-tax environment—and now there are more plans and higher contribution limits that make our strategies even more advantageous. We are also convinced that many IRA owners will still be well served by a series of Roth IRA conversions. With the shift in focus to saving income taxes, the Roth IRA could become an even more useful tool, though you should also know the legitimate reasons some experts are less enthusiastic about the Roth IRA conversion. I am, however, happy to report that clients and readers who have followed my advice for Roth IRA conversions in the past have benefited handsomely.

In our first edition (2006), we introduced readers to Lange's Cascading Beneficiary Plan (LCBP) for their estate planning. We still think it is the best, most flexible, estate plan for married taxpayers. We have drafted over 1,900 estate plans that have elements of or even an entire plan based on LCBP. It has worked out exceedingly well for the heirs of those clients who have died—always a sad event for a family and also for me as I usually develop a close professional relationship with my clients. It does, however, provide a certain satisfaction knowing things are set up just right to help the heirs get the most out of what they are left. I am also proud to say, estate planners across the country are beginning to understand the benefits of the strategy and are implementing it in their own practices. Since the book was first published, I have been asked to teach thousands of CPAs, attorneys and financial advisors about the benefits of Roth IRA conversions and Lange's Cascading Beneficiary Plan. I am awed by the number of references to "Cascading Beneficiary Plan" that currently pop up on Google search!

We have always stressed the importance of deferring taxes by contributing to retirement plans and limiting IRA withdrawals to the mandatory minimum both during your lifetime and the lifetime of your heirs. An IRA and/or retirement plan that keeps withdrawals to the minimum, thus deferring income taxes, is commonly referred to as "a stretch IRA." Unfortunately, our strategy for prolonging "the stretch" over multiple generations is facing a hostile Congress and our ability to create tax-deferred, and in the case of the Roth IRA, tax-free dynasties is threatened. While the current laws still prevail, we fear Congress will eliminate the stretch IRA for non-spouse heirs, perhaps during this next session. Therefore, this edition compares and contrasts strategies under the current law with what we think the future law will be, specifically in relation to inherited IRAs and inherited Roth IRAs. We correctly predicted changes regarding Roth IRA conversions in our last edition and readers who implemented our strategies benefitted handsomely. I really encourage all readers to pay attention to the potential "death of the stretch IRA" and potential "death of the stretch Roth IRA," in Chapter 13. Each of the issues presented in *What's New!* are covered in more detail in the book. This section, however, offers an overview for readers who may want to jump to the sections of the book that give the details supporting our most recent recommendations.

The Accumulation Years: The Best Ways to Save for Your Retirement

Congress is getting more and more generous by allowing **higher IRA, Roth IRA, 401(k) and Roth 401(k) contributions,** and we review these new limits. Contributing the maximum possible to retirement plans at work remains a great place to beat the tax blues. Furthermore, with the higher contribution limits and options for multiple plans, wealthy taxpayers and taxpayers of more modest means can invest a considerable sum in tax-deferred accounts and ultimately, tax-free Roth accounts. There are few options available to high-income taxpayers who are still working that allow them to reduce their taxes, but contributing the maximum possible to their retirement plan at work is for most, the best place to start.

That said, **what about Roth contributions?** Considering a Roth contribution foregoes the tax deduction for making a retirement plan contribution, does it make sense for a high-income taxpayer to contribute to the Roth? Those questions are answered in Chapter 3.

Unfortunately, our slowly recovering economy has pushed people to take **loans out against their retirement plans**; we're seeing more and more people doing this to pay for college educations for their children. This strategy can have some serious consequences, and we address that in Chapter 1. Also discussed in Chapter 1 is the growing problem of insolvent pension plans, and we offer strategies to protect yourself and your spouse if you participate in such a plan.

Roth IRAs have come under fire in recent years, with President Obama asking that owners be required to take Required Minimum Distributions (RMD) as they are required to do with their traditional IRAs. I came under fire, too, because some readers felt that the rates of return used in my calculations comparing the benefits of Roth IRAs to traditional IRAs in edition two reflected an asset allocation that was too risky for a retiree. (My justification, however, is that since Roth IRAs have the longest investment time horizon, you most likely should invest the Roth IRA more aggressively). That said, **my calculations have been amended to reflect more conservative rates of return**, and guess what? The Roth is still a better option for most – but not all – people. You'll have to read Chapter 2 to see if someone in your situation will benefit from owning one.

The Distribution Years: Spending the Right Funds First, and Other Critical Retirement Decisions

Over the years, I have met with countless clients who have far too much of their portfolio in the stock of one company (generally their previous employer). Many of these clients have told me that the fear of the capital gains tax on highly appreciated stocks keeps them from diversifying their holdings. Yikes! The risk of keeping all your eggs in one basket dramatically outweighs the tax liability—especially now when the tax hit on selling highly appreciated securities is reduced. **Changes to the tax laws in 2012 reduce the impact of the capital gains tax.** For lower income taxpayers, the capital gains tax is eliminated. So, if you're one of those people who have steadfastly refused to diversify because of the capital gains tax, please read Chapter 4. And consider diversifying your portfolio before the government changes the laws again and before your undiversified portfolio plummets.

Chapter 5 discusses the **Required Minimum Distribution rules from retirement plans, and they have not changed significantly – yet.** As indicated above, President Obama is trying to "harmonize" the rules for Roth IRAs (which do not require minimum distributions) with traditional IRAs (which require minimum distributions beginning at age 70 ½). How will this affect owners of Roth IRAs? My thoughts are presented in Chapter 5. This chapter also contains an interesting tip for avoiding income tax on required distributions for those who are charitably inclined. It also contains a little-known strategy for IRA owners who are taking RMDs to stop paying their estimated tax payments without penalty and getting an interest-free loan from the IRS.

Chapter 6 is worth reviewing because it discusses **the pros and cons of rolling retirement plans into IRAs after you retire.** Sometimes it is a good idea, and sometimes it is a very bad idea—you need to know when it is a good idea and when it will hurt you. Please note you will not receive the standard advice you would get from advisors who want to manage all your money. Be advised that a manager who pushes that idea a little too aggressively should raise a red flag. It also covers the details of a 2014 IRS ruling that allows some people to convert a portion of their old retirement plan into a Roth IRA, *completely tax-free.*

Roth IRA conversions have been a cornerstone of many of the retirement and estate plan recommendations I have made to my own clients. So much has changed in the past few years! High income taxpayers are now subject to higher tax rates, and there is continuing pressure from our President to eliminate a key benefit to the Roth—no RMDs. **So, does converting money from a traditional IRA to a Roth still make sense?** Chapter 7 provides all of those details.

Decisions about retirement finances, protecting your surviving spouse, and leaving money to your heirs need to be based on solid information. Multiple scenarios should be evaluated and we particularly stress the importance of running the numbers. In Chapter 8, we discuss **the advantages and disadvantages of annuity based guaranteed-lifetime-income options,** and we also cover a 2014 change to the tax laws that makes it possible for individuals who are currently working to receive a guaranteed lifetime income from their retirement plans at work. Please don't fear this is a disguised attempt to sell you a commercial tax-deferred annuity. We have never been fans of commercial tax-deferred annuities and that hasn't changed.

If your retirement plan at work allows you to contribute on an after-tax basis, or if you can purchase stock through your plan, then you must read Chapter 9. It's short, but the information can save you a lot of money when you retire. It also discusses the steps you have to take in order to take advantage of a 2014 ruling that allows certain taxpayers to convert a portion of their plan in to a Roth IRA, without paying any tax at all.

Estate Planning: It is Never Too Early (or Too Late) to Start

We've updated our famous case study of Eddie and Emily (Chapter 10). This case study has received a lot of attention. I've even received a call from an engineer and his wife who said "We are basically Eddie and Emily, can you help us implement all the strategies that you recommended for them?" It is a plan that has helped many people sleep better at night!

Chapter 11 is required reading for those of you who may have been told in the past that you need to worry about federal estate taxes. **Because of major changes in the tax laws, federal estate taxes now affect far fewer people,** and your old estate planning documents may be out-of-date and potentially dangerous. Many readers don't even know their existing wills and trusts are like a ticking income-tax bomb. That's a strong statement, but I stand by it. Please, if you haven't thought about your estate plans recently, read the section in this chapter titled "The Cruelest Trap of All." But don't let complacency over estate taxes allow you to drop your guard. You may find the assets you leave to your heirs threatened by an old enemy with sharpened fangs—the federal income tax.

Although some readers may cringe at the mention of life insurance, I discuss it in detail in Chapter 12. **Life insurance, as an income-tax reduction tool, takes on new importance now that we have higher tax rates and the "death of the stretch IRA" seems imminent.** Life insurance remains the most tax-efficient way to pass wealth from one generation to the next—by efficient, I mean completely tax-free. One area that may be of interest to my cynical readers is a demonstration that even if you live a long time paying insurance premiums over your lifetime, it is less expensive than the additional taxes your heirs would have to pay if you don't buy insurance!

Or, you may align yourself with my other clients who think, "I paid for their braces, I paid for their college, and anything I leave them is a bonus." You may also prefer the majority position which is "I am happy to implement many of the strategies in *Retire Secure!* because it will make me and my spouse more secure and as a bonus—and at no additional cost to me—my children and grandchildren will reap enormous benefits."

Chapter 13 addresses **the potential demise of the stretch IRA in some detail**. What can you do to avoid the income taxes and maintain the tax-deferred status of your IRA for as long as possible? Read this chapter for some cutting-edge strategies. If you like your family and your charities benefitting all at the expense of the IRS, you should consider the solution presented if the "death of the stretch IRA" becomes a reality.

I have always been an advocate of **disclaimers,** because they permit maximum flexibility when a death occurs. In my own practice, I've found that the vast majority of survivors are worthy of the deceased's trust, and disclaimers have worked as planned. But, a 2014 Supreme Court ruling affects how inherited IRAs are treated **in the event of a non-spouse beneficiary's bankruptcy**. This means that additional strategies should be considered if a surviving spouse intends to disclaim to a child or grandchild who has or might have creditors.

Also, a change in the tax law in 2011 introduced a concept called portability, which allows the executor of an estate to transfer any unused estate tax exemption to the surviving spouse. For some beneficiaries, it now makes more sense to disclaim only part of an asset. Read Chapter 14 for more information on how disclaimers can benefit your family.

Chapters 15 and 16 discuss the beneficiaries for your IRAs and retirement plans. You might say, "I'm not going to read that, I know who I want my beneficiary to be!" I say, "If you want to make sure that the law agrees with who you think your beneficiary is, please read Chapters 15 and 16." **Inaccurate beneficiary designations can trigger massive income taxes,** and family feuds that last for generations. More IRA and retirement plan owners get this wrong than get this right.

Many new clients are surprised at the very personal questions I ask when preparing recommendations for an estate plan. My questions often boil down to a common theme—**do you trust your spouse, do you trust your children, and do you trust your children's spouses?** We have been drafting more of the "I don't want my no good son-in-law to inherit one red cent of my money" trust than ever before. You can learn how you can protect your inheritance from your no good son-in-law, creditors, and even your loved ones from their own bad judgment. If any of these thoughts resonate with you, or even if you have young grandchildren, you should read the discussion on trusts in Chapter 17.

I will never understand our government's rationale for penalizing individuals who choose to donate a portion of their income to **charity,** but this is precisely what happened in 2014 when they implemented a phase-out of itemized deductions for high-income taxpayers. Chapter 18 offers a nifty trick that allows some charitably inclined taxpayers to receive a tax benefit for their donations, regardless of their income. Also discussed are the mechanics of the Charitable Remainder Unitrust, a possible alternative to continue the tax deferred status of retirement accounts if the government does kill the stretch IRA.

Conclusion

We hope that readers of previous versions of *Retire Secure!* will find this overview builds on what you have learned in the past and that it directs you to changes that might be particularly relevant to you. For new readers, we hope it gives you a strong sense of just how seriously we take this subject—we try to leave no stone unturned. Now, time to move onto the details and into the journey toward a secure retirement.

Introduction

The fear of running out of money has grown from a lingering, nagging concern to widespread dread. People ask themselves "Will we have enough to live comfortably for the rest of our lives? What kind of legacy will we leave our children and grandchildren? Are we proactively taking the right steps to get the most out of what we've got?"

Unfortunately, many people devote too much time worrying about the day-to-day fluctuations in the market and lose sight of the big picture. They need long-term effective tax-savvy strategies and good advice to implement now. Effective strategies are even more important for IRA and retirement plan owners because of the heavy tax burden on these plans. The difference between effective and ineffective tax planning for IRA and retirement plans can be the difference between prosperity and financial ruin.

To provide direction in the IRA and retirement plan field, I have authored several books, and write a monthly IRA and retirement planning newsletter that goes to over 4,000 professional advisors. I also deliver more than 150 presentations each year—all in an effort to provide much-needed advice to both consumers and professional advisors on how to build, preserve and protect their retirement savings.

Jim Lange shares my passion and vision in this area. He is making a powerful impact by providing cutting-edge advice for IRA and retirement plan owners and their advisors. Jim's valuable analysis and recommendations are unique to *Retire Secure!* You won't find his combination of information and analysis anywhere else—not even in my published work.

But don't think for a minute that Jim's recommendations are new and untested. In 1998, Jim wrote a ground breaking, peer-reviewed article on Roth IRA conversions for the American Institute of CPAs. In that same article, Jim outlined his comprehensive and now-famous cascading beneficiary plan; an estate plan that many IRA and retirement plan owners should consider. Fortunately for you, the details are all in this book. Jim's advice has stood the test of time and has been thoroughly vetted.

Retire Secure! covers all of the classic directives for sound retirement and estate panning, but the book evaluates them in light of the most recent tax laws. Thankfully, it is also spiced with humor. There are numerous cartoons, fun quotes, and flashes of Jim's good sense of humor.

Jim's overarching recommendation to "Pay Taxes Later" is as valid today as it was when the first edition of *Retire Secure!* was published. This simple phrase applies to all three stages of retirement planning: accumulating retirement assets, spending your assets in retirement, and planning for your heirs.

But let's not forget whose book this is. Jim is a champion of Roth IRAs, Roth 401(k)s, and Roth IRA conversions, and those investments reflect the one place where Jim makes an important exception to his "Pay Taxes Later" mantra. Fortunately for us, Jim succeeds in untangling the myriad of complexities of IRAs and Roth IRAs that can derail even the best of intentions. Jim also delves into an area that deserves much more attention than it's getting—Roth IRA conversions for high-income taxpayers. Due to changes in the 2010 tax laws, Jim and I agree that Roth IRA conversions are going to become a game changer for many families.

I highly recommend that you do yourself and your family a big favor and read *Retire Secure!* Planning for the future is not something to leave to chance. Knowledge is the first defense against mistakes, and taking action is what wins the game. Use *Retire Secure!* to effectively plan for your future.

— Ed Slott, CPA,
Author and Speaker,
www.irahelp.com

Part One

THE
ACCUMULATION
YEARS

The Best Way to Save for Retirement

1

⑊⑊⑊⑊⑊⑊⑊⑊⑊⑊⑊⑊⑊⑊

Fund Retirement Plans
to the Maximum

The most powerful force in the universe is compound interest.

— Albert Einstein

Main Topics

- Why contributing the maximum to a retirement plan is so important
- The clear advantage of pre-tax IRA and retirement plan savings
- Why you should contribute to your plan even if your employer doesn't match your contribution
- Why you must always contribute to plans with employer-matching
- The two principal categories of retirement plans
- Ten major types of retirement plans and their contribution limits
- When you can access the money in your retirement plan
- Pension decisions that could give you income for life (or not)
- Options for contributing to more than one retirement plan
- Minimizing your life insurance costs to maximize your retirement contributions
- Making retirement plan contributions when you think you can't afford it

> ## KEY IDEA
>
> Everyone who has access to an employee retirement plan should contribute the maximum amount his or her employer is willing to match or even partially match. If you can afford more, make nonmatched contributions.

Why Contributing the Maximum to a Retirement Plan Is So Important

A trusted client of mine recently referred to me as her "guardian angel." At first I was totally taken aback—no one had ever called me a guardian angel before. She continued, "Twenty years ago you advised me to put the maximum into my retirement plan. I didn't know if it was a good idea or not, but I trusted you and did what you recommended. Now I have a million dollars in my retirement plan. What should I do now?"

Ultimately, her question is answered in this book. But her comment also compelled me to complete a comprehensive analysis of why it was such good advice. I wanted to be able to persuasively convince anyone who harbored the least little doubt about the advantages of saving money in a retirement plan over saving money outside of a retirement plan.

I set out to evaluate the outcomes of two different scenarios:

1. You earn the money, you pay the tax, you invest the money you earned, and you pay tax on the dividends, interest, and capital gains.

2. You invest money in your retirement plan and you get a tax deduction. The money grows tax-deferred, and you don't pay taxes on that money until you take it out.

So, which is better: saving inside the retirement plan or outside the retirement plan? The answer: it is better to save within the retirement plan. Why? This isn't a touchy-feely issue. It comes down to numbers. Let's take a look.

The Clear Advantage of Pre-Tax IRA and Retirement Plan Savings

Mr. Pay Taxes Later and Mr. Pay Taxes Now are neighbors. From the outside, you wouldn't be able to tell them apart: they own the same type of car; their salaries are the same; and they are in the same tax bracket. Their savings have the same investment rate of return, and they even save the same percentage of their gross wages every year.

They have one big difference. Mr. Pay Taxes Later invests as much as he can afford in his tax-deferred retirement plan—his 401(k)—even though his employer does not match his contributions. Mr. Pay Taxes Now feels that putting money in a retirement account makes it "not really his money" as he puts it. He doesn't want to have to pay taxes to take out his own money, or put up with other restrictions that limit his access to "his money." Thus, he contributes nothing to his retirement account at work but invests his savings in an account outside of his retirement plan. Mr. Pay Taxes Now invests the old-fashioned way: earn the money, pay the tax, invest the money, and pay the tax on the income that the invested money generates (dividends, capital gains, etc.).

Both men begin investing at age 30.

- In 2015, they start saving $8,000 per year, indexed for inflation.

- Mr. Pay Taxes Later has his entire $8,000 withheld from his paycheck and deposited to his tax-deferred 401(k). (The analysis would be identical if he contributed the money to a traditional deductible IRA).

- Mr. Pay Taxes Now chooses not to have any retirement funds withheld but rather to be paid in full. He pays income taxes on his full wages—which includes the $8,000 he chose not to contribute to his retirement plan. After the 25 percent income tax is paid, he has only 75 percent of the $8,000, or $6,000, left to invest.

Now look at Figure 1.1 on the following page. Mr. Pay Taxes Later's investment is represented by the lighter curve, and Mr. Pay

Taxes Now's by the darker curve. Look at the dramatic difference in the accumulations over time.

Figure 1.1
Retirement Plans and Tax-Deferred Savings vs. After-Tax Savings Accounts

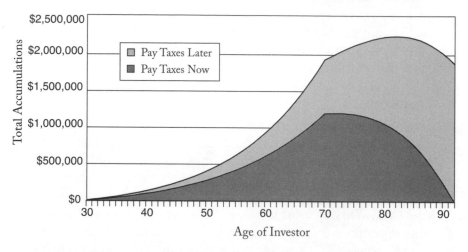

The assumptions for this graph include the following:

1. Investment rate of return is 6 percent including 70 percent capital appreciation, with a 15 percent portfolio turnover rate, 15 percent dividend income, and 15 percent interest income.

2. Mr. Pay Taxes Later contributes $8,000 per year to his pre-tax retirement savings plan. Mr. Pay Taxes Now invests $6,000 (25 percent less due to taxes). Both amounts are indexed for 2.5 percent annual raises, starting at age 30 until age 70.

3. Starting at age 71, spending from both investors' accounts is equal to the Required Minimum Distributions (RMDs) from Mr. Pay Taxes Later's retirement plan, less related income taxes.

4. Mr. Pay Taxes Later withdraws only the RMD, pays the 25 percent income tax due on his distribution, and spends the rest. Mr. Pay Taxes Now spends the same amount plus he pays income taxes due on his interest, dividends, and realized capital gains.

5. Ordinary tax rates are 25 percent.

6. Capital gains tax rates are 15 percent.

7. Dividends are taxed as capital gains.

Now, to be fair, Mr. Pay Taxes Later will have to pay taxes eventually. When he is retired, for every dollar he wants to withdraw, he has to take out $1.33. He pockets the dollar and pays $0.33 in taxes (25 percent of $1.33). If Mr. Pay Taxes Now withdraws a dollar, subject to some capital gains taxes, it's all his, just as he wanted. At age 92, however, Mr. Pay Taxes Now has depleted his funds entirely whereas Mr. Pay Taxes Later has $1,867,865 left in his retirement plan.

Given reasonable assumptions and all things being equal, following the adage, "Don't pay taxes now—pay taxes later" can be worth almost $2 million over your lifetime.

> **All things being equal, following the adage, "Don't pay taxes now— pay taxes later" can be worth almost $2 million over your lifetime.**

After spending your life working hard, paying the mortgage, paying the bills, raising a family, and putting your kids through college, you may never have expected to have such a substantial IRA or retirement plan and be so well off in retirement. For many of my clients, it seems like a fantasy. But it isn't a fantasy, and you need to think about the best ways to manage that money.

Many readers are afraid they will make costly mistakes and/or mismanage their retirement money. The fear is paralyzing, so they do nothing—literally, nothing. They procrastinate and avoid making important planning decisions for their IRA and/or retirement plan. That may have been you until now.

You have already made a great start by buying this book. Now, please read it and know that I have done everything in my power to provide you with the best information available on planning for your IRA and/or retirement plan. After all, your future and your financial security are dependent upon you handling your retirement finances properly. After reading this book, *please take action*. Promise yourself that reading this book will be more than an academic exercise. Promise yourself that it will motivate you to take action—take the critical steps that will put you and your family in a much more financially secure position than you are in today.

Make Those Nonmatched Contributions to Retirement Plans

What conclusion can we draw from Mini Case Study 1.1? Don't pay taxes now—pay taxes later. Even if your employer does not offer the additional advantage of matching contributions, you should contribute the maximum to your retirement plan, assuming you can afford it. Money contributed to a retirement plan, whether a 401(k), 403(b), SEP, SIMPLE, 457, deductible IRA, or another type of retirement plan, is a pre-tax investment that grows tax-deferred. There are no federal income taxes on the wages contributed.

Some taxpayers view contributions as tax-deductible. Whichever way you look at it, you are getting a tax break for the amount of the contribution multiplied by the tax rate for your tax bracket. Furthermore, once the contribution is made, you do not pay income taxes on the interest, dividends, and appreciation *until you take a distribution* (i.e., withdrawal) from the retirement plan. In other words, you pay taxes later.

By not paying taxes up-front on the wages invested, you reap the harvest of compounding interest, dividends, and capital gains on the money that would have gone to paying taxes—both on the amount contributed and on the growth had the money been invested outside of the retirement plan.

In the real world, not only is there a tax advantage to saving in a retirement plan, but doing so builds in the discipline of contributing to your retirement plan with every paycheck. The example above assumes that if you are not putting the money in your retirement plan, you are saving and investing an amount equal to what your retirement contribution would have been. But can you trust yourself to be a disciplined saver? Will the temptation to put it off until the next paycheck undermine your resolve? Even if you do put it in savings, knowing you have unrestricted access to the money, can you be confident that you would never invade that fund until you retire?

In my practice, the clients who usually have the most money saved at retirement are the ones who religiously contributed to a retirement plan over the course of their long careers.

The idea of paying taxes later and contributing the maximum to your retirement plan(s) is something that I have preached in my practice for over 30 years. Many of my long-standing clients took my advice 20 or 30 years ago—even if they didn't completely understand why—and now they are thanking me.

> **In my practice, the clients who usually have the most money saved at retirement are the ones who religiously contributed to a retirement plan over the course of their long careers.**

The Employer Matching Retirement Plan

Money won is twice as sweet as money earned.

— Paul Newman, *The Color of Money*

With all due respect, broadly speaking, you have to be pretty "simple" (that's a nice word for "stupid") not to take advantage of a retirement plan where the employer makes a matching contribution.

The Cardinal Rule of Saving for Retirement

If your employer offers a retirement plan matching contribution, the cardinal rule is: contribute **at least** the amount the employer is willing to match—even if it is only a percentage of your contribution and not a dollar-for-dollar match. Imagine depositing $1,000 of your money in a bank, but instead of getting a crummy toaster, you receive an extra $1,000 to go along with your deposit. To add to the fun, imagine getting a tax deduction for your deposit and not having to pay taxes on your gift. Furthermore, both your $1,000 and the gift $1,000 grow (it is to be hoped), and you don't have to pay income tax on the interest, dividends, capital gains, or the appreciation until you withdraw the money. When you withdraw the money, you will have to pay taxes, but you will have gained interest, dividends, and appreciation in the meantime. That is what employer-matching contributions to retirement plans are all about. If the employer matches the employee contribution on a dollar-for-dollar basis, it is the same as a *100 percent return on the investment in one day* (assuming no early withdrawal penalties apply and the matched funds are fully vested).

Over the years, I have heard hundreds of excuses for not taking advantage of an employer-matching plan. With few exceptions, all those reasons come down to two words: *ignorance* and *neglect*. If you didn't know that before, you know it now. If you are not currently taking advantage of your employer-matching plan, run—don't walk—to your plan administrator and begin the paperwork to take advantage of the employer match. Matching contributions are most commonly found within 401(k), 403(b), and 457 plans. Many eligible 403(b) plan participants also may have access to a 457 plan. You can, in effect, enjoy double the ability to tax-defer earnings through participation in both the 403(b) and 457 plans. Even if your employer is only willing to make a partial match up to a cap, you should still take advantage of this opportunity. For example, a fairly common retirement plan agreement may provide that the employer contribute 50 cents for every dollar up to the first 6 percent of salary you contribute. Keep in mind: This is free money!

> Many eligible 403(b) plan participants also may have access to a 457 plan. You can, in effect, enjoy double the ability to tax-defer earnings through participation in both the 403(b) and 457 plans.

Again, this isn't touchy-feely stuff. It is backed by hard numbers.

MINI CASE STUDY 1.2

Running the Numbers for Employer-Matched Retirement Plans

Scenario 1

- Bill earns $75,000 per year and is subject to a flat 25 percent federal income tax (for simplicity, I ignore other taxes and assume a flat federal income tax: 25% x $75,000 = $18,750 tax).

- He spends $50,000 per year.

- He doesn't use his retirement plan at work, so he has $6,250 available to invest: ($75,000 income – [$18,750 tax and $50,000 spending] = $6,250 available cash).

Scenario 2

Bob also earns $75,000 per year, has the same tax rate and spends the same amount. But, his father is a very wise man—he bought **Retire Secure!** After reading this chapter, he advises his son, Bob, to contribute the maximum amount to his retirement plan that Bob's employer is willing to match. Uncharacteristically, Bob listens to his dad and contributes $5,000 to his retirement account. Bob is fortunate because his employer matches his contribution 100 percent. Thus $10,000 goes into his retirement account.

Under current tax laws, Bob will not have to pay federal income tax on his retirement plan contribution or on the amount his employer is willing to match, until the money is withdrawn from the plan. By using his employer's retirement plan, Bob's picture changes for the better as follows:

- Bob pays tax on only $70,000.

    ($75,000 income – $5,000 tax-deferred)

    (25% x $70,000 = $17,500 tax)

- He now has $57,500 ($75,000 income – $17,500 taxes).

- He makes his plan contribution of $5,000, leaving him with $52,500 outside the plan.

- His employer matches the $5,000 (also tax-deferred).

- He now has $10,000 in his retirement plan (growing tax-deferred).

- He spends $50,000 per year.

- He is left with $2,500 in cash.

Which scenario strikes you as more favorable: Scenario 2, with $10,000 in a retirement plan and $2,500 in cash, or Scenario 1, with no retirement plan and $6,250 in cash? The extreme cynic can figure out situations when a little extra cash and no retirement plan would be preferable, but the rest of us will take advantage of any employer-matching retirement plan.

Please keep in mind that the money in the retirement plan will continue to grow, and you will not have to pay income taxes on the earnings, dividends, interest, or accumulations until you (or your heirs) withdraw the money. But, even without weighing in the advantages of the long-term deferral, at the end of the first year, assuming the employer-matched funds are fully vested, the comparative values of these two scenarios are measured by after-tax purchasing power as follows:

	Scenario 1	*Scenario 2*
After-tax cash available	$ 6,250	$ 2,500
Retirement plan balance	0	$10,000
Tax on retirement plan balance	0	($ 2,500)
Early withdrawal penalty	0	($ 1,000)
Total purchasing power	**$ 6,250**	**$ 9,000**

Even if Bob has a financial emergency and has to withdraw money from his 401(k) prior to age 59½, resulting in tax and an early withdrawal penalty, he still has $2,750 more than Bill, who saved his money in an after-tax account. And if Bob is older than 59½ when he needs to make the withdrawal, the penalty doesn't apply and the difference is even greater. Obviously, it is better to take advantage of the retirement plan and the employer's matching contributions.

Figure 1.2 demonstrates that the long-term advantages of the employer match are even more dramatic using the same basic facts and circumstances as in Mini Case Study 1.1, but adding in a 100 percent employer match of annual contributions. Figure 1.2 compares stubborn Bill who refuses to use the retirement plan versus compliant Bob who contributes to his retirement plan.

Spending from both accounts is higher than in Figure 1.1, since the retirement plan's larger balance requires larger RMDs (more about RMDs in Chapter 3). Unfortunately, the higher distributions deplete stubborn Bill's unmatched funds even faster—he runs out of money at age 80 instead of at age 92 as in Mini Case Study 1.1, while compliant Bob's matched retirement savings plan has $4,455,077 remaining! And despite the large distributions being made after age 80, compliant Bob's savings are still growing when he reaches 82. The obvious conclusion again is, if you are not already taking advantage of this, run—don't walk—to your plan administrator and begin the paperwork to take advantage of the employer match.

Figure 1.2
Retirement Assets Plus an Employer Match vs. After-Tax Accumulations

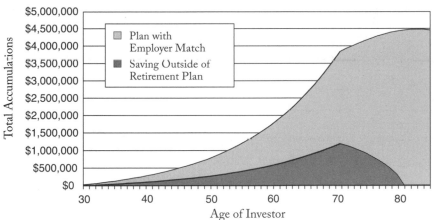

Occasionally, clients moan that they literally can't afford to make the contribution, even though their employer is willing to match it. I am not sympathetic. I would rather see you borrow the money to make matching contributions. Beg, borrow, or steal to find the money to contribute to an employer-matching plan.

There is an interesting option available if you want to see your child's retirement plan grow, but your child claims he or she isn't making enough to contribute to his or her retirement plan, even though the company offers a 100 percent match. You may want to consider making a gift to your child in the amount that your child would be out of pocket, if they contributed to the plan. Your child can then use the money you give him for spending, which allows him to maximize his retirement plan at work. In this example, you could make a gift of $3,750 ($6,250 − $2,500 tax savings). For your $3,750 gift, your adult child would end up with $10,000 in his retirement plan. That is an example of a leveraged gift. Lots of bang for your gifted buck!

Two Categories of Retirement Plans

Generally all retirement plans in the workplace fall into two categories: *Defined-Contribution Plans* and *Defined-Benefit Plans*.

Defined-Contribution Plans

Defined-contribution plans are relatively easy to understand, and usually offer a wide variety of tax-favored investment options. In a defined-contribution plan, each individual employee has an account that can be funded by either the employee or the employer, or both. Employers frequently tell their employees that their contributions are tax-deductible, which is not technically correct. The employee's taxable income is reduced by the amount that they contribute to the plan, which means that employees who do not have enough deductions to itemize at tax time, will still realize a tax benefit from contributing to the plan. At retirement or termination of employment, subject to a few minor exceptions, the money in a defined-contribution plan sponsored by the employer represents the funds available to the employee that can be rolled into his or her own IRA. In a defined-contribution plan, the employee bears the investment risks. In other words, if the market suffers a downturn, so does the value of your investments. Conversely, if the market does well, you are rewarded with a higher balance. The plan illustrated in Figures 1.1 and 1.2 is an example of a defined-contribution plan.

A growing number of employers are now offering Roth account options within their defined contribution plans. More information on the advantages of each option is covered in Chapter 2. If offered, the employee can direct all of their contributions to the Roth account, or split them between the Roth and traditional accounts. The Roth accounts are excellent options that provide tax-free growth within defined-contribution plans. But unlike employee contributions to traditional accounts, Roth contributions do not reduce taxable income. In addition, employer matching contributions cannot be added to the employee's Roth account; they must be credited to the traditional account so that they are taxed when withdrawn.

Common Defined-Contribution Plans

401(k) Plan: This plan can accept both employee and employer tax-deferred contributions. The contributions to the plan and the earnings are not federally taxable until they are withdrawn. Employee contributions to 401(k)s are usually determined as a percentage of salary or wages, and are limited to a prescribed amount. In 2015, for taxpayers under age 50, that limit is $18,000. For taxpayers age 50 and older, the IRS permits additional "catch-up contributions" of $6,000 for a total of $24,000. These limits are generally increased for inflation. The company—that is, the employer—is responsible for providing the employee with investment choices, typically six to ten choices in either one or two families of mutual funds. Some large employers offering 401(k) plans also allow their employees to purchase individual stock shares in their plans. Fortunately, after the spectacular collapse of Enron, companies are no longer permitted to *require* that their employees own company stock inside their retirement plans. The employer is also responsible for setting the basic rules of the plan – for example, whether they will offer a matching contribution, or if they will permit loans against the plan. They are also responsible for choosing the investments that are made available to the employee, and for plan administration. The employee is responsible for choosing his or her own investments from the options made available by the employer.

403(b) Plan: This plan is similar to a 401(k) plan but is commonly used by certain charitable organizations and public educational institutions, such as universities, colleges, and hospitals. Like a 401(k), the maximum contribution is limited in 2015 to $18,000 for employees under age 50, or $24,000 for those over 50. 403(b) plans also have a special "15 years of service" catch-up provision – so even if you're not age 50 or older, you may be able to contribute more than $18,000 to your plan. One big difference between a 401(k) plan and a 403(b) plan is that, for non-church employees, 403(b) plans can only invest in annuities and mutual funds. TIAA-CREF is the best known and most common 403(b) provider.

457 Plan: After the Economic Growth and Tax Relief Reconciliation Act of 2001 (EGTRRA), 457 plans have become more similar to 401(k) plans. They are commonly used by state and local governmental employers and certain tax-exempt organizations. Typical 457 employees are police officers, firefighters, teachers, and other municipal workers.

An interesting side note is that many eligible 457 plan participants don't realize they are eligible to make a 457 plan contribution. They may have a 403(b) plan and don't know they can "double" their tax-deferred earnings through participating in both a 403(b) and a 457 plan. A perfect candidate for using both plans would be a married teacher whose spouse has income and their combined income is more than sufficient for their needs. If they have enough income and if they are age 50 or older in 2015, the teacher could contribute a maximum of $18,000 to his or her 403(b), $18,000 to a 457 plan, and make an additonal catch-up contribution of $6,000. By doing that, the couple could reduce their taxable income by $42,000. Some 457 plans provide a "catch-up" provision for employees who are within three years of normal retirement age, which allows them to contribute even more.

SEP: SEP is an acronym for Simplified Employee Pension. These plans are commonly used by employers with very few employees, and self-employed individuals. Under a SEP, an employer makes contributions to IRAs, which are not taxable for federal income tax purposes, on behalf of employees. Contribution limits are higher with SEPs than with IRAs. Maximum allowable contributions equal 25 percent of the employee's compensation, up to $53,000 in 2015. If considering a SEP, you must be careful to look at how *compensation* is defined. After you go through the technical hoops, the contribution actually works out to about 20 percent of what most self-employed people think is compensation.

SIMPLE: SIMPLE is an acronym for a Savings Incentive Match Plan for Employees. They provide an attractive defined-contribution plan option for small companies that do not sponsor a retirement plan, or self-employed individuals. The maximum allowable contribution ($12,500 in 2015) is lower than that of a SEP, and the employer is required to make either a two percent (2%) non-elective contribution for each eligible employee, or a three percent (3%) matching contribution for all participating employees. These plans also allow additional "catch-up" contributions to be made by employees over age 50.

Single-K or One-Person 401(k): The Single-K is commonly used by self-employed individuals (with no employees) who want to contribute the most money possible to their own retirement plan. The business owner who has this kind of plan wears two hats – he can contribute to his personal 401(k) as an employee, and then make an additional contribution as the employer. Employee contributions are limited to $18,000 in 2015 ($24,000 if age 50 or over), or up to 100% of compensation if earnings are lower than $18,000. As the employer, the business owner can also make an additional maximum contribution equaling 25 percent of his or her annual compensation. (As with a SEP plan, be careful to define compensation accurately.) Between his employee and employer contributions, a business owner could contribute $53,000 in 2015 ($59,000 if he is age 50 or older) to his own retirement plan. For an example of the power of the Single-K and a calculation, please see Judy's example in Mini Case Study 1.3. These Single-K plans can also be set up to contain a Roth savings option. This is also the type of plan I usually prefer for the new self-employed retiree.

Payroll Deduction IRA: This is a relatively new savings option created in 2013, and it works for businesses of any size. It is probably the simplest and least expensive retirement plan option available to employers, but the contribution limits are low. The employee is responsible for opening an IRA account (either a traditional or Roth) with any financial institution that offers one. The employer is then responsible for deducting IRA contributions from the employee's pay, and depositing the funds into the employee's IRA account. The employer is not permitted to make matching contributions. The 2015 contribution limit for this type of account is $5,500, with an additional catch-up contribution of $1,000 allowed for employees age 50 and over. If you think this sounds a lot like a regular IRA, you're right; the major difference is that the payroll deduction by the employer forces the employee to contribute to his or her account.

My Retirement Account (myRA): The myRA was created in 2014 to help low-and middle-income employees who do not have retirement accounts, start saving for retirement. Accounts can be opened with as little as a $25 investment and automatic contributions of as little as $5 can be made by payroll deduction. Contributions are not tax-deductible. The withdrawal rules are a little complicated, but here is an overview. The maximum balance the accounts are allowed to hold is $15,000. Once the balance goes over that (or if 30 years pass), it has to be transferred to a Roth IRA. At that point, the withdrawals follow Roth withdrawal rules. However, if withdrawals are made before five years have passed, or before age 59½ (which might happen if the owner needs the money), the gains are taxed but contributions are not. Unlike all of the other options listed above, there are no fees associated with setting up these accounts. The only investment choice, however, is U.S. Government bonds, so participants can never lose money. And unlike all of the other options listed above, the employee's contributions can be withdrawn at any time, for any reason, without penalty. The earnings are subject to stricter rules; if withdrawn prior to age 59½ and before the account has been in existence for five years, then a 10% penalty applies. The government first began accepting applications for myRA participants at the end of 2014.

Deferral Contribution Limits Compared

As a result of a series of tax law changes starting with the Economic Growth and Tax Relief Reconciliation Act of 2001 (EGTRRA), the new deferral contribution limits for employees and owners of many of these individual and defined-contribution plans have grown substantially more generous. The government now allows us to put more money in our retirement plans and provides greater tax benefits. I recommend that we take the government up on its offer to fund our own retirement plans to the extent we can afford it.

The maximum deferral contribution limits for 2015 are shown in Table 1.1 on page 19. (The maximum contributions for individuals younger than age 50 appear in the first line and the maximum contributions for those age 50 and older are in the second line and in italics).

Please remember that, with the exception of the Roth accounts discussed more fully in Chapter 3, every one of the retirement plans listed above works basically the same way. Subject to limitations, your taxable income is reduced by the amount you contribute to your plan. Your employer's contribution is not subject to federal income taxes when it is made, nor is your deferral contribution. You pay no federal income tax until you take a withdrawal from the plan, and your money can only be withdrawn according to specific rules and regulations. Ultimately, the distributions are taxed at ordinary income tax rates. These plans offer tax-deferred growth because as the assets appreciate, taxes on the dividends, interest, and capital gains are deferred—or delayed—until there is a withdrawal or a distribution.

It is important to know that states tax retirement plans differently. Some states, such as Pennsylvania, do not give employees a tax deduction for their retirement plan *contributions* but they don't tax retirement plan *distributions*. So, Pennsylvania becomes a less desirable state to work in, but a more desirable state to retire to. California, on the other hand, does give employees a tax

Table 1.1: Maximum Deferral Contribution Limits for 2013-2015

	2013	2014	2015
SIMPLE Plans [a]	$12,000	$12,000	$12,500
50 and older	*$14,500*	*$14,500*	*$15,500*
401(k), 403(b), 457 [b]	$17,500	$17,500	$18,000
50 and older	*$23,000*	*$23,000*	*$24,000*
Roth 401(k) + Roth 403(b)	$17,500	$17,500	$18,000
50 and older	*$23,000*	*$23,000*	*$24,000*
SEP [c,d]	$51,000	$52,000	$53,000
50 and older	*$51,000*	*$52,000*	*$53,000*
Single-K [One-Person 401(k)] [c,d]	$51,000	$52,000	$53,000
50 and older	*$56,500*	*$57,500*	*$59,000*
Traditional and Roth IRA	$5,500	$5,500	$5,500
50 and older	*$6,500*	*$6,500*	*$6,500*
Payroll Deduction IRA	$5,500	$5,500	$5,500
50 and older	*$6,500*	*$6,500*	*$6,500*

[a] SIMPLE plans are for enterprises with 100 or fewer eligible workers.

[b] 403(b) plans are for nonprofits; 457 plans are for governments and nonprofits. In the last three years before retirement, workers in 457 plans can save double the "under age 50" contribution limit.

[c] Overall plan limits for business owners include total of all contributions by the employer (self-owned business), employee (self), and any forfeitures.

[d] Plus amounts for inflation-related adjustments.

deduction for their retirement plan contributions, but California taxes IRA and retirement plan distributions, which presumably over time would mean more revenue for the state because the distributions would include appreciation. A bad scenario for tax purposes is to live in Pennsylvania, not get a tax break for your retirement plan contributions and IRAs, and then retire to California where your IRA and retirement plan distributions would be taxed. A better plan would be to work in California, get the tax break for your retirement plan and IRA contributions, and then retire to Pennsylvania, with no taxes on retirement plan distributions. You could also retire to a state that doesn't have an income tax, like Texas or Florida.

There are important tax considerations for which state you live in and which state you retire to, and sometimes you have to take appropriate action before you even pack up your belongings and move. For example, a Pennsylvania resident who is moving to California should consider making a Roth IRA conversion while still a Pennsylvania resident because that conversion will not be taxed for PA purposes, and he can later take income-tax free Roth IRA distributions while a California resident.

Timing and Vesting of Defined-Contribution Plans

It is important to understand when employers are required to make their deposits to your retirement plan, and when your interest in the plan becomes vested.

First, your employer is not allowed to hang on to the money they deduct from your paycheck indefinitely. Department of Labor rules require that your employer deposit your contributions to your retirement plan "as soon as possible, but no later than the 15th business day of the following month." There are more restrictive rules in place for employers having fewer than 100 plan participants – these employers are required to deposit your contributions within 7 business days. Note, however, that the rules are different for the employer contribution; employers must make their contributions to an employee's retirement plan by the due date of the employer's federal tax return (including extensions). As a result, if your employer is on a calendar-year-end, you might not see the match portion of your 401(k) until well after year-end. Other employers match immediately when a contribution is made.

Also, just because the money is credited to your account doesn't necessarily mean it is all yours immediately. The portion you contribute will always be yours, and if you quit tomorrow, your contribution remains your money. The employer's contribution might only become available to you after working a certain number of years—once you have put in your time. Your employer may refer to this as being "vested" in the plan. A common vesting schedule is 20 percent per year that an employee remains with the company until five years have passed. At that point, the employee is 100 percent vested. This is called graded vesting. Other plans allow no vesting until the employee has worked for a certain number of years. Then, when he or she reaches that threshold, there is a 100 percent vesting in the employer's contributions. This is called cliff vesting.

A Quick Note about Retirement Plan Loans

Loans against IRAs and IRA-based plans (SEPs and SIMPLEs) are prohibited by law, but loans are permitted against 401(k), 403(b), 457(B), profit sharing and money purchase plans. Some employers offering these types of defined contribution plans allow their employees to take loans against their retirement accounts. Federal tax laws specify that, if loans are permitted, the amount can't be more than 50% of the participant's vested account balance, up to a maximum of $50,000. Federal laws also specify that the loan must be repaid within five years, unless the proceeds were used to buy your main home. Remember, the employer is responsible for setting the rules of their own plan, so some employers might only permit loans in the event of financial hardship and some might not permit them at all. If loans are permitted, the employee has to sign a written loan agreement that specifies the repayment schedule. Most employers require that the loan be repaid through payroll deductions.

If someone needs a loan, many people prefer to take one against their retirement plan because the interest rates are generally lower than what they can get from a bank, and they pay that interest back to themselves. There are some negatives about this strategy that you need to be aware of though. The money taken out of the plan is no longer earning an investment rate of return and, even if the loan is repaid with interest, the interest rate will likely not be as high as the investment rate of return that would have been earned if the money had remained in the account. Because most employers require repayment via payroll deduction, many employees can't afford to continue their 401(k) contributions while they are repaying their loan – which affects their ability to reach their long-term retirement goals. And if your employer offers a matching contribution, you lose their matching contribution (which I call free money) during the time you are not contributing to the plan.

While these might seem like relatively minor points, I think you will really regret taking a loan from your retirement plan if you are separated from service before it is repaid. If you lose your job for any reason, you generally have to repay the full balance remaining on the loan, within 60 days. What do you think the chances are of a bank giving you another loan to repay your retirement plan loan, when you are unemployed? If you are unable to repay it, then your employer is required to treat the loan as a distribution, and you will receive a 1099-R that you will have to include on your tax return the following year. In addition to having to pay taxes on the unpaid balance of the loan, you will also owe a 10 percent penalty if you are under age 59½. And while you might not plan on leaving your job, that decision could be made for you by something as simple as your company relocating, being sold, or going out of business. Then, you are left with a tax problem that you didn't see coming when you were filling out your paperwork for your loan.

Defined-Benefit Plans

With a defined-benefit plan, the employer contributes money according to a formula described in the company plan to provide a promised monthly benefit to the employee at retirement. Many people refer to these types of plans as "my pension." While most commonly offered by federal, state and local governments, there are a few private employers who still offer them. The amount of the benefit is determined based on a formula that considers the number of years of service, salary (perhaps an average of the highest three years), and age. Defined-benefit plans usually do not allow the employee to contribute his or her own funds into the plan, and the employer bears all of the investment risk. When it is time for the employee to collect his monthly benefit, the employer is responsible for paying the benefit—regardless of how the investments have done from the time of the employer's contribution to the time of the employee's distribution.

Defined-benefit plans were far more common 30 years ago than they are today. For people with defined-benefit plans, there are not many opportunities to make strategic decisions during the working years to increase retirement benefits. It might be possible to increase the retirement benefit by deferring salary or bonuses into the final years, or working overtime to increase the calculation wage base. These opportunities, however, depend on the plan's formula, and they are often inflexible and insignificant.

At retirement, the employee is often given a wide range of choices of how to collect his or her pension. Distribution options generally involve receiving a certain amount of money every month for the rest of one's life. Receiving regular payments for a specified period, usually a lifetime, is called an annuity. (Please don't confuse this type of annuity with a tax-deferred annuity or a 403(b) plan, which is also often called an annuity). The annuity period often runs for your lifetime and that of your spouse. Or it might be defined with a guaranteed period for successor beneficiaries; maybe it is guaranteed for the life of the longest living spouse, or perhaps for a 10-year term regardless of when you die or your wife dies. (A further discussion of annuities can be found in Chapter 8).

Guaranteeing Income for Life

Employees who have defined-benefit plans have some very important options to consider at the time of retirement. For example, let's assume that you are in good health and want the highest monthly income for the rest of your life. That often seems like the best option. However, choosing this option means that, if you die first, your surviving spouse is out of luck because your monthly pension payments stop at your death. More times than not, if we need to protect the income for both spouses' lives, I will recommend a reduced pension but with a 100% guarantee for the surviving spouse.

Sometimes pension plan owners take my usual advice and choose a lower monthly payment because it will last through their life and their spouse's life. Sometimes the owner will take a large annual payment and his or her surviving spouse will receive a fraction, perhaps half or two-thirds throughout his or her life. But there is another option to consider. One of the options frequently pushed by insurance agents is to buy a one-life (not two-life) annuity and use some of the extra income to purchase life insurance on the owner's life. Should the owner die, the life insurance death benefit can go toward the surviving spouse's support. When you look at the numbers, as we have, this usually isn't the best strategy if you still have the option to choose a pension benefit that protects your spouse after your death.

You can see that there are many important decisions to be made at your retirement. In these situations, "running the numbers," that is, comparing different potential scenarios, can provide guidance towards making a decision that is right for your family. And if you have already retired and made an irrevocable choice, it might not be too late to improve your situation. For example, if you already decided to take the highest pension without a survivorship feature, it might not be too late to get insurance, if you are still insurable. In other words, if you are retired and, after reading this book, are now concerned that by taking a one-life annuity with the highest monthly payment you did not sufficiently provide for your surviving spouse, you might want to consider purchasing life insurance. In many, if not most situations, it is often simplest and best to choose a two-life option ensuring full income to you and your spouse. But these questions are so complex that I strongly encourage you to consult with someone who is a retirement planning specialist, and who can objectively "run the numbers." That way, you can make a decision with full knowledge and understanding of the alternatives available for your family.

One other issue to consider—although hard to quantify and antici-pate—is companies failing to make their promised payments. The number of announcements about reduced payments and no payments has reached crisis proportions and is getting worse. Retirees in many industries have suffered serious reductions in their pension income, and many people who are not yet retired have been notified that their plans have been frozen, meaning that they will get the benefit accrued up to the frozen date, but no additional credit for more years of service or increases in pay. The Pension Benefit Guaranty Cor-poration is a federal agency that administers the pensions of companies that cannot meet their obligations to their employees, but even they are stretched to the limit because of the sheer number of pension plans that are inadequately funded. If you are a participant in such a plan, you might want to consider establishing a defined-contribution account in addition to this plan, to supple-ment your retirement income.

Failing pension plans may soon be the cause of another financial crisis in this country. As if the inadequate funding (formally known as the stated defi-cit) isn't enough to scare the daylights out of many pension plan participants, what about the understated liability? Many defined benefit plans use interest rate assumptions of 7 percent or higher, which is not realistic. If a plan is cur-rently paying out to pensioners, as most are, it is extremely imprudent for the plan assets to be invested aggressively. A safer strategy would be to invest the plan assets in a mix of stocks and bonds. So let's assume that the plan has 50 percent of its assets in stocks, and 50 percent in bonds. If stocks pay 7 percent over the long term and bonds pay 2 percent over the long term, the plan as a whole won't earn a 7 percent rate of return. It will earn an average rate of return of 4.5 percent. There are also costs associated with pension plan administra-tion – maybe 0.5 percent to 1 percent - that have to be considered as well. The solution, unfortunately, is not to try and earn a higher rate of return by invest-ing all of the plan assets in stocks. Pension plan owners, especially government agencies, have to bite the bullet and contribute more to the pension plan. And when they don't have the money in their budget to do so, they make the plan deficit disappear (on paper, anyway) by increasing the assumed rate of return.

I really feel the problem of underfunded pension plans is going to blow up on us and, to a large extent, it already has. If you don't believe me, google the words "underfunded pension plan" and look at the list of names that come up! It wouldn't surprise me at all to see that this will be the cause of the next major taxpayer bailout.

Cash Balance Plan

A relatively new and unique version of a defined-benefit plan is known as a *cash balance plan*. Technically, this is a defined-benefit plan, but it has features similar to a defined-contribution plan. Though on the rise, this type of plan is not common. Each employee is given an account to which the employer provides contributions or pay credits, which may be a percentage of pay and an interest credit on the balance in the account. The account's investment earnings to be credited are usually defined by the plan, and the employer bears all downside risk for actual investment earnings shortfalls. The increase in popularity of the cash balance plan has been spurred by the increasingly mobile workforce in the United States. Employees may take their cash balance plans with them to a new employer when they change jobs or roll them into an IRA.

> **There is a good possibility that you have the opportunity to invest more money in your retirement plan or plans than you realize.**

How Many Plans Are Available to You

There is a good possibility that you have the opportunity to invest more money in your retirement plan or plans than you realize. For many readers who are still working, applying the lessons of this mini case study could save you thousands of dollars a year.

MINI CASE STUDY 1.3

Contributing the Maximum to
Multiple Retirement Plans[1]

Tom and his wife, Judy, both 55, want to make the maximum retirement plan contributions allowable. Tom earns $51,000 per year as a guidance counselor for a school district that has both a 403(b) plan and a Section 457 plan. Judy is self-employed, has no employ-

---

[1] We have used 2015 amounts for this example. The retirement plan contribution limits for future years are likely to be even higher. The current year contribution limits are available on our website at **www.paytaxeslater.com**. You can also receive these updates as soon as they happen, by signing up for our free e-mail newsletter.

ees, and shows a profit after expenses on her Schedule C, Form U.S. 1040, of $80,000 per year. Tom and Judy have a 16-year-old computer-whiz child, Bill, who works weekends and summers doing computer programming for Judy's company. Bill is a legitimate subcontractor, not an employee of Judy's company. Judy pays Bill $24,000 per year. What is the maximum that Tom and Judy and Bill can contribute to their retirement plans for calendar year 2015?

Tom:
Calculating Maximum Contributions to Multiple Plans

Under EGTRRA, Tom could contribute $24,000 to his 403(b) plan in 2015 ($18,000 normal limit plus another $6,000 because he is over 50). Please note that under EGTRRA, Tom's retirement plan contribution is not limited to 15 percent of his earnings as it would have been under prior law. Under a special rule specifically relating to 457 plans, he could also contribute another $18,000 to his 457 plan in 2015. He is also eligible to contribute $6,500 to a Roth IRA ($5,500 per year limit plus $1,000 because he is over age 50). (Roth IRAs are discussed in more detail in Chapter 2). Please note the new law allows contributions to all three plans—something not previously permitted. Ultimately, Tom was able to contribute almost all of his entire income to retirement plans.

Judy:
Calculating Maximum Contribution to a Single-K

After rejecting a more complicated and more expensive defined-benefit plan, Judy chooses the one-person 401(k) plan, or the Single-K plan. Judy could contribute as much as $38,870 into her personal 401(k) plan. This plan for self-employed taxpayers has the equivalent of an employee and employer share. The first component is the 401(k) elective employee deferral amount that is limited to $24,000 in 2015 (the same limits as Tom's 403(b) plan). Most Single-Ks are set up so that you can deduct this portion on your tax return and have it taxed like a regular 401(k). If you want this portion to enjoy the tax-free benefits of a Roth IRA, which we generally recommend, you can set up a Roth Single-K, and elect to put this $24,000 into the Roth Single-K. So, she has options—traditional Single-K or Roth Single-K. Please see Chapter 3 for a detailed comparison of a Roth 401(k) vs. a traditional 401(k).

The second component is a $14,870 discretionary profit- shar-ing, or employer's contribution. Please note that, as with a traditional 401(k) plan, the *employer* contribution *cannot* be made to the Roth account. To arrive at the $14,870, Judy's net self-employed income of $80,000 must be reduced by half of her computed self-employ-ment tax, which is $80,000 x 92.35% x 15.3% = $11,304 x 50%, or $5,652. Then that amount is subtracted from her net income, $80,000 ($80,000 − $5,652 = $74,348). The $74,348 is multiplied by the 20% contribution rate limit (for self-employed individuals, and equal to 25 percent of earnings net of the contribution itself) to yield the maximum profit-sharing contribution amount of $14,870. (If Ju-dy's income had been higher, the total of both the employer and employee contributions to her Single-K could be as high as $59,000 in 2015. The maximum contribution allowed to the plan is $53,000 and she can also make a $6,000 catch-up contribution). Judy also can make an additional $6,500 contribution to her Roth IRA.

Bill:
For Parents Who Are Considering Funding Retirement Plans for Their Children

Although Bill is young, if he can afford it, he should use his $24,000 income to begin making contributions to his retirement plan. Bill will owe $3,672 of self-employment tax, half of which is deductible, so his net earned income for the purposes of retirement plan contribu-tions is $22,164.

Bill could open up a SIMPLE plan and contribute $12,500, plus a three percent (3%) SIMPLE matching contribution, which would be $665 (3% of $24,000 x .9235). The net earned income less these amounts is $10,835 which is enough to fully fund his Roth IRA with $5,500. If he already spent some of his income, his parents could make him a gift of the money.

The tax-free benefit of the Roth IRA and the tax-deferred ben-efit of the SIMPLE plan are so important to a child during his or her lifetime that some parents who have sufficient money are willing to fund their child's retirement plan. This is a wonderful idea. However, in order to contribute to a retirement plan or IRA, the child must have earned income. Some parents will be tempted to create a sham business for their child or even put their child on the payroll as a sham transaction. I do not recommend this approach. I advocate that the child do legitimate work, complying with all child labor laws. All retirement plan contributions should stem from legitimate businesses, and if based on self-employed earnings, be a real business. (I had to say that in case the IRS reads this. In all seriousness, however, there are also non-financial benefits in having a child do legitimate work to receive money).

I have seen parents paying infants to model, characterizing the payment to the infant as self-employment income and making a retirement plan contribution for the infant. I think that goes too far. Any situation where a child younger than 11 years old receives employment compensation is highly suspect. Even at age 11, legitimate compensation should not be too high.

Let's assume that Tom, Judy, and Bill max out their retirement plan contributions. Even though Tom and Judy earned only $131,000 and Bill earned only $24,000, the family could contribute almost $113,000 into their retirement plans and Roth IRAs. For subsequent years, the contribution limits are likely to be even more generous. Is this a great country or what?

This example intentionally exaggerates the family's likely contributions. The point is to show the maximum contribution limits and the variety of plan options available. In this particular case, Tom and Judy and Bill may choose not to maximize their contributions because they may not receive any income tax benefits beyond a certain level of contribution. It is worthwhile, however, to review this case study to help with choosing and implementing a new plan.

How to Minimize Your Life Insurance Costs to Maximize Your Retirement Contributions

Many old classic whole life insurance agents are going to hate me (some already do) for writing this chapter. Often, our younger clients will complain that they cannot maximize their retirement plan contributions because of the cost of their life insurance. Although whole life or guaranteed universal life can be a great vehicle for high income earners to save more money, term insurance is often a better solution for individuals whose budgets don't stretch to afford both the high whole life insurance premiums and maximized retirement plan contributions.

The objective of term life insurance is to protect a family from the financial devastation that can ensue from the untimely death of the primary bread winner(s). It is also important to insure the value of the services of a stay-at-home parent. It is critically important insurance, but it is also to your advantage to try to get the appropriate level of coverage for the most reasonable price. The following section, though by no means complete, presents my favorite idea for many young families to protect themselves in the event of an early, unexpected death, but to do so relatively cheaply. I am working from the premise that I do not like to see people underinsured, but I also want everyone to be thinking ahead to retirement.

One of the most common mistakes my younger clients make is not having sufficient term insurance. Most healthy young people survive until retirement and paying for term insurance is not something anyone really wants to do. In my practice, however, I have known young healthy people who died much too early. In my experience, it is rarely the result of a catastrophic car or plane accident, but more frequently because of the sudden onset of cancer or some other fatal disease.

Most people, however, also have this vague sense that the responsible thing to do is to purchase insurance to protect their families. Some people seek out an insurance provider and initiate a policy; others do something when they are approached by a life insurance professional. In either case they usually end up with some kind of policy. The key is to find a policy that balances adequate insurance and minimum premiums. I don't like to see people, especially younger people who are working on a limited budget, pay high life insurance premiums.

It isn't my intention to present a detailed prescription for determining your life insurance needs. For my purposes here, I will ask you to think about "How much income will your survivors require to live comfortably?" Let's say that after some analysis, you decide that an appropriate income is $60,000 per year in today's dollars. Please note I did not derive this number as a multiple of current salary; it is based purely on projected need.

I am not going to delve into the intricacies of calculating a safe withdrawal rate—that is to say, how much as a percentage of principal you can withdraw and have the money last for a lifetime—but I would say for young people with a long life expectancy, four percent (4%) would probably be on the high side for a safe withdrawal rate. This means if there is no other source of income, an individual will need at least $1,500,000 of life insurance ($60,000/4% = $1,500,000).

First, I hope I didn't just bum you out and make you realize you are vastly underinsured because $60,000 of income doesn't sound that high, and you don't have anywhere near $1,500,000 of insurance. Admittedly, whatever resources you have can be used to reduce the need for life insurance. If both spouses work, the income of the survivor can certainly be factored in. If you have significant investments or savings, they can also be used to reduce the need for insurance.

But to keep things simple, let's assume there aren't significant additional resources and the need is $1,500,000. Also, in this basic example, I am not factoring in the additional money that would be required for living expenses, and education or day care if there were young children involved.

Let's also assume that at least one member of the couple is working and he or she receives some life insurance as a job benefit. For discussion's sake, we will assume the salary is $100,000 and the insurance benefit is equal to three times the salary. You might say, "Well, that's a start. Now I only need $1,200,000 more." Sorry, that's the wrong answer. What if you get sick and can't perform your job? You lose your job, you lose your insurance, and because you are sick, you can't get life insurance. (Hopefully, you either have disability insurance through work or you have your own policy, but that is something I don't cover in this book). Whereas group insurance at work is a blessing for people who are uninsurable and can't get life insurance on the open market for a reasonable rate, there are two problems with group life insurance. The first, I just mentioned: If you lose your job, you lose your insurance. The second is that if you are healthy, you can almost always get insurance more economically on the open market.

For young people with cash flow problems, keeping the premiums affordable is critical. Many insurance professionals make a convincing case for permanent insurance, which is a type of policy that ultimately has cash value. There is a payout when you die, or sometimes upon reaching a certain age. Term insurance, on the other hand, is not designed to pay out if you reach a normal life expectancy. It is designed to pay if you don't survive to a normal life expectancy.

Permanent insurance is expensive. The insurance company will ultimately have to write a check to your beneficiaries, so it costs more. Many of my young working clients come in with some measure of permanent insurance—in some ways, it feels better to them. They are paying money into insurance, but they know there will be a payback. However, since it is so much more expensive, many of these same young people are significantly underinsured. If you have permanent insurance of even $500,000, you are still $1,000,000 underinsured even though you have a big premium every year. I would rather see the money going toward sufficient term insurance so the surviving spouse and other family members are protected.

Let's assume that you have a good job and marketable skills. You are prudent and thrifty, putting money into your retirement plan at work and maxing out your Roth IRAs. You do projections and determine that you will have sufficient money to retire at 60 (assuming you are 30 now). You might logically think "Okay, I need a 30-year level term policy (premiums are guaranteed never to go up) for $1,500,000."

Well, that is a reasonable start, but you are likely to find that the guaranteed premium for a level term policy for 30 years for $1,500,000 is more than you want to pay for insurance. Well, are you really going to need that much coverage for the whole time? Perhaps not. If you work and save for 10 years, you may only need $1,000,000 at that point in time. Perhaps in the 10 years beyond that, your need may drop to $500,000. I am trying to keep it simple to make a point. As you change, your insurance needs will change, and thinking within this more flexible framework offers some new options.

Since I am being frugal with your insurance budget, consider the following set of policies, assuming the above situation.

- Get a 30-year term policy for $500,000 coverage
- Get a 20 year term policy for $500,000 coverage
- Get a 10-year term policy for $500,000 coverage

If you die between the date the policy is issued and year 10, your heirs get $1,500,000, which is what we determined was the needed amount. At the end of 10 years, the first policy ends and you will only have $1,000,000 of coverage. That is okay. By this point you should have $500,000 in retirement plans and savings. In addition, the need for insurance will be down a little bit because your heirs will have a shorter life expectancy.

After 20 years, the second policy ends and you will only have $500,000 of coverage remaining. That is okay because by this time you should have $1,000,000 of retirement and savings, and your need will only be $500,000. At the end of 30 years, you will have no coverage, but again, that is okay because hopefully by then you will have accrued sufficient resources for your surviving spouse.

Of course in the above example, I have kept things really simple. I have not included relevant factors like inflation, children's needs, the ability of the surviving spouse to work, and so forth.

But you get the idea. We have helped a number of our clients reach their goal of adequate coverage through this layered system. Frequently, a 30-year level term policy costs more than individuals might want to pay or can afford, so they compromise by not getting the insurance coverage they really need. I would prefer to see you get the coverage you need using some variation of the layered approach that I have suggested. Remember, the goal is sufficient coverage for a reasonable cost. That said, my recommendation for many younger clients is to have most of your coverage through term insurance, but also add a small permanent policy to the mix.

In all fairness, I didn't invent this layered approach. I learned it from Tom Hall, an excellent broker I work with in Pittsburgh. This brings up another point. After you decide to get the insurance you need, I recommend purchasing your insurance through an ethical insurance broker (someone who can purchase insurance from many different companies). In our experience, working with a broker is the way to get the best policies at the best rates. (For more on working with brokers and qualifying for the best insurance rates, read Chapter 12). If you don't have or know an appropriate insurance broker, please see the back of the book.

When You Think You Can't Afford to Make the Maximum Contributions

Maybe now I have helped you rethink your insurance-retirement savings quandary. But you still feel you cannot afford to save for retirement. The truth is you may very well be able to afford to save, but you don't realize it. That's right. I am going to present a rationale to persuade you to contribute more than you think you can afford.

Let's assume you have been limiting your own contributions to the amount that your employer is willing to match and yet you barely have enough money to get by week to week. Does it still make sense to make nonmatched contributions assuming you do not want to reduce your spending? Maybe.

If you have substantial savings and maximizing your retirement plan contributions causes your net payroll check to be insufficient to meet your expenses, I still recommend maximizing retirement plan contributions. The shortfall for your living expenses from making increased pre-tax retirement plan contributions should be withdrawn from your savings (money that has already been taxed). Over time this process, that is, saving the most in a retirement plan and funding the shortfall by making after-tax withdrawals from an after-tax account, transfers money from the after-tax environment to the pre-tax environment. Ultimately it results in more money for you and your heirs.

A final point worth mentioning is that you should consider your personal tax bracket when making contributions to your retirement plan. Your tax bracket will likely change over the course of your lifetime because of your marital status, and changes in your income. While I still want you to contribute the maximum you possibly can to your retirement plan, in some instances it may make more sense to contribute to the traditional account rather than the Roth account, and vice versa. These strategies are covered in detail in Chapter 3.

> **Maybe now I have helped you rethink your insurance-retirement savings quandary. But you still feel you cannot afford to save for retirement. The truth is you may very well be able to afford to save, but you don't realize it.**

MINI CASE STUDY 1.4

Changing Your IRA and Retirement Plan Strategy after a Windfall or an Inheritance

Joe always had trouble making ends meet. He did, however, know enough to always contribute to his retirement plan the amount his employer was willing to match. Because he was barely making ends meet and had no savings in the after-tax environment, he never made a nonmatching retirement plan contribution. Tragedy then struck Joe's family. Joe's mother died, leaving Joe $100,000. Should Joe change his retirement plan strategy?

Yes. Joe should not blow the $100,000. If his housing situation is reasonable, he should not use the inherited money for a house — or even a down payment on a house. Instead, Joe should increase his retirement plan contribution to the maximum. In addition, he should start making Roth IRA contributions (see Chapter 2). (This solid advice freaked out a real estate investor after he read it in the first edition. He thought the money should have been used to invest in real estate. Being that aggressive, however, is a risky strategy, unsuitable for many, if not most, investors).

Assuming Joe maintains his pre-inheritance lifestyle, between his Roth IRA contribution and the increase in his retirement plan contribution, Joe will not have enough to make ends meet without eating into his inheritance. That's okay. He should cover the shortfall with withdrawals from the inherited money. True, if that pattern continues long enough, Joe will eventually deplete his inheritance in its current form. But his retirement plan and Roth IRA will be so much better financed that in the long run, the tax-deferred and tax-free growth of these accounts will make Joe better off by thousands, possibly hundreds of thousands, of dollars. The only time this strategy would not make sense is if Joe needed the inherited money to pay personal expenses or even to liquidate debt.

A Key Lesson from This Chapter

You should contribute the maximum you can afford to all the retirement plans to which you have access.

2

||||||||||||||||||||

Traditional IRAs versus Roth IRAs

All days are not the same. Save for a rainy day.
When you don't work, savings will work for you.

— M. K. Soni

Main Topics

- How traditional IRAs and Roth IRAs differ
- Contribution limits for both Roth and traditional IRAs
- Eligibility rules for both Roth and traditional IRAs
- Distribution rules for both Roth and traditional IRAs
- The principal advantages and disadvantages of a Roth IRA
- Choosing between opening a Roth IRA and a traditional IRA

KEY IDEA

The Roth IRA is always preferable to a nondeductible traditional IRA and is usually better than a deductible traditional IRA contribution.

What is the Difference between an IRA and a Roth IRA?

Individual Retirement Accounts (IRAs) allow individuals who are under age 70½ and who earn income to make contributions to their own retirement accounts. There are two major types of IRAs, the traditional and the Roth. Traditional IRAs were created in 1974, as an incentive for taxpayers to begin saving for their retirements. Owners of traditional IRAs enjoy tax-deferred growth on their investment, but the contributions and earnings are taxed at the federal level when a qualified withdrawal is made. IRA owners can also take a tax deduction for their contributions if they meet either of these two requirements:

- They (and their spouse, if married) do not have a retirement plan at work.

- They earn less income than the Adjusted Gross Income (AGI) limit for deducting IRA contributions. (Please see discussion following regarding traditional IRA eligibility rules).

If IRA owners have income above the limit for which they are permitted to deduct the contribution, they may still contribute to an IRA, but without the benefit of a tax deduction. These are commonly referred to as *nondeductible IRA contributions*.

With the exception of the Roth IRA (discussed below) and the Defined Benefit Plan, all the other retirement plans mentioned in Chapter 1 can usually be rolled into an IRA, income tax-free, at retirement or service termination.

Roth IRAs were first established by the Taxpayer Relief Act of 1997. The main characteristic of the Roth IRA is that the investment grows tax-free, and is not taxed when qualified withdrawals are made. However, unlike the traditional IRA, there is no income tax deduction up front. The Roth IRA income limit on contributions is much higher than the traditional deductible IRA income limit on contributions. This allows many higher income earners who are not eligible for a deductible IRA, to participate in a Roth IRA.

The main characteristic of the Roth IRA is that the investment grows tax-free, and is not taxed when qualified withdrawals are made.

Here is a comparison of the differences between Roth and traditional IRAs:

	Roth IRA	IRA
Investment	Grows tax-free	Grows tax-deferred
Withdrawals (qualified)	Tax-free	Taxed as ordinary income
Contributions	Income level	Income level
Income Limits	Affects ability to contribute	Affects deductibility of contribution
Contribution Limits	Same as IRA	Same as Roth IRA
Required Distributions	Not if you are the original owner*	Yes

* Note, at the time we went to press, there was some discussion among our lawmakers about requiring minimum distributions from Roth IRAs. While it might eventually happen, I don't believe that they would pursue such an unpopular course of action any time soon. Therefore, all of the illustrations that follow assume that there are no Required Minimum Distributions (RMDs) from Roth IRAs.

The essence of a Roth IRA (in contrast to a traditional IRA) is that you pay tax on the seed (the contribution, because you don't get a tax deduction), but you can reap the harvest tax-free (the distribution). With a traditional IRA, you deduct the seed, but pay tax on the harvest.

Contribution Limits for Both Roth and Traditional IRAs

The permitted contribution amounts are the same for both Roth IRAs and traditional IRAs. Note that the *total* permitted contribution amount applies both to IRAs and Roth IRAs, which means that for 2015, you can only contribute a total of $5,500 ($6,500 if you are 50 or older) to IRAs and Roth IRAs. The total IRA and/or Roth IRA contributions cannot exceed your *earned* income, and, as with traditional IRAs, a married individual filing a joint return may make a Roth IRA contribution for the nonworking spouse by treating his or her compensation as his or her spouse's. The contribution limits for 2011 through 2015 are shown in Table 2.1 on page 38.

> **The essence of a Roth IRA (in contrast to a traditional IRA) is that you pay tax on the seed (the contribution, because you don't get a tax deduction) but you can reap the harvest tax-free (the distribution).**

Table 2.1
IRA Contribution Limits for 2011 through 2015

Year	Annual IRA/Roth IRA Contribution Limits	Catch-Up Contribution Limits for Individuals 50 and Older
2011	$5,000	$1,000
2012	$5,000	$1,000
2013	$5,500	$1,000
2014	$5,500	$1,000
2015	$5,500	$1,000

Sharp-eyed readers may notice that, while the IRS found it necessary to adjust the maximum contribution limits for most employer-sponsored qualified retirement plans for inflation in 2015, they left the maximum contribution limits for traditional and Roth IRAs unchanged.

Traditional IRA Eligibility Rules

1. All taxpayers under age 70½ who have earned income are allowed to contribute to a traditional IRA without regard to income level.

2. If neither you nor your spouse participates in an employee-sponsored retirement plan, you both can deduct the full amount of your traditional IRA contributions.

3. If you are covered by a retirement plan at work, there are AGI limits for allowing full deductions, partial deductions, and limits above which no deductions are permitted. They are shown in Table 2.2 on page 39.

4. A spousal contribution can be made for a nonworking spouse if the other spouse has earned income, and a joint tax return is filed. A spousal IRA has been around for decades, but as of 2013, it has a new name: the Kay Bailey Hutchison Spousal IRA. And while the dollar amounts for contributions were increased for inflation, the basic rules for spousal IRAs are still the same. IRA contributions for both spouses are still limited by the amount of income earned by the working spouse. If the working spouse earns $8,000, then the maximum that can be contributed to both IRAs combined, is

Table 2.2
2014 and 2015 AGI Limitations for Deducting a Traditional IRA
if You Are Covered By a Retirement Plan at Work

		Fully Deductible	Partially Deductible	Not Deductible
Single & Head of Household	2014	$60,000 or less	$61,001 - $69,999	$ 71,000 +
	2015	$61,000 or less	$60,001 - $70,999	$ 70,000 +
Married Filing Jointly	2014	$96,000 or less	$96,001 - $115,999	$116,000 +
	2015	$98,000 or less	$98,001 - $117,999	$118,000 +
Married Filing Separately	2014	n/a	less than $10,000	$ 10,000 +
	2015	n/a	less than $10,000	$ 10,000 +

$8,000. Please note "contribution amounts" and "deduction amounts" are two different things. If the working spouse is not covered under a retirement plan at work, the non-working spouse's IRA contribution (maximum of $5,500 - $6,500 if over age 50 – in 2015) is fully deductible. If the working spouse is covered under a retirement plan at work, the nonworking spouse can still contribute the same amount, but the tax deduction may be limited, as shown in Table 2.3 on the following page.

If you have too much income to deduct your traditional IRA contribution, you can still make a nondeductible IRA contribution if you are otherwise eligible. You won't get the income-tax deduction up front, but you will still gain the advantage of the tax-deferred growth in the account.

Roth IRA Eligibility Rules

1. Unlike a traditional IRA, an individual can contribute to a Roth IRA after reaching age 70½ as long as he or she has earned income. Earned income includes wages, commissions, self-employment income, and other amounts received for personal services, as well as long-term disability benefits received prior to normal retirement age, taxable alimony, and separate maintenance payments received under a decree of divorce or separate maintenance.

Table 2.3
2014 and 2015 AGI Limitations for Deducting a Traditional IRA
if You Are Covered By a Retirement Plan at Work

		Fully Deductible	Partially Deductible	Not Deductible
Single & Head of Household	2014	no income limit	-	-
	2015	no income limit	-	-
Married Filing Jointly or Separately, Spouse Does Not Have a Plan at Work	2014	no income limit	-	-
	2015	no income limit	-	-
Married Filing Jointly, Spouse Does Have a Plan at Work	2014	$181,000 or less	$181,001 - $190,999	$191,000 +
	2015	$183,000 or less	$183,001 - $192,999	$193,000 +
Married Filing Separately, Spouse Does Have a Plan at Work	2014	-	less than $10,000	-
	2015	-	less than $10,000	-

2. Individuals must meet the income tests, which exclude higher income taxpayers from contributing to Roth IRAs. (See Table 2.4 on page 41).

3. A married individual filing a joint return may make a Roth IRA contribution for the nonworking spouse by treating his or her compensation as his or her spouse's, but must exclude any of his or her own IRA contributions from the income treated as his or her spouse's. (For example, in 2015, if you are not yet age 50 and make $8,000, you can contribute $5,500 to your Roth, but only $2,500 to your spouse's Roth.) Total contributions cannot exceed your income.

Table 2.4
2014 and 2015 Income Eligibility Rules

		Full Contribution	Reduced Contribution	No Contribution
Single & Head of Household	2014	up to $114,000	$114,001 - $128,999	$129,000 +
	2015	up to $116,000	$116,001 - $130,999	$131,000 +
Married Filing Jointly	2014	up to $181,000	$181,001 - $190,999	$191,000 +
	2015	up to $183,000	$183,001 - $192,999	$193,000 +

Advanced Distribution Rules for Traditional IRAs

1. Traditional IRA withdrawals are generally taxable at the federal level, but not necessarily at the state level. If you make nondeductible contributions to your IRA, you will have *basis* (in other words, money that you put into the account, that you already paid tax on, and on which the IRS can't tax you again). If all of your IRA contributions were tax deductible, you have no basis in the account. It is important to know if you have basis in your nondeductible IRA, because you don't want to pay more taxes on your IRA withdrawal than are required. The burden of proving that a portion of the withdrawal is not taxable falls on you, so I hope you filed a Form 8606 to keep track of the basis in your IRA. This form should be filed every year as an attachment to your tax return once you have any basis in your IRA. When a withdrawal is made from an IRA with basis, a calculation is made to determine what percentage of the money in the account is your contribution, and what percentage reflects earnings on your contributions. Let's say your non-deductible contributions were $20,000 and the value of your IRA at year-end after taking a $10,000 withdrawal is $90,000. In this case, 20 percent of the withdrawal is considered a return of your own money, and is not taxable. The remaining $8,000 is taxable. (My book, *The Roth Revolution*, covers in detail a great technique for

converting after-tax or nondeductible IRAs or after-tax dollars inside a traditional 401(k) to Roth IRAs without paying any tax. Please visit www.paytaxeslater.com, for more information about that book).

2. All traditional IRA withdrawals prior to age 59½ are subject to an additional 10 percent penalty (for amounts exceeding basis) unless the withdrawal falls under one of the following exemptions:

   • They are made to a beneficiary (or the individual's estate) on or after the individual's death.

   • They are attributable to the individual being totally and permanently disabled.

   • They were used for qualified first-time home purchase expenses.

   • The distributions are not more than your qualified higher education expenses.

   • They were used for qualified medical expenses that exceed 10 percent (or 7.5 percent, if you or your spouse was born prior to January 2, 1949) of AGI.

   • The distributions are not more than the cost of your medical insurance due to a period of unemployment.

   • They are part of substantially equal periodic payments over the life of the participant—that is, distributions qualifying under Section 72(t) (which we do not cover in this book) for exemption from the premature distribution penalty.

   • They are due to an IRS levy on the account.

   • The distribution is a qualified reservist distribution.

3. All traditional IRAs are subject to RMDs after age 70½.

Distribution Rules for Roth IRAs

1. In order to take completely tax-free (or qualified) withdrawals from a Roth IRA that has grown in value, five years must have elapsed since opening the account. There is a separate five-year holding period for

each Roth IRA conversion as well (conversions are discussed in more detail in Chapter 7). Distributions must be made on or after age 59½, unless one of the following special circumstances applies:

- A distribution is made to your beneficiary (or your estate) on or after your death.

- A distribution is attributable to your being disabled.

- A distribution is made for a qualified first-time home purchase expense up to $10,000.

2. This restriction also applies to the beneficiary of a Roth IRA whose owner dies before the five-year period has ended. The beneficiary may withdraw funds tax-free as long as they do not exceed the contribution amount, but he or she must wait until the five-year period has passed before being able to enjoy tax-free withdrawal of the Roth IRAs earnings.

3. Withdrawals prior to age 59½ may be taken without tax or penalties to the extent of previous annual contributions.

4. Withdrawals in excess of previous contributions made before the five-year holding period is met are taxable, but penalty-free under the following circumstances:

- For qualified college expenses.

- For qualified medical expenses that exceed 10 percent of AGI (or 7.5 percent if you or your spouse was born before January 2, 1949).

- For health insurance premiums paid for certain unemployed individuals.

- If withdrawals are part of substantially equal periodic payments over the life of the participant.

- If the distribution is part of an IRS levy.

- You are the beneficiary of a deceased IRA owner.

5. All other withdrawals prior to age 59½ that are in excess of previous contributions are taxable and subject to a 10 percent penalty.

6. Roth IRA amounts are not subject to RMDs during the original owner's lifetime.

Furthermore, a Roth IRA owner can designate his or her spouse as the beneficiary who, upon the Roth IRA owner's death, would have the option of postponing RMDs until the second death. After the surviving spouse's death, the subsequent beneficiary (usually a child) would be required to take nontaxable minimum distributions of the inherited Roth IRA based on her own long life expectancy. (Please see Chapter 13 for distribution rules for inherited IRAs and inherited Roth IRAs).

The five-year holding requirement for Roth IRAs is intended to promote long-term savings. The five-year clock starts ticking on January 1 of the tax year associated with the first contribution or conversion, which actually results in making the five-year waiting period less than five years. The period begins on the first day of the tax year for which a contribution is made. If you open a Roth IRA account for the 2015 tax year by making a contribution on April 15, 2016 (the last day you can make your Roth IRA contributions for 2015), the five-year period is from January 1, 2015, to December 31, 2019. To achieve the same five-year period start date when opening a Roth IRA account using a Roth IRA conversion, you must make the conversion by December 31, 2015 (the last day you can make your Roth IRA conversions for 2015). Pursuant to these Roth IRA rules, if you suddenly need the money the day after or at any time after you make the contribution, you can take out the amount you contributed, free of tax. Any interest or gains, however, have to remain in the account for five years, in order to become tax free. Note, however, that the IRS has a process called "ordering rules" that determine if there is tax due on your distribution. Distributions are ordered as follows:

- your contributions

- conversion and rollover contributions, on a first-in, first out basis (generally, taken from the earliest year first)

- earnings on contributions

Assume you converted $80,000 from a traditional IRA to a Roth IRA in 2011, and that $20,000 of that amount was your basis. At the time of the conversion, you would have included $60,000 in your taxable income. In 2012, you made a $5,000 contribution to the Roth IRA. In 2015, at age 60, you take a $7,000 distribution from the Roth IRA. How much of your distribution is taxable? Well, our office can always figure it out for you, but if you'd rather do it yourself, use the above rules. The money you contributed is considered first. You contributed $5,000, so $5,000 of the $7,000 is not taxable. The next $2,000 isn't taxable either, because that was part of your conversion and it was taxed in 2011. There is no early withdrawal penalty because you are over 59½. But suppose that your Roth IRA has grown to $150,000 and you want to withdraw everything so that you can buy a yacht. Following the same rules, the $5,000 you contributed is not taxable, and the $80,000 conversion amount is not taxable. The gain of $65,000 is taxable because your yacht is not a qualified exception to the five-year holding period rule. You should wait until 2016 to withdraw the final $65,000 because it will not be taxable then.

Advantages and Disadvantages of Roth IRAs

The principal advantages:

- With limited exceptions, they grow income tax-free.

- More liberal contribution rules are in place. Taxpayers may also elect to convert all or part of their traditional IRAs to Roth accounts, by paying the taxes at the time of the conversion. The future growth on the converted amount is tax-free.

- They are not subject to the RMD rules mandating withdrawals beginning at age 70½. As of this writing, you are not required to take distributions during your lifetime. (You may *choose* to, but you don't *have* to). If you die and leave your Roth IRA to your spouse, your spouse will not have to take RMDs either.

- If needed, all of your after-tax annual contributions are always eligible for withdrawal at any time without tax consequences.

- If you have earned income after age 70½, you can keep contributing money to your Roth IRA (and so can your spouse, based on your income). This is not an option for a traditional IRA; contributions must stop at 70½.

- In cases where maximum retirement contributions are made and there are also after-tax savings, forgoing a tax deduction helps to lower the amount of after-tax savings while putting more value in the tax-free environment. Keep in mind that after-tax savings have inefficient tax consequences on their investment returns.

The result of the many advantages of the Roth IRA is that, in many cases, the heirs receive income tax-free distributions for their entire lives.

The principal disadvantages:

- You do not receive a tax deduction when you make a contribution. You will then have less money to invest in after-tax funds or to spend. But remember, after-tax funds are not tax efficient due to taxes on income. And if you simply spend the tax savings, the Roth alternative will look even better because it forces you to save and build a more valuable IRA.

- If you drop into a lower tax bracket once you begin taking your IRA distributions, you may sometimes do better with a traditional IRA. In this case, the tax savings from the deductible contribution would exceed the taxes paid upon withdrawal. Sometimes this disadvantage can be offset by a longer period of tax-free growth.

- The Roth IRA account may go down in value. In that case, if the decline becomes large enough, you would have been better off with a deductible IRA because at least you would have received a tax deduction on your contributions. If you have lost a lot of money in a Roth IRA, however, there is some relief. While I wouldn't recommend doing this, if you liquidate all your Roth IRAs and recognize a loss, the loss can be claimed as a miscellaneous itemized deduction, subject to phase outs, on Schedule A (assuming that you itemize). Losses suffered in an account that was converted from a traditional IRA to a Roth IRA can be recharacterized so that you do not have to pay income tax on the entire converted amount, a much better alternative which is discussed in greater detail in Chapter 7. As always, I recommend that you use prudent investment strategies so that the possibility of losses in your Roth account are minimized.

- If Congress ever eliminates the income tax in favor of a sales tax or value-added tax, you will have given up your tax deduction on the traditional IRA. And since the distribution will be tax-free anyway, in retrospect, the choice of a Roth IRA would have been a mistake.

This situation is similar to the extreme example of having lower tax brackets in retirement.

People who have earned income, and who are ineligible to make traditional deductible IRA contributions because their income is above the limits, can still make contributions to an IRA, but *without* the tax deduction. These nondeductible IRAs are also available for people who are above the income limits to make Roth IRA contributions.

Nondeductible IRAs

If your income is below the threshold and you are eligible to make Roth IRA contributions, it is important to understand that the Roth is always a much better choice than the *nondeductible* IRA. Remember, you don't get a tax deduction for either, but the money in the Roth IRA will be tax-free when the money is withdrawn, and the nondeductible IRA will be taxable to the extent of growth in the account. Roth IRAs can provide a much better result over the long term. Many people make the mistake of contributing to the nondeductible IRA instead of the Roth IRA when they have a choice. Although the mistake can be mitigated if caught in time, this mistake results in needless taxes in the future.

Nondeductible IRA contributions that provide tax-deferred growth, however, are still of great benefit for many high income people who do not qualify to make Roth IRA and deductible IRA contributions. Better yet, as of this writing, high income individuals are still eligible to convert their nondeductible IRA accounts into Roth IRAs with little or no tax cost. A recent IRS ruling also permits individuals who have both deductible and non-deductible contributions in their retirement plans, to split the plan assets. This means that the pre-tax portion of the plan can now be rolled into a traditional IRA, and the after-tax portion can be rolled into a Roth IRA – effectively allowing a tax-free Roth IRA conversion. (See Chapter 7 for more information on Roth IRA conversions). This is opportunity knocking, given a little forethought.

> The Roth is always a much better choice than the nondeductible IRA. Remember, you don't get a tax deduction for either, but the money in the Roth IRA will be tax-free when the money is withdrawn, and the nondeductible IRA will be taxable to the extent of growth in the account.

What Makes a Roth IRA So Great When Compared with a Traditional IRA?

The advantages of compounding interest on both tax-deferred investments and on tax-free investments far outweigh paying yearly taxes on the capital gains, dividends, and interest of after-tax investments. As you saw in Chapter 1, you are generally better off putting more money in tax-deferred and tax-free accounts than in less efficient after-tax investments. Remember that with regular after-tax investments, you have to pay income taxes on annual dividends, interest, and, if you make a sale, on capital gains.

The advantage that the Roth IRA holds over a traditional IRA builds significantly over time because of the increase in the purchasing power of the account. Let's assume you make a $6,000 Roth IRA contribution. The purchasing power of your Roth IRA will increase by $6,000, and that money will grow income tax-free. On the other hand, let's assume you contribute $6,000 to a deductible traditional IRA and you are in the 25 percent tax bracket. In that case, you will receive a tax deduction of $6,000 and get a $1,500 tax break (25% X $6,000). This $1,500 in tax savings is not in a tax-free or tax-deferred investment. Even if you resist the temptation to spend your tax savings on a nice vacation and put the money into an investment account instead, you will be taxed each year on realized interest, dividends, and capital gains. This is inefficient investment growth. The $6,000 of total dollars added to the traditional IRA offers only $4,500 of purchasing power ($6,000 total dollars less $1,500 that represents your tax savings). The $1,500 of tax savings equates to $1,500 of purchasing power, so the purchasing power for both the Roth IRA and the traditional IRA are identical in the beginning. However, in future years, the growth on the $6,000 of purchasing power in the Roth IRA is completely tax free. The growth in the traditional IRA is only tax-deferred, and the $1,500 you invested from your tax savings, is taxable every year.

One of the few things in life better than tax-deferred compounding is tax-free compounding. If your income is not over the limit and you can afford to do so after making your employer-matched contribution and the appropriate nonmatched contributions to your retirement plan, I generally recommend making additional annual contributions to a Roth IRA. Although you don't get an income tax deduction for your contribution to a Roth IRA, as you might with a traditional IRA, the tax savings you realize from a traditional IRA contribution are neither tax-free nor tax-deferred. When you make a withdrawal from your traditional IRA, the distribution is taxable. But when you (or your heirs) make a qualified withdrawal from a Roth IRA, the distribution is income-tax free.

> One of the few things in life better than tax-deferred compounding is tax-free compounding.

Should I Contribute to a Traditional Deductible IRA or a Roth IRA?

As stated earlier, a Roth versus a nondeductible IRA is a no-brainer: if given the choice, always go for the Roth. But for those individuals with a choice between a Roth IRA (or work retirement plan) and a fully deductible IRA (or work retirement plan), how should you save? The conclusion is, in *most* cases, the Roth IRA is superior to the deductible IRA [and nonmatched retirement plan contributions like 401(k)s].

To determine whether a Roth IRA would be better than a traditional IRA, you must take into account:

- The value of the tax-free growth of the Roth versus the tax-deferred growth of the traditional IRA including the future tax effects of withdrawals.

- The tax deduction you lost by contributing to a Roth IRA rather than to a fully deductible IRA.

- The growth, net of taxes, on savings from the tax deduction from choosing a deductible traditional IRA.

In most circumstances, the Roth IRA is significantly more favorable than a regular IRA. (A number of years ago, I published an article in *The Tax Adviser*, a publication of the American Institute of Certified Public Accountants, that offered the mathematical proof that the Roth IRA was often a more favorable investment than a regular IRA).

> The conclusion is, in most cases, the Roth IRA is superior to the deductible IRA and nonmatched retirement plan contributions like 401(k)s.

The Jobs and Growth Tax Relief Reconciliation Act of 2003 (JGTRRA) and subsequent tax legislation changed tax rates for all brackets and reduced tax rates for dividends and capital gains. After these tax laws changed, I incorporated the changes into the analysis of the Roth versus the traditional IRA. The Roth was still preferable in most situations, although the advantage of the Roth was not quite as great as before JGTRRA. However, our country is currently facing unprecedented financial challenges, and I would be surprised to hear that our government intends to reduce our tax rates any time soon. And, if the tax rates on dividends and capital gains, or even the ordinary tax rates increase, the Roth's advantage will be even greater.

Figure 2.1
Roth IRA Savings vs. Traditional IRA Savings

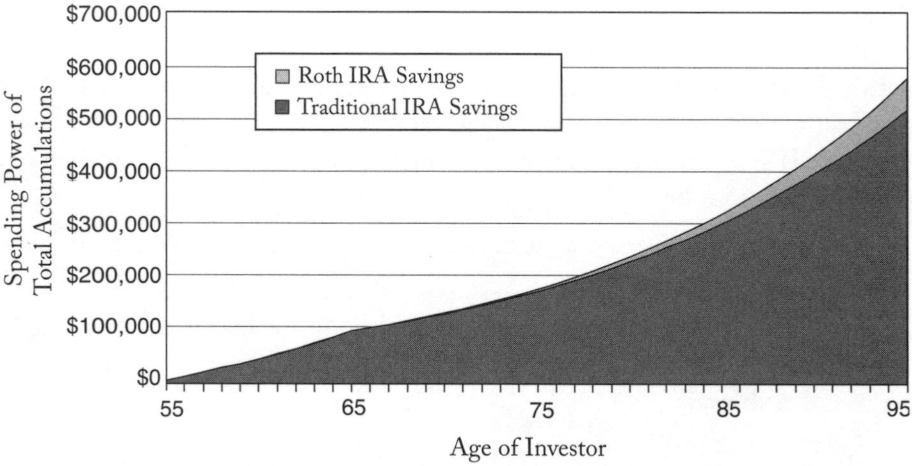

Figure 2.1 shows the value to the owner of contributing to a Roth IRA versus a regular deductible IRA measured in purchasing power.

Figure 2.1 reflects the following assumptions:

1. Contributions to a Roth IRA are made in the amount of $6,500 per year, beginning in 2015, for a 55-year-old investor, for 11 years until he reaches age 65.

2. Contributions to a regular deductible IRA are made in the amount of $6,500 per year by a different 55-year old investor, for 11 years until he reaches age 65. This investor's IRA contribution creates an income tax deduction for him of 25 percent, or $1,625. I will give the best-case scenario and say that this investor did not spend his tax savings. Instead, he invested his tax savings into his after-tax investment account and did not spend it.

3. The investment rates of return on the traditional IRA, the Roth IRA and the after-tax investment accounts are all 6 percent per year.

4. For the after-tax monies, the rate of return includes 70 percent capital appreciation, a 15 percent portfolio turnover rate (such that much of the appreciation is not immediately taxed), 15 percent dividends, and 15 percent ordinary interest income.

5. Ordinary income tax rates are 25 percent for all years.

6. Tax rates on realized capital gains are 15 percent.

7. Beginning at age 71, the RMDs from the traditional IRA are reinvested into the after-tax savings account.

8. The balances reflected in the graphs reflect spending power, which is net of an income tax allowance of 25 percent on the remaining traditional IRA balance. If the full amount was actually withdrawn in one year, however, the tax bracket may be even higher and make the Roth IRA appear more favorable.

The amounts reflected in the graph show that saving in the Roth IRA is always more favorable than saving in the traditional IRA, even if the contributions are made for a relatively small number of years. If tax rates become higher in the future, or if a higher rate of return is achieved, the overall Roth IRA advantage will be larger. Given a long time horizon (such as when monies are passed to succeeding generations), the Roth IRA advantage becomes even bigger. The spending power of these methods at selected times is shown in Table 2.5 below.

Table 2.5
Total Spending Power of Traditional vs. Roth IRA

End of Year Age	Traditional IRA	Roth IRA
55	$ 6,692	$ 6,695
65	$ 99,438	$100,235
75	$174,895	$179,506
85	$303,289	$321,468
95	$516,283	$575,700

This table may seem to show that there is not a significant difference between the two, but keep in mind that this illustration was purposely created using a very limited (11-year) contribution period and very conservative (6%) rate of return. In short, it demonstrates that, even with minimal contributions, shorter time frames and very conservative rates of return, the Roth IRA will still provide more purchasing power than a traditional IRA.

The Effect of Lower Tax Brackets in Retirement

I will usually recommend the traditional IRA over a Roth IRA if you drop to a lower tax bracket after retiring and have a relatively short investment time horizon. Under those circumstances, the value of a traditional deductible IRA could exceed the benefits of the Roth IRA. It will be to your advantage to take the high tax deduction for your contribution and then, upon retirement, withdraw that money at the lower tax rate.

For example, if you are in the 25 percent tax bracket when you are working, and you make a $6,000 tax-deductible IRA contribution, you save $1,500 in federal income taxes. Then, when you retire, your tax bracket drops to 15 percent. Let's assume that the traditional IRA had no investment growth – not an unrealistic assumption for a taxpayer who chooses to invest her IRA in a certificate of deposit which, at the time of writing, paid historically low interest rates. If she makes a withdrawal of $6,000 from the traditional IRA, she will pay only $900 in tax – for a savings of $600.

> **I will recommend the traditional IRA over a Roth IRA when you drop to a lower tax bracket after retiring and have a relatively short investment time horizon.**

$	1,500	(Initial tax savings from IRA contribution)
	− 900	(Tax due on IRA withdrawal)
$	600	(Final tax savings)

With that caveat, however, my analysis shows that the Roth can become more favorable when a longer investment period is considered. The tax-bracket advantage diminishes over time. So I ran the analysis again, starting with the same assumptions as in the previous example, except that, beginning at age 66, the ordinary income tax bracket is reduced from 25 to 15 percent.

The spending power of these methods at selected times is shown in Table 2.6 below. You can see that, under this particular set of circumstances, the traditional IRA would be more beneficial to you during your lifetime. Note, however, that the Roth offers more spending power from age 100 on. Of course, most people will not survive until 100, but we show the analysis to point out that even facing a reduced tax bracket, the Roth IRA will become more valuable with time—an advantage for your heirs.

Table 2.6
Total Spending Power of Reduced Tax Bracket in Retirement

End of Year Age	Traditional IRA	Roth IRA
55	$ 6,692	$ 6,695
65	$ 99,438	$ 100,235
(Lower Tax Bracket)		
75	$193,216	$ 179,506
85	$336,783	$ 321,468
95	$577,168	$ 575,700
100	$751,200	$ 770,416
105	$974,773	$1,030,990

If you anticipate that your retirement tax bracket will always remain lower than your current tax rate and that your IRA will be depleted during your lifetime, I will usually recommend that you use a traditional deductible IRA over the Roth IRA. Unfortunately, once the RMD rules take effect at age 70½ for tax-deferred IRAs and retirement plans, many individuals find that they are required to withdraw so much money from their IRAs, that their tax rate is just as high as their pre-retirement tax rate. And, when their RMDs are added to their Social Security income, some taxpayers find themselves in a higher tax bracket than when they were working. For these people, a Roth IRA contribution is usually preferable to a traditional IRA.

These numbers demonstrate that even with a significant tax-bracket disadvantage, the Roth IRA can become preferable with a long enough time horizon. Furthermore, when you consider the additional estate planning advantages, the relative worth of the Roth IRA becomes more significant.

(Please see www.paytaxeslater.com/reading.php for a free report on Roth IRAs and Roth IRA conversions).

Comments on Your Actual Tax Brackets: A Subtle Point for the Advanced Reader

The above analyses reflect simple assumptions of 25 percent income tax savings on your deductible IRA or retirement plan contributions. This is in essence the cost of the Roth IRA or Roth 401(k)/Roth 403(b) in the comparisons above. However, the U.S. tax code has several complications that create actual incremental tax brackets that are much higher than the tax brackets listed on the federal tax tables based on your taxable income. These items must be considered in the context of measuring the advantages of Roth IRAs to deductible IRA contributions.

These tax code complications can have extreme effects on the actual tax bracket for some people, most notably retirees with Social Security income and itemized deductions that involve medical expenses. For example, consider Fred Jones, a single 65-year-old retiree who had pension income of $36,000, Social Security income of $25,000, and part-time wage income of $5,000. He also has itemized deductions of $16,038, including $10,000 of medical expenses which, because he was 65, are deductible this year to the extent that they exceed 7.5 percent of his AGI. After looking at Table 2.5, Fred is considering the potential advantages of using his wage income to make a $5,000 Roth IRA contribution, rather than a $5,000 deductible IRA contribution. If he makes the traditional deductible IRA contribution, he pays $5,063 in federal income tax. If he chooses the Roth IRA his tax is $7,538 or $2,475 more. This is nearly 50 percent of the IRA contribution amount. This means his actual tax bracket is almost 50 percent even though the IRS tables indicate he is in the 25 percent tax bracket! The main reason that this happened is because the additional income from losing the IRA deduction caused much more of his Social Security income to be taxable. He also lost some of the medical expense deduction, due to its 7.5 percent of AGI limitation. Thus, Fred felt the cost of choosing the Roth IRA was too high that year and wisely chose the deductible IRA.

Although Fred's future situation may not always be so extreme, his numbers did not appear to be that unusual. Fred's example illustrates why careful tax planning is so important. There are many things in the tax code that result in a different actual tax bracket than the IRS tables would indicate. Before finalizing Roth contribution or conversion decisions, it is best to run the numbers or see a competent tax advisor to determine the actual effects.

When we analyze Roth IRA advantages and disadvantages for our clients (when compared to deductible contributions), we keep referring to the marginal tax rates to help us decide if the conversion makes sense in the long term. For most people, the current actual marginal tax rate is not hard to determine, and is similar to what the IRS tables would indicate. Therefore, we will continue to use simply calculated tax bracket rates in our analyses of Roth accounts. But please keep in mind that it is prudent to calculate the actual current year tax cost of the Roth.

In addition, our analyses do not reflect any additional advantages of the Roth IRAs when held in retirement due to these actual tax bracket variances. Fred's situation can be turned around to result in an extreme advantage for him. Suppose Fred is in need of an additional $5,000 in income for December, and he is comparing the effects of a withdrawal from either a taxable traditional IRA account or a Roth IRA account. Being able to get his money tax-free will then save him from paying an additional 50 percent tax when he files his return. This kind of situation gives the Roth IRA a potential advantage that our analyses in this book do not reflect. Instead we refer to a simple measure of the tax bracket, both when the Roth account is established and during retirement.

Wealthy clients and readers raise a lot of questions about the five-year holding period. What I really want to do when I hear that question is yell, "Why do you care?" It is extremely unlikely that anyone would need to spend all of their money at one time. Let's face it – if you did, you'd be broke, and the five-year holding period on the Roth account would be the least of your worries. Realistically, most people will spend their retirement savings over a period of many years. And, the people who have a Roth IRA as part of their retirement accumulations generally have at least some after-tax money and some traditional IRA or retirement plan funds – at least, this would be my advice. But because the Roth IRA is the last money I want people to spend, it should not matter that there is a five-year waiting period to achieve tax-free growth. The Roth's advantages almost always more than make up for any lack of liquidity resulting from the five-year rule.

> **Wealthy clients and readers raise a lot of questions about the five-year holding period. What I really want to do when I hear that question is yell, "Why do you care?"**

The fact that individuals can continue to contribute to a Roth IRA if they continue working past age 70½ is a great opportunity to continue saving, especially since more and more people continue to earn income well after the traditional age of retirement. The no-RMDs rule gives rise to significant estate planning opportunities to stretch savings for those willing to leave the money in the tax-free account for a long time. As with traditional IRAs, heirs must take RMDs, but they generally are extended over a lifetime. Depending on the lifespan of the beneficiary, the funds can grow tax-free to their great advantage.

A Key Lesson from This Chapter

Roth IRAs have significant benefits over traditional deductible IRAs:

1. No taxes are due upon the eventual distributions.

2. No required distributions are necessary during the owner's lifetime.

3. Withdrawals prior to age 59½ are free from any tax and penalties to the extent of previous annual contributions.

3

||||||||||||||||||||||

Traditional 401(k)s and 403(b)s versus Roth 401(k)s and Roth 403(b)s

The question isn't at what age I want to retire,
it's at what income.

— George Foreman

Main Topics

- What are Roth 401(k)s and 403(b)s?

- How do Roth 401(k)/403(b) accounts differ from a Roth IRA?

- Advantages and disadvantages of Roth 401(k)/403(b) contributions

- Availability of the Roth 401(k)/403(b)

- Contribution limits for both Roth and traditional 401(k)s/403(b)s

- Choosing between the Roth and traditional 401(k)/403(b)

- Additional advantages for higher income taxpayers

- Effects of a higher liquidation tax rate

- What if tax rates drop in retirement?

- A higher liquidation rate may be appropriate

- Extremely lower tax brackets in retirement
- What if you need the money: spending down the Roth assets
- Conclusion
- Making it happen

KEY IDEA

The Roth 401(k) and Roth 403(b) plan options offer high income participants an entrée to the world of tax-free wealth accumulation that was previously unavailable to them via traditional plans.

What Are Roth 401(k)s and Roth 403(b)s?

In Chapter 1, we touched on some of the basic differences between traditional and Roth 401(k)s and 403(b)s. The Roth 401(k) and Roth 403(b) combine the features of a traditional 401(k) or traditional 403(b) with a Roth IRA. Employees are permitted to deposit part or all of their own contribution, which is the amount deducted from their paychecks, as a contribution to a Roth account, meaning it will receive tax treatment similar to a Roth IRA. The laws governing retirement plan contributions, however, require that the employee always have the option to defer money into the traditional deductible account when the Roth account is offered as an option. No one is forced to use the Roth account if they prefer to take the tax deduction.

> **Unlike traditional contributions to a 401(k) or 403(b) plan, employee contributions to a Roth 401(k)/403(b) account do not receive a federal tax deduction. But the growth on these contributions will not be subject to taxes when money is withdrawn, because the Roth account grows tax-free.**

Unlike traditional contributions to a 401(k) or 403(b) plan, employee contributions to a Roth 401(k)/403(b) account do not receive a federal tax deduction. But the growth on these contributions will not be subject to taxes when money is withdrawn, because the Roth account grows tax-free. In short, if you have two options for your retirement plan, one a traditional account and the other a Roth account, with the same amount of money in each, the Roth account will be of greater value since the income taxes imposed on withdrawals from the traditional 401(k) greatly reduce its overall value. By this, I do not mean to imply that the Roth retirement plans are better than the traditional plans for everyone, but they are for many. The choice is similar to deciding whether to make a Roth IRA contribution or a *deductible* contribution to a traditional IRA as discussed in Chapter 2.

Roth retirement plans were first offered in 2006, but under temporary rules. Many employers did not add the Roth feature to their existing plans because of the additional paperwork, plan amendments, reporting, and recordkeeping involved. More recently, the law has become permanent and more employers are now offering Roth 401(k) and 403(b) features. These significant additions to the retirement planning landscape offer many more individuals an extraordinary opportunity to expand, and, in many cases, to begin saving for retirement in the Roth environment where their investment grows *tax-free*. Coupled with the increased contribution limits for the traditional 401(k) and 403(b) plans, employees and even self-employed individuals will be able to establish and grow their retirement savings at a rate greater than ever before.

> **These significant additions to the retirement planning landscape offer many more individuals an extraordinary opportunity to expand, and, in many cases, to begin saving for retirement in the Roth environment where their investment grows *tax-free*.**

How Do Roth 401(k)/403(b) Accounts Differ from a Roth IRA?

One of the most significant advantages of the Roth 401(k)/403(b), and the one that distinguishes it from a Roth IRA, is that Roth 401(k) and Roth 403(b) plans are now available to a much larger group of people. Roth IRA contributions are only available to taxpayers who fall within certain Modified Adjusted Gross Income (MAGI) ranges. The 2015 income limit for Roth IRA contributions for married couples filing jointly is $193,000 and for single individuals and heads of household, less than $131,000. If your income exceeds these limits, you are not permitted to contribute to a Roth IRA. These restrictive MAGI limitations do not apply to Roth 401(k) or 403(b) plans, providing higher income individuals and couples with their first entrée into the tax-free Roth environment.

This increased accessibility is really big news. Roth IRAs have always appeared to be ideal savings vehicles for wealthier individuals, but up until January 1, 2006, or more recently if their employers just began offering the Roth 401(k) and 403(b) options, wealthier individuals had been precluded from establishing Roth accounts due to the income limits.

The longer the funds are kept in the tax-free Roth environment, the greater the advantage to both the Roth IRA owner and his or her heirs.

In Chapter 2 we demonstrated how Roth IRAs can be of great advantage as part of the long-term retirement and estate plan, and these wealthier individuals are the folks who can generally afford to let money sit in a Roth account and gather tax-free growth. The longer the funds are kept in the tax-free Roth environment, the greater the advantage to both the Roth IRA owner and his or her heirs.

Advantages and Disadvantages of Roth 401(k)/403(b) Contributions

The Roth 401(k)/403(b) plan option offers advantages and disadvantages similar to those of Roth IRAs discussed in Chapter 2, but they are worth repeating and expanding upon here:

Advantages of the Roth Plans

1. By choosing the Roth, you pay the taxes up front on your contributions. While you might have taken the tax savings from your traditional plan contribution and invested the money in after-tax investments, over time, you will receive greater value from the tax-free growth.

2. If your tax bracket in retirement stays the same as it was when you contributed to the plan, you will be better off (assuming the Roth account grows, and possibly even if it goes down in value somewhat).

3. If your tax bracket in retirement is higher than when you contributed to the plan, you will be much better off. (Please note that we will look more closely at the effect of higher and lower tax brackets in retirement later). There are many reasons why you could move into a higher tax bracket after you retire. Here are a few examples:

    a. The federal government could decide to raise tax rates.

    b. You need to increase your income with taxable withdrawals from your traditional IRA plan, perhaps because you have medical expenses that were not covered by insurance.

    c. You own or inherit income-producing property or investments that begin to give you taxable income.

    d. You own annuities or have other lucrative pension plans that begin paying you income because of Required Minimum Distributions (RMDs).

    e. The combination of your pension, Social Security, and RMDs are higher than your former taxable income from wages.

4. While you are alive, there are no RMDs from the Roth IRA accounts. Roth *401(k)s/403(b)s* are subject to RMDs, but, as of this writing, these plans can easily be rolled into a Roth IRA upon your retirement. Traditional plans have RMDs beginning at age 70½ for retirees. The Roth IRA provides a much better long-term, tax-advantaged savings horizon, as shown in Chapter 2.

5. Your heirs will benefit from tax-free growth if the Roth is left in your estate. They can extend the tax-free growth over their lifetimes by taking only the required withdrawals. Whatever advantage you achieved with the Roth can be magnified by your heirs over their lifetimes.

6. The Roth provides greater value for the same number of dollars in retirement savings. This may lower federal estate and state inheritance taxes in an estate with the same after-tax spending power.

7. If you are in a low tax bracket now, or even if you have no taxable income (possibly because of credits and deductions), contributing to the Roth plan instead of the traditional plan will not cost you a significant amount now, but it will have enormous benefits later.

8. If you were previously unable to consider Roth IRAs because your income exceeded the income caps, you are now eligible to consider Roth accounts.

9. If you need to spend a large amount of your retirement savings all at once, withdrawals from a traditional plan would increase your marginal income tax rate. The Roth has a significant advantage in these high spending situations. Because Roth withdrawals are tax-free, they do not affect your marginal tax rate.

10. Having a pool of both traditional plan money (funded by the employer contributions and taxable upon withdrawal) and Roth plan money (funded by the employee and tax-free) to choose from, can give you an opportunity for effective tax planning in retirement. With both types of plans, the Roth portion can be used in high income years and the traditional plan can be used in lower income years when you are in a reduced tax bracket. These low tax brackets may occur during years after retirement, but before the RMDs from the employer's contributions begin.

Disadvantages of the Roth Plans

1. Your paycheck contributions into the Roth 401(k)/403(b) are not tax deductible, as is a traditional 401(k)/403(b) contribution. You will get smaller net paychecks if you contribute the same amount to a Roth account, rather than a traditional account, because of increased federal income tax withholding. Losing the tax-deferred status means that by the time you file your tax return, you will have less cash in the bank, that is, in your after-tax investments. (Keep in mind, however, when compared to tax-deferred or tax-free retirement savings accounts, after-tax investments are the least efficient savings tool).

2. The retirement investments may go down in value. If the decline becomes large enough, it is possible that you would have been better off in a traditional tax-deferred plan, because, at the very least, you would have received a tax deduction on your contributions.

3. If Congress ever eliminates the income tax in favor of a sales tax or value-added tax, you will have already paid your income taxes. However, it seems unlikely that such a system would be adopted without grandfathering the rules for plans in place to prevent such inequities.

4. If your tax bracket in retirement drops, and you withdraw funds from

your retirement assets before sufficient tax-free growth, the taxes you save on your Roth 401(k) plan withdrawals are less than the taxes you would have saved using a traditional plan. This can be the case if you earn an unusually high amount of money from your employer in one year, maybe from earning a large bonus that puts you in a very high tax bracket, but ultimately you do not end up with such high income after retirement. If that were the case, a better approach might be to use the traditional account for deferrals in that year or other years where your income is unusually large. (Please note that later we will look more closely at the effect of lower tax brackets in retirement).

Availability of the Roth 401(k)/403(b)

Employers who now offer a 401(k) plan or a 403(b) plan may choose to expand their retirement plan options to include the Roth 401(k) or Roth 403(b), but they are not required to do so. Some companies were early adopters; others may take more time to incorporate the new plans into their offerings; still others may never offer them.

Employers who now offer a 401(k) plan or a 403(b) plan may choose to expand their retirement plan options to include the Roth401(k) or Roth 403(b), but they are not required to do so.

Contribution Limits for Roth and Traditional 401(k)s/403(b)s

For 2015, the traditional and Roth 401(k)/403(b) employee contribution limits are $18,000 per year, or $24,000 if you are age 50 or older). Employer matching contributions don't affect this limit.

In 2015, a 50-year-old employee cannot make a $24,000 contribution to a traditional 401(k) account and a $24,000 contribution to a Roth 401(k) account; the contributions to both accounts combined cannot exceed $24,000. The Roth 401(k)/403(b) contributions will be treated like a Roth IRA for tax purposes.

Perhaps an example would help.

Joe, a prudent 55-year-old employee, participates in his company's 401(k) plan. He has dutifully contributed the maximum allowable contribution to his 401(k) plan since he started working. Until his employer adopted the new

Roth 401(k) option, his expectation was to continue contributing the maximum into his 401(k) for 2015 and beyond.

Now Joe has a choice. In 2015, he can either continue making his regular deductible 401(k) contribution ($24,000); he could elect to make a $24,000 contribution to the new Roth 401(k); or he could split his $24,000 contribution between the regular 401(k) portion and the Roth 401(k) portion of the plan. His decision will not have an impact on his employer's contribution—the employer's matching contribution remains unchanged and goes into a traditional tax-deferred account.

With Joe's $24,000 contribution, however, there is a fundamental difference in the way his traditional 401(k) is taxed and the way his new Roth 401(k) is taxed. With the traditional 401(k), Joe gets an income tax deduction for his contribution to the 401(k). After Joe retires, however, and takes a distribution from his traditional 401(k), he will have to pay income taxes on that distribution. If Joe contributes to the Roth 401(k), he will not get a tax deduction for making the contribution, but the money will grow income-tax free. When Joe takes a distribution from his Roth 401(k), he will not have to pay income taxes, provided other technical requirements are met. These other requirements are usually easy to meet, and include such things as waiting until age 59½ before making retirement account withdrawals and waiting at least five years from the time the account is opened before the first withdrawal.

Because Joe has some after-tax savings already and does not really need more income tax deductions, he is advised to contribute to the Roth 401(k). Assuming Joe takes my advice and switches his annual contributions to the Roth 401(k), he will have three components to his 401(k) plan at work. He will have the employer's matching contributions in his traditional account, plus the interest, dividends and appreciations on those contributions, to the extent that he is vested in the plan. He will have his own (the employee's) traditional portion of the plan, which consists of all of his contributions to date plus the interest, dividends, and appreciation on those contributions. Then, starting in 2015, he will have a Roth 401(k) portion for his Roth contributions.

If Joe is married filing a joint tax return and his 2015 adjusted gross income is less than $193,000, he may have already been making contributions to a Roth IRA outside of his employer's retirement plan. In 2015, he would have been able to make the maximum Roth IRA contribution of $6,500 ($5,500 for people under age 50) to the plan. And remember that Joe can contribute the maximum ($24,000) to his Roth 401(k), plus the maximum

($6,500) to his Roth IRA, assuming that his income is below the exclusion limits. As long as Joe is working, the Roth 401(k) at work will remain separate from any Roth IRA he may have outside of his employer's plan.

If his 2015 adjusted gross income was more than $193,000, he would not have been allowed to contribute to a Roth IRA (the income phase-out range is between $183,000 and $193,000). What is much different for Joe is that the amount of money he will be allowed to contribute into the income tax-free world of the Roth will see a dramatic increase, because there is no income limit for employees who want to contribute to a Roth 401(k) or 403(b) plan at work.

Choosing between the Roth and Traditional 401(k)/403(b)

The following analysis is equally important for individuals considering a Roth IRA conversion. I do not repeat this analysis in Chapter 7, but people who are considering a Roth IRA conversion, or interested in learning more about them, should read this material with the Roth conversion in mind.

Many clients come to us wondering whether they would be better off making contributions to a Roth account or to a traditional retirement account. If the choice is between using a Roth IRA versus a nondeductible traditional IRA, it is pretty easy to make the case for the Roth. However, because of the nature of the Roth's advantages and disadvantages, which are contingent on your current and future income tax brackets, there is no one size fits all answer if the choice is between a traditional deductible IRA and a Roth. So I have formulated some different scenarios showing how the Roth accounts become advantageous for some people and a bad idea for others.

Assume that we have an employee named Gary who is 55 years old, and who is able to contribute $24,000 to his 401(k) plan for eleven years, until he retires at age 66. His employer offers a Roth account in their 401(k), and Gary wants to know if he should direct his contributions to the Roth or the traditional side of the plan. We ran the numbers using the following assumptions:

1. Gary earns a conservative rate of return of 6 percent annually on all of his accounts.

2. At age 70, Gary rolls the Roth 401(k) part of his plan over to a Roth IRA to avoid RMDs. (This is a very important step; we'll cover more about it later).

3. Gary knows that he will save a significant amount in taxes if his contributions are made to the tax-deductible traditional account. Gary is more disciplined than most savers. He is willing to take all of the money that he saved on taxes and contribute it to an after-tax brokerage account environment.

4. In this scenario, Gary's income tax rates are as follows:

   a. 25 percent ordinary incremental tax rate during his working years.

   b. 25 percent ordinary incremental tax rate during his retirement years.

   c. Capital gains tax rates are 15 percent.

5. Gary's RMDs from his traditional 401(k) plan begin at age 70. He pays ordinary income taxes on the distributions, and uses the rest of the money to pay his living expenses. The Roth account has tax-free spending withdrawals taken in the same amount.

6. The calculated income tax rate on all growth of the after-tax account averages 16.5 percent.

7. At the end of each year, we measure the spending power for each scenario. To measure the spending power of pre-tax traditional 401(k) plan balances, an allowance is made for income taxes. The tax rate of this allowance or liquidation rate is, initially, 25 percent, comparable to the ordinary tax rate.

Now we are able to run the numbers and see the resulting spending power of remaining assets as shown in Figure 3.1 on the following page.

Figure 3.1 shows that there is an increasing advantage from investing in the Roth 401(k) instead of the traditional 401(k) plan. Although it's difficult to see, the advantage begins in the first year. At Gary's retirement age of 66, the advantage has grown to $6,101, or 1.45 percent. By age 75, after RMDs have begun, the advantage is 4.11 percent; by age 85, it is 9.68 percent; and by age 95, it is a 22.00 percent advantage resulting in an additional $162,680 for the Roth owner.

Figure 3.1
Roth 401(k) Savings vs. Traditional 401(k) Savings RMD is Spent Annually

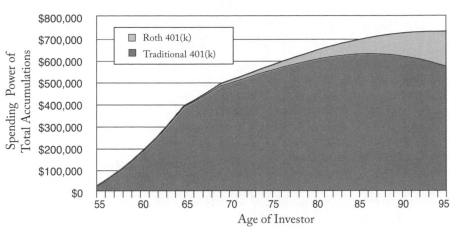

For an individual person whose circumstances match the assumptions above, the cumulative advantage over the 40-year projection period should provide the incentive to use the Roth rather than the traditional 401(k). And if a rate of return greater than six percent is assumed, the advantage to the Roth owner increases significantly.

Under current rules, if Gary should pass away and leave his Roth account to his surviving spouse, she will not have to take RMDs from the account over her lifetime. If he leaves the Roth account to someone other than his spouse, perhaps a child, they can still extend the period of the tax-free growth by limiting distributions to the RMDs over his or her normal life expectancy. The rules regarding RMDs are discussed in detail in Chapter 5, but for now it's important to know that RMDs force money out of a tax-deferred or tax-free environment, into a taxable environment. And remember Mr. Pay Taxes Now and Mr. Pay Taxes Later from Chapter 1? Mr. Pay Taxes Later was the clear winner.

If you're trying to figure out the most opportune strategies for naming beneficiaries of your IRAs, you should refer to Chapter 13 for an in-depth discussion on the subject, but here is a simplified explanation of the inheritance rules for a spouse:

- if you leave behind a traditional IRA, your spouse can treat the IRA as his or her own and ultimately take RMDs based on his or her own life expectancy.

- if you leave behind a Roth, your spouse is never required to take RMDs.

The rules are not as generous if your beneficiary is not your spouse, and they may even change for the worse. (In fact, these rules could provide an incentive for committed couples who have not legally married, to do so.)

> **Even though we are not talking about Roth IRA conversions at this point in the book, the reasoning that goes into deciding to put money in a Roth 401(k) versus a traditional 401(k) is conceptually similar to the reasoning that goes into deciding to make a Roth IRA conversion. So, although you may be retired, the following analysis is relevant for retirees thinking about a Roth IRA conversion.**

Additional Advantages for Higher Income Taxpayers

One great feature of the new Roth 401(k)/403(b) plan is that it allows higher income taxpayers to save money in the Roth environment. How does the advantage change in their situation? Figure 3.2 uses the same assumptions as Figure 3.1; except that Gary's ordinary income tax rate has been increased to the current maximum of 39.6 percent, including the liquidation tax rate used for measurement.

In Figure 3.2, we discover that the Roth 401(k) advantage for a higher income taxpayer is greater than for the lower income taxpayer in the 25 percent tax bracket (Figure 3.1). The advantage has now become a huge 40.4 percent, or $338,352, after 40 years. Why such a large difference? There are several reasons why this happened, and they relate to the ever-changing tax laws. First, the maximum federal income tax rate was increased from 35 percent, to 39.6 percent. Second, there were several new taxes imposed on high income taxpayers. Higher earners (in 2014, single individuals whose adjusted gross income exceeds $200,000 or married taxpayers filing jointly whose income exceeds $250,000) are now subject to the Net Investment Tax, which adds on an additional 3.8 percent tax to certain investment income earned outside of the Roth account. High earners are also subject to a phase-out of their standard deductions and personal exemptions, which effectively increases their average tax rate. These and other factors all combine to make the Roth an even more attractive option for higher income taxpayers than in prior years.

Figure 3.2
Roth 401(k) Savings vs. Traditional 401(k) Savings RMD is Spent Annually

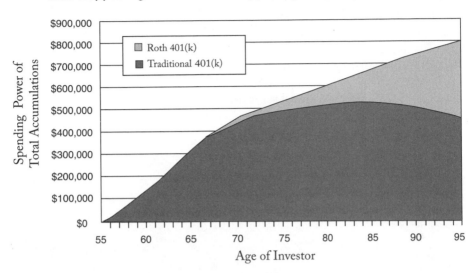

And guess what? The higher income taxpayer is more likely not to need to spend the Roth investments, thus making the long-term benefits more achievable. The bottom line is that the Roth 401(k) is dollar for dollar more valuable for the higher income retirement plan owner than a middle income retirement plan owner. The counter argument is that the amount of savings to middle income taxpayers, though smaller, is more meaningful in terms of the impact on their lives.

Effects of a Higher Liquidation Tax Rate

Let's further consider the liquidation tax rate. This is a tax rate applied to remaining amounts in your traditional pre-tax retirement accounts if you were to liquidate your entire account. By applying the liquidation tax rate, you get a measure of what the account would be worth in after-tax dollars. You can think of it as a measure of the total amount you could withdraw from the traditional 401(k), an amount that changes as each year passes and your retirement plan grows. Suppose you didn't handle your 401(k) rollover correctly – something we'll cover in Chapter 6 – and you had to pay income tax on your entire 401(k) balance on April 15. Wouldn't all this extra income you'll have from cashing out the plan put you in a higher tax bracket? What happens to Figure 3.1 if we use a higher liquidation tax rate of 39.6 percent, for an average income level taxpayer? Figure 3.3 still reflects ordinary income tax rates of 25 percent on withdrawals, but incorporates a liquidation withdrawal taxed at 39.6 percent. The money that is withdrawn from the traditional IRA has been immediately reinvested in the same funds as the Roth IRA, but in an after-tax account. This line is called Traditional 401(k) with Liquidation on Figure 3.3.

Figure 3.3
Roth 401(k) Savings vs. Traditional 401(k) Savings
Ordinary Tax Rate of 25%
Liquidation Tax Rate of 39.6%

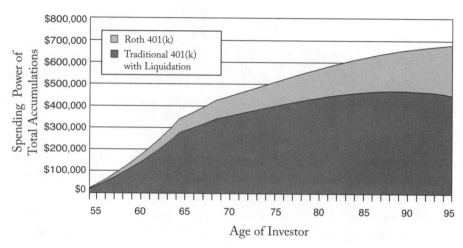

What we find is that the graphs are similar in their general trends. However, we can also see that the Roth now has a larger comparable advantage than in Figure 3.1. Not surprisingly, the tax consequences of liquidating the account at age 55 aren't so bad because the balance in the 401(k) is relatively low. But if Gary liquidates his 401(k) when he is 95, the difference is significant. He would pay over $225,000 in additional income taxes if the account he liquidated is a traditional IRA as opposed to a Roth IRA. This shows that using a Roth 401(k) protects our nest egg from additional income tax costs should we need to spend an unexpectedly large amount of money in the middle of retirement, which might be the scenario for a retiree who needs to liquidate a large portion of his retirement plan in order to move into a retirement home or life care community.

The Roth 401(k) provides a level of safety from the income tax burden if a large liquidation is necessary, for any reason. Whatever the financial problem is, it need not be worsened by extra-high marginal income tax brackets.

What if Your Tax Rates Drop in Retirement?

A situation that makes a Roth 401(k) less appealing is when the employee earns a high income and is in a high tax bracket while working, but when he retires, he is in a lower tax bracket. Let's assume that Gary has saved enough after-tax money from his paychecks that he is able to survive by spending only his savings, Social Security and the RMDs from his traditional 401(k), beginning at age 70.

If we now make a graph similar to Figure 3.2, but instead of continuing the 39.6 percent ordinary tax bracket throughout his retirement, we use a lower 28 percent tax bracket, and we also use a liquidation rate equal to the ordinary tax rate of 28 percent in retirement, we find the graph looks like Figure 3.4 below.

Figure 3.4
Roth 401(k) Savings vs. Traditional 401(k) Savings
Ordinary Tax Rates 39.6% Before Retirement, 28% After Retirement
Liquidation Tax Rate of 28%

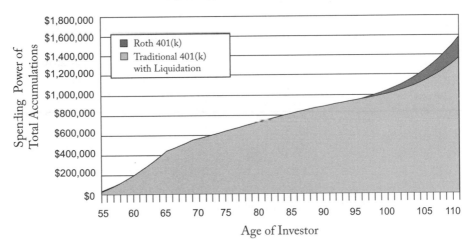

Figure 3.4 illustrates that, in the early years, the traditional IRA has a definite advantage. The line for the traditional IRA hides the line for the Roth IRA, so I'll tell you what you can't see in the earlier years. After one year, the traditional IRA has an advantage of more than 10 percent. At age 65, the advantage declines to less than eight percent, and at age 75 to slightly more than six percent. The breakeven point happens at age 94, after which the Roth IRA has the advantage. Even more interesting is the fact that, after age 94, the Roth advantage grows at a much faster rate. The traditional IRA began with an

advantage of more than 10 percent, and it took more than 40 years for the Roth IRA to overtake it and gain the advantage. Once the advantage was reached, though, it took only eleven years (age 106) before the Roth's value is more than 10 percent greater than the traditional IRA. And at age 110, the Roth's advantage has grown to more than 15 percent. It is not likely that you will live long enough to see the Roth's advantage in this scenario, but if your plan is to keep the money in the tax-free Roth environment and then leave it to heirs who will do the same, the Roth is clearly the preferred vehicle.

Figure 3.4 is hard for many people to believe. How can the Roth become better with lower taxes in retirement? The answer lies in the fate of the original income tax savings generated by using the traditional 401(k). This money went into the after-tax investment pool where its growth became subject to income taxes. These taxes don't seem like much: ordinary taxes on interest and smaller capital gains tax rates in retirement than were paid while working. But these taxes, even at their reduced rates, are disadvantaged over the long term in contrast to the Roth 401(k) where growth is entirely *tax-free*.

A Higher Liquidation Rate May Be Appropriate

Some readers may be skeptical of the fact that we used a 28% liquidation rate in Figure 3.2. Remember, the *liquidation rate* is the marginal tax rate that you would incur upon withdrawing, or cashing in, your entire IRA or retirement plan. What happens if you have a very large IRA or retirement plan? We have to apply a higher marginal rate to the traditional plan balances to allow for higher marginal rates if the entire IRA or retirement plan is cashed in at once, because the additional income from the IRA withdrawals will likely push you into a tax bracket that is higher than 28 percent.

A higher rate could also be used to illustrate the potential advantage your heirs could realize after your death from the continued tax-free growth of an inherited Roth IRA. The advantage to your heirs can be more than a few percent if the maximum tax-free growth is maintained over their life expectancy. We have extended these calculations over three generations, and have found in those cases that a Roth inheritance received by a grandchild can eventually be worth over 50 percent more than a comparable pre-tax fund inheritance. So, under the current rules, your heirs would be better off inheriting a smaller Roth account than a larger amount of pre-tax money. But those rules might change, as you will see in Chapter 5.

In any case, let's look at what happens if we assume that the withdrawal pushes the taxpayer into the highest possible tax bracket, which at this writing is 39.6 percent.

Although it is difficult to see on the graph, the Roth has an advantage of $131 after the end of the first year. And by age 95, the Roth's advantage has only grown by 5.83 percent, or about $50,000.

So the bottom line is that, for moderate to high income taxpayers, the Roth 401(k) is better.

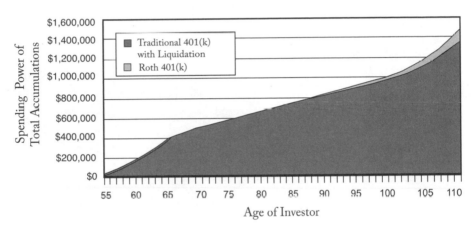

Figure 3.5
Roth 401(k) Savings vs. Traditional 401(k) Savings
Ordinary Tax & Liquidation Tax Rates of 39.6%
Retirement Tax Rate of 28%

Extremely Lower Tax Brackets in Retirement

In a sobering illustration, however, we can see where the Roth 401(k) is not advantageous. Figure 3.6 assumes an individual in the 39.6 percent tax bracket while working and the 15 percent tax bracket in retirement. Maybe they were extravagant spenders during their early working years and neglected to save much in traditional retirement accounts. Maybe most of what they have is Roth IRAs and little else, for whatever reason. Figure 3.6 shows a different story.

Here the Roth 401(k) contributor went too far. The Roth is disadvantaged from the very first year, because the income tax savings afforded by the contribution to the traditional account in the early years offer a greater benefit than the income tax savings in the later years. And the disadvantage continues to grow, the longer the account is held. Some readers might argue that this scenario is not realistic, because an individual who is in the maximum tax bracket while working is not likely to be in the minimum tax bracket in retirement. Such individuals would more than likely be eligible to receive the maximum Social Security benefits possible, which when combined with other sources of taxable income, will push them into a higher tax bracket. So I created this worst-case scenario for the readers who believe that the Social Security system will be bankrupt by the time they retire, and their retirement income will come solely from their own savings.

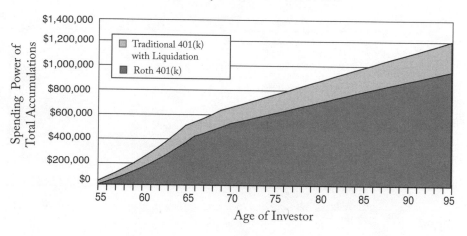

Figure 3.6
Roth 401(k) Savings vs. Traditional 401(k) Savings
Ordinary Rate of 39.6%
Retirement & Liquidation Tax Rate of 15%

This graph does show that your retirement plans should include having an income that is not too much less than your income while working, if you want to get the tax benefits from the Roth. It may seem obvious that everyone should hope to avoid a significant decline in income during their retirement, but this is a point worth mentioning because there is a lot being published about the benefits of retiring to third-world countries where the cost of living is less than in the United States. If that is your plan, the tax deduction from traditional 401(k) contributions might be too good to pass up.

When Higher Liquidation Rates Should Again Be Considered

Even if you do fall into a much lower tax bracket after retirement, your heirs may not. And, if they were to inherit the Roth under current law, they could potentially reap continued tax-free advantages for decades. So let's look at what happens if we have a taxpayer who is in the highest income tax bracket, who leaves a Roth account to an heir who is in the lowest income tax bracket. If the heir liquidates the account after decades of tax-free growth, a liquidation tax rate of 39.6 could be appropriate.

Figure 3.7 and related calculations show the Roth 401(k) retains an advantage of almost three percent until age 69, when the traditional plan begins to recover. By age 76, the traditional plan has the advantage due to lower taxes paid by the heirs upon withdrawals. Again, if these substantially lower income tax rates persist for long enough after retirement, the traditional plan ends up being significantly better as shown in Figure 3.6.

Figure 3.7
Roth 401(k) Savings vs. Traditional 401(k) Savings
Ordinary Tax & Liquidation Tax Rates of 39.6%
Retirement Tax Rate of 15%

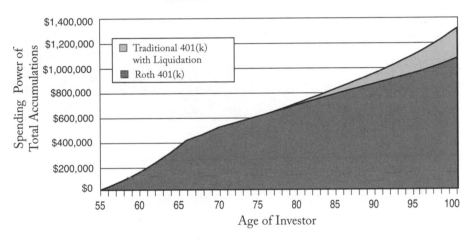

What if *You* Need the Money, Not Your Heirs: Spending Down the Roth 401(k)

All the above figures may indicate that the Roth 401(k) is a good idea and can eventually result in huge gains for the family. But what if you need to spend your Roth account during your own lifetime? The quick answer is, if that is all you have to spend, without taxable income from any other source, you may be better off taking the original tax deductions on the traditional 401(k) as shown in Figure 3.6.

But what about a more balanced situation, where you have a pension income as well as Social Security, and your tax rate is 25 percent all along, as in Figure 3.1, but you need to tap into your nest egg, taking more than the RMD.

Would it have been a mistake to have contributed to a Roth if you have to systematically deplete the account over time?

To answer this question, we prepared the graph in Figure 3.8, which is similar to Figure 3.1, but instead of taking only the RMDs from retirement accounts, we take $20,000 from the traditional 401(k) during ages 66 to 69, and $20,000 more than the resulting RMDs for each year thereafter.

Figure 3.8
401(k) Savings vs. Traditional 401(k) Savings
Moderate Additional Spending

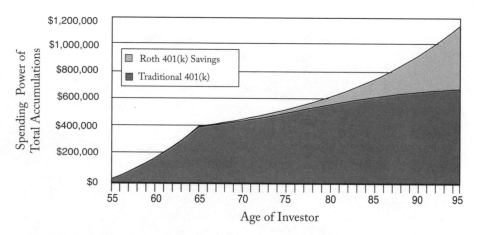

Figure 3.8 still indicates an advantage to the Roth 401(k) due to the tax savings which began in Year 1. The level of spending is higher in the earlier years, but actually becomes lower in the later years. This is because the larger withdrawals in the earlier years have reduced the account balance, so the RMDs in the later years are lower.

The result of this sooner-than-expected withdrawal rate is not significant to the decision of which is better. The Roth still grows its advantage to more than 66 percent, or $449,050, by age 95.

Let's assume that your spending needs are even greater. This time we will begin to take $40,000 at age 66 and increase the withdrawal every year for inflation: This creates the graph shown in Figure 3.9.

Now the Roth advantage is less apparent. The traditional 401(k) plan runs out of money before age 82, but the Roth 401(k) plan runs out before age 84—a period of about eighteen months. It might seem like an insignificant difference, but if you were in this situation at age 83 and had no other money available to you, I think you would be glad you chose the Roth. The bottom line is that despite the excessive spending in retirement, the Roth 401(k) is still better than the traditional 401(k) plan.

Figure 3.9
Roth 401(k) Savings vs. Traditional 401(k) Savings
Substantial Additional Spending

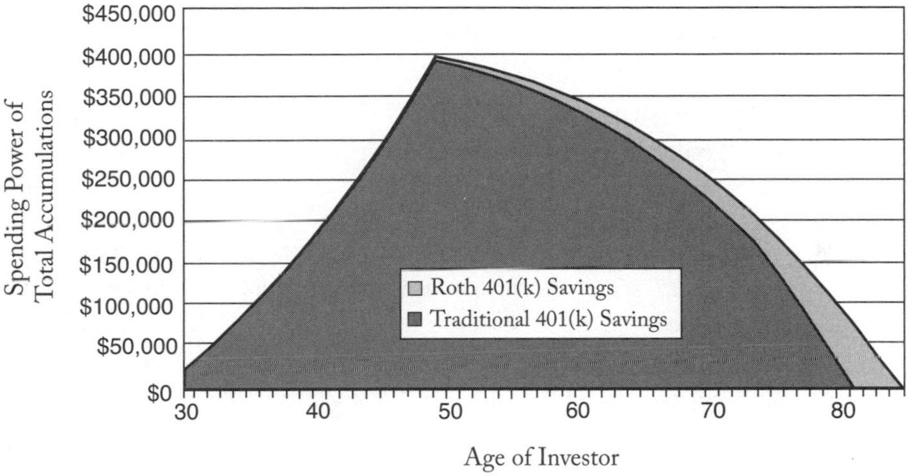

Conclusion

It is unlikely that the assumptions made in the above analyses will reflect your exact personal situation. The assumed rate of return I have used is very conservative (6%), and the differences between the Roth and traditional IRA will be even more pronounced if you earn a higher rate of return on your own investments. There will always be uncertainty regarding future investment rates, tax rates, and even your own spending. However, there is value in seeing objective numbers in different scenarios, and hopefully the above information can help you make decisions regarding your own retirement and estate plan. Seeing a qualified financial advisor who can personalize the advice for you would be the preferred course of action.

The Roth savings options can change people's lives for the better. Subject to a few exceptions discussed above, if you have access to a Roth option in your retirement plan at work, I highly recommend that you take advantage of it, and if you can afford it, contribute the maximum allowed. Also, please keep in mind that this analysis is also quite valuable for someone interested in Roth

IRA conversions because there are a lot of similarities in the calculations and the sensitivity of tax brackets.

Making It Happen

The Roth savings options can change people's lives for the better. Subject to a few exceptions discussed above, if you have access to a Roth option in your retirement plan at work, I highly recommend you take advantage of it, and if you can afford it, contribute the maximum allowed.

Notice, however, there is a caveat. I said, "If you have access." Though Congress has made Roth 401(k)s and Roth 403(b)s available for employers to use, that doesn't mean your employer has adopted these features or has made plans to do so. Speaking as an employer, the additional paperwork seems insignificant to me. I suspect the biggest reason more companies haven't added a Roth 401(k) component to their plan is inertia. If you are an employee who is not being provided with options for a Roth 401(k) or Roth 403(b), you should gently (or not so gently depending on your personality and the office politics) suggest that your employer adopt the Roth 401(k) or Roth 403(b) plan and allow you to participate.

In Notice 2006–44, the IRS provides a sample amendment for Roth elective deferrals, which should ease the burden for plan sponsors. If you are a retirement plan administrator or owner of a small business and if you have not already considered implementing a Roth 401(k) or Roth 403(b), you should strongly consider it. We did it in our own business and now, in addition to what I contribute to my employee's retirement plan, each employee has the option of a Roth 401(k) or a traditional 401(k). The paperwork and costs were minimal.

A Key Lesson from This Chapter

For most readers, the expansion or entrée into the tax-free world of Roth 401(k)s and Roth 403(b)s is well advised and over the long term will be one of the best things you can do for yourself and your family.

Part Two

THE DISTRIBUTION YEARS

Spend the Right Funds First and
Other Critical Decisions You
Face in Retirement

4

||||||||||||||||||

Optimal Spending Strategies for Retirees

I am having an out-of-money experience.

—Author Unknown

Main Topics

- The optimal order for spending assets

- Four mini case studies

- Spend your after-tax money first

- Capital gains may affect spending order

- Your marital status may produce different recommendations

- Does it matter which accounts you leave to your children?

- Using tax planning to determine the optimal spending order

KEY IDEA

Spend after-tax dollars first, then spend tax-deferred and Roth dollars strategically to optimize tax results.

Which Assets Should I Spend First?

The topic of which dollars to spend first is becoming increasingly difficult to simplify into general rules of thumb. Under the old laws, it was much easier and and generally more accurate to recommend spending after-tax dollars first, then IRA dollars, and then spend Roth dollars last. Even under the old laws, that wasn't always accurate for everyone, but it was more accurate back then than it was today.

With recent tax law changes that affect capital gains and tax brackets, and new taxes aimed specifically at high income individuals, this simplistic advice is no longer accurate for an ever growing number of taxpayers. Sometimes it is the best course of action, but sometimes it now makes sense to spend Roth IRA dollars before traditional IRA dollars in order to stay in a lower tax bracket. In order to get the best answer for your specific situation, you should have a qualified advisor "run the numbers" for you. However, it would not be helpful for me to tell you that you have to run the numbers, and not give you general guidelines which illustrate the points I'm talking about. Therefore, please understand that the information presented in this chapter is just that – general guidelines – that may not produce the optimal result for your own situation.

At retirement an individual moves into distribution mode—that is to say, he begins to spend retirement savings. This is *not* to say that accumulation stops. Income and appreciation on the investments, Social Security funds, and any pension plan proceeds might still be exceeding your expenses.

You may be fortunate enough to find that your Social Security, pension, Required Minimum Distributions (RMD) from your IRA (if any), and dividends and interest on your after-tax investments provide enough funds for your living expenses. Let's assume, however, that isn't the case, and you need to either tap into your after-tax funds (you might think of that as your "nest egg") or make additional taxable withdrawals from your IRA or retirement account to make ends meet.

In general, it is preferable to spend principal from your after-tax investments rather than taking taxable distributions from your IRA and/or retirement plan.

In general, it is preferable to spend principal from your after-tax investments rather than taking taxable distributions from your IRA and/or retirement plan.

I've been in business for over thirty years. Most of my clients actually listen to me, but I always have a few who don't. Instead of following my recommendations, they choose to spend their IRAs first. It drives me crazy. When I review their tax return, I see it. You can't hide it because it's an IRA distribution, and you have to pay taxes on it. With this one particular client, every year, when I delivered his tax return, I would include a personal note saying, "I really hate to see you pay income taxes on this." I would also call him. He said his stockbroker wanted to maintain a balance between his IRA and after-tax dollars. Now, I'm all for an appropriate and well-balanced portfolio. I agree that you don't want to have all your eggs in one basket. But I'm not into this allocation between IRA and non-IRA dollars at the expense of considerable extra taxes right now. If you're older than 59½, you don't have to worry about maintaining the liquidity of your after-tax dollars because you can take money out of an IRA whenever you want without a penalty. I would much rather that, subject to some exceptions, most taxpayers follow my "pay taxes later" rule.

Mini Case Study 4.1 and Figure 4.1 (on page 84) provide a comparison of the benefits of spending after-tax savings before pre-tax accumulations.

MINI CASE STUDY 4.1

Spend Your After-Tax Money First

Both Mr. Pay Taxes Now and Mr. Pay Taxes Later start from an identical position in 2015. They are both 65 years old and both have $300,000 in after-tax funds and $1,100,000 in retirement funds. They both receive $25,000 per year in Social Security income. They want to spend $86,000 per year, after paying income taxes. Their investment return is 6 percent and the rate of inflation is 2.5 percent. Income tax assumptions include ordinary income and capital gains tax rates established by the American Taxpayer Relief Act of 2012 and subsequent tax laws. State income taxes are ignored.

Mr. Pay Taxes Now does not spend any of his after-tax funds until all the retirement funds are depleted. By spending his retirement funds first, he triggers income taxes on the withdrawals, reducing the tax-deferral period, and his balance goes down. He also subjects a larger share of his after-tax funds to income taxes on the dividends, interest, and potential capital gains. All income taxes due on the retirement funds and the after-tax funds cause a greater amount to be withdrawn from his retirement account. In 28 years, by paying taxes prematurely, he has sacrificed a fortune in tax-deferred

Figure 4.1

Benefits of Spending After-Tax Savings Before Traditional Retirement Plans

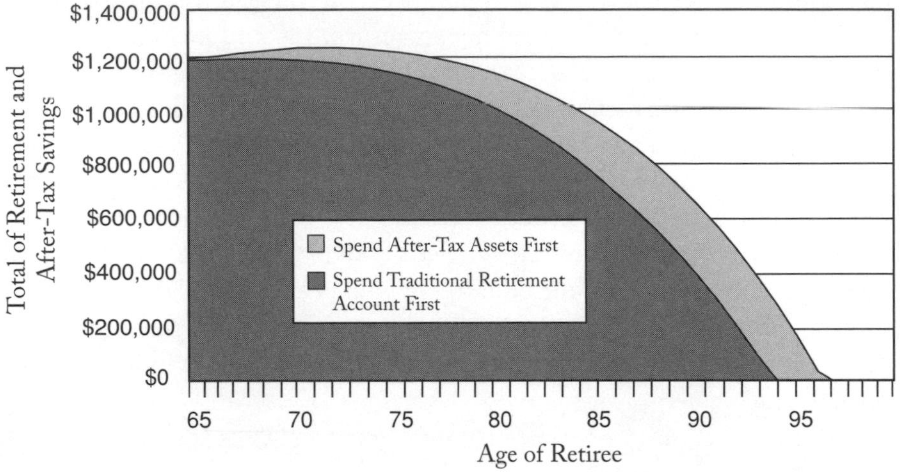

growth. Shortly after his 93rd birthday, Mr. Pay Taxes Now is out of money.

Mr. Pay Taxes Later first uses his after-tax funds to meet expenses. Only when the after-tax funds are depleted are withdrawals made from the retirement accounts. He fully uses the tax-deferred features of the IRA. Mr. Pay Taxes Later has over $390,000 on his 93rd birthday. Both he and Mr. Pay Taxes Now enjoyed an identical lifestyle, investments, and so forth, but there is a significant difference in the amount each has remaining at their age 93. Mr. Pay Taxes Now is broke, and Mr. Pay Taxes later has enough funds to support himself for an additional 3 years. In states such as Pennsylvania that do not tax retirement income but do tax after-tax investment income, the benefits of spending the after-tax money first is even greater. The conclusion would most likely be the same for any reasonable set of assumptions in terms of how much money each individual has, and what rate of return you want to assume. The principle stands: don't pay taxes now—pay taxes later!

Once the after-tax money is spent, there is no longer a one size fits all answer as to whether it is more advantageous to spend traditional IRA or Roth IRA money. In late stages of spending and under certain other circumstances, it does not hold true that no Roth dollars should be spent while traditional IRA dollars remain. If you live long enough to fully deplete your traditional IRAs and are left with only Roth dollars and little taxable income other than Social Security, you will likely be in the zero percent tax bracket. From that point on, you will be missing out on what could have been tax-free traditional IRA withdrawals. It would be a mistake to have completely wiped out your traditional IRA before spending your Roth. Before the traditional IRA is all gone, it makes sense to spend a combination of traditional and Roth IRA dollars so that zero percent tax brackets never get wasted. In 2015, a married couple filing a 2014 tax return jointly could withdraw up to $18,150 from their traditional IRA and, if they have no other taxable income, would pay zero tax on the withdrawal! Also, there are strategic times when spending Roth dollars can save more in taxes than the 15 percent tax bracket you expect to be in. Your actual taxes on incremental additional IRA withdrawals may be 27 percent or more because of the phase-in rules on the taxability of Social Security and the addition of the new Net Investment Tax. There may be other situations where spending some Roth dollars before traditional IRA dollars could benefit you in retirement.

The Big Picture

MINI CASE STUDY 4.2

Capital Gains May Affect Spending Order

What follows is a detailed mathematical analysis regarding whether it is a good idea to spend highly appreciated dollars that will incur a capital gain or spend IRA dollars. We try to be even handed and use a "running the numbers approach" to come up with recommendations. The problem in real life, however, is that the highly appreciated assets often comprise a large percentage of the portfolio. Furthermore, frequently those assets have been good performers in the past and clients often have strong emotional ties to the stock, especially if it is the stock of their former employer. Though hard to quantify, there is significant value that might even exceed any tax disadvantage in reducing your exposure to any concentrated positions in stocks or funds, even if you have to incur a capital gain.

One of the primary reasons people think it may be better not to spend the after-tax money first is because of capital gains. Changes to the capital gains tax rules in 2012 make this an issue for far fewer people than in the past. Capital-gains tax rates now vary depending on whether the gains are short-term or long-term, and they no longer apply *at all* to taxpayers whose taxable income falls in the 10 percent or 15 percent marginal tax bracket. High income taxpayers who fall into the 39.6 percent tax bracket are subject to a 20 percent capital gains tax. Taxpayers whose income falls into a bracket higher than 15 percent but less than 39.6 percent are subject to a 15 percent capital gains rate. Let's assume that the after-tax assets in the previous example have a zero cost basis, and that the entire $300,000 will now be taxed as capital gains. Is that a problem? The answer is, not necessarily.

Mr. Pay Taxes Later is a single man in Figure 4.1, so let's assume he's single here too. If he liquidated 100 percent of his after-tax stock account all at once, he would have a $300,000 capital gain. That's nowhere near enough to put him into the highest income and capital gains tax brackets, but 85 percent of his Social Security is now taxed. The tax he owes on just his Social Security and the capital gain is $42,722. It doesn't stop there, though. Because his income is so high, he's subject to a phase out of his personal exemption amount. Instead of being able to reduce his income by the full amount normally allowed for a single person, only $1,638 of his income is not taxed. (If he itemized his deductions, those would also be limited because his income is so high. We're going to try and keep it simple, though, and we're assuming he does not itemize). He also has to pay two additional taxes - the Alternative Minimum Tax ($4,053) and the Net Investment Tax ($4,608). Since he has such a high income this year, Mr. Pay Taxes Later is going to have to pay the IRS $51,383 on April 15th.

If Mr. Pay Taxes Later had talked to us before liquidating all of his stock, we would have told him that he could save a lot of money in taxes by liquidating only as much as he needs to meet his expenses each year. Let's assume that he cashed in only $69,000 of his stock each year. This is approximately the amount he has to withdraw if he needs $86,000 to live on after he pays his taxes. 85 percent of his Social Security will still be taxed, but he's in a lower tax bracket because his total income is significantly lower. His income is so much lower, in fact, that he does not have to pay the additional Alternative Minimum Tax or the Net Investment Tax at all, and he's entitled to deduct the full amount of his personal exemption too. This year, he will owe the IRS only $7,395. If he liquidates the $300,000 stock account at an equal rate over four years, the tax savings compared to liquidating it all at once are significant.

The really surprising news, though, comes if we make Mr. Pay Taxes Later a married man. We're going to assume that he has a wife who is his age, and that she collects the same amount of Social Security that he does. In this scenario, they will have more to spend (almost $90,000) by liquidating less (only $40,000) of the after-tax stock account each year. When he was a single man, he had to liquidate $69,000 each year in order to be able to spend $86,000. How on earth is that possible?

One obvious reason is that his wife is receiving her own Social Security benefits (I used $25,000 for purposes of this illustration), and they can use that money toward their spending needs. The not-so-obvious reason lies in their tax return. Their standard deduction and personal exemption amounts are double that of a single person, which reduces their taxable income. Because their taxable income is lower, only 48 percent (as compared to 85 percent) of their Social Security benefits are taxed. Their taxable income for the year is only $63,850 (as compared to $92,250 when he was single), and the tax due on their income is only $146. In this scenario, Mr. Pay Taxes Later liquidated $40,000 of after-tax stock with a zero cost basis, paid almost nothing in tax, and still has more spending money than he needs! They have $50,000 in Social Security benefits and $40,000 in proceeds from the sale of the stock, which leaves them with $89,854 after they pay the IRS! And if they did want to limit their spending to $86,000, they could liquidate just $36,000 of their stock each year and pay nothing – yes, zero – in federal income tax on 100 percent of their income.

Let's even go so far as to consider what happens if the married Mr. Pay Taxes Later decides to listen to his buddy, Mr. Pay Taxes Now, instead of me, and withdraws the additional money he needs from his retirement plan instead of his after-tax account. He didn't know that the money he takes from his retirement plan is subject to ordinary income tax rates. If he withdraws the exact same amount, $36,000, from his retirement plan instead of his after-tax account, he will owe the IRS $4,399 on April 15th. If he had cashed in his after-tax stock that had a cost basis of zero and the income was from a $36,000 capital gain, he would have owed the IRS nothing. Zero. Nada. Unfortunately, he doesn't have enough money to pay the tax bill, because his Social Security and the $36,000 retirement plan withdrawal were just enough to cover his normal monthly expenses. That means that he has to withdraw even more from his retirement plan to pay the tax, which is going to increase his tax bill next year. The amount he needs to withdraw to cover his spending needs in addition to the tax due on his retirement plan distribution is $42,200, which increases the tax amount due to $6,116. And as you can imagine, paying all of these unnecessary taxes will cause him to burn through his retirement plan very quickly. For higher income taxpayers, the outlook is even gloomier, because they are in higher income tax brackets and are potentially subject to the additional Alternative Minimum and Net Investment taxes as well.

When considering spending in retirement, there are many factors that have to be taken into consideration in order to make sure that there are no unpleasant surprises by the time April 15th rolls around. This is one area where it is well worth your time and money to consult with an accountant who is highly skilled in tax planning. It is a specialty in my practice, and it allows us to make recommendations concerning Roth IRA conversions to our clients with confidence. But above all, I hope I have made it very clear that the old assumption that you can never cash in highly appreciated investments without getting hit with a huge tax bill is simply no longer true.

There is one point to consider, though, which may be of interest to readers who have more than enough income from other sources, and who expect to have money in their estates to leave to their children. The step-up in basis rule states that, if property is inherited, it assumes a basis equivalent to its fair market value at the date of the decedent's death. It is referred to as a step-up because frequently the fair market value of the property at the date of death is greater than the decedent's basis—which was the cost when it was first acquired. If you have $100,000 of Google stock for which you paid $10,000, your basis is $10,000. If you sold the stock, you would have to report a $90,000 capital gain. If you leave the stock to a child, though, his basis in the stock would be $100,000 because that was the value at the time of your death.

So if you are preparing an estate plan assuming that your life expectancy is short, it may be advantageous for you to not spend highly appreciated after-tax investments before your retirement funds. If you anticipate being in a situation like this, consult with a qualified advisor who will run some numbers for you. Most of the numbers we have run indicate that unless you are going to die in a few years, you are usually better off spending your after-tax dollars first, even if you will incur capital gains tax and give up your step-up in basis.

MINI CASE STUDY 4.3

Which Accounts Should I Save For My Children?

Phyllis Planner is 65 years old and widowed (though the conclusion would be basically the same for a married taxpayer). She is thinking ahead. She wants her money to provide her with a comfortable standard of living, and she also wants to leave some money to her three children. How should Phyllis evaluate which pool of money to spend first and which to save for as long as possible?

There are four general categories of money to support her retirement. They are ranked in order of how I recommend Phyllis spend her money, exhausting each asset category before breaking into the next asset category.

1. After-Tax Assets Generated by Income Sources:
   - Pension distributions
   - Dividends, interest, and capital gains
   - Social Security

   Of course when Phyllis is 70½, she will be required to take minimum distributions from her IRA. Since she will have to pay income taxes on the distributions, the proceeds that remain after she pays taxes on the IRA distributions could also be spent before any of the following assets or sources of income.

2. After-Tax Assets (investments that are not part of a qualified pre-tax retirement plan that would generate income subject to taxes annually):
   - Investments that will either sell at a loss or break even
   - Then, more highly appreciated investments

3. IRA and Retirement Plan Assets (assets subject to ordinary income tax):
   - IRA, 403(b), 401(k), and so forth, dollars over and above required minimum distributions

4. Roth IRA:
   - Roth IRA dollars

The assets in the income category should be spent first, since she has to pay tax on that money anyway. But let's assume that Phyllis' Social Security, and the pension, dividends, and interest are not sufficient to meet her spending needs. Then the question becomes, "Which pool of money should be spent next?" If we keep in mind the premise of "don't pay taxes now—pay taxes later," the answer is obvious: the after-tax dollars. If we spend our after-tax dollars, except to the extent that a capital gain is triggered on a sale, those dollars will not be subject to income taxes and the money in the IRA can keep growing tax-deferred. Then, when Phyllis has exhausted her after-tax funds, she can delve into her IRA or pre-tax funds.

Whenever you make a withdrawal from an IRA, you are going to have to pay income taxes. To get an equivalent amount of spending money from the IRA assets and the after-tax assets, you have to take the taxes into consideration. Assuming that you are in a 25 percent tax bracket, you need $1.33 from the IRA assets to get $1.00 of spending money ($1.00 cash + $0.33 to pay the taxes). (We get $0.33 cents because $1.33 x 25 percent = .33.) On the other hand, the after-tax money is withdrawn tax-free, so to get $1.00, you withdraw $1.00 unless capital gains tax applies. Even if you are subject to capital gains tax, the rate is 15 percent for taxpayers who are in the 25 percent tax bracket. You are still ahead by .18 for every dollar you withdraw.

Finally, when Phyllis exhausts her IRA and pre-tax funds, she spends her Roth IRA. Why should she spend her traditional IRA before her Roth IRA? If tax-deferred growth is a good thing, then tax-free growth is even better. By spending taxable IRA money before Roth IRA money, she increases the time that the Roth IRA will provide income tax-free growth.

If your plan is to leave money to your heirs, their tax situations should be considered as well. If you have heirs who have tax deferral/avoidance as a goal and their tax bracket is the same as yours or higher, then the Roth assets are the best assets for them to inherit. The opposite conclusion may be reached if you have other heirs who plan on spending the money soon after they inherit it, and are in a lower tax bracket. If that is the case, you could be better off spending the Roth IRA yourself. The facts of each case should be considered.

MINI CASE STUDY 4.4

Using Tax Planning to Determine the Best Spending Order

One possible exception to spending after-tax dollars first is to make small IRA withdrawals, or small Roth IRA conversions if your current tax bracket is lower than your tax bracket will be once you retire. This strategy saves some taxes since you are getting some money out of your IRA before you have to take required minimum distributions (RMD), which will be taxed at your higher post retirement rate. If you withdraw just enough to take you to the top of your current (low) tax bracket, then you get that money out at a lower tax rate without pushing yourself into a higher tax bracket. But first, let me clarify a common misunderstanding about taxes and tax brackets.

What many people don't understand is that tax brackets are tiered. A married couple who is filing their joint tax return in 2016 (for their 2015 taxes), and who has taxable income up to $18,450 is taxed at 10 percent. If they earn more than that, then the next tier of their income is taxed at the next bracket (income from $18,451 to $74,900 is taxed at 15 percent for married filing jointly), and so on. Some people are deathly afraid of getting one more dollar. They think, "Oh no! If I get one more dollar I'm going to be thrown into the 25 percent tax bracket, and my taxes are going to explode." But that's not right. What happens is that *the one additional dollar* will be in the 25 percent bracket. This is illustrated in Table 4.1 on the following page, which shows the tax brackets for returns filed for the tax year 2015. You can see that a taxpayer, who falls into the maximum tax bracket of 39.6 percent, does not actually lose 39.6 percent of his income to taxes.

> **Determining a strategy for the distribution years is where the rubber meets the road. I've had clients who, while beginning their planning, get upset because they have not accumulated as much as they could have, or for mistakes made along the way. That's water under the bridge. If that's you, it's okay. Properly planning the optimal strategy for the distribution years will help you make up for mistakes made during the accumulation years.**

Let's look at a hypothetical example. Though Joe and Sally Retiree, aged 65, have an estate of $1.5 million, their taxable income is only $30,000. (Taxable income is arrived at after subtracting itemized deductions and personal exemptions and dependents). Right now, they are in the 15 percent tax bracket, but when Joe reaches age 70½, his minimum distribution will push his income well into the 25 percent tax bracket. Joe decides to make voluntary withdrawals from his IRA every year until he reaches his RMD date as follows.

The top income limit of the 15 percent bracket for married filing jointly (using 2015 tables) is $74,900. Joe and Sally already have $30,000 in taxable income before any IRA withdrawal. If Joe makes a voluntary $44,900 IRA withdrawal now, he still pays tax on the withdrawal at the same 15 percent

Table 4.1
2015 Tax Brackets for use in filing 2015 returns in 2016

MARRIED FILING JOINTLY
and SURVIVING SPOUSES

If Taxable Income is between:	*The Tax is:*
$ 0 - 18,450	10% of taxable income
$ 18,451 - 74,900	$1,845 plus 15% of the excess over $18,450
$ 74,901 - 151,200	$10,312.50 plus 25% of the excess over $74,900
$151,201 - 230,450	$29,387.50 plus 28% of the excess of $151,200
$230,451 - 411,500	$51,577.50 plus 33% of the excess over $230,450
$411,501 - 464,850	$111,324 plus 35% of the excess over $411,550
more than $464,850	$129,996.50 plus 39.6% of the excess over $464,850

SINGLE

If Taxable Income is between:	*The Tax is:*
$ 0 - 9,2250	% of taxable income
$ 9,226 - 37,450	$922.50 plus 15% of the excess over $9,225
$ 37,451 - 90,750	$5,156.25 plus 25% of the excess over $37,450
$ 90,751 - 189,300	$18,481.25 plus 28% of the excess over $90,750
$189,301 - 411,500	$46,075.25 plus 33% of the excess over $189,300
$411,501 - 413,200	$119,401.25 plus 35% of the excess over $411,500
more than $413,201	$119,996.25 plus 39.6% of the excess over $413,200

rate as the rest of his income. If he waits until age 70½, when he is required to make a withdrawal, much of the later distributions will be taxed at 25 percent. Depending on the circumstances, it might be a reasonable strategy for him to begin distributions before he turns age 70½. Calculations reveal that the higher distribution yields a slight long-term advantage, although not as much as you might think because of the simultaneous loss of some tax deferral.

For many clients, particularly frugal clients, I would prefer a variation of this strategy that provides better long-term benefits. Instead of making an IRA withdrawal of $44,900, paying tax on the funds, and then being left with after-tax dollars that will generate taxable income, I would recommend Joe make a $44,900 Roth IRA conversion. Many clients will resist this advice, but I urge you to at least consider it. My wife and I have made Roth IRA conversions well into the six figures of our own money, paid an enormous tax bill, and I still recommend that clients take advantage of the lower tax bracket this way. This advice is perfectly consistent with Jonathan Clements' article in *The Wall Street Journal*, in which Jonathan quoted me giving this identical analysis. We will cover the reasons to consider Roth IRA conversions in more detail in Chapter 7. For now, suffice it to say that I am a big fan of Roth IRA conversions.

If Joe doesn't want to make a Roth IRA conversion, he should at least consider taking IRA distributions even before he is required to, based on his tax bracket. Please note that adding income in the form of extra IRA distributions and/or Roth IRA conversions may have an impact on the taxability of Social Security benefits and other items (refer back to "Comments on Your Actual Tax Brackets" in Chapter 2), which should be worked into the numbers for the amount to withdraw or convert.

A Key Lesson from This Chapter

Leaving money in the tax-deferred environment for as long as possible confers advantages that almost always outweigh concerns over paying capital gains on your after-tax assets. Depending on the specific circumstances, it maybe preferable to spend either traditional or Roth IRA dollars next.

5

||||||||||||||||||||||

Required Minimum Distribution Rules

There was a time when a fool and his money were soon parted, but now it happens to everybody.

— Adlai Stevenson

Main Topics

- An overview of the Required Minimum Distribution rules (RMD)

- How to calculate your RMD

- An explanation of the IRS tables

- A possible compromise for taxpayers who don't need their RMD for income

- How to get your interest-free loan from the IRS

> # KEY IDEA
>
> If you can afford it, take only the minimum the government requires you to withdraw from your retirement plan or IRA. This distribution pattern retains more money in the tax-deferred account and is consistent with our motto, "Don't pay taxes now—pay taxes later." Note that after taking the Required Minimum Distribution, you can always withdraw more money should the need arise.

Eventually Everyone Must Draw from Retirement Savings

Even if you stick to the game plan to spend your income and after-tax dollars first, eventually, by law, you will have to withdraw funds from your traditional IRA or qualified retirement plan (Required Minimum Distributions (RMDs). Roth IRAs are currently exempt from this requirement, but that may change if President Obama has his way. For now, though, I will limit the discussion to the rules governing traditional retirement plans.

You will usually be required to take the annual RMD by April 1 of the year following the year that you reach age 70½. The key word here is *minimum*. Keeping in mind the "Don't pay taxes now—pay taxes later" rule of thumb, I want you to continue to maintain the highest balance in your IRA. If you take a RMD the year you turn 70½ and a distribution the following year, you may remain in a lower tax bracket which would be advantageous. You can always take out more if you need it.

During the financial crisis of 2009, the federal government temporarily suspended the RMD rules. The reasoning was that older retirees shouldn't be forced to sell their investments when the value of the investments is low. That reasoning didn't make sense to me because investors have always been allowed to take their RMD in stock instead of cash, if they prefer – it's called an in-kind distribution. So, if the investments in your IRA have decreased in value, you can have the investment shares transferred directly to a non-IRA account, and leave them alone until they increase in value again. You still have to pay

Eventually, by law, you will have to withdraw funds from your traditional IRA or qualified retirement plan.

tax on the amount of the transfer, but the only reason you would be forced to sell when the value is low would be if you did not have a lot of cash on hand, and need to sell some of the securities to pay the tax on the RMD. Another point to consider is that, while the IRS requires that you calculate the RMD for every IRA account that you own, you are not required to withdraw a minimum distribution amount from every IRA you own. You can add up all of your RMDs and take the total amount from one account, preferably from one that has not gone down in value. Hopefully, being aware of these little-known rules will help you avoid having to take a loss on your investments if you need to take a RMD when the markets are down.

Calculating Your RMD after Age 70½

Currently, RMDs are calculated by taking your projected distribution period, based on your age and the age of a beneficiary deemed to be 10 years younger than you, and dividing that factor into the balance of your IRA or qualified plan as of December 31 of the prior year. Bear in mind that your projected life expectancy factor or the projected distribution period is not based on your personal eating and exercise habits or even your genetic history! It is an actuarial calculation from the IRS determined solely by age. Many large financial institutions offer tools on their websites that automatically calculate RMDs. If you would like to do the math yourself, the IRS's Supplement to the Publication 590 contains worksheets that you can use to work through the calculation, as well as the tables that you will need to use to find your RMD factor. For those who would just like a quick glance, the tables are published in the appendix at the end of this book.

The IRS provides three life expectancy tables. The most frequently used table is Table III, not Table I. I present them here in the reverse order.

1. **Table III: Uniform Lifetime Table** (for use by unmarried IRA owners and married owners whose spouses are not more than 10 years younger). This table is available in the appendix of this book.

2. **Table II: Joint Life and Last Survivor Expectancy Table** (for IRA owners with spouses 10 or more years younger). This is not covered in the appendix of this book because it is too long. See IRS Publication 590.

3. **Table I: Single Life Expectancy Table** (for IRA beneficiaries). This table is available in the appendix of this book.

Table III: Uniform Lifetime Table for IRA Owners

Generally speaking, most IRA owners will use Table III. In effect, the age-dependent projected distribution periods in Table III are based on joint life expectancy projections of an IRA owner and a hypothetical beneficiary not more than 10 years younger. Using a joint life expectancy is advantageous because the longer joint-life expectancy factor reduces the annual RMD. But rather than using the actual life expectancy of the beneficiary for the calculations, the IRS simplifies the terms. Table III deems all beneficiaries—from children to grandmothers—to have a life expectancy 10 years longer than that of the owner. At age 71, the projected distribution period is 26.5 years (roughly the single life expectancy from Table I plus 10 years, although you must refer to the tables for the precise factor).

MINI CASE STUDY 5.1

RMD Calculation for IRA Owners

Bob turns 75 in 2015. As of December 31, 2014, he has two IRAs that are each worth $500,000. He names his son, Phillip, as the beneficiary for one IRA and his 72-year-old wife, Mary, for the other. To calculate his 2015 RMD for the IRA with his wife as beneficiary, he takes the life expectancy at his age 75 from Table III, 22.9, and divides that into his balance, $500,000, to arrive at $21,834. He uses the same table and the same factor to arrive at the same RMD from the IRA that has his son as the beneficiary. When Bob dies, the amounts that his wife and son will be required to take from the IRAs they inherited from him will be different. I'll go into more detail about that later in this chapter.

Table II: Joint Life and Last Survivor Expectancy Table for IRA Owners with Spouses 10 or More Years Younger

Because nothing that the government does is ever without complications, there is an exception for married individuals when the IRA owner is 10 or more years older than his or her spouse. Those individuals are permitted to use their actual joint life expectancy factor, which will result in smaller RMDs.

Table 5.1

| | IRS Table III | | | IRS Table II | | |
| | Spouse Who Is Not 10 Years Younger (or Child) as Beneficiary | | | Spouse Who is 10 Years Younger as Beneficiary | | |
Bob's Age	IRA Balance ($)	Factor	RMD ($)	IRA Balance ($)	Factor	RMD ($)
75	500,000	22.9	21,834	500,000	24.3	20,576
76	478,166	22.0	21,735	479,424	23.4	20,488
77	456,431	21.2	21,530	458,936	22.5	20,397
78	434,901	20.3	21,424	438,539	21.7	20,209
79	413,478	19.5	21,204	418,329	20.8	20,112
80	392,274	18.7	20,977	398,217	20.0	19,911
81	371,296	17.9	20,743	378,307	19.1	19,807
82	350,554	17.1	20,500	358,500	18.3	19,590
83	330,053	16.3	20,249	338,910	17.5	19,366
84	309,805	15.5	19,987	319,543	16.7	19,134
85	289,817	14.8	19,582	300,409	16.0	18,776
86	270,235	14.1	19,166	281,634	15.2	18,529
87	251,069	13.4	18,737	263,105	14.5	18,145
88	232,333	12.7	18,294	244,960	13.8	17,751
89	214,039	12.0	17,837	227,209	13.1	17,344
90	196,202	11.4	17,211	209,865	12.4	16,925

MINI CASE STUDY 5.2

RMD Calculation with IRA Owner and Spouse More Than 10 Years Younger

Bob will have to use a different calculation for the RMD for the IRA with his wife as the beneficiary if Mary is only 63 years old. According to Table II, Bob's and Mary's joint life expectancy factor based on their ages they will be on their birthdays in 2015 is 24.3. Bob calculates his RMD by dividing 24.3 into his balance of $500,000 to arrive at $20,576. Bob's RMD for the account with his wife as the beneficiary is lower than for the account with his son as the beneficiary because Bob and his wife were permitted to use their actual *joint* life expectancy factor for his calculation.

We will cover more about IRA beneficiaries in Chapter 13. For now, please look at the table on preceding page to see how the age of his spouse affects Bob's RMD.

Table I: Single Life Expectancy Table for IRA Beneficiaries

When a spouse dies before age 70½, the younger spousal beneficiary of the IRA has two options. He or she can roll the inherited IRA into his or her own IRA, and begin RMDs when he or she reaches age 70½. Or, he or she can decline to treat the IRA as his or her own and simply defer distributions until the year that the original IRA owner would have attained age 70½. At that point, he or she would begin distributions based on his or her Table 1 life expectancy factor. This is an extremely important decision that you will have to make if your spouse predeceases you, and the advantages and disadvantages of each option are covered in detail in Chapter 13.

Nonspouse beneficiaries of inherited IRAs have no options. They must begin to take distributions based on their own life expectancy (as projected in Table I) as of the year following the year of the IRA owner's death. For each subsequent year, the non-spouse beneficiary subtracts one (1) from his original factor, because his life expectancy is diminished by one year for every year he survives. This is frequently referred to as the "minus one method."

Calculating Your Life Expectancy after the Initial Year

It is interesting to note that Table 1 life expectancies are reduced by one full year as each year passes. Tables II and III, however, reduce the life expectancy of the IRA owner by less than one year. This is analogous to the old double recalculation method. (Readers who remember those rules get bonus points). The idea is that as we age, our life expectancy declines, but it does not decline by an entire year.

So, if you are a surviving spouse who inherits an IRA, but you don't treat the inherited IRA as your own IRA, your life expectancy is recalculated each year based on the life expectancies shown in Table I (the full year decline).

When you die, your nonspouse heirs must use your life expectancy at the time of your death, reduced by one for each subsequent year, for their RMD calculation. For a discussion on whether a spouse should treat an IRA as his or her own IRA, refer to Chapter 13.

Timing Your First Required Distribution

Retirement plan owners born between July 1, 1944, and June 30, 1945, will have to take one distribution in 2015 and one in 2016, or two distributions in 2016 if they fail to take a distribution in 2015. If you fail to take a distribution in 2015, the first distribution in 2016 will have to be taken prior to April 1, 2016 (in effect, for what should have been taken in 2015), and the second distribution will have to be taken by December 31, 2016.

A retirement plan owner born between July 1, 1945, and June 30, 1946, will reach age 70½ during 2016. Technically, he or she could delay taking the first RMD until April 1, 2017. The rule was, and remains, that the required beginning date for taking RMDs is April 1 of the year following the year the owner turns 70½. However, if the owner was born between July 1, 1945, and June 30, 1946, and he or she waits until 2017 to take the first distribution, then that person must take two distributions in 2017. The first distribution would be due before April 1, 2017, and the second distribution would be due by December 31, 2017. Annual minimum distributions would continue for the rest of the participant's life.

Failing to take a minimum distribution when required, or not taking a large enough minimum distribution has very expensive consequences. The IRS charges a 50 percent excise tax on the amount that was not distributed as required. So if you were required to take a $10,000 minimum distribution and didn't do so, you will owe $5,000 in excise tax. And that's in addition to the normal income tax you will owe on the distribution, as well as general penalties for underpayment of tax.

For participants born July 1, 1946, or afterward, there is no RMD for 2016. Unless the participant needs the money or is pursuing the early distribution of an IRA because of a lower income tax bracket or estate plan strategy, he or she is better off leaving the money in the IRA and taking the first RMD in 2017 or later.

So, if you have a choice, should you limit your distributions to one per year, or should you wait and then take two the following year? If you take a minimum distribution the year that you turn 70½ and only one distribution the following year, you may remain in a lower tax bracket, which would be advantageous. Taking two distributions in one year, though, could push you into a higher tax bracket and possibly accelerate the phase-out of certain tax credits or deductions. If that is the case, you will likely be better off violating our "Pay taxes later" rule by taking one distribution and paying some tax before you have to. On the other hand, if you will remain in the same tax bracket even with two distributions, then it makes no difference if you wait until you are required to begin distributions. This allows you to take advantage of the additional period of tax-deferred growth.

Special Rule for Qualified Plan Owners Who Are Still Working Past Age 70½

RMD rules apply to traditional IRAs (not Roth IRAs) and qualified plans [401(k)s, 403(b)s, Roth 401(k)s, and Roth403(b)s, etc.). However, the rules governing 401(k)s and 403(b)s are slightly different than for IRAs.

- If you are still working after age 70½, the IRS does not require you to take a distribution from the retirement plan connected to your current job as long as you do not own more than five percent of the company. Remember, though, that your employer is responsible for setting the rules for your plan. Even though the IRS doesn't require you to take a distribution, your employer might.

- If you have a plan such as a 401(k) associated with a job from which you have retired, the IRS says you will have to take your initial RMD by April 1 of the year following the year in which you reach age 70½. Some employers allow you to keep your retirement plan with them when you start to take withdrawals, and some employers require that you roll the account into an IRA before you start to take withdrawals.

- If you have two or more retirement plans associated with jobs from which you have retired, the IRS requires that each plan calculate a minimum distribution for you when you reach age 70½. This is different from their rules for calculating RMDs on IRAs, which allow you to add up the values of all of your IRAs, calculate the RMD, and then take the full distribution from one account. This can be a very important consideration for people whose old plans happen to include stock in the company they worked for, because the RMD requirement might cause you to have to sell stock when the value is low. As long as you have enough other assets to pay the tax on the RMD, though, you can take your company stock as an "in-kind" distribution and keep it in a brokerage account until the time that it increases in value again. The one exception to this rule is for 403(b) plan owners. The IRS allows participants in 403(b) plans to add up the values of all their accounts, calculate the RMD, and then take the full distribution from one account. For individuals such as retired university professors who have multiple 403(b) plans, this makes the paperwork much simpler to deal with at year end.

• If you had a 401(k) plan from a former job and rolled that 401(k) plan into a plan associated with the job at which you are still working, then you will have to check with the plan administrator of your current plan to see whether you will be forced to take RMDs upon attaining age 70½ from the portion of that 401(k) plan that is attributable to your former employment. PLR 200453015, published in January 2005, states that the IRS permits deferral of the RMDs on all of the funds in the new employer's account *including the rollover contributions* from the former employer until April 1 of the year after the employee retires from the new employer. You must, however, make sure that your employer's plan will allow you to do what the IRS will allow you to do.

MINI CASE STUDY 5.3

RMD if Still Working Past Age 70½

Joan continues to work although she is older than 70½. She has a total of $1 million in her 401(k) plans: $500,000 associated with her current job and $500,000 from a former job. She has never consolidated the two plans. Her new plan includes both her and her employer's most recent contributions.

By April 1 of the year after she turns age 70½, she will be required to take minimum distributions from the $500,000 associated with the job she left, but not from the account that is still active due to her employment. Whether she could take the money from the 401(k) from the job she retired from, roll it into her current plan (by trustee-to-trustee transfer), and avoid an RMD is not clear. The

IRS will allow it, but her current employer may not. If your employer does permit it, this may be an incentive for someone still working after age 70½ to consider rolling money out of their IRA and into a retirement plan at work. Usually, I prefer money going the other way, which is from 401(k) to IRA, or my current preferred strategy, from a work 401(k) or IRA to a one-person 401(k) plan that you control.

I have a client who became really excited about the prospect of avoiding his minimum distribution. He wanted to start his own retirement plan [actually a one-person 401(k)] based on his small self-employment income. Then he wanted to roll his IRA into a one-person 401(k) and suspend his RMDs on his IRA. It was a good thought, but with a fatal flaw. He is more than a five percent owner of his consulting business, and the rule about deferring the RMD after 70½ if you are still working does not apply to individuals with a five percent or greater ownership in the company.

Special Rules for 403(b) Participants

Participants in 403(b) plans are subject to some special rules that do not apply to participants in other types of plans. Both employee and employer contributions to a 403(b) plan made before January 1, 1987, are not subject to RMDs until age 75. As a result, the balance that was in your 403(b) as of December 31, 1986, is not subject to RMDs until you reach age 75, not age 70½, even if you have retired. If you fall into this special category of 403(b) account holders, you should consult with your organization's benefits office to determine the balance in the account as of December 31, 1986. Surprisingly, many institutions, including TIAA-CREF, do a good job of tracking that balance. If your 403(b) plan included pre-1987 contributions and you roll it into an IRA, the "grandfathered" status of those contributions is lost, and you will be required to take minimum distributions on them at age 70½. Contributions made on January 1, 1987 and later are subject to RMDs at age 70½. Note, however, that the growth and appreciation on pre-1987 dollars is not grandfathered and is treated like a regular 403(b).

On the other hand, when you actually calculate the tax advantage of keeping the funds in the 403(b) to defer a portion of the minimum distribution, it is relatively small. If you think you could get even a slight investment advantage by doing a trustee-to-trustee transfer from your 403(b) to an IRA to gain additional investment options, it would still be worthwhile.

Retired public safety officers, including law enforcement and firefighters, have a special exception to the distribution rules. They can receive a distribution of up to $3,000 completely tax-free from their 403(b), as long as the proceeds are used to directly pay for accident, health or long-term care insurance.

Would you like more cutting-edge information on distribution planning for TIAA-CREF participants? Go to:

www.financialfreedomforfaculty.com

Request our free report called *The Best Retirement and Estate Plan for University Faculty*. Please do it now, while it's fresh on your mind.

A Possible Compromise for Those Who Don't Need Income and Are Charitably Inclined

Although there is no way to avoid taking RMDs from traditional (not Roth) IRAs, there is an option available to those individuals who do not need that income for living expenses, and who are inclined to donate to charity. The Pension Protection Act of 2006 created something called a Qualified Charitable Distribution, which allows IRA owners to specify that a payment of up to $100,000 from their RMDs be sent directly to a **qualified** charity. Here is how it works. IRA owners electing this option are still required to take their RMD, but the amount of the distribution that is sent directly to the **qualified** charity can be excluded from their gross income. For individuals who are charitably inclined, this can make a lot more sense than having the RMD sent to them, and then issuing a separate check to the charity, particularly if the taxpayer can't itemize deductions. (Married couples who have incomes in excess of $309,900 in 2015 will be subject to a limitation on their total itemized deductions, including their charitable contributions). So, if you can't itemize, the charitable contribution isn't tax deductible, and the IRA distribution is taxable. With a Qualified Charitable Distribution (QCD), you still can't deduct the charitable donation, but at least you're not taxed on the IRA distribution. In addition, ther are many potential tax benefits from reducing your adjusted gross income using a QCD:

- Less of your Social Security income may become taxable

- The phase-out of medical expenses you claim as itemized deductions is reduced

- The phase-out of total itemized deductions is reduced

- The Net Investment Income tax surcharges can be reduced

- You may avoid future increases in your Medicare premiums

- Your Alternative Minimum Tax may be reduced.

QCDs were originally supposed to be effective only in 2006 and 2007, but Congress has extended them on a temporary basis every year, through 2014. Although they are not in the law for 2015 and beyond, they could very well be extended into future years. Decisions about extending QCDs have historically been done very late in the year. If you plan to wait until a definite decision has been made about QCDs before requesting your RMD, your retirement plan custodian might not have time to process your request. Since failing to take your RMD when required is a very expensive mistake, I recommend making all customary charitable donations directly from your IRA. If Congress extends the QCD provisions, you were able to take advantage. If they aren't extended, then there is no harm done. The full amount of your IRA distribution will be treated as taxable income, which is what would have happened anyway.

Qualified Charitable Distributions have three criteria that you must be aware of:

1. You have to make sure that the charitable organization is a *qualified* charity. A qualified charity is one that has a valid tax-exempt status, according to the US Treasury. There are some very good causes that I personally donate to, but they do not meet the definition of a qualified charity. As such, I cannot deduct those contributions nor could I send them a QCD. The organization will be able to tell you if they're tax-exempt or not, or, if you want to be 100 percent sure, you can ask the IRS.

2. You have to be at least 70½ to make a QCD.

3. QCDs are only available for IRAs, or inactive SEPs and SIMPLE plans. QCDs from an employer-sponsored retirement plan are currently not permitted.

When Should You Schedule Taking Your RMD?

Theoretically, you should take your RMD on December 31 to delay as long as possible withdrawing money from the tax-favored environment. In the real world, however, it is difficult to get any work done with financial firms in December, and trying to comply with a deadline between Christmas and the last day of the year is a total nightmare. Remember, if you miss taking a withdrawal by year-end, you face the 50 percent penalty for failing to take your RMD—an expensive penalty. If you don't need the cash, I recommend scheduling your distribution for Thanksgiving or early December. If you need the RMD for your spending needs, it may be best to schedule 12 equal monthly distributions throughout the year.

> **If you don't need the cash, I recommend scheduling your distribution for Thanksgiving or early December.**

Schedule your IRA distribution
for Thanksgiving

How to Get Your Interest-Free Loan from the IRS

I do not understand why anyone would have extra tax taken out of their paycheck to ensure that they get a big refund. Why on earth would you give the IRS an interest-free loan? It should be the other way around! Would you like to get an interest-free loan from the IRS? One way to do so is to take your RMD in December and have federal income tax withheld from it, rather than paying quarterly estimated taxes on your retirement income throughout the year. From the IRS's perspective, tax that is withheld is treated as if it has been withheld at an even rate throughout the year as opposed to being treated like a single estimated tax payment you made late in the year – so you won't get penalized for paying all of the tax due in December. Here's an even better idea for those of you who hate paying estimated taxes and who love being "floated" by the IRS. If you are currently paying quarterly estimated taxes on your non-IRA income, you can forgo your estimates completely and instead ask your IRA custodian to do up to a 100 percent tax withholding on the RMD you take at the end of the year. Let's say that you have been paying estimates of $1,500 each quarter, and you've been told that you will have to take a RMD of $6,000 this year. In December, you can instruct your IRA custodian to withhold federal income tax from your RMD at a rate of 100 percent, and have them send the entire $6,000 directly to the IRS. This strategy allows you to earn interest on the money you are required to take from your IRA for as long as possible, and also allows you to earn the interest on the estimated tax payments that you were going to send to the IRS. The best part is that, under current rules, as long as the amount of taxes withheld from your RMD is sufficient to cover the amount of tax you owe for the entire year, there is no penalty for paying 100 percent of your tax liability in December!

A Key Lesson from This Chapter

Keep your RMD to the required minimum. Do not take out more money than you need so that you keep the balance in your tax-deferred accounts as large as possible.

6

||||||||||||||||||||||

Should You Transfer Your 401(k) to an IRA at Retirement?

Rollovers Versus Trustee-to-Trustee Transfers and Other Strategies

They say it is better to be poor and happy than rich and miserable, but how about a compromise like moderately rich and just moody?

— Diana, Princess of Wales

Main Topics

- Options for handling your retirement plan after you leave your job

- Assessing the flexibility of your retirement plan

- Advantages and disadvantages of:
  1. keeping old retirement plans
  2. transferring old retirement plans to IRAs
  3. trustee-to-trustee transfers
  4. IRA rollovers

- The mechanics of initiating the transfer or rollover

KEY IDEA

In most cases retirees should consider a trustee-to-trustee transfer of the majority of their company 401(k) plan to an IRA or, alternatively, a one-person 401(k) plan. There are circumstances, however, where a retiree will be well served by retaining at least a portion of his or her retirement plan in the original company 401(k).

When someone retires or is "service terminated," the big question is: "What should I do now?"

Without getting into specific investment ideas, let's consider whether it makes sense for you to keep your money in your existing retirement plan, transfer it to an IRA, take a lump-sum distribution or, make a trustee-to-trustee transfer into your new one-person 401(k) plan. Contingent on the specifics of any given retirement plan, the basic options are as follows:

1. Transfer the money into a separate IRA.

2. Leave the money in your current plan.

3. Annuitize the balance (for more information on annuitizing, see Chapter 8).

4. Use some combination of options 1, 2, and 3 (often my favorite choice).

5. Take a lump-sum distribution.

6. Transfer money to a one-person 401(k) plan.

Rolling Over to an IRA

Retirees often talk about rolling over to an IRA or rolling money out of a retirement plan and into an IRA. Technically we should use the term *transfer*, simply because the IRS makes a significant distinction between the mechanics and regulations of a rollover versus a trustee-to-trustee transfer. The trustee-to-trustee transfer is simpler, and what I usually recommend. I'll explain the distinctions between rollovers and transfers later in this chapter. (In keeping with common usage, when referring to a transfer I will use the terms *rollover* and *transfer* interchangeably throughout this book, but please understand that what I am referring to is following the technical procedures of a trustee-to-trustee transfer). (See the section in this chapter called *The Mechanics of IRA Rollovers and Trustee-to-Trustee Transfers*).

Though there are a few downsides, transferring retirement plan accumulations into an IRA or into your own one-person 401(k) via a trustee-to-trustee transfer is usually the best option. As with most decisions, there are advantages and disadvantages.

> **Retirees often talk about rolling over to an IRA or rolling money out of a retirement plan and into an IRA. Technically we should use the term *transfer,* simply because the IRS makes a significant distinction between the mechanics and regulations of a rollover versus a trustee-to-trustee transfer.**

Tax Advantages of Transferring a Company 401(k) (or Other Retirement Plan) into an IRA

Proper planning requires taking the appropriate steps while you are alive and having in place the appropriate procedures after you and your spouse have died. If done correctly, your heirs could stretch taxable distributions from an inherited IRA and certain retirement plans for decades. Under the current laws, it is potentially possible to stretch retirement plan distributions for as long as 80 years after you die. (Stretching the IRA is discussed in detail in Chapter 13). If, however, your employer's retirement plan document stipulates the wrong provisions, the stretch may be replaced by a screaming income tax disaster. Your heirs could be in for a tax nightmare if you never transferred your 401(k) retirement plan into an IRA. Different rules apply if a spouse inherits a 401(k) versus someone other than your spouse—say a child—so it is important to understand how your decisions can affect the outcome.

Some employees prefer to keep their retirement plan balance where it is rather than transferring it to an IRA simply because their 401(k) plans may offer favorable fixed-income investments, (often called Guaranteed Income Contracts, or GICs) and/or the possibility of lower transaction fees. Unfortunately, many employees fail to realize that the specific plan rules that govern their individual 401(k) or other retirement plan take precedence over the IRS distribution rules for inherited IRAs or retirement plans. The distribution rules that come into play at the death of the retirement plan participant are found in a plan document created by the employer that few employees or advisors ever bother to read. You would like to think that, since employers participate in the plans they offer to their employees, they would design the rules of the plan to be as beneficial as possible. Unfortunately, that is not necessarily the case. Most people wouldn't even think that the rules that their employers set could affect their estate distribution after their death, but, since the plan rules always take precedence over the IRS rules, it is possible that your employer's decisions could haunt your beneficiaries long after your death. Here's how it works.

The IRS provides three options if you inherit your spouse's 401(k) or retirement plan. The first option is to leave the money in the plan. You have to change the name on the account, but sometimes there are advantages to keeping it where it is. For instance, even if you are not yet age 59½, you can take withdrawals and not have to pay the 10 percent penalty. You might also like the investment choices that the plan has. If you elect this option, though, you cannot change the beneficiary designations that were chosen by your spouse. They would continue to apply after your death. The second option is to roll the money over into an inherited IRA. You would be required to take (at least) the Required Minimum Distributions (RMD) based on your own life expectancy. Withdrawals would not be subject to the 10 percent penalty even if you are not yet age 59½, and you can name your own beneficiaries. The third option is to roll the 401(k) into your own IRA. This is the best option if you don't need the income, because you will not be required to take distributions until you reach age 70½. You can also name your own beneficiaries with this option.

The rules for a non-spouse beneficiary will depend on how old the employee was at the time of his or her death. If the employee was older than age 70½ (and had begun taking RMDs), a non-spouse beneficiary must continue to take at least the RMDs. The distribution can be based on either the employee's (or decedent's) life expectancy, or on the beneficiary's life expectancy, whichever is longer.

If the employee was not yet 70½, the plan rules could specify either of two options. You might be allowed to take RMDs based on your own life expectancy, thus stretching the tax deferral for as long as possible. Or, you might be required to take all of the money out of the plan no later than December 31st of the fifth year following the employee's death. If this is the case, you can take some out each year, or wait until the last year and take it all at once. Plans that have this requirement cause a huge acceleration of fully taxable income, even if the withdrawals are made over a period of five years. Let's assume you inherit a $1 million 401(k), and the plan requires that you withdraw all of the money within five years. Even if you have no other income at all, and you spread the withdrawals evenly over five years, the distributions will be taxed at a minimum rate of 28 percent. The taxes on distributions totaling $1 million would amount to over $280,000, leaving $720,000 outside of the protection of the inherited 401(k).

Many 401(k)s used to require beneficiaries to remove 100 percent of the proceeds of the plan within one year after the death of the owner, which meant that the beneficiaries had to pay tax on the entire plan balance. In prior years, those kinds of rules provided an enormous incentive to roll the money into an IRA rather than keeping it in a 401(k). Employers are no longer permitted to require that beneficiaries withdraw the money from the plan within one year. The stretch IRA concept permits beneficiaries to limit distributions from an inherited IRA to the required minimum, which allows them to maintain money in the tax-deferred environment for as long as possible after the death of the IRA owner. I discuss the implications of the stretch IRA in detail in Chapter 13, but you should know that most experts agree that the rules are likely to change.

Rolling the 401(k) into an IRA

MINI CASE STUDY 6.1

True Story of the Disastrous Consequences of Not Making a 401(k) Rollover to an IRA *(Details adapted)*

Even before the divorce papers were final, the mother of a young son had her divorce attorney draft a new will and retirement plan beneficiary designation. In her will and in her retirement plan, she cut out her ex-husband and left everything to her son via a trust that provided for his education, among other things. Making provisions for her son was particularly important because she was in poor health and was no longer able to work.

She saw a financial planner about the possibility of rolling her retirement plan into an IRA. She hated to pay fees and found the idea of moving the account particularly distasteful because she liked the fixed-income account of her former employer's 401(k) plan. She was not aware that the rules of her retirement plan, as stated in the plan document, stipulated that the entire plan balance must be withdrawn within a year of her death. Her retirement plan would not permit her son to use his own life expectancy for RMD purposes.

The financial planner used only investment-related reasons to try to convince her to roll over her 401(k) into an IRA, and was not successful. The attorney who prepared the will and the beneficiary designation of the 401(k) never recommended an IRA rollover at all.

The mother died with over $250,000 in her former employer's retirement plan. Because the plan rules said that the money had to be taken out by the last day of the year after her death, the trust she established for her son had to pay massive income taxes on the entire balance of the retirement plan. Even worse, the trust for her son had a much higher income tax rate than he would have had individually, which meant the retirement monies were taxed at the highest rate – which at the time was 35 percent.

Had the mother taken her retirement plan and rolled it into an IRA the day before she died, and if she had used the appropriate beneficiary designation, the money would have remained in a tax-deferred environment as an inherited IRA. Distributions and thus taxation could have been spread over the son's life expectancy. For at least a portion of that money, income tax could have been deferred for more than 80 years.

If the client, the attorney, or the financial advisor had read *Retire Secure!*, they would have seen the potential for the problem of accelerated income taxes lurking in the rules of the employer's plan. The advisor could have pointed to compelling reasons to transfer the money into an IRA that went beyond investment issues. They might have considered rolling everything but the fixed-income fund into an IRA, but they didn't. The result of the lack of planning and the lack of a knowledgeable advisor left the son financially handicapped, in addition to suffering the loss of his mother.

> **Retirees who still have their money in a retirement plan that doesn't allow the stretch should strongly consider rolling their retirement plan, or at least a major part of their retirement plan, into an IRA.**

The moral of the story: If you are unaware of your plan's death distribution rules, please inquire about them right away. It could save your family a bundle in the long run.

Reasons to Transfer an old 401(k) to an IRA or to a One-Person 401(k)

One of the most compelling reasons to transfer money out of a 401(k) retirement plan and into an IRA is the opportunity to take advantage of the universe of investment choices offered by IRAs. The challenge facing most IRA owners is choosing among the thousands of available investments such as mutual funds, stocks, bonds, etc. Leaving the money in the company plan will limit your options to those your employer makes available to you. The argument for greater investment choices becomes even more critical if your plan does not offer good investment choices. A second reason to consider moving an old 401(k) is that, nowadays, most people don't stay employed with one company for their entire career. Most people have several – even many – employers over the course of their careers. This might lead to the existence of several 401(k) plans, all of which are likely to have different rules and maybe even different beneficiaries. If you have a good plan where you work, you can ask your plan administrator if the plan accepts rollover contributions. If so, you can transfer your old 401(k) into your current 401(k). If not, you can roll your old 401(k) in to an IRA. Some financial writers, like Jonathan Clements of *The Wall Street Journal*, feel that naive retirement plan owners are likely to be the victims of unscrupulous financial advisors. The argument goes that if you stay in your 401(k) plan, you will avoid some of these unscrupulous advisors. I hate it when I see an "advisor" who has convinced their client to transfer their 401(k) to an IRA, and then has invested that money in products that pay them a high commission while charging high fees to the client. But, in general, if you hold stocks or alternate investments—other than a much-better-than-average type of fund that you could not replicate outside your retirement plan—I would like to see you make a trustee-to-trustee transfer out of the retirement plan and into an IRA or a one-person 401(k) (subject to other exceptions coming up).

Advantages of Retaining a 401(k) Rather than Rolling It into an IRA

1. *Superior credit protection:* Many ERISA (Employee Retirement Income Security Act of 1974) type plans enjoy federal protection against creditors and bankruptcy that IRAs do not enjoy. It should be noted, however, that the Bankruptcy Abuse Prevention Act of 2005, signed in April 2005 by President Bush includes an exemption for contributory IRAs and Roth IRAs. At the time we went to press, the exemption is $1,245,745. It further exempts all rollovers from retirement plans to IRAs. There is one exception to this rule. In 2014, the US Supreme Court determined that *inherited* IRAs and retirement plans are not subject to this exemption, and therefore are not protected from creditor claims. Because there are two different types of creditor protection, I usually advise owners of large IRAs to keep their rollover IRA in a separate account from their contributory IRA. IRAs usually have state law protections, but over time, even these state law protections have diminished. For the vast majority of participants, a good umbrella insurance policy providing coverage of at least $1 million or possibly $2 million or more (to protect against unexpected liabilities) is the best solution. For participants with personal liability issues, such as emergency room doctors or surgeons, the superior credit protection may be more important than the investment and estate planning advantages of the IRA. For example, I recently worked with a physician who decided not to terminate his qualified retirement plan for these reasons, when it would have been easier to terminate the plan and roll the plan balance into an IRA. For the physician, the additional protection of keeping his 401(k) plan from work intact was more

important than the simplicity and reduced fees of an IRA. Recent case law has held that one-person 401(k) plans are not ERISA plans, so they are not federally protected against bankruptcy claims. Depending on the state you live in, though, your state laws may provide creditor protection to your personal 401(k) that is somewhat superior to that of an IRA.

2. *Deferred Required Minimum Distributions:* Special rules allow employees of companies whose ownership interest is five percent or less, to defer taking their RMDs until they retire, even after they turn age 70½. For example, let's assume you are such an employee, aged 72, and still working. Half of your retirement assets are in a 401(k) where you currently work. The other half is in an IRA, which came from a rollover from a previous employer. There is no RMD from your current employer's plan, as long as you continue to work there. You must take your annual RMD from your traditional IRA, even though you are still working. Even if the company allows you to transfer a portion of the 401(k) into an IRA, there is at least an argument for leaving it in the 401(k) to continue deferring taxes until the time arrives for RMDs.

3. *Borrowing privileges:* The 401(k) plan may have provisions that allow you to borrow against the plan. I talked about the dangers of 401(k) loans in Chapter 1, but there can be situations when it may be handy to borrow money from a 401(k) plan. Borrowing from an IRA is not permitted, with one caveat. The IRS does permit you to *withdraw* funds from an IRA and, as long as the funds are re-deposited within 60 days, there is no tax consequence. This is not a loan. If you do not redeposit the funds within 60 days, the distribution is fully taxable, and penalties apply if you are under age 59½.

4. *Net unrealized appreciation:* Before you initiate a trustee-to-trustee transfer out of a 401(k) into an IRA, you might be giving up an enormous opportunity if you do not check to see if there is any net unrealized appreciation (NUA) stock, or any after-tax money. This might be applicable to you if you purchased stock inside the plan that has increased in value, or if your plan rules specify that you can contribute to both a pre-tax and after-tax account. If you are considering rolling your 401(k) into an IRA, please make sure that there is no NUA or after-tax money in the plan. If there is any NUA stock

or after-tax money in the retirement plan, then special treatment is highly recommended because you can save an enormous amount of money. (Please see Chapter 9 for more on NUA).

5. *Roth IRA conversion possibility for non–spouse beneficiary:* Notice 2008–30 provides a unique opportunity for a non-spouse beneficiary to do a Roth IRA conversion of an inherited 401(k) or 403(b) plan. Non-spouse beneficiaries of inherited IRAs are not allowed to do Roth IRA conversions, so the ability for non-spouse beneficiaries of qualified plans to convert is an additional reason to retain assets in a qualified plan. This could be a huge opportunity if you are in a higher income tax bracket than your beneficiaries.

6. *Direct Roth IRA conversion from 401(k) and 403(b) plans:* It used to be that you had to transfer your 401(k) balance into a traditional IRA before you could convert that traditional IRA to a Roth IRA. Under current laws, it is possible to transfer your 401(k) account directly to a Roth IRA, eliminating the need for the extra step. But the good news doesn't stop there. For years, taxpayers who had after-tax contributions in their 401(k) accounts tried to roll those directly into their Roth IRA too. The IRS rules weren't clear, and the process was complicated. Many 401(k) plan sponsors simply issued one check for the amount in the traditional account, and another check for the amount in the after-tax account, and passed the responsibility for the legality of the rollover on to the new custodian. Some taxpayers were audited because of the transaction, and some weren't. In September of 2014, the IRS issued a ruling that formally permits what taxpayers have been trying to do all along. If you have after-tax contributions in your 401(k), you can now directly roll those contributions in to a Roth IRA, tax-free.

Music to the Ears of a CD Investor

I bet all you CD investors are tired of hearing everyone talk about the benefits of a well-balanced portfolio, aren't you? You don't want to hear that inflation will eat at the purchasing power of your CD investments. You just want some good advice on how to manage your CDs. Okay. Fair enough. This is for you.

Maybe you just don't want to be in the market no matter what all the financial advisors say. Many people feel this way in light of the recent market volatility. If you feel this way, you will be happy to know that the FDIC insurance for CDs has been increased from $100,000 per person to $250,000 per person. Those seeking additional security can add a transfer on death designation to the CDs adding $250,000 of FDIC insurance protection per beneficiary named on the transfer on death designation.

Conservative retirees are also attracted by the offers made by some banks to allow seniors to upgrade their CDs annually to a higher interest rate and for a longer term. When the maximum term, typically 10 years, is reached, the annual upgrade in rates is still permissible, but you have to ask for it. Conservative investors should also be aware of the one-year rule, which restricts IRA owners from transferring their IRAs from one bank to another, to take advantage of higher CD rates. This type of transfer is only permitted once per year. Choosing CDs with a term of five to 10 years should alleviate some of the worry about market ups and downs, but is certainly not advisable when interest rates are as low as they are when we went to press. Also, many retirees are unaware that most banks permit annual RMDs to be taken from CDs without breaking the CD or incurring any penalty or loss of earnings. Virtually all institutions follow this rule when taking RMDs (as compared to voluntary distributions) from IRA CDs. But, don't just arbitrarily roll over a sizeable portion of your 401(k) into CDs that you buy from your current bank. It would be better to get quotes from at least three or four banks. Share the quotes with the bank manager you really want to do business with, and ask him/her for their best and final rates.

Weighing the Investment Advantages versus the Threat of Income Tax Acceleration

My clients who have good guaranteed investment contracts in their 401(k) plans often tell me they understand about the stretch IRA and the acceleration of income taxes for their heirs, but they don't want to give up the security of their fixed-income account that is paying higher-than-current interest rates on comparable investments. At least to some extent, they are right. What should you do if you are in that situation? For one thing, just because a GIC is paying a higher rate now, please don't assume that will be an indefinite arrangement. As the old bonds and paper mature, the GIC will be forced to lower its return in keeping with the lower current rates. Therefore, the investment advantage, while real, will likely only be temporary. Beyond the investment issue, I think it is important to revisit the distinction between spouse and non-spouse beneficiaries.

As with the previous section on the tax advantages of transferring a 401(k) (or other retirement plan) into an IRA, the information in this section may also be dated if there is a change to the rule regarding income tax acceleration of the inherited 401(k). To get an update on this law, please visit www.paytaxeslater.com.

Let's assume you have named your surviving spouse as the primary beneficiary of your 401(k). Your strategy is that after your death, your spouse will choose to retain the retirement plan as his own rather than disclaiming to your children. (See Chapter 14 for more information about disclaimers). In that case, your surviving spouse will be allowed to inherit your retirement plan with no obligation to withdraw it all immediately and pay the income taxes. By naming your spouse as beneficiary, he or she will be able to stretch distributions over his or her lifetime even if the money remains in the 401(k). Income tax acceleration will be avoided at the first death.

Depending on the rules of the plan, a problem may arise upon the death of the second spouse, when the money is left to the children or any non-spouse beneficiary. The income tax could be accelerated at the death of the second spouse. Over time, this income tax acceleration could cost the beneficiaries of the second spouse (presumably the children) a lot of money. The only rational justification for paying so much more in tax is that you prefer the fixed-income account of your 401(k), and the projected time frame for the income tax acceleration problem seems very far removed. Both you and your spouse have to die before the income tax is accelerated.

In trying to prepare for the death of the second spouse, the general strategy might include having the surviving spouse transfer the 401(k) into an IRA when the first spouse dies. The reason for thinking ahead is that you never want to be in a situation where there is only one life separating the family from accelerated income taxes. The strategy might even include the idea that if the 401(k) owner gets sick, he or she would abandon taking advantage of the fixed contract, guaranteed investment advantage. The plan might be to transfer the money into an IRA to avoid the massive income tax hit in the event of the employee's death and the subsequent death of the employee's spouse. If we use this straddle plan, that is, leave the money in the 401(k) but be prepared to roll it over into an IRA on short notice, you could argue that you are getting the best of both worlds. You and your spouse get the higher fixed-income fund interest during your life and the stretch afterwards for your children. You count on being prepared to jump into action at the first sign of trouble. This solution is comfortable.

Is it a reasonable strategy? Not really. Too many things could go wrong. Failing health and advanced age seriously complicate the picture. In addition, my experience has been that people don't like to acknowledge how sick they are, and putting decisions off until you reach that state is not wise. A sick person often pushes financial matters aside. I have often seen sick clients who just were not up for dealing with money. Justifiably, they want to devote all their remaining time and energy on their health and family.

The strategy above would fail if upon the first death (it could be either spouse) the surviving spouse fails to make the transfer from the retirement plan to the IRA. After a death, I have seen surviving spouses freeze, that is to say, become afraid to do anything. If this happens and the surviving spouse dies before the transfer to an IRA is made, then we have the income tax acceleration disaster. If there is a sudden or unexpected death, the trauma can be even more paralyzing.

If you are currently a participant in a plan that accelerates income at your death for non-spouse beneficiaries, you must transfer this money to an IRA before the non-spouse beneficiary inherits the funds to avoid the acceleration. If you do not, the non-spouse beneficiary will face massive taxation. I recommend moving the money out of the 401(k) while everyone is healthy and choosing the appropriate investments to compensate for the loss of the fixed income fund.

One compromise might be to leave the fixed asset portion of your portfolio that is currently invested at higher-than-current market rates in your 401(k) and transfer the rest into an IRA. I would consider this approach the minimum that you should do to avoid the income tax acceleration.

My New Recommendation: The One-Person 401(k) Plan

Throughout this chapter and in other parts of this book, I have mentioned the possibility of creating a one-person 401(k) plan and using that as your primary retirement plan vehicle as many people now use IRAs. The difficult part to using this strategy is that you need self-employment income to open your own one-person 401(k) plan. Many retirees, by definition, don't have self-employment income. If that is your case, the best solution might be to roll the money into an IRA or if your retirement funds are in an IRA now, to leave them there.

If possible, it would be better if you could get some self-employment income. Do some consulting, work on a project, do something where you earn some income and based on that self-employment income, set up a one-person 401(k) plan. You will have control of the plan, and you can do a trustee-to-trustee transfer of all your retirement plans to this one-person 401(k) plan.

If you are retired and still have money in your former employer's 401(k) plan, subject to exceptions mentioned in this chapter, I would consider rolling at least a portion, if not all, of your existing 401(k) plan from your former job into your new one-person 401(k) plan. I would even suggest that you consider rolling your IRA to your new one-person 401(k) plan. This offers the following benefits:

- extremely flexible investment choices

- your beneficiaries would still be able to make a Roth IRA conversion of the inherited 401(k)

- expanded Roth IRA conversion possibilities (new)

- depending on the state you live in, you may have better protection from creditors than with a traditional IRA

Having a lot of money in a company 401(k) or even a traditional IRA is not bad, but having it in a one-person 401(k) plan that is completely under your control is, for many retirees, a better strategy. If you don't have any self-employment income and have no realistic way of getting self-employment income, the classic trustee-to-trustee transfer to an IRA will usually be best with at least the majority of your retirement assets.

However, to be fair (as mentioned above), there are some advantages to leaving your company 401(k) plan where it is and not rolling the money into an IRA or one-person 401(k).

A Quick Note About the Aggregation Rules

Under the old Section 408(d)(2) IRA aggregation rules (also called the pro-rata rule), a retirement plan participant who wanted to transfer the balance of his plan, including the basis from after-tax contributions, to a traditional IRA was not permitted to isolate the after-tax contributions and convert that money to a Roth IRA, and then transfer the balance of the account to a self-employed retirement plan or a qualified retirement plan with another employer without first considering the balances of his other existing IRAs.

It was unbelievably complicated, so I want to give you some historical perspective. Think of all of your retirement assets as being different pots of money. In the past, you would have needed to first determine the value of all of your after-tax contributions to your IRA and retirement plan. Second, you would have needed to add up the value of all of your traditional IRA accounts – Roth IRAs are not included. Finally, you needed to figure out the ratio of the after-tax contributions to the traditional IRA accounts. That ratio was the percentage of your Roth IRA conversion that was not taxed. Let's look at an example.

Assume you had a $1,000,000 IRA with no basis, and had an old $300,000 401(k) with basis of $50,000 from your after-tax contributions. You wanted to convert the $50,000 to a Roth IRA. Under the IRA aggregation rules, if you wanted to convert the $50,000 of after-tax contributions in your 401(k) to a Roth IRA, you would have had to previously convert the entire balance of the other traditional IRAs as well as the $300,000 401(k). This would have caused a whopping income tax bill in the neighborhood of $437,500 ($1,250,000 total conversion amount with taxes at 35 percent) to get the $50,000 of after-tax contributions into a Roth IRA. That would have made no sense.

Many retirees tried to circumvent the aggregation rules by taking advantage of a special rule that allowed them to roll the pre-tax contributions in their 401(k) directly to an IRA, and take the after-tax contributions back. The plan administrator would issue two checks for the distributions, and the idea was that the pre-tax contributions would be rolled into an IRA, and the after-tax contributions would be deposited into a brokerage account where they would presumably earn taxable interest and dividends. What actually happened was that retirees would roll the pre-tax contributions directly to an IRA, and then try to roll the after-tax contributions directly to a Roth IRA – in effect, giving themselves a tax-free Roth IRA conversion. The IRS fought this strategy for years and said that the pro-rata rule should still apply to those transfers. In October of 2014, though, they finally gave up and issued a clarification stating that the after-tax amounts can, assuming certain requirements are met, be rolled directly in to a Roth IRA.

This ruling gives high-income taxpayers an unprecedented opportunity to save money which ultimately can end up in a Roth environment. In the past, there was little incentive for them to contribute to the after-tax account in their 401(k)s, and their contributions to the pre-tax accounts were limited ($18,000 in 2015, or $24,000 if they were age 50 or older.) Assuming that their plans allow it, they can now contribute the maximum to their pre-tax account and the maximum to their after-tax account (in 2015, the total contribution limit is $53,000 or 100 percent of compensation below $53,000). Thanks to this new ruling, they may be able to roll the after-tax amount in to a Roth IRA at retirement.

It is important to know the pro-rata rules still apply to partial withdrawals. Let's say that you have a $1,000,000 401(k) that is still with your former employer and $200,000 of that is your after-tax contributions. You heard about this new ruling and you want to convert the $200,000 to a Roth IRA. If you request a distribution of only $200,000, then $160,000 will be considered pre-tax contributions and $40,000 will be considered after-tax contributions, because the pro-rata rules apply. If you want to move the entire $200,000 to a Roth IRA, then you have to take the entire $1,000,000 out of the plan. If you transfer $800,000 to a traditional IRA and $200,000 to a Roth IRA, the transfer to the Roth IRA will be tax-free.

The rules on this topic are very complicated. If you have any basis from after-tax contributions in your qualified plan account, you should consult with a qualified advisor who can review your situation prior to completing a rollover to an IRA. To download a free report that examines this new strategy, or more accurately one of my old secret strategies applied to the new law, visit **www.paytaxeslater.com**.

Combining Distribution Options

Frequently, my clients who have been associated with TIAA-CREF decide to leave the fixed-income component of their retirement plan (TIAA) in their 403(b) plans because of the favorable rate of return. Incidentally, I agree with that reasoning. Some of them will choose to transfer their CREF balances to an IRA because of the diversity of investment options. Finally, some participants will annuitize part of their TIAA-CREF balance to guarantee a set amount of income regardless of how long they live. (Please see Chapter 8 for more information about annuitizing). Although not all plans offer an option to annuitize, it is still beneficial for retirees to consider splitting their retirement accumulations between their 401(k) plans and their IRAs in situations where there are investment and/or tax reasons to maintain a separate IRA and 401(k) plan account.

Many of my Westinghouse retiree clients follow a similar strategy. They opt to keep the fixed-income portion of their 401(k) plan in the Westinghouse plan and transfer the remaining funds into an IRA. Although not all plans offer the annuitization option, it is still beneficial for retirees to consider splitting their retirement accumulations between their 401(k) plans and their IRAs in situations where there are investment and/or tax reasons to maintain a separate IRA and 401(k) plan account.

Lump-Sum Distribution

First, let's get the terminology straight. When I refer to the *lump-sum distribution,* I am referring to the special tax treatment afforded retirees when they withdraw their entire account and pay income tax on the entire amount. Ouch!

Many retirees say they "took the lump sum," but what they really mean is that they chose *not* to annuitize their retirement plan accumulations—that is, not to accept regular monthly payments for the rest of their lives. (For more information on annuitizing, see Chapter 8). What actually happened was that they rolled or transferred the money into an IRA or left the money in the existing retirement plan. Few retirees actually elect the special tax treatment per Internal Revenue Code (IRC) Section 402(d), which is the proper meaning of *taking a lump-sum distribution.*

So why is a lump-sum distribution significant? The advantage of a lump-sum distribution is that it qualifies for a special tax calculation. The tax calculation is called 10-year averaging, and it is available only to individuals born before 1936. The essence of the 10-year averaging calculation is that you may withdraw your entire retirement plan balance and pay income taxes on it immediately, but at a reduced income tax rate. In addition, a capital gains tax rate is applied to the amount attributable to pre-1974 contributions to the plan. This amount will often be less than the ordinary income tax that would otherwise be due.

A lump-sum distribution is only permitted when the employee reaches 59½, or is separated from service, or dies. If the owner is self-employed and becomes totally or permanently disabled, they may take a lump-sum distribution as well. Lump-sum distributions must be made within a 12-month period from the triggering event for the distribution (i.e., death, attainment of age 59½, separation from service), subject to certain exceptions, to qualify as a lump-sum distribution.

Ten-Year Averaging is a Hellish Calculation

Do you qualify? Should you do it?

The answer in both cases is usually no. I will spare you the details. Even assuming you are willing to jump through enough hoops to qualify, for most employees, it will result in a needless acceleration of income taxes, though admittedly at a lower-than-normal rate.

In practice, I have never recommended a 10-year averaging plan but have preferred to take advantage of the net unrealized appreciation (NUA) provisions when available (described in more detail in Chapter 9) and roll the rest into an IRA. My reason for not getting too excited about the 10-year averaging is not the restrictions, but the fact that you must come up with money to pay the taxes now. Remember: pay taxes later. Nonetheless, asking your financial professional to run the numbers for you is a prudent approach.

The general idea behind the lump-sum distribution is that if you successfully jump through a series of hoops, the IRS will discount your taxes. That said, even at a reduced tax rate, it would require some very compelling arguments to persuade me that accelerating taxes is a good idea—especially if large sums of money are involved, which is often the case.

In theory, I can picture the lump-sum distribution (LSD) being useful in two situations.

1. You have a phenomenal use for the money. Some physicians, who have pensions in addition to a 401(k), have taken a LSD and used the money to speculate in real estate. They paid the reduced tax on the LSD and used the remaining proceeds as a down payment on commercial real estate. If the rent covered the mortgage, the idea was that the building appreciation would be on the entire purchase price of the real estate and not the amount invested (the down payment). During the boom real estate markets of past years, that strategy actually worked for a number of taxpayers. Unfortunately, it also leads to unrealistic expectations for the next generation of would-be landlords. During the best of times, that strategy was too aggressive for me, and in today's environment, I would not even think about it.

2. I could picture considering the LSD if the retirement plan owner was rich and either terminally ill or extremely old and if the value of the total estate was worth well more than the estate tax exemption equivalent amount ($5.43 million in 2015). In that case, he might want to consider the LSD to avoid the combined income and estate taxes on the IRA after death.

Other professionals certainly disagree with me. My natural bias is toward keeping retirement assets in IRAs or retirement plans rather than withdrawing the money and paying the tax earlier than necessary, except if you are making a Roth conversion. If there were a good reason to make early IRA or retirement plan withdrawals, then the LSD becomes attractive. I just hate paying taxes up-front.

There could be times when the LSD may be a good choice, but I suggest that you approach it with a predisposition against the LSD and make a qualified financial professional prove to you with hard numbers that it would be a good thing to do in your specific situation. If you take that approach, you will likely be safe from making a bad decision.

Deciding on a good strategy for handling your retirement assets is an area where a good financial advisor can be worth his weight in gold, particularly if he is a number

> **Deciding on a good strategy for handling your retirement assets is an area where the appropriate financial advisor can be worth his weight in gold.**

runner. Getting good advice at this point can have a significant impact on your future.

The Mechanics of IRA Rollovers and Trustee-to-Trustee Transfers

Let's assume the goal is to move your retirement plan funds from one retirement plan to either another retirement plan or an IRA or your new one-person 401(k) plan (what I generally recommend). Most people call this kind of transfer a rollover. But you need to be aware that according to the proper terminology, there are, in fact, rollovers and trustee-to-trustee transfers.

Individuals planning to move money from a 401(k) retirement plan (or similar plan) to an IRA generally will want to conduct a trustee-to-trustee transfer.

A rollover from a 401(k) or other type of qualified retirement plan into an IRA is tax-free, provided you comply with the rules. IRC Section 402 states that retirement plan distributions are not taxed if rolled over to a retirement plan or an IRA. Technically, a rollover is a distribution from one retirement plan or an IRA to the owner and then taken by the owner to the new retirement plan. If you affect a transfer of funds through a rollover, you have to worry about the following rules:

- The 60-day rule
- The 20 percent withholding-tax rule
- The one-rollover-every-12-months rule

The best way to avoid the problems of the 60-day rule, the 20 percent withholding-tax rule, and the one-rollover-per-12-months rule is to complete a trustee-to-trustee transfer of a retirement plan to an IRA. In a trustee-to-trustee transfer, you never touch the actual money. It is an electronic blip; a few pieces of paper (not green) pass from one financial institution to another. Some institutions make the check payable to the new trustee but send it to the participant who is then responsible for forwarding the check to the new trustee. Although this is a permissible method of completing a trustee-to-trustee transfer, please speak to a qualified advisor and the plan administrator before completing a trustee-to-trustee transfer under these circumstances.

The following three sections provide a short description of the problems you may encounter if you do not do a trustee-to-trustee transfer. If the merit of doing the trustee-to-trustee transfer rather than a rollover is established in your mind, you may safely skip the next three sections and jump to "What You May Roll Over and What You May Not."

Avoiding the 20 Percent Withholding-Tax Rule

When someone elects to roll over a 401(k) or other retirement plan to an IRA without using a trustee-to-trustee transfer, the transferring company must withhold 20 percent of the amount rolled over and send it to the federal government as an estimate of what you will owe on April 15th. (If you live in a state that taxes retirement income, they might be required to withhold state income tax as well). This can be a nightmare if your intent was to roll over the entire amount. By not doing a trustee-to-trustee transfer, you create an unnecessary 20 percent withholding of income taxes. This withholding trap has caught many unwary 401(k) owners off guard. Since your former employer is required to withhold 20 percent, the only way you will not have to pay any income taxes on the rollover is for you to come up with the 20 percent amount yourself, from other sources. If you don't have the 20 percent amount to restore to your retirement plan, you'll have even more headaches because you will have to pay income taxes on the rollover to the extent that the 20 percent withholding is insufficient to cover the tax that you owe based on your final situation at year end. The best way to avoid the 20 percent withholding-tax rule is by simply doing a trustee-to-trustee transfer.

Note, that the 20 percent withholding-tax rule does not apply when transferring one IRA to another.

The 60-Day Rule

Let's assume you can get around the 20 percent withholding problem. Another problem remains. You must comply with the 60-day rule. You must restore the funds to another retirement plan or an IRA within 60 days of receiving the distribution. Otherwise, income taxes must be paid on the entire amount; furthermore, if you are 59½ or younger, you have the added 10 percent premature distribution penalty—a nightmare.

Are there exceptions? A few—but basically, you don't want to go there. If you are planning to do a rollover as opposed to a trustee-to-trustee transfer, you have to get the money back in a retirement plan or IRA within 60 days.

Most of the reasons the IRS will accept as excuses for not doing so are so terrible that you would never want to plan for any of them to happen. If you do miss the 60-day rule accidentally, then you can start looking at the reasons the IRS will waive the rule, but don't expect to obtain relief.

In practice, people who want to do a rollover versus a trustee-to-trustee transfer may be looking for a short-term loan, and the only source of money is the IRA or a qualified plan. Loans are not permitted against IRAs, and the amount of the loan that was allowed by their qualified plan might not be enough, and some people who think they are clever might choose to withdraw their IRA or retirement plan and attempt to repay the money within the 60 days. That might work, but it is risky at best.

The classic reason for trying to finesse the system is to use the money for some type of real estate transaction. However, that is what bridge loans at the bank are for. If avoiding those fees is so critical, and you are certain that there will be no hang-ups with either the sale or purchase of whatever the money is needed for, good luck. But if the deal goes sour because of some unforeseeable event, don't expect the IRS to have any sympathy.

Perhaps the Horse's Ass Award goes to the guy who wants to take advantage of some type of financial tip on an investment that isn't listed on one of the popular exchanges. He is told he can double his money in a month. The Horse's Ass has no other funds to invest except his IRA or retirement plan. He goes to his retirement plan, withdraws funds as a loan, invests in his sure winner, and plans to restore the retirement plan before 60 days pass. The sure winner implodes, and the Horse's Ass has not only lost money on his investment, but he will have to pay income taxes on money he doesn't have anymore. The $3,000-per-year loss limitation on deducting the capital loss will virtually make the tax benefits of the loss meaningless, and the income tax he must pay on the retirement plan withdrawal will be draconian.

If the hot tip were a stock or mutual fund that is traded over any of the recognized stock exchanges, he would have been better off rolling the money into an IRA and purchasing the security in his IRA account. That way, when the account gets clobbered, at least he will not face the tax liability in addition to the loss.

The One-Rollover-Per-12-Months Rule

An individual is allowed only one rollover per any 12 month period, but the number of trustee-to-trustee transfers anyone can make is unlimited. If you have different IRAs or different retirement plans, you may have one rollover per separate IRA or separate retirement plan.

Also, the one-rollover-every-12-months rule applies only to IRAs. For example, a reader who initiates a direct rollover from a 401(k) to an IRA on January 2, 2015, can roll over to another IRA on January 15, 2015, if he or she so desires. This move is permissible because the first distribution was not from an IRA.

Again, life is complicated enough. Do a trustee-to-trustee transfer, and don't worry about this rule, the 60-day rule, or the 20 percent withholding-tax rule.

What You May Roll Over and What You May Not

The general rule of thumb under the new expanded portability rules is that an individual can roll anything into anything. Of course, that is a slight exaggeration, but the general idea now is that, if the paperwork is done correctly, funds can go from one qualified plan to another without taxation, though some restrictions may apply.

Most of the recommended rollovers—or to be more technically correct, trustee-to-trustee transfers—will be from taxable retirement plans to IRAs. For example, a retired or service-terminated employee owning a fully taxable account, such as a 401(k), a 403(b), a 457 plan, a SEP, a Keogh, and so on, will usually be well served to institute a trustee-to-trustee transfer to an IRA. The employee is allowed to transfer from account to account if he or she likes. For example, if you leave your university job and go into the private sector, you might think it's a good idea to consolidate your old 403(b) with your new company's 401(k). You can, but it may not be in your best interests. I generally prefer that you transfer the old 403(b) into a separate IRA or your own one-person 401(k) and then start new contributions in the 401(k), which will eventually leave you with balances in an IRA, or your own 401(k) and a 401(k) from work.

> The general idea now is that, if the paperwork is done correctly, funds can go from one qualified plan to another without taxation, though some restrictions may apply.

There will be times when it might be advisable to go backwards. For instance, if a working or self-employed IRA owner wanted to use retirement funds to purchase life insurance, he or she might take his or her IRA (through which he or she is not allowed to purchase life insurance), transfer it into a different qualified plan, and then purchase his or her insurance inside the qualified plan. Caution is advised, however, for retirement plan owners who want to purchase life insurance inside a retirement plan. We do not cover that risky strategy in this book.

In summary, you cannot do the following:

- Transfer or roll over the Required Minimum Distributions (RMD) from a retirement plan or an IRA into another retirement plan. You must pay tax on that money.

- Make a Roth IRA conversion from your RMD.

- Open a Roth IRA with your RMD.

- Transfer or roll over inherited IRA distributions.

- Transfer or roll over Section 72(t) payments (a series of substantially equal payments distributed from a qualified plan for the life of the employee or the joint lives of the employee and his designated beneficiary that qualifies for an exception from the 10 percent penalty otherwise imposed on 72(t) payments).

Special Exception for 403(b) Owners with Pre-1987 Balances

Even if retired, a 403(b) owner's pre-1987 balance is not subject to RMDs until he is age 75, *not* age 70½. To qualify for this exception, the plan sponsor has to have separately accounted for and kept records for the pre-1987 contributions. If records were not kept for the pre-1987 contributions, then the entire plan balance is subject to the age 70½ RMD rules. If there are pre-1987 contributions, retirees might want to keep their 403(b) plans with their previous employer because the RMDs at age 70½ would be less. If the 403(b) is rolled into an IRA, you will be required to take the RMD at age 70½ on the entire balance in the account (including the pre-1987 dollars).

If the terms of the 403(b) retirement plan allow the non-spouse beneficiary to keep the assets in the plan for five years, then there is no tax incentive to do the rollover (assuming the retiree is happy with the investment accounts offered). In fact, there is a tax disincentive because of the acceleration of the RMD. The tax disincentive ends up being so minor, however, that if you think you can do even a tiny bit better by investing outside of the 403(b) with an IRA, then don't worry about the minor acceleration of income you will make by losing the option to defer the pre-1987 RMD until you would have reached age 75.

Would you like more cutting-edge information on planning distributions from a 403(b) plan? Please go to www.financialfreedomforfaculty.com for a free report. Please sign up now while it's fresh on your mind!

Inexact Language on a Beneficiary Form Can Spell Disaster

If you do decide to roll your 401(k) in to an IRA, or transfer your IRA to a new custodian, you will have to fill out new beneficiary forms. Most people take this step for granted, but I have to caution you about it because sloppy titling could ruin the entire stretch IRA concept for your non-spouse beneficiaries. I discuss this in detail in Chapter 16, but for now it is important to know that the deceased IRA owner's name must remain on the account.

MINI CASE STUDY 6.2

The Difference between Proper and Sloppy Language on a Beneficiary Form

Grandpa and Grandma both name a well-drafted trust for their grandchild, Junior, in the beneficiary designations of their respective IRAs. They both die during the same year. Due to a quirk in estate administration, Detailed Danny becomes the administrator for Grandpa's IRA, and Sloppy Susan becomes the administrator for Grandma's IRA. Detailed Danny, when transferring the inherited IRA to the trust for Junior, follows the advice of Grandpa's financial planner and titles the account "Grandpa's IRA (deceased, December 2008) Trust for Benefit of Junior." Junior, being only 10-years-old at Grandpa's death, ends up stretching Grandpa's IRA for his entire lifetime. Even when Junior is 70-years-old, the account continues to have Grandpa's name. Because the inherited IRA makes a tremendous difference in Junior's life and since his financial security is assured, he often thinks of Grandpa's thoughtfulness and also appreciates Detailed Danny's care in handling the inherited IRA.

Sloppy Susan, when doing similar work for Grandma's IRA, titles the account "Trust for Junior." The trust is audited, and the IRS requires the trust to pay income tax on the entire balance. If the titling of the account does not make it clear that the IRA is inherited from the deceased IRA owner, the income tax on the inherited IRA is accelerated. The trust is then required to pay income tax on the entire balance and, to make it worse, at the higher trust income tax rates. When Junior turned 21, he found out what happened and his attorney suggested he sue Sloppy Susan for negligence in the handling of his IRA.

Junior decides not to sue Sloppy Susan because it isn't nice to sue your mother. His mother, Sloppy Susan, did, however, deprive Junior of the stretch for Grandma's IRA, which will end up costing him over $1 million. His only consolation is that he will still receive inherited IRA benefits from Grandpa's IRA for the next 60 years. When Junior is age 70, he shakes his head while thinking of his grandmother. Grandma's legacy, of course, has long since vanished—ravaged by taxes due to sloppy titling.

Make sure that your executor or administrator knows how to title the inherited IRA correctly. If you are a financial planner, I hope I have made a compelling case for the correct titling of an inherited IRA. If you are in charge of internal office procedures at a financial institution, create a policy that ensures that all inherited IRAs retain the name of the deceased IRA owner; you will do a lot of beneficiaries much good.

Also, please don't assume that your financial professional, whether a CPA, financial planner, or (with all due respect) an attorney, will know about proper titling and act accordingly. A number of years ago, I received a call from a planner in California. This is a true story. He said, "Jim, my client died, with more than a million dollars in an IRA. The IRA owner left the IRA to his son. When my secretary saw that the son was the beneficiary, she took the money and transferred it to his son's account. Is that okay?" Oh no! She just accelerated the income tax on $1 million. He said to me, "Oh, Jim, I'm sure the IRS will understand that it was just my secretary, and she didn't mean to do it."

Sloppy titling could ruin the entire stretch IRA concept for non-spouse beneficiaries of an IRA. It is imperative that the deceased IRA owner's name remain on the account.

No. The IRS won't understand. The client's son had to pay tax on $1 million instead of stretching that million out over the course of his life. Boom! Income tax on the whole thing. So instead of having $1 million, the son now has only $600,000. I hope the planner's malpractice premiums were paid up. Whether he actually gets sued or not, the planner has to live the rest of his life knowing that that mistake cost his client a bundle.

Do you have a trusted advisor to help you with your retirement plan? Do you feel confident he or she is qualified and experienced in distribution and estate planning for IRAs and retirement plans? If you do, great. Please—finish reading this book; make a list of questions, comments, and concerns; and set up an appointment as soon as possible.

If, however, you don't have a trusted advisor and can't find anyone who you feel has the appropriate expertise in retirement plans and IRAs, there is another option for some readers. I and some of the CPAs and attorneys in my office are offering a number of free IRA assessments, and taking on a limited number of private clients who will work with us directly. If you are interested in working with one of us one-on-one, please visit www.paytaxeslater.com or refer to the end of the book for more information.

Other Titling Notes

If there are multiple beneficiaries (as is typical with accounts left to "children equally"), the accounts should be split after death and the inherited IRAs should then be kept separate. Please note that under the new rules, each child will be able to take RMDs from the inherited IRA based on his own life expectancy. In addition, although the deceased IRA owner's name will remain on the account, the Social Security number of the beneficiary should be used.

A Key Lesson from This Chapter

For most individuals approaching or at retirement, initiating a trustee-to-trustee transfer of a qualified retirement plan to an IRA or a one-person 401(k) is a good decision. With proper titling, you can preserve the stretch, and you can offer your heirs the continued advantage of tax-deferred growth and take advantage of a wider variety of investment choices during your lifetime. That said, you still have to weigh the decision carefully and look at the particular circumstances of your situation. Deciding how to manage your retirement assets at the time you retire is important and deserves your full attention.

7

||||||||||||||||||||||

Roth Conversions

Did you ever notice that when you put "THE" and "IRS"
together it spells "THEIRS"?

— Author Unknown

Main Topics

- The Roth conversion rationale

- "The secret" to valuing IRAs and Roth IRA conversions

- Factors to consider before a Roth conversion

- Mini Case Study 7.1: Benefits of a Roth conversion for You and Your Beneficiaries

- Mini Case Study 7.2: Take Advantage of Windows of Opportunity for Conversions

- Mini Case Study 7.3: The Roth Advantage to the Beneficiary

- Mini Case Study 7.4: The Effect of the Proposed Five-Year Distribution Rule

- Tax-free conversions are possible

- Opportunities and challenges for high income taxpayers

- The downside of Roth conversions

- Recharacterizing a Roth conversion

KEY IDEA

A Roth conversion of even a portion of your traditional IRA or retirement plan can offer significant financial advantages.

The Roth Conversion Rationale

The Roth IRA was created as an incentive for Americans to save more for their retirements and was written in to law in 1998. Since that time, our office has made thousands of financial projections comparing the benefits of traditional retirement savings accounts to the Roth accounts. It has become apparent to us that, in general, Roth IRAs, Roth 401(k)s, Roth 403(b)s, and Roth conversions from traditional accounts usually result in more purchasing power for IRA owners and their families than traditional plans because they create tax-free growth. This is true even taking into account the tax expenses of a Roth conversion and the tax-deferred savings foregone by using a Roth account instead of a traditional tax-deductible retirement account. A traditional retirement plan, whether it is an IRA, a 401(k), 403(b), KEOGH, SEP, or 457 plan is funded with tax-deductible contributions from both you and/or your employer.

The money in these plans grows tax-deferred and is taxed when withdrawn. You may need to withdraw money from your IRAs and retirement plans to meet your living expenses before age 70½, in which case you will be taxed at that time. If you are fortunate enough to have enough after-tax dollars or other income that you don't need to withdraw from your IRAs or retirement plans, you may continue deferring the taxes until you reach age 70½, at which time you will be required to begin withdrawing money from your retirement plans. In general, the distributions from your IRA and retirement plans are added to your other income, and you pay taxes on the total. You will have to pay income taxes on the withdrawals at your existing tax rate, or possibly a higher tax rate if the additional income pushes you into a higher tax bracket.

With a Roth conversion, you can change a traditional IRA or retirement plan, or just a portion of your IRA or traditional plan, to a Roth account. When you make the conversion, you have to add the amount of the Roth conversion to your income, and pay taxes on it. After paying the tax, you will have converted your traditional retirement account (or the partial amount) to a Roth account. And in doing so, you pay tax on your retirement income now. Why on earth would anybody want to do that?

The reason you might be willing to pay income taxes now is because all of the growth on the account from the day of the conversion and all withdrawals from the Roth by you or your heirs will be completely tax-free (after certain conditions are met). Maintaining the status quo and doing nothing is usually a less attractive alternative. Withdrawals from your traditional IRA, which will include your own contributions as well as the growth, will be taxed at future ordinary income rates.

Unlike a traditional IRA, there are currently no Required Minimum Distributions (RMD) from a Roth IRA for you or your spouse. With good planning, a Roth account will give you years of tax-free growth on the total investment. After you and your spouse both die, it is likely that you will have some Roth IRA dollars remaining in your estate. At that point, your children and/or the trusts you have established for your grandchildren will be required to withdraw money from their inherited Roth account. Those distributions might happen years after you converted the account, and they will be tax-free.

You may still be asking, "Who in their right mind would write the government a check when they don't have to?" The answer is me, many of my readers and clients I have advised over the years, and, hopefully after reading this chapter, you too. The reason bears repeating: Under current law, the Roth IRA will grow income-tax free for the rest of your life, income-tax free for the rest of your spouse's life, and income-tax free for the lives of your children, your grandchildren, and potentially even your great grandchildren.

To use an agricultural analogy, a Roth IRA conversion requires you to pay tax on the seed. In this case, the seed is the amount of the traditional IRA that you want to convert to the Roth IRA. You plant the seed (invest in your new Roth IRA) and, over many years, it blossoms and grows. Then when you, or your heirs, harvest the crop (the original investment and all of the growth), the harvest is income-tax free. The advantages of the Roth conversion, when circumstances warrant one, should not be under-estimated; it could mean hundreds of thousands of dollars – sometimes millions of dollars – of additional purchasing power for your family. And it even offers significant advantages to you, too.

The Secret to Understanding Roth Conversions: Valuing Wealth in Terms of *Purchasing Power* Instead of *Total Dollars*

The following section puts IRAs and Roth IRAs in a new perspective and may require a second reading to cement the concept. It is the key to understanding IRAs in general, and the Roth conversion illustrations that follow in this chapter. I call it "the secret" because very few people, including CPAs, financial planners and advisors, attorneys, and even Roth IRA commentators, know it. I believe understanding "the secret" is the first step in understanding Roth IRA conversions, and the nature of IRAs and retirement plans in general.

> **I believe that the best way to measure wealth, or affluence, is by assessing your total purchasing power, not your total dollars.**

In the world of money, the general rule is that whoever has the most, wins. Right? We all want the most money we can possibly get our hands on. Well, I'm going to go out on a limb and suggest to you that having "the most money" is not the best way to measure your affluence or wealth. Don't panic! I'm not getting metaphysical with you and suggesting people who have no money, but who have good health or a wonderful family, are rich (though they might well be). I believe that the best way to measure wealth, or affluence, is by assessing your total *purchasing power*, not your *total dollars*.

Let's say you have $1 million in a traditional IRA. Even though you have that amount in dollars, you do not have $1 million in purchasing power. This is because the money in the traditional IRA is tax-deferred, not tax free, and you will have to pay income tax when you cash in that IRA. So, even though the face value of your account is $1 million, you have far less than $1 million available to you to travel the world, pay for your grandchildren's education, give to charity, or to do whatever you choose. (I'm assuming that sending a big fat check to the IRS is not on your priority list)! Understanding the concept of purchasing power is critical to truly understanding the benefits of a Roth IRA conversion.

The Simple Math (Arithmetic) Behind the Secret

Let's assume for discussion's sake that you have $100,000 in a traditional IRA or retirement account. I typically refer to the money in those accounts as *pre-*

tax dollars. Let's also assume that the only other money you have is $25,000 outside of the IRA in a CD or other taxable investment. I refer to that money as *after-tax dollars.* For this example, I am also going to assume that you are in the 25 percent tax bracket. Your own tax bracket, while very important for determining whether and/or how much to convert to a Roth account, is not important for the purpose of understanding "the secret."

The Key to Unlocking the Secret

When measuring money the conventional way, we would say that you have a total of $125,000 dollars: $100,000 in your retirement plan (pre-tax dollars), and $25,000 outside of your retirement plan (after-tax dollars). That is all well and good, and I agree that, in this simple example, $125,000 does represent the total number of dollars you have. I, however, submit to you that the more appropriate measuring tool of your wealth is purchasing power.

Continuing with the previous scenario ($100,000 of pre-tax money and $25,000 of after-tax money), let's assume that you want to buy something that costs exactly $100,000. (Not a wise decision, certainly, but this is only an example)! You would have to cash in the IRA and pay taxes on the withdrawal. Assuming that you are in a 25 percent tax bracket, the tax due on the $100,000 withdrawal would be $25,000. In this example, conveniently, you have enough money in your after-tax account to pay the tax due on the withdrawal. And after you pay the taxes, you are left with $100,000 that you can use to make your purchase. So what does that mean? Well, even though you had $125,000 total dollars, after withdrawing the money from the retirement account and paying the required taxes, you have only $100,000 left to spend on whatever it was that you really wanted to buy.

In contrast, let's assume you are starting with the same assets above ($100,000 in an IRA and $25,000 of after-tax dollars). You make a $100,000 Roth IRA conversion and use your $25,000 of after-tax dollars to pay the taxes on the conversion. That leaves you with a $100,000 Roth IRA and no after-tax dollars. On paper, you have less money than you did in the first example, but in this example, the money can be withdrawn tax free, so you also have $100,000 available to spend.

Do you see why I consider the two accounts that total $125,000 to be worth only $100,000 when measured in terms of their purchasing power? I would maintain that, at least on day one, the two investors have equal purchasing power. But if you just look at the numbers on paper, you might think that the guy who has $125,000 is richer than the guy who has the $100,000 tax-free Roth account.

Let's compare Mr. Status Quo, who sits there with his $100,000 Traditional IRA and $25,000 after-tax account, to his identical twin brother, Mr. Roth IRA Conversion. Mr. Status Quo laughs when his brother converts his $100,000 traditional IRA to a Roth IRA, and liquidates his $25,000 after-tax account so that he can send money to the IRS to pay his large tax bill. Mr. Status Quo tells his brother that he should have his head examined. But on day one, Mr. Roth IRA Conversion still has the same purchasing power as Mr. Status Quo:

	Roth IRA value after conversion	Traditional IRA
	$100,000	$100,000
Non-IRA money*	25,000	-0-
Total Dollars	$125,000	$100,000
Less taxes paid on IRA when withdrawn	(25,000)	-0-
Purchasing Power	$100,000	$100,000

Mr. Roth Conversion used his non-IRA money of $25,000 to pay tax on the conversion.

For this example, we assume the liquidation rate (which is the rate of tax we have to pay when we withdraw our traditional IRA) is equal to the conversion rate (the rate of tax we have to pay to make a Roth IRA conversion). On day one, Mr. Status Quo and Mr. Roth IRA Conversion are equals when their wealth is measured in purchasing power. And, while Mr. Status Quo's IRA (the $100,000) will grow tax–deferred, that growth will be taxed when he withdraws money from the account. The dividends, interest and capital gains on his after-tax account (the $25,000) will also be taxable. Mr. Roth IRA Conversion's Roth account will continue to grow income-tax free.

Now let's take this concept and apply it to you. Let's assume that you are considering the advisability of making a Roth IRA conversion. Rather than using total dollars as your measurement tool, consider using purchasing power instead. You and/or your financial advisor complete the appropriate paperwork, and what used to be your $100,000 traditional IRA is now a $100,000 Roth IRA. (Please note that, in most cases, you don't even have to change your investments to convert your traditional IRA to a Roth IRA). Sometime in February of the year following the year that you make the conversion, you will receive a Form 1099 that in effect says, "Please add $100,000 to your taxable income for the year you made the Roth IRA conversion." Continuing with our simple example, you pay your $25,000 tax (or 25 percent) on your additional income. In this case, you have $25,000 of after-tax money to pay your tax bill. The analysis would be significantly different if you had to pay the tax by withdrawing money from a traditional IRA or retirement plan, but we'll talk more about that later in this chapter.

So what do you have now? You have $100,000 in your Roth IRA. If you cash in your Roth IRA, how much tax do you have to pay? None, as long as you meet the conditions that are discussed in Chapter 3. After making the conversion, you have $100,000 of purchasing power. Without the conversion, you would have $125,000 but only $100,000 of purchasing power because of the taxes that you will owe when you cash in your IRA. Can we agree that, if your measurement tool is purchasing power rather than total dollars, and the tax rate is constant, making a Roth IRA conversion will not diminish your purchasing power as of day one? (I think I have hammered that home)!

This is a critical concept. Critics, analysts, and even some authors who hold themselves out as IRA experts hold that Roth IRA conversions are great for young people because young IRA owners have so many years going forward for tax-free growth. Traditional thinking also holds that a Roth conversion for an IRA owner who is 60, 70 or 80+ is a bad idea because the IRA owner will not have enough years of tax-free growth to make up for paying the income tax on the conversion. That's what most financial writers think, and I take great exception to this traditional thinking. The common flaw in their logic is that many software programs (including software programs from huge financial companies that should know better) compare the results using total dollars, rather than purchasing power. When you use purchasing power as your standard, it is clear that, on day one, the individual who made the conversion is no better off, but also no worse off. And if the account grows in value, the individual who made the conversion is clearly better off, because the gains on the Roth account are tax-free.

Does this suggest to you that, perhaps, even for an older individual, a Roth IRA conversion might be an acceptable transaction? You could be 90 years old, do a Roth IRA conversion and, given the previous assumptions, you would have a level of purchasing power equivalent to your pre-conversion purchasing power. You could be 110 years old, and it might be very appropriate for you to make a Roth IRA conversion. Admittedly, it is more beneficial for a younger person to make a Roth IRA conversion than an older IRA owner, because the younger person will likely have more years to enjoy tax-free growth. But, just because the results are better for a younger person doesn't mean that a conversion is a bad idea for an older IRA owner. Furthermore, while older IRA owners are likely to derive some benefits from the conversion during their lifetime, their heirs might enjoy life changing increases in wealth because of their action.

This does not mean that Roth IRA conversions are a good idea for everyone. Roth IRA conversions can be a very bad idea, given a specific set of circumstances. Before we recommend that our clients make a Roth IRA conversion, we run the numbers first to make sure that the conversion will benefit them and also to determine what the optimal amount for them to convert would be. What follows next is a discussion of who qualifies to make a conversion, and the factors we need to take in to consideration before recommending a conversion for you. The illustrations that follow later in this chapter show how those factors can produce dramatically differing results for our clients.

Who Qualifies for a Roth Conversion?

Prior to 2010, individuals with adjusted gross incomes in excess of $100,000 were not permitted to make Roth IRA conversions. This law was permanently repealed in 2010, and now anyone, regardless of their taxable income, can convert any portion of their traditional IRA to a Roth. In addition, you may now convert your retirement plan such as a 401(k) or 403(b) directly into a Roth IRA if you are retired. Under current laws, an inherited 401(k) retirement plan may also be converted to Roth 401(k) status; however, an inherited IRA is not eligible for conversion. And as discussed in Chapter 3, if your plan allows it, you may now also convert some of your own 401(k) or 403(b) into a Roth 401(k) or 403(b) while you are still working. So, if you were ineligible to convert in the past because of the income limitations, or because all of your retirement assets were or still are in your 401(k) or 403(b) plan at work, you may want to revisit the concept again.

Factors to Consider before Converting to a Roth IRA

The potential for tax-free growth is so compelling that *all* taxpayers who have substantial IRA or retirement plan balances should consider converting at least a portion of them. As I mentioned at the outset of this chapter, a Roth conversion is one of the rare actions that contradicts my advice "Don't pay taxes now, pay taxes later." This is because by paying the associated taxes *now*, you *avoid* additional taxes later. However, many factors must be considered pertaining to both you, as the IRA or retirement plan owner, and to your beneficiaries, before making a Roth conversion. Let's look at the major factors.

> **The potential for tax-free growth is so compelling that all taxpayers who have substantial IRA or retirement plan balances should consider converting at least a portion of them.**

If you are the IRA or retirement plan owner, you need to consider all of the following:

- Your current and future income tax rates

- Your projected Medicare premiums if you will be covered by Medicare Parts B and D including income related increases

- The rate of return on your investments

- Your age and life expectancy

- Your anticipated spending needs during retirement

- Your other sources of income (including any pensions, Social Security, wages, or other income)

- The balances in your IRAs and retirement plans

- The balances of other investments including after-tax money and investments

- Other assets and liability balances you may have, such as real estate and loans

Regarding your IRA's probable beneficiaries, you need to consider these factors:

- Their age and life expectancy

- Their planned use of the IRA and retirement plan funds after inheritance

- Their future income tax rates

- The amounts of your IRAs or retirement plans that have charities as beneficiaries

That is quite a list of things to consider, which is why we strongly recommend that you consult with a qualified financial advisor or CPA who can "run the numbers" prior to making any decisions about how to proceed. In our practice, we typically have the client in the room while we are running the numbers. This way, the client sees what we are doing and can insert their own "what if" scenarios as we work.

Also Consider Current and Future Income Tax Laws

Obviously, income tax laws are significantly important for you and your heirs when planning for Roth conversions, including potential future tax rates and laws. If you are considering a conversion, one thing you need to be aware of is that President Obama would like to see some of the benefits of the Roth accounts eliminated. Historically, his budget proposals have included a provision to "harmonize" the rules of Roth IRAs with those of traditional IRAs, requiring that the original owners start mandatory withdrawals at age 70½. To make matters worse, President Obama and the Republican House would also like to force beneficiaries of IRAs or Roth IRAs to withdraw the balance within five years of the original owner's death. This provision will be introduced as part of the President's 2016 budget proposal. If it is passed, the outcome will be that your children (or any other non-spouse beneficiary) will only be able to enjoy the tax-free growth in the Roth account for five years after your and your spouse's death. However, even if the law does pass, the Roth IRA conversion will, for many if not most taxpayers, still be very favorable but admittedly not as favorable as with existing laws where the heirs can continue the Roth's tax-free growth for the rest of their lives. Billions of dollars have been converted from traditional IRAs to Roth IRAs and, if these changes are made in to law, my opinion is that the beneficiaries of existing accounts would have to be grandfathered under the old rules—meaning that, if a beneficiary inherits an account *before* the law is changed, they will be subject to the old rules. Many clients and readers would like the "grandfathered" accommodation to apply to anyone who established a Roth prior to the proposed law's passage. That won't do it. The IRS doesn't care. If you are kicking when they change the law, your heirs will have to suffer with the five year rule. If you die before they pass the law, then your heirs may continue to "stretch" either the inherited IRA or inherited Roth IRA over the life of the beneficiary.

Is the law likely to change? I don't know, and I hate to bet on what Congress may or may not do. I do, however, think there is at least a 50 percent chance that the ability to stretch both traditional and Roth IRAs will be repealed within this generation's lifetime. To be fair, similar proposals were included in previous budgets and they did not pass, but remember what happened in 2013. The President wanted the stretch IRA and stretch Roth IRA to be repealed, and the Republican House voted for the proposal. Only the Democratic Senate stopped the repeal. Now that we no longer have a Democratic Senate, if the proposal comes up again, as I suspect it will, it will likely pass.

So, how does this potential change in the treatment of the inherited Roth IRA impact your Roth IRA decisions? What we do in our office is try to convert only an amount that will help or, at worst, be a breakeven for the IRA owner and their spouse. Any additional benefit your heirs will realize should be regarded as a bonus, not the main reason for the conversion. None-the-less, it is true that even if the law is changed and the stretch is repealed, and you made conversions with the intention of only benefitting you and your spouse, your children or other heirs will still be better off. What I no longer recommend is that you factor in the long-term "stretch Roth IRA" that the kids and grandchildren would enjoy for their entire lives in determining how much you convert. For example, let's assume the appropriate person "runs the numbers" and determines you are a little worse off if you make a conversion, but under current law, your children and grandchildren would be better off. In the past, I might have leaned toward the conversion, but now I would lean against it.

The Roth Conversion Decision Analysis

Should you keep your traditional IRAs, or should you convert them to Roths? The examples that follow, quantifying the Roth's advantage over not making a conversion, will span three generations of Roth IRA owners: the original IRA owner (most likely you), the child of the original owner, and the grandchild of the original owner. While many factors need to be taken in to consideration, including weighing the advantages to each generation, the bottom line is that the future tax savings on the tax-free growth of the Roth IRA generally outweigh the benefits of a tax-deferred traditional IRA combined with after-tax investments—assuming those after-tax investments are used to pay the income tax on the conversion.

Readers have questioned our math. They say that if all our assumptions are steady (interest rate, tax rate, growth, etc.), then the Roth IRA conversion ends up being a breakeven or even a loss for the IRA owner. I agree that would be true if you paid the tax on the conversion from the IRA itself. However, if you pay the tax on the conversion with after-tax dollars, the math favors the conversion - especially if the benefit is measured in terms of purchasing power. This becomes even more apparent once the traditional IRA owner turns age 70½ and is required to take minimum distributions from the account. The Roth account continues to grow tax-free. It even grows in cases where the tax on the conversion was paid from the IRA itself. The longer the time horizon for tax-free growth, the greater the benefit a conversion can provide.

If you are like many of our clients, however, your wealth is primarily in your retirement plans and traditional IRAs. If you do not have the money to pay the income tax on the conversion from funds outside the IRA, then my advice would change—don't do a conversion, or do a much more conservative conversion. Another instance where I would not recommend making a Roth IRA conversion would be if you plan to leave all your money to charity. The charity doesn't have to pay taxes anyway and will not benefit from the tax-free growth of the Roth IRA, so you will have paid tax on the conversion needlessly.

If you do not have the money to pay the income tax on the conversion from funds outside the IRA, then my advice would change—don't do a conversion.

A Series of Small Conversions Rather than One Big Conversion

In Chapter 2, we introduced the advantages tax-free Roth IRAs have over traditional tax-deferred IRAs. There were two important points to remember:

1. The growth in the Roth IRA is tax free.

2. The Roth eliminates the problem of the taxable growth on the tax savings from a deductible IRA contribution.

These advantages also apply to Roth conversions. A conversion, with time, results in more purchasing power than in a tax-deferred IRA account that is combined with other nontax-sheltered, after-tax investments (but even on day-one is a breakeven). Additionally, there are no RMDs from the Roth IRA (for either you or your spouse) as there are with traditional IRAs. If you don't need the money, the Roth account keeps growing tax-free in contrast to a traditional IRA which has RMDs—eventually forcing the IRA owner to pay the tax and then to invest whatever is left in after-tax investments.

Depending on the circumstances of the individual contemplating the Roth IRA conversion, I often recommend a series of partial conversions of their traditional IRA to a Roth IRA—one every year over a period of years. How much to convert is a significant decision because if you convert a large amount, it could result in a high tax rate on the conversion. Your best strategy might be to convert just enough to bring your taxable income to the top of your present tax bracket, and then repeat that process in subsequent years. This keeps the conversion-related taxes to a reasonable amount, and it prevents you from paying income taxes on the conversion at a high rate.

> **Your best strategy might be to convert just enough to bring your taxable income to the top of your present tax bracket, and then repeat that process in subsequent years.**

For families in the right situation, even a modest conversion could mean tens of thousands of dollars (in today's dollars) in additional purchasing power for your family.

MINI CASE STUDY 7.1

Benefits of a Roth IRA Conversion

Suppose you have a financially identical twin, and you are both 65. Because you read **Retire Secure!** and after consulting with your financial advisor, you decided to make a series of Roth IRA conversions that total $250,000. Your twin, however, never even learns about the possibility of a Roth IRA conversion. Every year for five years from the time you are 65 to 69, you convert $50,000 (growing at 6 percent each year) from the traditional IRA to a Roth IRA. Your conversion amounts add to your taxable income each year. For this example, we will assume your total income (and perhaps Medicare premium increases) causes you to pay 28 percent tax on each conversion amount. (We use 28 percent because we assume you are usually in the 25 percent bracket. The extra income from the conversion will generally increase your tax bracket in the year of conversion). You pay the tax on the conversion from money outside of your IRA. Your financial twin, on the other hand, doesn't make the conversion. He keeps his after-tax money and invests it in a diversified portfolio, and enjoys investment income on the same amount of money that you sent to the IRS. For simplicity, we will assume 75 percent of the investment income is taxed at the preferred rates for long-term capital gains and qualified dividends. The other 25 percent of investment income is taxed at ordinary tax rates.

You and your twin invest identically, and you each receive a 6 percent return on your investments. For purposes of comparison, though, I do not want you to compare the total dollars in each of your accounts. Doing that would make no sense, because the withdrawals from his traditional IRA account will be taxable, and withdrawals from your Roth IRA account will be tax-free. Instead, I want you to think in terms of that very important concept called purchasing power, or the amount of goods and services that you and your twin can each buy, after you have both paid any income taxes on traditional IRA balances. The graph in Figure 7.1 on the next page shows the amount of purchasing power over time for both of you.

The graph in Figure 7.1 reveals that, after the very first conversion, your Roth account has a small advantage over your twin's traditional IRA. This advantage grows over time. When all of your IRA is converted after five years, you will have $7,330 more in spending power than your twin. At age 90, you will have $113,601 in more spending power.

This is a significant advantage but, remember, you paid the higher tax rate of 28 percent on the amounts you converted because your income was higher than usual during those five years. If you had left the money in the traditional IRA like your twin and withdrew only your RMD, the tax rate on those with-

Figure 7.1
The Roth Conversion Advantage

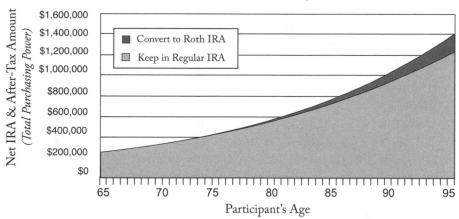

The assumptions for this graph include the following:

1. Each investor starts on 1/1/2015 with $250,000 in an IRA and $68,400 in after-tax investments from which the taxes on the conversions are paid.

2. Investments earn a 6 percent rate of return.

3. Ordinary federal income tax rates are 25 percent for regular IRA minimum distributions and on one-quarter of the investment income on the after-tax accounts.

4. Federal taxes on the other three-quarters of the investment income in the after-tax accounts is taxed at the preferred 15 percent rate.

5. State income taxes of 3 percent are levied against after-tax investment income, but not on the conversion amount or IRA withdrawals (similar to tax laws in Pennsylvania).

6. Tax on the conversion and for measuring the purchasing power of the remaining traditional IRA balances is 28 percent.

7. Required Minimum Distributions from the regular IRA are reinvested with the after-tax investments.

8. No withdrawals from the investments are made.

drawals would have been only 25 percent. The results in Figure 7.1 show that, even if you are pushed in to a higher tax bracket during the years of conversion, the conversions can still result in an advantage over time.

MINI CASE STUDY 7.2

Take Advantage of the Window of Opportunity for Roth IRA Conversions

Many new retirees find themselves in the fortunate position of being in the lowest tax bracket they will ever be in for the rest of their lives. You no longer have the income from your job. If you use our recommended strategies for taking your Social Security benefits (please see www.paytaxeslater.com for details on those), you will likely delay applying for your benefit until at least age 66. If you do receive benefits earlier, they might be lower than they will be when you turn 70. As we talked about in Chapter 4, you will be spending after-tax dollars first, which is likely to result in a smaller tax impact than if you spent IRA dollars. Assuming you have not reached age 70, you will have no RMDs on your IRA. When all of these factors are taken in to consideration, there is a good possibility that your income will be much higher when you are 70.

These years of low income tax rates between the time you retire and the time you are required to begin taking minimum distributions can be an optimal time to make Roth conversions. There could also be other times when your income is temporarily lower than at other times. One example might be a lay off where you aren't working for a year. Another might be a significant medical expense that will lower your taxable income. We call these times, as well as the more common occurrence of the time between retirement and age 70½, a "window of opportunity" to make Roth conversions at lower income tax cost.

The following example shows what happens if, during the conversion years, you are in a lower tax bracket than you might expect to be during your later retirement years. This can happen if you delay starting your Social Security benefits, and you do not need to take taxable IRA withdrawals to meet your spending needs. Using the same starting point as in Mini Case Study 7.1, we will assume half of the conversion amounts are taxed at 15 percent and half at 25 percent for an average conversion tax rate of 20 percent. This gives your financial twin a small advantage in the early years because his long-term capital gains and qualified dividends will escape federal income taxes completely during the five year period he is in the 15 percent tax bracket. Since your income is higher from doing the conversions, there is still the 15 percent tax for you on the long-term capital gains and qualified dividends during those years.

Figure 7.2
The Roth Conversion Advantage Using a Window of Opportunity

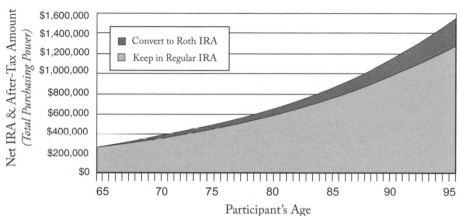

The graph in Figure 7.2 reveals that there is a larger advantage to the Roth conversions that grows over time. After five years, when all of your IRA is converted, you will have $28,546 more in spending power than your twin. At age 90, the conversion advantage has grown to $167,480. This is a much better advantage than in Figure 7.1 because you were able to take advantage of temporarily lower income tax rates before you would have been required to start distributions on your traditional IRAs and retirement accounts.

These results indicate that the Roth IRA can offer significant advantages over the course of a lifetime for the smart twin who made the conversion. The results shown in Figures 7.1 and 7.2 may even understate the advantages of the Roth IRA conversion because they do not consider *your beneficiary's time frame* for taking distributions from the inherited Roth IRA. Your beneficiary may continue to receive tax-free growth from the inherited Roth IRA, as compared to the tax-deferred growth of the traditional IRA and taxable growth of any after-tax accounts.

Looking at Figure 7.2, if you survive to age 95, the advantage would be $270,632. This advantage is even greater than the $250,000 beginning balance of the IRA! Even if you do not think you will live to that age, there will be continued advantages that can grow dramatically for your children or grand-children after they inherit your Roth IRA.

So, what will the situation look like if we extend the time frame to include a child as a beneficiary?

MINI CASE STUDY 7.3
Roth IRA Advantage to the Beneficiary

Figure 7.3
Roth IRA Advantage to the Child Beneficiary After Using the Window of Opportunity

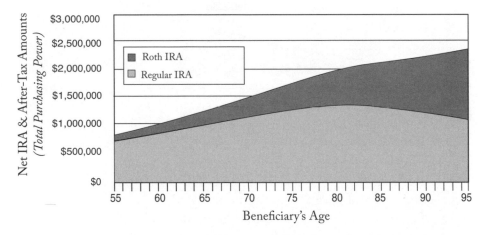

Let's return to our example of you and your financial twin. Suppose you convert your $250,000 IRA to a Roth IRA over five years as in the above examples for Figure 7.2, using the window of opportunity to lower the tax on the conversion. Your twin does not do the conversions and you both die at age 85, which is 20 years after you began your Roth IRA conversions. You and your financial twin both have a 55-year-old son, and you each leave your money to your son.

At the time he dies, your twin has assets with a *purchasing power* of $747,944. This consists of his traditional IRA of $399,563 plus after-tax funds of $460,259, minus an income tax allowance (how much tax will be owed) on the traditional IRA of $111,878. If you die on the same day, your purchasing power is $851,412. You'll have $801,784 in your Roth IRA and $49,628 of after-tax funds – the after-tax funds come from tax savings you realized from the conversion. And, since your account is a Roth, there is no deduction needed for an income tax allowance.

Figure 7.3 shows that your son, who inherited the Roth IRA, will eventually be left with nearly twice what your twin's son, who inherited the traditional IRA, will have. The numbers are even more compelling. By the time your son reaches age 85, he will have $2,145,237. Your nephew, whose father did not make the conversion, has only $1,352,565. The conversion created an advantage to your son of $792,672 which is *over three times* the amount of the original IRA. The benefits of Roth IRAs to the second and third generation can be so significant that much of our planning used to be done considering children and grandchildren, but that is no longer automatically the case. We'll cover the reasons why shortly.

Effect of the Proposed Five-Year Distribution Rule on Inherited Accounts

Remember President Obama's proposed law change which would require a non-spouse beneficiary of an IRA or Roth IRA to withdraw all the funds within five years? If it is passed, will making conversions have been a mistake? Figure 7.4 demonstrates what would happen if both children inherited the IRAs at their age 55 (as in Figure 7.3) and withdrew their RMDs over five years. The withdrawals made by your twin's son will be taxable and, in order to keep his tax rates as low as possible each year, he withdraws a relatively equal amount each year until the IRA is liquidated. Even though he tries to minimize the taxes, your twin's son's required distributions over the five years increases his income taxes on the distributions to 28 percent for each of those years. (Without the five-year rule, Figure 7.3 his income tax rate was 25 percent). Your son, however, doesn't have to worry about taxes. He keeps all of the money in the inherited Roth IRA account until the very last day of the fifth year, so that he can maximize the tax-free growth, and then withdraws the entire amount tax-free. (We have kept the same spending as in Figure 7.3).

Figure 7.4 on the following page shows that by the time the children reach age 85, the child of the twin who did not make the conversion has $1,091,930 in after-tax funds whereas the child who inherited the Roth IRA has $1,665,469 — a conversion advantage of $573,539. This advantage is less than in Figure 7.3, but is still significant even if the inherited IRAs and Roth IRAs must be liquidated in five years. If the five-year rule is implemented, the

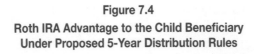

Figure 7.4
Roth IRA Advantage to the Child Beneficiary
Under Proposed 5-Year Distribution Rules

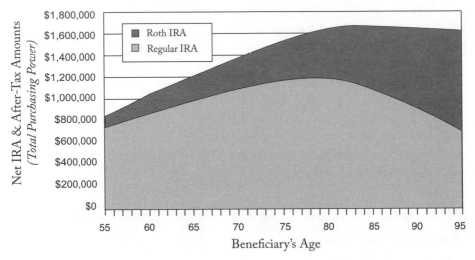

advantage to the Roth is 72.3% of the advantage that the beneficiary would be able to enjoy if he had been able to leave the money in the account.

The downside of the five-year rule is that the child ends up with much less money at age 85 than without the five-year rule. With the Roth IRA, he ends up with $1,665,469 instead of $2,145,237. This is because the money that had been in the Roth is forced into a taxable account. At age 85, the child will have paid an extra $479,769 in taxes that he otherwise would not have had to pay, if he had been able to leave the money in the Roth account.

I should point out that, with larger inheritances of traditional IRAs and Roth IRAs of perhaps $1,000,000 or more, the traditional IRA distributions could be so significant that, when all the child's income is considered, the child beneficiary may actually have his tax rates pushed as high as 35 percent during the years when he is forced to take distributions. If we had used the 35 percent tax rate on the traditional IRA withdrawals for the child in the above graph, the conversion advantage would be $690,757 by age 85. This is less than the $792,672 advantage without the five-year rule, but still maintains 87 percent of the significant conversion advantage.

The conclusion you should draw from this analysis is that the five-year rule is not welcome because it subtracts substantially from your children's IRA and Roth IRA inheritances. It should not, however, deter you from implementing a well thought out Roth conversion plan.

Additional Advantages of Naming Grandchildren as Beneficiaries

As I showed in Figures 7.3 and 7.4, the results of Roth conversions are quite favorable using a child as your beneficiary. However, under current rules, the results for a grandchild beneficiary are even better because of the lower RMDs of an inherited IRA or inherited Roth IRA for a younger person. If the five-year rule is made in to law, it would negate this additional advantage for the grandchild. However, there is the possibility that if the IRA or Roth IRA is inherited before such rule goes into effect, the five-year rule may not apply as existing inherited accounts may be exempt from the rules. In other words, existing inherited accounts would be grandfathered under the old rules assuming you or your spouse die before they change the rule. But, since we don't know when or if the law is going to change, let's look at what happens if a third-generation beneficiary inherits a Roth account.

Figure 7.5 shows the results if the beneficiary of your IRA is your 25-year-old grandchild instead of your 55-year-old child. The assumptions are similar in other respects to Figure 7.3, and your grandchild is assumed to have the same after-tax spending amounts as in the example of your 55-year-old child.

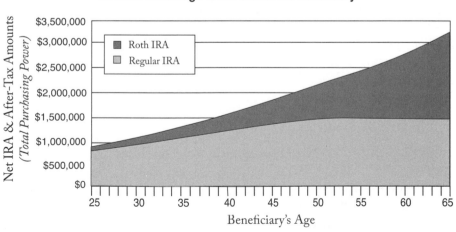

Figure 7.5
Roth IRA Advantage to the Grandchild Beneficiary

Figure 7.5 shows that your grandchild is much better off with your Roth conversion than without it. Let's revisit my "secret," or the idea of purchasing power, as it would apply to Figures 7.3 and 7.5. After 30 years from inheritance, and assuming an inflation rate of 3 percent, the relative purchasing power advantages from the Roth conversion are as follows:

	Advantage in Future Dollars	Advantage in Today's Dollars
Child as beneficiary	$ 792,672	$ 180,814
Grandchild as beneficiary	$ 1,042,281	$ 237,752

After 40 years from inheritance, the graphs show the relative purchasing power advantages from the Roth conversion are as follows:

	Advantage in Future Dollars	Advantage in Today's Dollars
Child as beneficiary	$ 1,263,174	$ 214,402
Grandchild as beneficiary	$ 1,889,653	$ 320,737

The advantages shown in the tables, even in today's dollars, are a large percentage of the beginning balance of the IRA converted for the child and even more than that for the grandchild. The conclusion here is that, under current law, there is much to be gained by your beneficiaries from Roth IRA conversions, especially when they are able to continue the tax-free growth in the inherited Roth IRA.

Tax-Free Roth Conversions Are Possible

Anyone who can convert in a tax-free manner an amount from a traditional IRA or retirement plan that is growing tax-deferred to a Roth account that will be tax-free should do so. There are almost no good reasons not to do so.

Anyone who can convert in a tax-free manner an amount from a traditional IRA or retirement plan that is growing tax-deferred to a Roth account that will be tax-free should do so.

New laws in 2014 allow retirement plans such as 401(k)s and 403(b)s to segregate your after-tax contributions with separate accounting. If your plan does this, and you have after-tax contributions (basis) in your own account, you may now be able to convert your basis to a Roth IRA without having to use the aggregation rules. If your plan rules permit you to do such a conversion, those basis amounts can be, and should be, converted to a Roth IRA tax free.

Also, there is no time limit on how long you must keep your money in a traditional IRA before you convert it to a Roth IRA. Taxpayers without other taxable traditional IRAs, whose incomes are too high to make a direct contribution to a Roth IRA can contribute the maximum to a non-deductible traditional IRA and then convert it immediately to a Roth IRA, tax-free! These rules are discussed in detail in Chapter 2.

Generally, the amount you convert from a traditional IRA to a Roth IRA is taxable, but if you have "basis" in your IRA from non-deductible contributions, a fraction of the total may not be taxable. It is usually prudent to have a professional calculate the amount of the conversion that is taxable because the IRS's aggregation rules consider the values of all of your traditional IRAs and ultimately make only a part of the conversion tax-free. And here is another important point. Please make sure you do not roll over a retirement plan to a traditional IRA in the same year that you do this tax-free conversion of an IRA contribution. The aggregation rules use end-of-year balances rather than at-the-time-of-conversion balances when calculating the amount of the conversion that is taxable, and your IRA balances will be higher after the rollover.

Even if you are subject to the aggregation rules, your basis in your IRAs will make part of the conversion tax-free. If the amount of your basis is significant, the taxes due on your conversion will be reduced. This provides an incentive to do the conversion sooner rather than later, because future growth of your traditional IRAs will make the conversion taxes higher.

Opportunities and Challenges for Higher Income Taxpayers to Move into the Roth Environment

For the very high income, top tax bracket individual, the benefit of a Roth IRA conversion is potentially phenomenal. Because of increased tax rates in 2013, high income earners are in a much better position to take advantage of the tax-free growth in a Roth than in previous years. By paying taxes on a conversion with after-tax money, they can reduce balances in their after-tax accounts that generate taxable income each year. This is a subtle but significant point. Those after-tax amounts are now subject to the higher capital gains tax rate of 20 percent instead of 15 percent and there is an additional 3.8 percent net investment income tax imposed on after-tax investment income. The top ordinary income tax rate has been increased to 39.6 percent, up from 35 percent. Higher income taxpayers also face a phase-out of itemized deductions and personal exemptions. It is these high taxes and limitations that make the cost of obtaining Roth IRAs a much more expensive proposition for high income individuals. Though we like to "run the numbers" for almost all Roth IRA conversion recommendations to optimize the amount and the timing, it is especially critical and frankly difficult for us, to do so for high income taxpayers.

For middle income taxpayers, large Roth conversions are relatively more costly as it can push their incomes up into those new higher tax rates. Lower or middle income individuals can also push themselves into a much higher tax bracket if they make a significant conversion.

The silver lining is that taxpayers who are already in the highest tax bracket cannot pay higher taxes! High income taxpayers are also likely to have the money to pay the taxes on the conversion from outside the IRA or retirement plan. Ultimately, the wealthy are also the most likely to be able to take advantage of a long time horizon of tax-free growth, because there is a reduced chance that they will need to spend that money. This means that high income taxpayers are frequently better candidates for large Roth conversions than middle or lower income taxpayers.

Prior to 2010, higher income individuals were not permitted to make Roth conversions as there was an income limit on conversions. Now there is no limit – but for how long? It is possible that new laws could limit Roth conversions again. And our analysis has shown that over a generation—passing the Roth from parent to child—a taxpayer's family could benefit by as much as twice the amount converted or more. So, I strongly recommend wealthy readers to "run the numbers" with the help of a qualified advisor, to see if they can take advantage of the opportunity to do a Roth conversion while they can.

Rates of Return Affect Conversion Advantages

It should be noted that the above examples calculating advantages to Roth conversions all assumed a 6 percent rate of return. If we had used a higher rate of return such as 8 percent or 10 percent, the advantages would be much higher. Since equities have averaged over 10 percent returns over the last 50+ years, it is possible, even probable, that long-term money invested in Roth IRAs could earn far more than 6 percent in the very long run.

Conversely, if your rate of return is less than 6 percent, the advantages will be smaller. If you were to invest in CDs or savings accounts and earn 1 percent on your Roth money, the benefits of conversion may not be worth it. If you are conservative and have a largely fixed income allocation for your traditional IRA and other assets, we generally recommend that you consider a more aggressive investment allocation for your Roth IRAs because of the likely longer time horizon for number of years invested before distributions are taken out.

Losing money in the Roth accounts is even worse. But a decline in investment values in a Roth account can also present a very interesting opportunity, called a recharacterization.

The Downside of a Roth Conversion

The analysis thus far has assumed that your investments will grow over time. Even if the rate of growth is slower than I assume, you would still be better off, just not by as much. But what if your converted investment drops significantly after you make the conversion? Then, you would not be a happy camper and my advice to make a Roth IRA conversion would have hurt you, not helped you. The fear of losing money on investments is on everyone's mind as we experience such volatility in the market.

The traditional response is that if you wait long enough the investment will recover. But, what if it doesn't? What if you just decide it was a mistake. Are there steps you can take if the investment goes down soon after you make the Roth IRA conversion?

Yes. In short, you can recharacterize your Roth IRA conversion. However, please note that you *cannot* recharacterize a conversion inside your 401(k) or 403(b) to a Roth 401(k) or Roth 403(b). *Recharacterize* is the formal jargon to describe undoing your conversion. You can recharacterize a Roth IRA conversion by October 15 of the year following the year of the conversion. Why would you do that? Recharacterizing doesn't help you recover the loss in your investment, but you can recover the taxes you paid on the original conversion by filing an amended return. Doing so would put you in a position similar to where you would have been if you had not completed the Roth IRA conversion in the first place. Your investment will have decreased in value whether it was in the traditional IRA or the Roth, but at least you will not have paid taxes unnecessarily on the conversion.

Now here's the exciting part. After you recharacterize your Roth IRA that has gone down in value, you can, after a waiting period, make another Roth conversion of the same account. Why would you go through all that paper-work again? The answer is simple. If the account is converted again while the value is down, your tax liability to the IRS is greatly reduced.

There are waiting rules regarding these "reconversions" of IRAs. You must wait until the next calendar year (or 30 days, whichever is longer) to do another conversion of the same money. You can avoid this restriction, though, if you do the second Roth conversion to a new Roth IRA account before you do the recharacterization of the first account. But wait! Here's another rule: you need to be careful not to move the recharacterized money back into the same IRA from which it was converted. If you do, the waiting periods will apply.

Partial recharacterizations are also permitted. I frequently have clients, even in good investment years, do a partial recharacterization. For example, let's say that we recommended you convert no more than $50,000. If you convert more, your income will come very close to the limit of $170,000 where you would owe additional Medicare premiums. Because of an unexpected year-end capital gain in one of your mutual funds, though, your income including the conversion amount ends up being $189,500.

Is there any way to avoid the increase in your Medicare premiums? You bet! You can recharacterize 40 percent (or $20,000) of your conversion amount. Then you would only be taxed on the $30,000 of the conversion you kept. Your income would be $169,500 and you would avoid additional Medicare premiums. Please note that, if you recharacterize a Roth IRA, you must move back to the traditional IRA not only the conversion amount you wish to undo but also any growth it earned. If it declined in value, less will be moved back. It makes sense to discuss recharacterizations with your tax advisor before you finalize your tax return if you do significant Roth conversions.

This hindsight created by the recharacterization option is a wonderful safety net and, if you are "on the fence" about whether to do a conversion or not, it provides incentive to do the conversion. You can wait to see if it grows or not, and if you change your mind, you can undo it.

It should be noted that some tax proposals set forth for discussion recently have included a rule to prohibit such recharacterizations of Roth conversions. Please consult a well-informed advisor to stay on top of any such rule changes that may occur.

Fair warning: Please don't overdo this Roth conversion and recharacertizing strategy unless you are prepared for a few headaches at tax-time.

MINI CASE STUDY 7.4

Recharacterizing the Roth IRA Conversion

Carrie Convert converts $100,000 of her traditional IRA in July 2015. She files her tax return in April 2016, reports an additional $100,000 in income, and pays the tax in a timely manner. The stock market goes down and by October 2016, her Roth IRA has decreased in value to $50,000. Carrie is disgusted and wants to strangle me for telling her how great it would be to make a Roth IRA conversion. Of course, she could stay the course and hope the investment will recover. Carrie does, however, have an even better course of action.

She should recharacterize (undo) the Roth IRA conversion by October 15, 2016. She would fill out the appropriate paper work with the IRA custodian to recharacterize the Roth IRA, returning it to a traditional IRA. After filling out the appropriate paperwork, she will have a $50,000 regular IRA instead of a $50,000 Roth IRA. Then, since she filed her tax return and paid the tax on the conversion, she should file an amended tax return, Form 1040-X, showing the necessary election is made under IRS regulations, and request a refund of the taxes she paid on the conversion. Or, if Carrie had filed an extension request on April 15, then she would not have to file an amended return at all—she would simply file her return, and disclose the transaction, but not pay tax on the conversion.

Granted, her investment is still $50,000 instead of $100,000, but even if she had not made the conversion, her investments would still be down in value. So, she is no better or worse off because she converted and recharacterized. If she then decides to convert another $50,000 after the 30 day waiting period, she would have the same value in a Roth IRA as she had before the recharacterization, but would only owe the IRS taxes on $50,000 of conversion income instead of on $100,000 of conversion income.

Over the years, our office has helped many clients recharacterize Roth conversions. The reason is that while we're quite sure that Roth conversions are a great retirement and estate planning strategy for many, we have no way of knowing how the stock market will perform on any given day or any given year (or any time period for that matter). Many of our clients who have made conversions, often on my advice, were then advised to recharacterize or undo the conversion after the investment lost money. The clients who took my advice and reconverted the same accounts at the lower values to new Roth IRAs, recovered quickly from their initial annoyance and are now very, very happy. The tax consequences of their conversion were less, and the record growth that the market has experienced after 2008 has resulted in substantial tax-free gains in their Roth IRA accounts.

The fact that the tax laws allow you to recharacterize a Roth IRA offers some protection against making a Roth IRA conversion and experiencing a significant downturn in the investment in the short term. The ability to recharacterize might give additional confidence to IRA owners considering a conversion.

I do concede however, that if you make a Roth IRA conversion and the investment inside the account loses money over the long term or even becomes worthless, then the conversion will have been a mistake. That is one of the risks of doing a Roth IRA conversion.

Other risks involve congressional changes to the tax laws, as noted above. I confess to having some concerns about this. It is written into the Internal Revenue Code that Roth IRA conversions will stay income-tax free. True, they said the same thing about Social Security, and we are now paying tax on Social Security. The difference is that the Social Security provision was never part of the Internal Revenue Code. It was not taxed in the early years of the program because of a series of administrative rulings issued by the Treasury Department (which is not law), but in 1983, Congress made it law by specifically authorizing taxation of Social Security benefits.

If Steve Forbes got his way and the United States switched to a value-added tax or national sales tax and eliminated income tax, then the tax you paid on the conversion would presumably be wasted. Currently, though, there is over $7 trillion dollars in the IRA and retirement plan system and most taxpayers are expecting to pay taxes on that amount. And since the government really needs the revenue, I can't see the taxes on IRAs and retirement plans being forgiven. What I think is more likely is a tax increase and, in that case, making a Roth IRA conversion while taxes are lower will yield even more benefits than my analysis shows.

At the time I am writing this, the market has returned to, and surpassed, the record highs it set before the financial crisis of 2008. Does this mean you should not make a Roth conversion unless the market goes down? Of course not! If you make a Roth IRA conversion and the market improves, you will be a happy camper. If it goes down, you can always do another conversion to a different Roth IRA and recharacterize the first one, allowing future gains to happen tax-free in the Roth.

> **After the first edition of** *Retire Secure!* **was published, I was invited to make presentations and train financial planners all over the country. One night, one of the financial planner attendees offered me a ride from my speaking engagement to my hotel. He told me that he read my book and talked to his parents about changing their wills and IRA beneficiary designations consistent with my recommendations. Even though both of his parents were in good health at the time, they listened to their son and changed their estate plan to the cascading beneficiary plan and made a series of large Roth IRA conversions. Unexpectedly, not long after making the recommended changes, his father died. In terms of benefits for the next generation, the planner conservatively valued the difference between the old plan and the new plan in millions of dollars. His "aha" moment was realizing that this advice works. But more important, he did something about it! If you think this advice is right for you, take action, preferably with the help of a qualified expert.**

This chapter is not meant to be a complete analysis of all issues and strategies related to Roth conversions, but to give you some guidance on why this is potentially a great opportunity for you and your family. My book, *The Roth Revolution*, is devoted to the entire spectrum of opportunities within the Roth environment. In that book, I delve much deeper into the discussion of when and how to effectively capitalize on Roth conversions. So to learn more about these conversion opportunities, I recommend this book for further reading. If you would like more details on *The Roth Revolution*, please visit www.paytaxeslater.com.

A Key Lesson from This Chapter

A Roth IRA conversion can provide the Roth IRA owner and his or her family with an exceptional vehicle for increasing purchasing power.

8

||||||||||||||||||||

Annuitizing Your Financial Accumulations

Does It Make Sense for You?

I advise you to go on living solely to enrage those
who are paying your annuities.

— Voltaire

Main Topics

- Defining annuitizing

- Types of annuities

- Picking among survivorship options

- Drawbacks of annuitizing

KEY IDEA

Annuitizing your retirement plan or after-tax accumulations
can be a method of making sure you don't outlive your money.
For some individuals, annuitizing part of their financial assets
is a totally reasonable choice.

What is Annuitizing?

An annuity refers to receiving a specified income payable at stated intervals for a fixed or contingent period. The opposite of an annuity is a lump sum.

Annuitizing your retirement plan accumulations or after-tax money involves surrendering all or a portion of your money to purchase an immediate annuity in exchange for receiving regular, recurring payments for a defined time period, most commonly the rest of your life or, if married, the rest of your and your spouse's life.

> **Annuitizing your retirement plan accumulations or after-tax money involves surrendering all or a portion of your money to purchase an immediate annuity in exchange for receiving regular, recurring payments for a defined time period.**

There are other annuities, such as nonqualified (or non-retirement) annuities, which are sold by life insurance companies. These products allow you to accumulate after-tax funds in a tax-deferred annuity vehicle, but they are not the same as annuities offered in your retirement plan. You do not have to take Required Minimum Distributions (RMDs) on a non-qualified annuity. At your retirement, you can still elect to annuitize the balance in the account, or you can pass the account on to your beneficiary when you die. These are often referred to as commercial annuities.

Commercial annuities can offer income guarantees that are attractive to retirees and their advisors, but many charge high fees and your investment options within them are limited. If tax-deferral is your goal, most people would be better off to open an IRA, or their own personal 401(k).

I will combine the discussion of annuitizing your retirement plan and purchasing an immediate annuity because, conceptually, they are quite similar. The basic concepts of annuitizing apply to both retirement funds and after-tax funds. The major difference is the income tax treatment of the annuity payments.

- The early distributions you receive from an after-tax (or commercial annuity) are partially taxable. This is because a portion of the distribution is considered a return of the money you paid in to the annuity and so it is not taxable until the entire original cost is recovered. The other portion of the distribution is considered ordinary taxable income, such as interest income. After the initial period of cost recovery, which can last for many years, the payments become fully taxable. The insurance company calculates how much of your payment you need to pay tax on.

- Distributions from annuities purchased with retirement funds, on the other hand, are fully taxable like pension income.

Readers who can't stand the roller coaster ride of the stock market may derive some comfort from purchasing an immediate annuity, which will provide a guaranteed income each month.

Payment Schedules

The terms and the duration of the annuity payments depend on what is offered and the choices made. Usually, the choices include receiving payments for:

- The remainder of your life

- The remainder of your and your spouse's life

- A fixed number of years

- One of the above plans with an extra provision to extend benefits to your heirs

There are many variations in payment schedules, including various guaranteed periods. For example, one option offers payments for life with 10 years of payments guaranteed. In that case, if you die within 10 years of annuitizing, the remaining payments within the 10-year period are paid to your heirs. Sometimes you can choose a higher payment while both you and your spouse are alive and a lower payment after your death, such as a 100 percent benefit initially and a 50 or 66 percent benefit for the surviving spouse. Remember, unless you pick a payment option that includes a survivorship or guarantee option, there will be no money left to pass on to your heirs. Your insurance company will be the big winner if you die at an early age, because they get to keep the rest of

Remember, unless you pick a payment option that includes a survivorship or guarantee option, there will be no money left to pass on to your heirs.

your money. On the other hand, the insurance company is required to pay you for as long as you live. So if you live longer than they expected you to, they will lose a lot of money on you.

Which is the better deal? It depends. An ideal candidate for an annuity is a healthy single person with a long life expectancy who doesn't care about leaving any money behind. If the person is married, then a joint life annuity to last through both lifetimes is often the best choice. Annuitizing a portion of a retirement plan is a reasonable choice in many situations, because it ensures that a portion of your money will last at least as long as you do. Annuitizing too much of your retirement money could result in a lack of flexibility that you might later regret, especially if you incur high medical expenses in your golden years.

Most insurance companies and retirement plans will calculate your annuity payment according to your actuarial life expectancy, which is based on your age and sex. Your actual physical condition does not enter into the calculation unless you ask the insurance company to rate you. This is the opposite of life insurance. When purchasing life insurance, you want to show the life insurance company how healthy you are, so that they give you the best possible rate for the coverage. The sooner you die, the better your decision to buy life insurance. With an immediate annuity, you want to show the life insurance company that you have a much reduced life expectancy, because they spread your payments out over a shorter period of time and the amount you receive in each payment will be higher. And if you live a long life after annuitizing, preferably well past the actuarial life expectancy that the insurance company used when calculating your monthly payments, the better it will work out for you and your family.

If you own an annuity and are considering annuitizing, I would not recommend it if you have a reduced life expectancy. Usually the annuity company or retirement plan does not give sufficient weight to the health of the applicant for me to recommend an annuity for someone with a dramatically reduced life expectancy. Occasionally, a company considers these factors, but not always. For example, I had a client with multiple sclerosis who was denied a favorable annuity rate in spite of her health condition. In her case, annuitizing did not make sense because the total of the monthly payments she would have received up to her likely life expectancy was far less than the total amount she had in the annuity. So if she had died at her expected age or sooner, her insurance company would have made a substantial profit, and her heirs would have received less money.

Annuitizing: A Conservative Strategy?

One view holds that annuitizing over a lifetime or joint lifetimes is a conservative strategy because it practically ensures that you will not outlive your money. Although you lose access to the large lump sum of money immediately after purchasing the annuity and the lifetime-based payments stop after your death, the payments will not run out in your lifetime, no matter how long you live.

Annuitizing a large amount of money is sometimes an emotionally hard choice to make. It feels like you are giving it all away despite the fact that you are actually ensuring a secure income source. One solution to the fear of annuitizing is to annuitize only a portion of the available funds. Annuitizing a portion, but not all, of your assets is probably sound for many situations. Jonathan Clements, a great financial writer and defender of the consumer, wrote the following in his column for *The Wall Street Journal*.

> *I often suggest that income-hungry retirees take maybe a quarter of their nest egg and use it to purchase an immediate fixed annuity, thus buying a lifetime stream of income. But if you really want to generate a lot of income and you think you will live to a ripe old age, here is an even better strategy. Buy that immediate annuity—but wait until age 75, so you get a generous income stream based on your shorter life expectancy.*

Some people do not like the idea of annuitizing because they are afraid that, if they die early, the money they paid into the account will be lost to the insurance company. There are some products that offer guarantees that will return some of the capital you invested, if you die early. For example, one option would be to choose payments for life with a guaranteed 10-year payout to your heirs if you die prematurely. Sometimes, the annuity contract will specify that a large portion of the original cost will be returned to the family if the owner dies early. Asking for these types of guarantees is common, but they come at a cost and the amount that you receive monthly will be reduced. Alternatively, you might want to consider forgoing the extra expense of an annuity guarantee feature, and instead buy a life insurance contract with money not spent on any guarantee feature. My personal preference is to keep it simple: If you choose to purchase an immediate annuity, make it for your life or the lives of both you and your spouse. The common advice among financial planners and attorneys is "Don't sell a client an immediate annuity without a guarantee feature, because if the client dies early, the heirs might sue you or at least give you plenty of grief." From a financial planner or insurance agent's viewpoint, that is probably good advice. For the client, however, it might not be the best advice.

If you haven't done it yet, please get out a pad of paper, a pen or pencil and/or your computer spreadsheet. A great start is making a list of all your assets (preferably on one sheet of paper) and all your income. Just the process of assembling this information could be eye opening. Ideally, you would then take that sheet of paper with you to your appointment with a financial professional who is qualified and experienced in distribution and estate planning for IRAs and retirement plans, and who inspires your confidence.

I know I sound like a broken record, but I hate to think you'll make a mistake and then really regret doing this completely on your own!

MINI CASE STUDY 8.1

When Annuitizing the Majority of Your Assets is a Good Choice

Ida is a retired 65-year-old woman in excellent health, with no children and no heirs. After her daily yoga and meditation routine, she enjoys her steamed organic tofu and broccoli sprinkled with ground flax seeds. After her breakfast, she swallows a host of vitamins and supplements with wheatgrass juice. Then she walks three miles to visit her 95-year-old parents who are both in excellent health.

She has a $400,000 CD and no other considerable assets. She receives $25,000 a year in Social Security. She hates thinking about money, but fears that she will become destitute or at least miserable if she invests unwisely and there is another downturn in the market. She spends $36,000 per year before taxes. Though she would prefer to be able to spend a little more, she never wants to be in a position where she has to spend less. Her five-year CD, however, is about to mature, and she discovers from her bank that she would only get two percent interest if she renews it.

If she continues to keep her money in 60-month CDs, based on a two percent interest rate, she would earn and receive only $8,000 of interest income. Her total income including her Social Security would be $33,000 per year. Her Social Security is nontaxable, so she pays only a small amount of state tax (her federal tax is zero because her interest income is below the level of her standard deduction and personal exemption. She must pay $240 to her state on the interest she earns on the CD). Her cost for Medicare insurance, which is deducted from her Social Security check, is $1,260 per year, and she is left with only $31,500 of net income. So she has to dip into the principal of her CD every year, if her minimum living expenses amount to $36,000. With principal deterioration and inflation to worry about, particularly in today's volatile stock market, she legitimately fears she will out-live her money. Though she has been advised about the advantages of diversification, she is not comfortable owning stocks and doesn't want to be an investor. Even with a diversified portfolio, there are no guarantees that she would meet her financial goals, and her fear of being forced to reduce her spending could become a reality.

What options does she have? She could purchase a $400,000 lifetime annuity, which would pay her income regardless of how long she lives. She will discover that there are an overwhelming number of varieties and choices. She could take an annuity over her lifetime only, or over both her and a beneficiary's lifetime if she chooses to name a beneficiary. She could have fixed payments, or could combat future inflation by asking for increasing payments, either at a flat rate of increase, or a variable increase based on stock market returns to some degree. The example below shows what would happen if she invested her $400,000 in a fixed annuity:

	Monthly Payment	**Paid Annually**
Fixed payments, no increases	$2,103.97	$26,033.93
First Year Payments (increasing 4% per year)	$1,465.09	$18,029.24

Taking inflation into account, Ida feels that increasing the payments by four percent per year should provide her with adequate safety. She does not have a spouse that she needs to provide for in the event of her death, and is not interested in lowering her payment to provide for an heir. She decides to purchase the increasing single life annuity providing $18,029 initially, which, combined with her Social Security, gives her an income of $43,029; it also generates a better cash flow and less tax than the CD option because only a portion of the annuity payment will be taxable. A comparison of the CD option and the annuity option is shown below:

	CD Option	Increasing Single Life Annuity Option
Social Security income	$25,000	$25,000
Interest income	8,000	0
Guaranteed annuity income	0	18,029
Income before taxes	33,000	43,029
Less income taxes	(148)	(0)
Less spending needs	(36,000)	(36,000)
Amount available for savings (or required savings withdrawal)	($3,148)	$7,029

Some sharp-eyed readers will look at this illustration and say, "Hey! He said the annuity would be partially taxable, and this shows zero tax!" In Ida's case, I am assuming that she has no other income or assets other than the $400,000. If she put all of that money into an annuity, a portion of the money that she will receive back each month is considered a return of her principal, and a portion of her payment is considered interest. The insurance company calculates that percentage – it's called the exclusion ratio. In Ida's case, the amount of her annuity payment that is taxable is $3,064.97 and that is lower than her federal standard deduction. She has no other taxable income, so she wouldn't even need to file a federal tax return. I also assumed that she is a Pennsylvania resident. Pennsylvania is a senior-friendly state that does not tax retirement income, and offers tax forgiveness to low-income residents. In Ida's case, the only income she has to report on her state tax return is interest. The interest portion of her annuity payment is only $3,064.97, so when the state receives her tax return showing only that income, they think she is nearly destitute and completely forgive the tax she would otherwise owe on that amount. If she invested in the CD, she'd earn $8,000 interest. In that scenario, the state doesn't think she's quite as poor, and they forgive only a portion of the tax she owes on her interest. Even if Ida has income from other sources, the tax consequence of the annuity would always be lower because the interest income itself is lower.

The annuity meets Ida's needs. She will have a guaranteed income stream that, with the four percent inflation adjustment protection, should be sufficient to meet her needs for the rest of her life. She earns guaranteed interest on her $400,000, and her monthly payments will increase annually by four percent. If she had to continue with CD investments, her future interest income would be reduced since her principal is deteriorating at $3,148 per year, and the deterioration will increase each year. On the other hand, with the annuity option, she is able to put $7,029 in savings each year.

Comparing the annuity option with the CD option, her annuity payments are always increasing four percent annually while the CD interest income decreases. This causes the CD balance to become fully depleted when Ida is about 86 years of age, at a time when there is a surplus balance of about $115,000 under the annuity option. Figure 8.1 on page 176 shows the principal balance remaining under these two options.

Figure 8.1 assumes that Ida's spending increases at a rate of 2.5 percent per year. You may not be able to see it in the figure, but the annuity option levels off very slightly when Ida is about 85years old. This is due to a slight increase in the income taxes associated with the annuity. Only 17.6 percent of the annuity is taxable income initially, but when the nontaxable amounts received exceed the annuity cost of $400,000, the entire annuity payment becomes taxable. Most of Ida's Social Security income, however, is still not taxable even when this happens, and her taxes never exceed 10 percent of her income. Though the annuity will end when she dies, she doesn't care because her needs are met and she has no heirs. This plan not only meets her psychological need for security, but it also is probably the best course of action for her.

Figure 8.1
Balance of Funds Available CD Investments vs. Lifetime Annuities

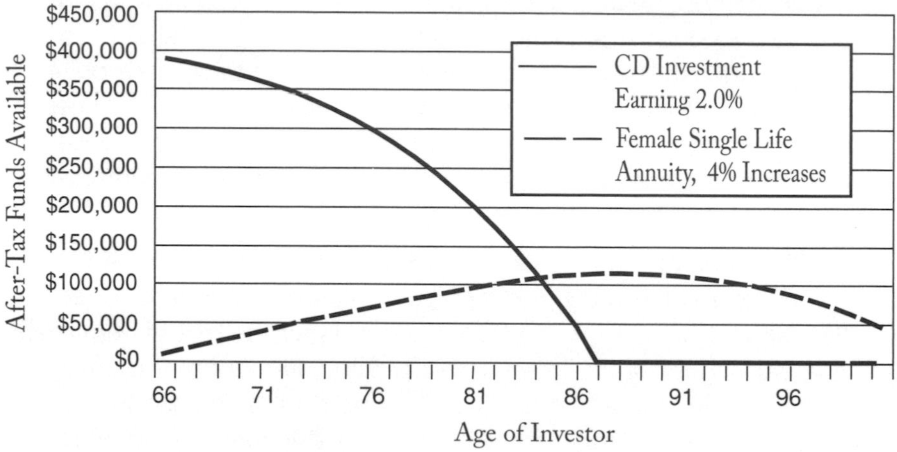

Perhaps your investment goals are somewhat more aggressive than Ida's. In other words, you feel that to make the example more meaningful, we should compare the annuity with after-tax investments earning a rate of return of five or six percent instead of just a two percent CD. Using the same assumptions except for the interest rate, the after-tax investment pool would not be fully depleted until the time Ida was 96 or 101 years old (for five or six percent rates of return, respectively). Some readers would point to that as proof that, when compared to investments earning higher interest rates, an annuity is clearly the inferior choice. Remember, this illustration assumes that the only withdrawals you make from the after-tax account are for your ordinary living expenses. In real life, you may find that you withdraw more than you planned – whether it is for medical bills not covered by insurance, or even to help an adult child who is having financial difficulty. In that case, the after-tax account would be spent down much sooner than shown here, and you would probably be very glad that you had the guaranteed income of the annuity.

Annuitizing Retirement Accumulations

Many people are faced with taking RMDs from their retirement plans once they reach age 70½, the required beginning date. Instead of taking these payments based on the annual value and life expectancy factors, they can choose to annuitize the balance. This way, they no longer have to worry about managing the money and what happens if the balance dwindles or becomes depleted. The risk and responsibility is transferred to the insurance company that provides the annuity. In many situations, annuitizing at least a portion of the retirement assets is a good choice. In the late 1990s, when the market was up and you could smell confidence in the air, annuitizing was frowned upon. "Why annuitize when you can make 25 percent in the market? Even if the market levels out at 10 percent, you could still do better than annuitizing."

After three years in a row of significant losses in the stock market between 2000 to 2002, and even greater losses from October 2007 to 2009, heightened fears of economic downturns, the price of energy, the mortgage foreclosure crisis, the failure of major financial institutions, terrorism, federal deficits, and stock market downturns, there is a new attitude toward annuities. Many people just want to make sure they have financial security for themselves and their spouse. I rarely recommend that someone with large accumulations annuitize everything. Even with Ida, I would probably advise that she only annuitize a portion of her assets and keep a portion of her assets outside of the annuity. In many real-life situations, annuitizing a portion of your retirement holdings is consistent with a desire for security. It provides a stable income that, combined with Social Security, will provide a minimum base of income and a sense of financial security not available with other strategies.

> In many real-life situations, annuitizing a portion of your retirement holdings is consistent with a desire for security. It provides a stable income that, combined with Social Security, will provide a minimum base of income and a sense of financial security not available with other strategies.

MINI CASE STUDY 8.2

When Annuitizing a Portion of the Retirement Plan is Appropriate

George and his wife Susan, both 65, retired three years ago with $2.2 million in their combined retirement plans. George didn't do a good job of diversifying their holdings and to make matters worse, against Susan's wishes, he invested too much of their money in the stock of the company that he worked for. The company went bankrupt and their stock became worthless, so now they now have $1.6 million. No longer do George and Susan talk of a worry-free retirement. At the moment, they are more concerned about whether they have enough money to last their lifetimes than they are about leaving any money for their children and grandchildren.

They have seen financial planners who have recommended a diversified portfolio striking a balance between income-bearing and growth investments. Still, Susan worries. The planners explain that if George and Susan invest too conservatively in an all-income port-folio, inflation and taxes will reduce the value of the principal and their estate will decline in purchasing power, something that makes Susan uneasy. George isn't as worried as Susan, but he would also like a long-term solution that would provide the possibility of an upside but with the assurance they will always have a roof over their heads, food on the table, and gas in the car.

I ask them if they have ever considered adding an annuity to their retirement plan, and explained that they may choose a one-life annuity, a two-life annuity with full benefits to the survivor, or three-quarters or half benefits to the survivor, an annuity with a guaranteed payment for five or 10 years, and so on. My purpose here is not to analyze all the annuity choices but to let you know that annuitiz-ing a portion of a retirement plan is often a reasonable option that can be customized for your needs and goals.

My preference for George and Susan is to combine the con-cepts of annuitizing and maintaining a retirement plan. If George and Susan annuitize one-fourth, or $400,000, of their $1.6 million in retirement funds, they would then be free to invest the remaining $1.2 million in a well-diversified portfolio and still look to enjoy the benefits of any future gains in the market. A $400,000 annuity would provide them with a retirement annuity income of $22,972 per year for as long as either of them lived. Even replacing the fixed income portion of their portfolio with an immediate annuity and investing the remainder of the portfolio is a safe strategy.

Changes in interest rates and inflation may affect the eco-nomic outcome of annuitizing. If interest rates are low, the quoted annuity payout amount may be lower in anticipation of lower invest-ment returns by the annuity-issuing company. If interest rates are low and going higher, and you like the idea of annuitizing, you may want to consider waiting for the interest rates to rebound somewhat so the payout gets better before annuitizing a portion of your retirement plan.

> **Would you like to determine if you are a good candidate for an immediate annuity for a portion of your portfolio? Please visit www.paytaxeslater.com for more advice, or fill out the request form in the back of the book to see if either I or someone in my office would be able to advise you, or refer you to someone who could help you determine whether an immediate annuity would be appropriate for your situation.**

Annuitizing Has Worked Out Well for Many Investors

Annuitizing has worked out well for many of my older clients who were forced to annuitize. Readers who work for non-profits, universities, or public school systems are probably familiar with a retirement program called TIAA-CREF. Most TIAA-CREF participants who retired in the 1980s or before were forced to annuitize most of their TIAA (bond) and CREF (stock) holdings. (They may also have been able to take some taxable withdrawals). Those retirees currently enjoy both a fixed payment stream from the TIAA annuity, and a variable payment stream from the CREF annuity. In addition to whatever they saved, they can count on a monthly income from their TIAA-CREF annuities and Social Security. They may not be rich, but they are usually comfortable. Usually they don't worry about money and, barring any unforeseen events, don't have to. There is no need for any trusts, no money management, and no messing around. When the market is up, they get larger distributions from CREF but still enjoy a steady income from the TIAA fixed annuity that has outperformed the guarantee. Although the CREF (stock) annuities have experienced periods of large declines over the years, the payment amounts received from CREF annuities greatly exceeded the TIAA annuity payments over the last 20 years. So over the long term, the CREF annuities have provided income, albeit a variable income, that surpasses the income provided by the TIAA annuities. This income, combined with their Social Security, will be something on which they can rely.

I am particularly familiar with this type of person because one of them was my mom. When she retired from her job as a professor of journalism (back then they had mandatory retirement at 70), she had to annuitize her retirement plan accumulations. My dad predeceased her, so I recommended she take out a one-life annuity without a guaranteed number of years. Since I preferred she get more income, I told her to forget the survivorship feature and just get the most possible for herself. Against my advice, she chose an annuity with a survivorship feature. If she died within 10 years of her retirement, my brothers and I would have received some income, but she died at age 95. The extra money she spent for the survivorship guarantee for her children was wasted, but she took great delight in knowing that the insurance company still lost a bundle of money on her. They calculated her monthly benefit assuming that she would only live until age 84, and they had to pay her for an additional 11 years! (By the way, my mother proofed the first two editions of this book. If you find any errors in this edition, it is entirely on me).

The above example is not limited to TIAA-CREF participants. It will apply to many taxpayers who either had to or have chosen to receive a regular payment for life in the form of a pension.

Annuitizing: A Risky Strategy?

Another view of annuitizing is that it is not conservative but rather a gamble. Since most annuities are based on an actuarial life expectancy, you are gambling that you will outlive your actuarial life expectancy, and the company holding the annuity is gambling that you won't. Evaluate your win/loss potential according to these criteria:

- If you have reason to believe that you will not survive your actuarial life expectancy, then annuitizing is probably a mistake.

- If you think, however, that you and your spouse are going to substantially outlive your actuarial life expectancy, then annuitizing will provide an assured income stream for a long life.

- If you have a terminal illness and your spouse has a long life expectancy, consider having your spouse purchase an immediate annuity on his or her life only.

Although annuitizing will provide fixed monthly amounts for a lifetime, there are other risks involved that make even this conservative strategy a gamble. One risk is that the issuing insurance company will go bankrupt and be unable to meet its obligations to pay the annuity. State governments provide some guarantees to protect against their insolvency, but, like the Pension Benefit Guaranty Corporation discussed earlier, some of those plans are stretched to the maximum because of insurer insolvencies. You can minimize your risk by choosing insurance and annuity companies with Standard & Poor's quality ratings of at least AA or preferably AAA, even if it means that the interest rate offered to you is not as high as through a lesser-rated insurance company.

Another way to reduce your risk exposure is to buy immediate annuities from more than one company. For example, if you want to purchase an immediate annuity of $300,000, which represents 25 percent of your portfolio, consider three separate annuities of $100,000 cach from three different companies.

Another risk involves the effect of inflation and the fixed nature of the fixed annuity payments. If the payout results in the same payment amount every month, the long-term effects of inflation can lead to the annuity income becoming inadequate to meet growing expenses in later years. Some annuities offer options that serve to offset inflation risks. One is choosing a payment stream that increases every year by a fixed rate of interest, although this option is not available for most retirement plan annuities, just after-tax annuities. This fixed rate of increase, however, is not directly tied to inflation, and could become insufficient in times of high inflation.

CREF annuities, for those in a TIAA-CREF plan or any similar plan, may help to protect your annuity payment stream from inflation by providing a payment that changes based on market investment returns. This can be both good and bad. If the stock market (or other investment index) does well, then you will be better off, but if the market returns are negative, you face the risk of the payments decreasing. Either can happen in times of high inflation. Pick your poison—do you risk the effects of inflation, or of a market decline? Although there is no single correct answer, diversification may be the key to help in such decision making.

If you do not need the money, then annuitizing retirement plan assets needlessly accelerates the payment of income taxes on your retirement accumulations. In theory, at least in the early years, the annuity payment

> **If you do not need the money, then annuitizing retirement plan assets needlessly accelerates the payment of income taxes on your retirement accumulations.**

will be somewhat higher than RMDs since it reflects a return of principal. This is unlike the favorable tax situation we saw earlier in Case Study 8.1 where Ida annuitized after-tax assets.

Also if you incur unexpected expenses and need more than your monthly annuity payment amount, but have no other savings, you are just plain out of luck unless you can borrow from a bank or other lending institution. If you are taking RMDs from a retirement plan, you can always eat into the principal for a large distribution when and if you need it. This is, of course, the fundamental risk of annuities.

A Variation on the Annuity Theme: The Longevity Annuity

If your most consuming, most sleep-depriving worry is running out of money before you die—despite all your best planning, perhaps a longevity annuity is something you should consider. In effect, a longevity *annuity* is a type of annuity that requires immediate payment for a deferred benefit. You buy the annuity now, but you receive nothing immediately other than the guarantee that, a number of years from your purchase date, if you are still alive, you will begin receiving annual or monthly benefits. An example might be helpful.

Assume you are age 65, healthy, and think you have a long life expectancy. You don't need any additional income now and you think you have more than enough money to last you for the next 20 years. Your fear is that you might very well live beyond those secure 20 years and then you would outlive your money. You don't want to buy an immediate annuity because you really don't need the income now. So, you purchase a longevity annuity that will provide you with an income 20 years from now. In its purest form, if you die before 20 years, too bad, you get nothing, your heirs get nothing from the insurance company, and buying the annuity would have been a mistake.

If, however, you live until 95, the decision to buy this type of annuity will have proven to be of tremendous benefit. Obviously, if you live longer, the annuity would be even more valuable. It is like many forms of insurance. If you need it, you will be very glad that you have it. Not needing it is the risk that you take because your money was wasted. But being the number runners that we are, let's look at specific examples to help quantify the benefits and drawbacks. As you would expect, you can purchase longevity annuities, also known as deferred immediate annuities, with various survivorship features.

MINI CASE STUDY 8.3
Buying a Longevity Annuity

Phil is age 65 and he is confident that he will have sufficient income for the next 20 years to maintain his standard of living. He also has $100,000 of discretionary after-tax dollars to immediately fund a longevity annuity. He is unmarried, but he does have a son to whom he would like to leave something. Phil is intrigued by the idea of the immediate deferred annuity, for which he would pay $100,000 now and receive no benefit from until he turned 85. He wants to look at the cost and benefits of the immediate deferred annuity and also compare and contrast the numbers for purchasing the longevity annuity on a life only basis versus an installment refund basis. If he opts for the life only option, and then dies before turning 85, there would be no benefit paid to his son and the insurance company gets to keep all the money Phil paid for the annuity. If he opts for the installment refund option, though, and then dies before turning 85, his son or other heirs will be guaranteed the monthly income for 15 months—guaranteeing some return of his original investment.

Once Phil reaches age 85, the longevity annuity with the life only option will provide him with a fixed lifetime monthly income of $4,356.21 ($52,274.52 per year). If he chooses to go with the installment refund option, his monthly income will be $2,854.30 ($34,251.60 per year). The interest rates used in these calculations were from 2014, and were relatively low at the time. If rates are higher when you're reading this, then the income would be even higher.

If we assume an inflation rate of 2.5 percent per year, these amounts provide an annual income in today's dollars of about $31,902 for the life only option or $20,903 for the installment refund option at age 85. Each year thereafter, the real income in today's dollars drops due to the continued effects of inflation.

These two amounts mean that, if we don't take into account interest or the time value of money, or if Phil lived 12 or 15 months beyond his 85th birthday, this would be a winner. However, that isn't a fair analysis. A fair analysis must take into account the time value of money and taxes on the annuity income. If we make certain assumptions and run the numbers, we have a much less favorable breakeven point.

Let us run the numbers assuming investment income on an alternative investment generating rates of return of four, six, or eight percent. The annuity income received at age 85 is taxable to the extent that the income exceeds the $100,000 investment. For example, let us also assume that the annuity company has determined that the income at age 85 is considered 28 percent withdrawal of cost basis and the rest is ordinary income (and therefore taxable) until the total cost of $100,000 is returned. Also assume an average tax rate of 23% for both scenarios. The following chart shows the various break-even points:

Figure 8.3
Longevity Annuity Illustration

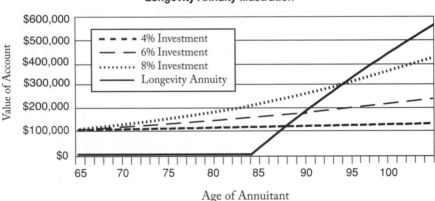

This graph illustrates that, if Philip dies before age 85, purchasing the annuity would have been a bad decision. But if Philip lives to age 90, he'll receive more money through the annuity than his after-tax investments paying 4% and 6%. If he lives beyond 95, the annuity beats his 8% investment as well. This graph also assumes that Phil does not spend any of his after-tax money. This may prove difficult in real life, especially if his assets are seized to pay for care in a nursing home. Philip also has the option to elect the return of premium guarantee option. This would reduce the amount he receives monthly, but also guarantees that his heirs will receive some money from the account.

Now that Phil has the numbers, his options are much better defined, but he still has to decide if his fear of running out of money outweighs the risk of not realizing a return on the investment.

That is a dilemma that people have to assess for themselves. But I offer this observation from Larry J. Kotlikoff, a Boston University economics professor and developer of important software that does a dynamic analysis of multiple variables affecting retirement spending. His model is superior to other models that use constant and static spending targets. Larry says if the whole point is to never run out of money, we should be willing to pay a premium over the actuarial break-even number—in effect, for peace of mind. The reason it has so much appeal to me and other advisors is that it helps alleviate the #1 fear facing most retirees—outliving their money. By the way, I would not recommend it in its simplest form if you are married. In that case, unless there are extenuating circumstances (such as one of you has life insurance or a pension or other resources), you should purchase the immediate deferred annuity for both lives so that your surviving spouse does not lose the income at your death. The above example does not analyze these numbers. For now, suffice it to say that the annuity payment would be reduced because the insurance company must continue paying until both the husband and wife die.

What Are the Disadvantages of a Longevity Annuity?

What are the biggest arguments against it? Well, right off the bat, you are writing a check for $100,000 (actually it could be for any amount), and you are not getting any immediate benefit. You could die before 85, and your decision would not have worked out well for your family. For many people with heirs to consider, that will be the end of the discussion. For you hearty souls who are worried about running out of money and are willing to take some extra risks to address your fear, please read on for even more reasons not to do it.

The insurance company that issued your annuity could fail, and you end up with nothing. However, almost every state has a guaranty fund, much like FDIC, that pays claims if your insurer becomes insolvent. During the bailout of AIG and other financial companies, stockholders suffered, but owners of their annuities and beneficiaries of life insurance policies were completely protected. Of course, I can't deny there is some amount of risk, even with highly rated companies.

Another reason not to buy it now is that today, interest rates are relatively low and as a result, the future annuity payments will be less than they would be if interest rates were higher. Perhaps the best solution to this issue is to keep your options open and when interest rates go back up and the benefit per dollar of the premium goes up, consider buying one then.

In addition, we could face hyperinflation and even if you survive, you would get paid in devalued currency.

On the other hand, if you think that the economy is not going to do well over the next 20 years and you want a guarantee of not running out of money, and you can live with the downsides that I pointed out, this is a great idea. But perhaps the best use for a longevity annuity comes not from purchasing one outright, but rather trading up.

The "Aha!" Moment with Respect to Longevity

I often rely on Tom Hall, an insurance broker with Pittsburgh Brokerage Services, LLC, to find my clients the best deals on life insurance. Tom often has astute recommendations. This "aha" moment came from Tom.

Before introducing Tom's idea, I have to give you some background information on one problem I often encounter as an estate planner. Many of my clients, at some point in their lives, have purchased a commercial, high commission annuity. A discussion of that type of annuity is beyond the scope of this chapter. In any event, sometimes they work out well, but sometimes retirees who have purchased a tax-deferred annuity don't have a good plan for their eventual disposition.

Tom Hall says, "That's fine. Do a tax-free exchange of your tax-deferred annuity for this longevity annuity." What a great idea! The reason this is such a good idea is a taxpayer can do a tax-free exchange disposing of an asset he or she did not want to keep in exchange for guaranteed payments in the future as long as the client lives. This could be a much better choice than electing the annuitizing option that is usually part of a tax-deferred annuity contract. The reason is, if you annuitize a tax-deferred annuity contract now, the payments will be much lower than if you elect to defer payments for a number of years in the future.

At the moment, the longevity or immediate deferred annuity is not a well-known option for many taxpayers. Until now, employees in the private sector could not purchase longevity annuities within their 401(k) plans – and this was largely because of the RMD rules. As of June of 2014, though, new tax rules will make it possible for all employees to buy qualified longevity annuity contracts (QLACs) within their retirement plans. QLACs purchased within retirement plans are exempt from RMD rules as long as the plan participant does not use more than 25% of their plan balance (or, $125,000, whichever is less) to buy the annuity. The distributions must start by age 85. Remember, it is up to your employer to decide what options are available to you within your 401(k), so you may have to suggest that they add a new option for longevity annuities. Even if they do not, you can transfer money to an IRA to purchase one on your own. Being able to avoid the RMD on $125,000 of retirement income is a significant estate planning tool, and the guaranteed income can provide you with a lifetime of financial security.

Special Idea: Using Annuities for Spendthrift Children

Over the years, our legal practice has drafted many spendthrift trusts for adult children as beneficiaries of wills and trusts and retirement plans (see Chapter 17 for more details regarding spendthrift trusts). We usually draft these trusts when a parent feels that an adult child is not capable of handling money responsibly. Sometimes it is drafted to make sure the no-good son-in-law doesn't get one red cent of mom and dad's hard-earned money. The trust is set up for the benefit of the irresponsible child (or the daughter who is married to the no-good son-in-law). A trustee is named to invest the funds and make distributions according to the terms of the trust.

Many times naming a spendthrift trust as a beneficiary is a good solution. Sometimes it isn't. There are multiple problems with spendthrift trusts, including aggravation; an additional tax return; and legal, accounting, and trustee expenses. Perhaps the biggest problem with the spendthrift trust is choosing a trustee. Usually, the parents of the adult child decide who should be the trustee of the spendthrift trust. Many of my clients do not want a bank or trust company as a trustee or, even if they did, the value of the trust isn't enough to get a bank interested. I personally will not act as a trustee and neither will a lot of attorneys. (We don't want to have to deal with whiney beneficiaries wanting more money than our prudent natures would allow). One logical choice of trustee is one of the spendthrift's siblings because the sibling is likely to have a greater understanding of the situation than a bank or other corporate trustee. Do you, however, really want to set the stage for family strife? What happens when the trustee doesn't give the spendthrift what he wants? What would Christmas dinner be like after Brother Trustee just said, "No, Sister Spendthrift, you can't use the money from your trust fund for a new sports car." Or "No, Sister Spendthrift, paying for tuition and room and board at the University of the Sun Devil Worshiper doesn't qualify as funds for education, and I won't pay tuition for that institution out of your trust!"

Naming a bank as trustee is often a problem, too. Often there isn't enough money in the trust for a bank to be willing to serve as trustee. Even if the trust is large enough for them to act as trustee, the fees they charge can be substantial, and ultimately many clients just don't want a bank involved.

One Solution to Providing for the Spendthrift Adult Child

Let's assume the goal is to provide an income stream for the adult spendthrift child for the rest of the child's life. Mom and Dad want the assurance that their child will be properly provided for. They may not see the need for the child to accumulate money. They also may not care about what happens to the money after the child dies.

One potential solution to the problem is to eliminate the trust entirely. Assume the parents have three children, and they want to treat all three equally. The parents could give a direction in their will or other document that the spendthrift's share would be used to purchase a life-time annuity for the benefit of the spendthrift. The annuity would be purchased from the estate after mom and dad die. An annuity will assure a future income stream and provide protection against the spendthrift's creditors.

MINI CASE STUDY 8.4

Using an Annuity in Lieu of a Spendthrift Trust (a True Story)

Concerned Parent is trying to figure out how to provide for his son, one of three children. He trusts his daughters completely and is planning to leave both of them their one-third of the inheritance directly. The issue is how to leave money to his son, whom he doesn't trust with money. If he leaves it to his son outright, he is afraid his son will deplete the principal through excessive spending or be vulnerable to potential creditors of both his son and his daughter-in-law. He also fears his daughter-in-law will put pressure on his son to spend more than he might be comfortable spending, or what may be prudent to spend, but he doesn't want to be too controlling from the grave or jeopardize his son's marriage.

If he leaves the money in some type of spendthrift trust, the money is tied up and perhaps overprotected. He would also have to choose a trustee. If the bank is a trustee (a corporate fiduciary), there will be fees and extra layers of administration. If he names one of his daughters as trustee, there is a good chance that he will harm the relationship between the son and the daughter. Then he would have to decide among the different possibilities for terms of the trust. Should the trust have a mandatory distribution? How much license should the trustee be authorized to use? Should it be a total-return trust? (Another subject, another day, but a total-return trust is a new type of trust that makes sense in some situations.)

Does Concerned Parent really want to control from the grave? No! The Concerned Parent doesn't want to control his son's life. He just wants to provide him with the highest degree of financial security.

At the Concerned Parent's death, the executor is directed to take all or a portion of what would have gone to the son directly to purchase an annuity with monthly annuity proceeds going to the son. Son gets an annuity for the rest of his life and most likely ends up with a larger monthly or annual distribution than he would have received had the inherited money been left in a trust. If you make this provision in your will or revocable trust, I recommend giving the executor the right to shop for the best deal on an annuity at the time of your death.

This idea of directing the executor to purchase an annuity has been used in practice to the total delight of the Concerned Parent and to even greater delight of the responsible sibling who doesn't have to be trustee for the spendthrift sibling. If the son was hoping to come into a windfall at his parent's death, he might not be too happy with being put on a budget, but hopefully will not argue too much at the prospect of a guaranteed lifetime income.

Some of my more advanced readers may ask, "Well, what about all those advertisements I see for companies that buy annuity payments for a lump sum? Can't the son just go to one of them and get his windfall inheritance in spite of Dad's wishes?" Hopefully the son won't try it because the fees charged by those companies are exorbitant, and he'll lose a lot of money that he'll never be able to get back. If you're still worried about your child doing it, though, your best option might be to establish a trust and write the terms to specify that payments cannot be directed to a third party.

Protection from Creditors

Another advantage of the immediate annuity is that it provides some protection from creditors. Once the annuity is purchased, the principal itself will be protected from creditors because it is gone—that is, outside the control of the annuitant. In some situations, a creditor may be able to reach the proceeds (a payment) of the annuity, but that is unlikely. For example, a creditor can't get an order directing an annuity company to pay the son's annuity directly to the creditor. It could, however, strategically levy a checking account where the proceeds of the annuity check would be deposited, in which case the son should learn to be an effective sleazebag and open a new checking account, or pay up.

This idea of buying an annuity is also a good idea for the father of a child who has substantial debts or who practices in a profession where there is significant personal liability, such as medicine. Of course, one of the downsides of annuitizing for the benefit of a child is that there will be nothing to pass on to the grandchildren.

To address that flaw, I offer several responses.

1. So what? With the exception of providing for education, most grandparents are much more interested in providing for their children than their grandchildren. Of course this isn't always the case, but it is in my experience.

2. You don't have to have the executor annuitize all the proceeds. You can have the executor annuitize just a portion.

3. Something could be set up for the grandchildren directly. If you purchase an annuity for your child, you could leave some portion of the Inherited IRA or other assets to a trust for the grandchildren.

A Key Lesson from This Chapter

Annuitizing a portion of your retirement plan or purchasing an immediate annuity for roughly 25 percent of your retirement assets is often a good strategy to help ensure that you never run out of money. A new strategy of purchasing an immediate deferred annuity will be very attractive to some individuals.

9

||||||||||||||||||||||||||||||||

Withdrawing Retirement Plans Funded with Company Stocks, and Net Unrealized Appreciation

*If you do not know how to ask the right question,
you discover nothing.*

—W. Edwards Deming

Main Topics

- What is Net Unrealized Appreciation (NUA)?

- Limits on funding qualified plans with employer stock

- Case studies (that save a bundle)

KEY IDEA

The difference between the market value of your company stock still invested in your retirement plan at the time of a distribution and its value at the time your employer made the contribution to your plan is called net *unrealized appreciation*, or NUA. At retirement, it is critical to check for NUA before rolling money into an IRA. NUA qualifies for favorable tax treatment.

The key to significantly greater overall wealth accumulation for you and your family is delaying, for as long as possible, taxes on distributions, of any amount, from the tax-deferred environment—in other words, pay taxes later. Unfortunately, I frequently see retirees pay tax unnecessarily when receiving stock distributions from their pension plans. Stock distributions potentially qualify for a favorable tax treatment that can save the owner a lot of money, if they follow specific rules when taking their distribution. This is particularly true if the capital gains tax and qualified dividends are taxed at 15 percent.

What is NUA, and Why Should I Care?

Some employees have the option to buy their company's stock within their 401(k)s or retirement plans. The strategy has paid off for over 10,000 Microsoft employees, who became millionaires as a result of their stock ownership in the company. Enron employees, however, did not fare as well – almost 60 percent of the assets in their 401(k) plan were invested in Enron stock, and most employees watched helplessly in 2001 as its value dropped by 99 percent.

The difference between the market value of your company stock invested in your retirement plan at the time of a distribution and its value at the time your employer made the contribution is called net unrealized appreciation (NUA).

Employers have been and, as of this writing, are still allowed to fund qualified plans with their company's stock, using the fair market value of the stock to value the contribution. However, a unanimous Supreme Court decision in 2014 might discourage employers from offering their employees a stake in the business in future years; they no longer have a key protection against lawsuits claiming that it is imprudent to allow employees to hold company stock in their retirement plan. Employers can now be held liable under the Employee Retirement Income Security Act (ERISA) if they offer company stock to employees, and the value of the stock drops. Employers are also liable under insider-trading laws if they dump the stock in their pension plan to avoid a loss to their employees, knowing that the company is in trouble. Even prohibiting the employees from purchasing new stock could be a signal to other investors that it's time to sell, thus driving the price down lower than it might otherwise go.

Currently there are no restrictions on the amount of company stock that can be held in a defined contribution plan, such as a 401(k). A defined benefit pension plan, however, is not permitted to have more than 10 percent of its assets tied up in the employer's company stock.

For some plans, such as stock bonus plans, all contributions are in employer stock. Profit-sharing plans may also have 100 percent of their assets invested in employer stock. If you participate in these kinds of plans where you work, you may have too many of your eggs in one basket. While it might seem like a good idea if your company and its stock are doing well, you expose yourself to the risk of the stock dropping suddenly. Remember, your employer writes the rules of your retirement plan, and most employees don't read those rules. It is common to see restrictions that limit the employee's ability to sell the stock for a certain period of time, or even until they reach a specific age. Blackout periods, when all activity in the account is completely frozen, can occur. Employers can announce a blackout period if they need to perform administrative tasks in the plan, or if upper management intends to make a major announcement about the company that might affect the price of the stock. Blackouts are usually for a short period of time — a few days or weeks — but it is possible that they could coincide with a drop in the price of the company stock. Enron employees found this out when the company stock declined 35 percent during a pre-scheduled two-week blackout period, and they were not permitted to make any transactions in their 401(k)s. No matter what company you work for, it is very risky to have more than 10 percent of your 401(k) in company stock.

But what happens if you do have some company stock in your retirement plan? When you retire and take a lump-sum distribution from a qualified plan, such as a 401(k), the distribution may include employer stock that (hopefully) is worth more than its fair market value at the time it was purchased in your plan. The difference between the market value of your company stock invested in your retirement plan at the time of the distribution and its value at the time it was purchased is called net unrealized appreciation (NUA). For example, if the stock in your plan was purchased at $10 per share, and is now worth $100 per share, each share has $90 of NUA. You should care about this because NUA receives favorable tax treatment and, if the financial institution handling your rollover doesn't do it properly, it will cost you a lot of tax money that you shouldn't have to pay. Before we look at how it works, though, you have to understand that the NUA rules apply only in two specific situations.

1. If the stock shares are distributed in-kind as part of a "lump sum distribution," then 100 percent of the NUA is non-taxable at the time of distribution.

2. If the stock withdrawal is not a "lump sum distribution," then only the NUA attributable to your own contributions is non-taxable. If 100% of the stock in your plan was purchased through your payroll deductions, then you don't really have anything to worry about. If you received stock from your employer as part of an incentive plan, though, you need to be very careful that you follow the lump-sum distribution rules.

If you do have employer stock in your retirement plan, you also need to be very careful to choose a new custodian who can accept the transfer of the stock. If they tell you that you "can't" transfer your stock out of your IRA, you should run out of their office screaming because that probably means that they are not licensed to handle individual stocks. Get a second opinion from a larger, well established financial firm, please – it could save you a lot of money.

If you transfer the stock portion of your plan into an IRA, you will be required to take minimum distributions from not only your regular IRA assets but also from your company stock, and you will have to pay tax on those distributions at your ordinary income tax rate. If you transfer the stock into a brokerage account, you get to treat the NUA portion as a special entity as long as the distribution initially qualifies as a lump-sum distribution as described in Chapter 6. If it does qualify, then your NUA is not taxed at the time of the lump-sum distribution. You pay tax only on the original value of the stock at the time it was purchased in your plan. The amount that you paid tax on becomes your basis in the stock. You do not have to pay tax on the NUA portion until you sell or otherwise dispose of the stock in a taxable transaction. When you do sell it, you pay tax at lower capital gains rates instead of ordinary income rates. No matter how long you have held the stock, the NUA portion is taxed as a long-term capital gain. The essence of the advantage of the NUA is that sales you make of company stock held in a non-IRA brokerage account will be taxed at capital gains rates, rather than ordinary income rates as with traditional

> **The essence of the advantage of the NUA is that sales you make of company stock held in a non-IRA brokerage account will be taxed at capital gains rates, rather than ordinary income rates as with traditional IRAs.**

IRAs. If you die, there is no step-up in basis for NUA, which means that tax is still due on the total amount of the long-term capital gain. Post-distribution gain, however, may get a step-up in basis.

Would you like to continue your IRA and retirement plan education? You can listen to my MP3 and read my special reports from the comfort of your home. Please go to the last several pages of this book for ordering information. In addition, this information can be accessed at www.paytaxeslater.com.

MINI CASE STUDY 9.1

When Checking for NUA Saves a Bundle

Joe Employee retires and takes a lump-sum distribution from his company's stock bonus plan, consisting totally of his company's stock, which had been contributed by his employer. He rolls the stock into a brokerage account instead of taking the distribution as cash. The total value of the stock at the time of the distribution is $500,000. The company's cost basis in the stock is $100,000.

At tax time, Joe gets a Form 1099-R from his employer showing a total distribution of $500,000; the taxable portion of which is $100,000. Since he didn't sell the stock, the amount of NUA is $400,000. Joe pays tax on $100,000 of ordinary income at the time of the distribution. If Joe sells the stock immediately for $500,000, he will also report a $400,000 long-term capital gain. If he doesn't sell the stock, the gain will be deferred until he does.

Already Joe is better off than if he had not followed the rules to allow it to be treated as a lump-sum distribution with NUA. If he had simply cashed out the plan and opened a $500,000 CD, for example, or cashed in a $500,000 IRA, he would have to pay income taxes on the entire amount at ordinary income tax rates. At the current top marginal rate, the tax is $500,000 x 39.6% = $198,000 of income tax on an immediate cash-out. This leaves Joe with $302,000 after taxes.

Since Joe's transaction qualifies for NUA treatment, he sells $400,000 at capital gains rates of 20 percent and $100,000 at ordinary income tax rates: ($400,000 x 20% = $80,000, plus $100,000 x 39.6% = $39,600), or a combined tax of $119,600. This leaves Joe with approximately $380,000 after taxes. Better yet, Joe can take his NUA assets as an in-kind distribution, keep track of the NUA status, and not pay income taxes on the gain until the time he sells the stock.

- If Joe holds the stock for three months and then sells it for $550,000, he will report a $400,000 long-term capital gain (the NUA portion) and a $50,000 short-term capital gain on the stock.

- If Joe holds the stock for a year after the distribution, and then sells it for $600,000, the entire $500,000 of gain on the stock, not only the NUA, qualifies as long-term capital gain.

- If he just sits on the NUA, hopefully the stock will continue to increase in value, but some day he will be subject to capital gains taxes. Even at death you can't escape the capital gain, and there is no step-up in basis other than the post-distribution gain.

In most cases, it is beneficial to roll over a distribution from a qualified plan into an IRA to get the benefits of tax-deferred growth. But Joe has done even better! While he holds the stock, all the appreciation is accumulating in a tax-deferred manner, since gain on the stock is not taxed until he sells it. And he will pay tax on the gain at capital gains rates when he sells the stock, rather than or-dinary income rates like distributions from an IRA. Joe also has the option of keeping part of the stock and rolling over the balance of the shares into an IRA. In this situation, Joe would pay income taxes only on the basis of the shares he keeps and would maintain NUA status on those shares. If Joe rolls the stock over to an IRA, and later takes a distribution in stock from the IRA, the taxable amount of the distribution is the fair market value of the stock, and Joe is taxed at ordinary income rates. Rolling shares into the IRA is a bad idea for Joe, because he loses the tremendous benefit of the capital gains rates for the NUA portion.

This is why it is critical when you retire and are considering an IRA rollover that you check to see if there is any NUA in your retire-ment plan. If you do not have company stock in your plan, and there was no type of stock swap, you will not have NUA. If you do own employer stock in your retirement plan, then you will have to find out from the payroll department whether you have NUA. If some of the

NUA on employer stock is relatively small due to the difference in the stock basis and fair market value at the time of the contribution, a rollover of those shares into an IRA may be a better approach. Preserving the tax-deferred status of those shares may outweigh the minimal long-term capital gains benefits derived from taking the distribution.

Getting a handle on NUA could present a tremendous savings opportunity. When you calculate how much money you can save in taxes, you will find you may be in a much better situation using the NUA rules to your advantage. We have used the simplest of calculations for our example, but you should seek the advice of a qualified tax expert to review your specific situation because there alternative methods permitted to calculate the tax.

MINI CASE STUDY 9.2

A Typical NUA Opportunity

It is rare for an employee to have a retirement plan funded 100 percent with employer stock. More typical is the case of Bob, who retires from his company and receives a lump-sum distribution from the company's pension plan consisting of $450,000 in cash and other securities and employer stock worth $50,000, of which $40,000 is NUA. That is to say, the stock value at the time the company contributed it to Bob's retirement plan was $10,000. This is a reasonable range that you might find for an employee who has worked at the same company for many years.

- Bob should roll over the non-company stock portion (the $450,000) to an IRA and keep the stock while still excluding the NUA portion from income—the best of both worlds.

- Bob will end up with a $450,000 IRA and $50,000 in company stock and will have current taxable income of $10,000. The $40,000 in NUA won't be taxed until Bob sells the stock. (Or, charitably inclined readers can read Chapter 18 for an idea that avoids the income tax completely).

If the employer contributed the distributed stock to the plan, then the deferral and capital gains treatment apply only if the distribution meets all the qualifications for a lump-sum distribution, other than the subsequent rollover of a portion of the plan to an IRA. Such a partial rollover would prohibit the 10-year averaging treatment as discussed in Chapter 6, but would not prohibit the special tax treatment for NUA. If the distribution does not qualify as a lump-sum distribution, then only the NUA of stock that the employee himself contributed to his plan would qualify for this special treatment of income deferral and capital gains.

If you have substantial NUA in your retirement plan, I highly recommend that you hire someone to run the numbers for you to help determine a long-term NUA plan. If the people you work with don't have this special expertise in NUA, I know of no one better than one of the top IRA and retirement planning expert in the country, Robert Keebler, CPA.

A Key Lesson from This Chapter

The difference between the market value of a stock when it was contributed to your IRA and its value upon distribution is called the net unrealized appreciation, or NUA, and NUA receives favorable tax treatment. The most important piece of information to carry with you from this chapter is that you should always check for NUA before rolling money into an IRA. If you have NUA, please, either get professional advice or dig further into the matter.

Part Three

ESTATE PLANNING

It's Never Too Early to Start

OVERVIEW

Over the course of my career, I have met many couples who are far too complacent about their retirement and estate plans. Once their wills and trusts are prepared, they feel that they are set for life and don't need to do anything else. The unfortunate truth is that the laws of the land are constantly changing. Some of those changes, like the Supreme Court ruling in 2013 that struck down the Defense of Marriage Act and permitted same-sex marriages, make international news. Other changes aren't interesting enough to earn the attention of the public eye, but they can have significant effects on the outcome of your estate after your death. The chapters that follow cover changes in the laws that have already happened, as well as a few that I believe are likely to happen, and how those changes can affect you. If you have not had your estate documents reviewed by an attorney since 2012, I recommend that you do so immediately. The illustrations in the following chapters will show you why.

10

||||||||||||||||||||||||||||||||||||

Eddie and Emily: A Retirement and Estate Planning Case Study*

*You can always amend a big plan, but you can never expand a little one.
I don't believe in little plans. I believe in plans big enough to meet a
situation which we can't possibly foresee now.*

— Harry S. Truman

Edward J. Engineer ("Eddie"), age 65, is a retired engineer. Eddie is married to Emily, age 65. Though Eddie made a reasonable salary as an engineer, it was difficult to save money. Taking care of the mortgage and maintenance on the house, buying groceries, braces, and raising their children took most of his paycheck. They also paid for their children's college education. Eddie did make regular contributions to his retirement plan, and when it was deductible, to a voluntary IRA. Emily has a small IRA.

Eddie and Emily have two married children and four grandchildren. Their son, Bill, is doing quite well financially and is in a solid marriage. Their daughter, Sarah, unfortunately, has significant marital problems, and to make life even more difficult, her finances are a mess because her husband is a spendthrift. This is a major concern to Eddie and Emily and, to make matters even worse, Eddie doesn't trust his son-in-law. Period.

Just 10 years ago, Eddie had $1,000,000 in total retirement assets. He was just hoping that the accumulations would provide for his and Emily's comfortable retirement. With time and compounding, however, Eddie's retirement assets grew to a high of $2,200,000 in his 401(k) and $280,000 in his IRA. The last twelve months of investment results have been rough for Eddie, though, and his balances have shrunk to roughly $1,800,000 in his 401(k) plan and $200,000 in his IRA. The Engineers do not think of themselves as wealthy, and they have not changed their spending habits. Eddie continues to drive his 10-year-old car. He would consider it absolutely foolish to spend money on a new car. His current one is reliable and certainly serviceable.

Eddie and Emily remain in their relatively modest house where they raised their children. Emily still clips coupons. After years of managing their money very carefully, Eddie and Emily have read that they might suddenly be facing enormous taxes on their retirement assets, both during their lifetime and after their death. They thought they knew what to do about filing for Social Security, but then they received confusing information that their strategy for taking their Social Security benefits might not be optimal. Their current income does not cover their expenses, and in order to make up the shortfall, they must make withdrawals from their portfolio. They wonder if they should spend their IRA or 401(k) funds first, or whether they should spend after-tax money first—money on which they have already paid taxes. Eddie was never really comfortable with the planning for his retirement plan or IRA. Among other things, he wasn't sure how the beneficiary form of the IRA and 401(k) plan should be filled out. And they weren't sure if they had enough life insurance, or even if they needed life insurance at all. So this couple came to me to see if it was possible to minimize those taxes, and if there was anything else that they could improve upon with respect to their estate planning.

The first thing I noticed was that Eddie and Emily have wills that are twenty years old. They were drafted at a time when the federal estate-tax exemption was only $600,000 and there was a legitimate risk of their money being subject to substantial federal estate taxes when Eddie and Emily died. Their wills include a trust that basically says that if Eddie predeceases Emily, a significant portion of his money will go into a trust which will provide Emily with the income it generates, and she will also have the option to invade the principal for her health, maintenance and support.

The Engineers have an approximate net worth of $2.5 million, including life insurance. A detailed list of the Engineers' assets is as follows:

Eddie's 401(k) plan	$1,800,000
Eddie's IRA	200,000
Emily's IRA	30,000
After-tax investments and savings	130,000
House	185,000
Cars and personal property	45,000
Whole life insurance	50,000
Term life insurance	60,000
Total estate	$2,500,000

In talking with Eddie and Emily, I discovered the following information about them.

- Eddie and Emily's first concern is providing for a comfortable retirement as long as they both live. Their second concern is providing for the survivor upon the first death.

- Though Eddie and Emily would prefer leaving money to their children rather than paying taxes, avoiding taxes is secondary to providing for each other.

- Eddie and Emily trust each other completely, although Eddie is a little tighter about money than Emily.

- Eddie and Emily wondered if life insurance should play a role in their planning, and, if so, what kind and how much?

- Eddie wondered if he should leave his old 401(k) where it was. The reason he never rolled it into an IRA was because one-third of his money is invested in a guaranteed income fund that used to pay a better rate than the prevailing bond market. Now that rate has dropped.

- Despite the fact that their children have widely disparate needs, Eddie and Emily want to treat the children equally, but he is adamant that he doesn't want his no-good son-in-law to get one red cent of his money. He is also worried about his daughter's bleak long-term financial situation.

- Eddie and Emily want to know more about optimal beneficiary designations for their retirement plans to pass that money on to their children and possibly their grandchildren.

- Eddie knew that with the higher exemption amounts (the amount in your estate that is exempt from federal estate taxes) the traditional trusts that were part of their wills might not only be unnecessary, but possibly financially disastrous, and he was not confident about their retirement plan and IRA beneficiary designations.

- Eddie, even more so than Emily, doesn't want to see his no-good son-in-law get one red cent of his money. The thought of that no-goodnik living off an inheritance makes Eddie sick. This problem, in addition to his daughter's bleak financial prospects, though not his primary concern, weighs heavily on Eddie's mind.

Even though Eddie has been thinking about all of these questions for several years, to get him to do anything outside his routine often takes a Herculean effort. Emily has always let Eddie take care of the investments and big picture planning, but Emily also knows it is time to secure their golden years by getting their IRAs, Social Security, and estate plan in order.

Some Good Ideas for Eddie and Emily

Retirement Planning

Eddie told me that he and his wife were planning to go to the Social Security office the following morning to apply for benefits, because they didn't want to have to tap into their savings to cover their budget shortfall every month. I asked them to delay their visit until we had an opportunity to run the numbers and see if that was the best strategy for them. I tell them that by using advanced strategies that allow their benefits to be permanently increased for Delayed Retirement Credits, and by using the Apply and Suspend method, the increase in their Social Security income over the long term might be far more advantageous than taking a lesser amount at age 65.

Advanced options such as Delayed Retirement Credits and Apply and Suspend option are techniques that allow retirees to claim the maximum amount of Social Security benefits possible. Unfortunately, maximizing Social Security benefits is such a complicated topic that an in-depth discussion about it would take up an entire book in itself. If you would like to read the peer reviewed article I wrote that covers this topic in more detail, please visit: **http://www.paytaxeslater.com/articles/trusts_estates_september_2014.pdf**

> **If you would like more information on maximizing Social Security benefits, please sign up for our newsletter at www.paytaxeslater.com. It is such an important topic that I'm considering writing an entire book about it.**

Tax Planning

I also talked to the Engineers about the advantages of using their $130,000 nest egg to meet their current budget shortfall, rather than applying for Social Security benefits now or by making withdrawals from their retirement plans. They were reluctant to do it because they'd always thought of that money as being their "nest egg." I pointed out that the money they withdraw from the IRA will be taxable. Even if they decide to not withdraw money now, they will be in a higher tax bracket after they turn 70 because they will be required to take minimum distributions from their retirement accounts, and the distributions will be taxed for federal income tax purposes.

They'd never really given it any thought, but from now until they turn 70, their taxable income is relatively low. If they choose to not make any IRA or 401(k) withdrawals and live off their after-tax funds [money not in his 401(k) or IRA], their taxes will be very low compared to the years when they have to start taking minimum distributions. He wonders if these "low tax years" create an opportunity for him and his family. I told them that they could do a series of Roth IRA conversions over the next five years, without affecting their tax bracket at all. Eddie is pretty sharp and he realizes that the years between entering retirement and being required to take minimum distributions will give him more control over his income than he has ever had. Specifically, he knows his income tax bracket is lower now than it will likely ever be again. With my help, Eddie decided to make a series of Roth IRA conversions based on their current and projected tax brackets.

This strategy cannot be looked at in a vacuum. We have to consider Eddie and Emily's final decision about their Social Security benefits and come up with an integrated plan for Roth IRA conversions that will keep their taxes as low as possible. Fortunately for Eddie and Emily, the massive changes passed by Congress in 2001 actually simplified projecting Eddie's Required Minimum Distribution (RMD). Though we are oversimplifying for this case study, Eddie realized that when he turns 70, his RMD would be roughly four percent (4%) of the balance of his account. As he and Emily age, they will be required to take out more and more money from their IRA and 401(k) and pay income taxes on those withdrawals, whether they like it or not.

Investment Planning

Eddie sensed that it might not be a smart thing to keep the majority of his retirement plan in his 401(k) any longer. He was still reluctant to change the status quo until I pointed out to him that he could make a partial transfer of his 401(k). At first, he assumed it would be rolled into an IRA but was delighted to find out the advantages for him and his family if he rolls that money into his newly created one-person 401(k) plan that he set up after earning $10,000 consulting for his old company. With his one-person 401(k), he can direct his investments himself, preferably in low-cost index funds, or have them professionally managed. He can also take advantage of a great technique to make a *tax-free* Roth IRA conversion of his after-tax dollars inside his 401(k) (see www.pay-taxeslater.com for a report on this technique) and his children will be able to stretch his personal 401(k) when he and Emily die. I also explained that even though you can never get out of paying income taxes on those traditional retirement plans and IRAs, it was usually advantageous to postpone paying taxes for as long as possible, via a stretch IRA. (See Chapter 13 for an in-depth discussion on the stretch IRA. For the purposes of this case study, though, you can probably get by with just knowing that the current stretch IRA rules will allow beneficiaries to defer income taxes over their lifetimes, which could be for 40 or even 80 years after the death of the IRA owner). Eddie and Emily's children will also be able to do a Roth IRA conversion of any money that is left in the inherited 401(k). As a potential bonus, Eddie may enjoy added creditor protection because the state that he lives in affords somewhat better creditor protection to 401(k)s than IRAs. (Many practitioners, including me, think the difference in creditor protection is not significant). For now, he can also take full advantage of Lange's Cascading Beneficiary Plan— which we think is the best estate plan on the planet for Eddie and Emily as well as most couples who have only been married once, and who have children and grandchildren.

Estate Planning[1]

Eddie's new estate planning/attorney team was quick to stress that the beneficiary designation of his IRA and his 401(k)—*not his will or living trust*—determine the disposition of the retirement plan funds upon his death. Most of Eddie's assets were in retirement accounts. Thus, focusing on the design of Eddie's retirement plan beneficiary designations was the single most important portion of Eddie and Emily's estate plan.

As mentioned, they were worried about the trusts they had drafted when the exemption amount was $600,000, and Eddie had concerns about the beneficiary designation of his 401(k) and his IRA. As time passes, Eddie begins to realize that his current planning is not appropriate for his family's needs.

Eddie and Emily found out that their will and retirement plan and IRA beneficiary designation severely limited the options available to survivors and/or heirs upon either Eddie's or Emily's death. In fact, given the increases in the exemption amount, Eddie's and Emily's current estate planning documents are a disaster waiting to happen. With their old A/B trusts, if Eddie dies first, his IRA and other assets in his name go into a trust for Emily's benefit. True, Emily can draw income and invade principal for health, maintenance and support, but as it turns out the trust as drafted for them years ago is

---

[1] A discussion of taxation at the state level is beyond the limited scope of this case study; thus, all references to taxes refer to taxes at the federal level.

now a monumental mistake. Please read the section in Chapter 11 called "The Cruelest Trap of All."

Eddie wanted to know if there was some type of protection for Sarah's inheritance, to protect the assets from their no-good son-in-law. He isn't worried about leaving money directly to his son and daughter-in-law, since they both have always shared Eddie's very conservative values about money. Since he's particularly concerned about Sarah, though, we talked to Eddie about establishing the "I Don't Want My No Good Son-In-Law to Inherit One Red Cent of My Money Trust." The trust is not funded until both he and Emily die, but Eddie will rest assured knowing that his no good son-in-law will never be able to get his hands on Eddie's money. By naming a trust for Sarah's benefit as the beneficiary of his 401(k) instead of naming Sarah outright, Eddie can make sure that her no-good husband won't be spending Sarah's inheritance on a brand new Harley.

> As I was saying good night to my daughter one evening, we talked about the most important thing about *Retire Secure!* I went on about how good our number running is and our ability to make projections. She commented, "Dad, what about all of the people who will be able to live better lives because of your book? Isn't that the most important thing?" My daughter made me stop and think. I often get so lost in the material that I forget about the impact *Retire Secure!* is having on people's lives.
>
> So, please don't just read this book as an intellectual exercise. After reading the material, please implement the appropriate strategies either on your own or with the help of an advisor and put yourself and your family in a better position for the future.

Protection Planning

During the planning conference, our attorney looked at Eddie and asked him point-blank, "Do you trust your wife?" After a little kidding, he answered, "Yes." The attorney asked Emily if she trusted her husband, and Emily also answered affirmatively. The attorney then took the opportunity to explain to Eddie and Emily the keystone of an estate planning technique that seemed tailor-made for their situation: *Lange's Cascading Beneficiaries Plan*. (See Chapter 15 for more details). Now that they were comfortable with the way their retirement assets will be left to Bill and Sarah, Eddie and Emily considered that those assets would be taxable to the children when withdrawn and used. Even with all this planning, the kids will face some big income tax bills as well as potential estate and inheritance tax issues. Taking a lot of money out of the retirement plan all at once after Eddie and Emily die would not only cut short the stretch but also create a higher tax rate. What if Eddie and Emily died prematurely? They only had $50,000 in whole life insurance, and the $60,000 of term life insurance was going to become increasingly expensive to maintain. They decided to review the costs and benefits of survivorship life insurance to address these concerns.

They investigated a survivorship life insurance policy with a death benefit of $1,000,000, which amounted to 40 percent of their total estate. This amount would provide the estate and the children with sufficient liquidity to pay taxes and other expenses. This solution also allows the stretch IRA and Roth IRA to continue as long as possible, even to the grandchildren. Using a broker to search for quotes from the top-rated companies, and following a process similar to the one cited in Chapter 12, they found their premium was going to be about $14,500 per year. They had hoped for a lower premium of about $12,400 per year—which would have been possible if they had received a preferred rating on their health assessment from the insurance company. However, Eddie's cholesterol readings and extra weight would not allow that.

Even so, the $14,500 was within their budget. They could still afford to give money to the children annually or on an as-needed basis during their lifetimes. To think their children (or in Sarah's case, Sarah's trust) would be guaranteed $500,000 each at their deaths, gave comfort to Eddie and Emily that their children would be well provided for even if their spending began to reduce the savings accumulations in later years. They also realized that should they die earlier than expected, Eddie and Emily's family would be very well provided for compared to not getting the survivorship policy. They also decided that they would cancel the term insurance policy so that the premiums could be used to pay for part of the survivorship policy.

We ran the numbers to show the outcome if they buy a survivorship policy compared to gifting money to the children directly. We assumed a four percent rate of return and a 28 percent federal and state income tax rate that the children would have had to pay on the growth of the gifted money. Assuming Emily lives longer than Eddie and that she reaches age 87 (her life expectancy), the gift fund would contain $589,249, but the insurance policy will guarantee the children $1,000,000. This is an additional $410,000 for the children! In addition, life insurance proceeds are income and inheritance-tax free upon receipt. They decided to commit to the $1,000,000 survivorship life insurance policy since it was not only a great deal for the family but they also felt much more secure in using their own savings and retirement money as they needed. (See Chapter 12 for a more detailed discussion of survivorship life insurance).

Conclusions

With expert guidance, Eddie and Emily designed a retirement and estate plan that optimized their assets for themselves and eventually their children. The Engineers were relieved. Finally they had made the decisions they had been delaying for years.

A Key Lesson from this Chapter

There is a reason that the words *retirement* and *estate planning* seem to just roll off the tongue—they belong together. It is important to understand that the consequences of your decisions may have immediate, short-term, and long-term tax ramifications. Plan with the big picture in mind, and keep things flexible when you can. Integrated planning always beats out something that is cobbled together.

---

* The information contained in this case study is not intended as legal advice. Due to the personal nature of retirement and estate planning, the fictional estate plan discussed in this case may not be appropriate for another situation.

11

||||||||||||||||||||||||||||||||||||||

The Best Ways to Transfer Wealth and Cut Taxes for the Next Generation

Collecting more taxes than is absolutely necessary is legalized robbery.

— Calvin Coolidge

Main Topics

- Defining income, estate and gift taxes

- Avoiding estate and gift taxes

- The importance of annual giving

- Different types of gifts

- Tax traps on the death of the second spouse

- The problem with B trusts intended for the benefit of the spouse

- The nastiest trap of all

- Funding trusts with retirement assets

KEY IDEA

For married couples whose assets will not exceed $10 million at their deaths, the main concern is no longer the federal estate tax, but income taxes on inherited IRAs and retirement plans.

Defining Income, Estate, and Gift Taxes

In previous editions of *Retire Secure!*, I wrote about the importance of proper estate planning in order to avoid or minimize estate taxes. In the past, the federal estate tax was a huge problem. One well-known horror story involved Elvis Presley, whose net worth was about $10 million when he died. Unfortunately for his heirs, Elvis had not planned well and, after taxes, probate costs and attorney fees, they were left with less than $3 million, the majority of which came from his famous home, Graceland. The executor put Graceland up for sale, but had no buyers. The estate didn't even have enough cash to continue paying the utilities on the property and, out of economic necessity, the decision was made to turn it in to a tourist attraction. Luckily, that worked out very well for his daughter, but if it hadn't, the property would likely have been foreclosed on and Elvis' estate would have been worth nothing. The IRS has made changes in recent years that make those taxes applicable to far fewer people. So it's important to understand how taxes affect you during your lifetime, and also how they impact your family after your death.

In its simplest form, the federal gift and estate tax system is a transfer tax levied when individuals transfer assets to others during their lifetime or at their death. It is rare that individuals pay gift taxes during their lifetime. Therefore, it is much more common for the transfer tax to be imposed on the transfer of assets at their death.

Assets that you transfer to a spouse are treated differently than assets you transfer to a non-spouse. If married, you are allowed to transfer an unlimited amount of property to your U.S. citizen spouse, during his or her lifetime or at death, free of transfer taxes. This is called the Unlimited Marital Deduction. If your spouse is not a U.S. citizen, the situation is more complicated and is beyond the scope of this book.

With respect to transfers to non-spouse beneficiaries, the IRS sets the upper limit on how much money individuals are allowed to transfer to others each year and during their lifetime before they incur a transfer tax. In 2015, you are allowed to give gifts of up to $14,000 each year to one individual and a total of $5.43 million over your lifetime. If you gift more than the annual amount allowed, you are required to file a gift tax return, and the excess gift reduces the amount of your estate that will be taxable at your death. The American Taxpayer Relief Act of 2012 (ATRA) provided that the annual gift limit will be increased for inflation. ATRA also provided that the lifetime limit, formally called the Lifetime Gifting Exclusion, will equal the federal estate tax exemption. In 2015, there is a $5.43 million federal estate tax exemption. So in 2015, the Lifetime Gifting Exclusion amount that an individual can use, which allows him to transfer to non-spouse beneficiaries during his lifetime without incurring a federal gift tax is also $5.43 million. Sometimes the terms are used interchangeably, but they're really two different things. It's just important to understand that if you gift more than the annual limit, the amount of your estate that can be excluded from federal estate tax is reduced by the amount of the excess gift. Please see additional discussion under Gift Taxes later in this chapter.

The amount that you are allowed to transfer at death without incurring a federal estate tax to non-spouse beneficiaries is referred to as the Applicable Exclusion Amount. The Applicable Credit Amount (formerly, and now often incorrectly, referred to as the Unified Credit Amount) is the amount of federal estate tax that would be due on the Applicable Exclusion Amount but for the existence of the credit. In 2015, the Applicable Exclusion Amount equals $5.43 million. The Applicable Credit Amount (the amount of federal estate tax that would be due on $5.43 million but for the credit) equals $2,117,800. Married individuals may each transfer an amount equal to the Applicable Exclusion Amount to non-spouse beneficiaries. Any reduction of the Lifetime Gifting Exclusion due to excess gifts in years prior to your death will also have the effect of reducing your Applicable Exclusion Amount for estate tax purposes. (We include the historical data as well as current data to highlight the fluctuations in the amount).

Applicable Exclusion Amounts

2001	$675,000
2002	$1 million
2003	$1 million
2004	$1.5 million
2005	$1.5 million
2006	$2 million
2007	$2 million
2008	$2 million
2009	$3.5 million
2010	Estate tax is repealed
2011	$5 million
2012	$5.12 million
2013	$5.25 million
2014	$5.34 million
2015	$5.43 million

George Steinbrenner, the owner of the famed New York Yankees franchise, died on July 13, 2010 – the only year in which the federal estate tax was repealed. If he had died one year earlier or later, his widow and children would have paid an estimated $500 million to $600 million in estate taxes.

The limits in 2011 and beyond are significantly higher than the limits allowed up to 2001, which never exceeded $675,000. This means that estate plans that were drafted prior to 2002, especially those that included Marital (or A/B) Trusts, are more than likely outdated and perhaps counterproductive. We will explore this idea further a little later in this chapter. With the inherent flexibility of the estate plans our law office drafts, we are less concerned about redrafting issues than other estate firms might be.

If our office did not draft your wills and trusts, or if you have not had your estate planning documents reviewed in more than ten years, you should put that on your "to do" list. It is quite possible that your old plan won't provide for your heirs in the way you intended, and worse, it is very likely that you will seriously constrain your spouse's access to the family money. Furthermore, you could dramatically increase income taxes for the next two generations. Please read on, this is very important.

As you have seen, the Applicable Exclusion Amount has changed frequently over the years, and it is likely there will be further changes in the exemption amounts during our lifetime. Fortunately for our clients, the estate plans that we draft will survive intact in the face of most changes to the exemption amount. Let me show you how to build a flexible estate plan that accommodates scheduled changes and adapts for changes about which we can only speculate.

Please note, this book does not address the potential impact of estate taxes assessed by individual states because they are far too varied.

Prediction is very difficult, especially if it's about the future.

— Niels Bohr

Given that the Applicable Exclusion Amount is a moving target, I think the safest way to plan is to recognize that your family may or may not be subject to the federal estate tax in the future. Whether your estate will be subject to federal tax will be determined by the combination of what your estate happens to be worth at the time of your death, what the Applicable Exclusion Amount equals in the year of your death, and how well you plan. That said, unless the Applicable Exclusion Amount drops precipitously, for most readers, it will not be a significant issue—the greater challenge will be minimizing income taxes on IRAs and retirement plans.

Avoiding Estate and Gift Taxes

In the United States there are several common ways to avoid federal gift and estate taxes. The first is simply to die with less than the Applicable Exclusion Amount (subject to exceptions) in your estate. That sounds obvious, but with the shifting Applicable Exclusion Amount, it becomes problematic, and planning for individuals with total estates over $5.43 million, or estates that have the potential to grow greater than $5.43 million, becomes more challenging. Alternatively, if Congress in its infinite wisdom decides that it needs to collect even more tax revenue from its citizens, we could see lower exemption amounts again in the future. If that happens, retirees who thought they did not have enough money to worry about estate taxes may find themselves with an enormous tax problem—and they didn't even have to hit the lottery to do it.

Another way to minimize estate taxes is to make sure that you take advantage of the unlimited marital deduction. The unlimited marital deduction allows you to transfer, tax-free, an unrestricted amount of assets to your spouse at any time, even after your death. At a minimum, the unlimited marital deduction leads to a deferral of federal gift and estate taxes, and may even lead to avoiding the taxes entirely depending on your spouse's spending and the federal estate tax exemption at the time of your spouse's death. As long as your spouse is a U.S. citizen, he or she is entitled to inherit an unlimited amount of money from you, without paying any federal estate taxes. This applies to retirement plans, IRAs, and every other type of asset. As mentioned above, the state rules vary.

I will discuss additional ways to minimize and perhaps avoid federal gift and estate taxes (and state inheritance taxes) later in this chapter.

How You Can Save Millions without Spending a Nickel on Attorney Fees: The Importance of Annual Gifting

A lawyer is a learned gentleman who rescues your estate
from your enemies and keeps it himself.

— Henry Peter Brougham

I had an uncle who planned to take his money with him. Why else wouldn't he make annual gifts to his deserving children and grandchildren? Why would he allow that money to be taxed at 50 percent and make his family wait until after he died to enjoy what was left?

If your estate could possibly approach the Applicable Exclusion Amount (in 2015, $5.43 million or $10.86 million if you are married), or if you are afraid that Congress will lower the exemption amount, gifting can be an excellent strategy. Control is nice, staving off the fear of running out of money is important, but saving what could be hundreds of thousands of dollars in estate taxes for your children is also important. Of course you have to consider your own individual circumstances. If you are in a position where gifting is advisable, I offer a short description of the most basic types of gifts.

Different Types of Gifts

I like to focus on three important forms of gifts:

The most important estate planning tool for many people is simple gifting.

1. The classic maximum allowed per year per beneficiary ($14,000 in 2015), usually given to children

2. Gifts of education

3. Gifts of Second-to-Die insurance

The most important estate planning tool for many people is simple gifting. Before you even look at all the more sophisticated gifting models, seriously consider plain old, non-sexy gifts of the maximum allowed per year per beneficiary (or more, if you buy my argument below).

MINI CASE STUDY 11.1

The Measurable Benefits of Simple Gifting

Tom and Judy, both 60 years old, have two children and four grandchildren. Even though they have grown their estate to $4 million, they are relatively frugal. They live comfortably on their pensions and Social Security and they don't want Uncle Sam to get any of their hard-earned money at their deaths. At the very least, they want to drastically reduce the taxes their children will owe upon their death. Let's assume they reject all of the more sophisticated gifting techniques. They opt for simple gifts of $14,000 per year per beneficiary (with adjustments for inflation). They have six beneficiaries and each parent may give $14,000 per year per beneficiary. Thus they give away $168,000 (6 x $28,000 per donee) per year. Their plan is to continue making these gifts as long as they are comfortable with their own finances. They know that if they do nothing, they run the risk of growing too old and too rich, and may have no options left to reduce taxes.

Of course, one of the reasons this example can be debated is because we really have no way of predicting what future estate taxes are going to be. This lack of predictability is a terrible problem for estate planners, and they have different methods of handling it.

Let's consider another aspect of simple gifts. If you are married and you have sufficient assets to do so, you and your spouse can give $28,000 in 2015 to your child without eating into your combined Applicable Exclusion Amount ($10.86 million in 2015). If your child is in a committed relationship, you and your spouse can also give an equal gift to your child's partner or spouse. In 2015, that means you can give a total of $56,000 to that couple without triggering the federal gift tax currently, or affecting your Applicable Exclusion amount. But suppose that, for whatever reason, you want to give your child $100,000. Assuming that you can afford to, go ahead and give it to him.

But wait, you cry, if I give $100,000 to my child, I will eat in to my Applicable Exclusion Amount. So what? If you give a $100,000 gift to your child and only $28,000 is exempted, it is true that $72,000 of your credit will be used. If your taxable estate is not likely to reach the Exclusion Amount, does it matter if the credit is used during your lifetime or after your death? Yes, you will be required to file a separate gift tax return when you make the gift, but that is not a big deal. The significance of this is that, assuming that you can afford it, you can now give as much money as you want to your children, grandchildren, or any other person.

Notice that I said "assuming that you can afford it" when saying that it is okay to give your child a large gift. If you're the child who receives such a gift, it's a good idea to first make sure that

> **The significance of this is that, assuming that you can afford it, you can now give as much money as you want to your children, grandchildren, or any other person.**

your parent can afford to give it to you. Some people might think that it's okay to use an aggressive gifting strategy in order to prevent their assets from being seized to pay for nursing home care. That's a really bad idea. If your parent does not have nursing home insurance, they are required to use their own assets to pay for their care. Nursing home stays are very, very expensive. If your parent does not have sufficient assets to pay for their care, Medicaid will "look back" at any gifts or transfers they have made within the past five years. If any gifts were made during that period, the value is used to calculate an equivalent period of time for which your parent will be ineligible for Medicaid. If you want your parent to continue to have nursing home care, that means you'll be paying their bill out of your own pocket.

I still see a lot of parents who give gifts that are limited to the annual maximum, and I don't know why because they have more than enough money to comfortably make larger gifts. If you exceed the annual gift maximum, you have to file a gift tax return, but I don't think that's a big deal. Some people choose to limit their gifts to the annual maximum because they are afraid that the government will lower the federal exemption amount, and they'll have used up more of their lifetime limit than they planned. That's possible, but it would have to be a huge reduction in order to affect most people. I would still rather take that chance and get the money to the kids when they need it most rather than at your death. They might be too old and rich to really appreciate it like they would now.

I don't want to get into the psychology of whether it harms a child or grandchild to receive too much money too early in their development. I think that is actually a critical issue, and I have had several experts who discussed these issues on my radio show. (Please see **www.paytaxeslater.com** and click on "Listen on Demand" and scroll down to the shows that feature Roy Williams and Neale Godfrey). In my example above, I have assumed that isn't an issue for the purposes of the gift. To make it clear, I would feel better about large gifts if your children are old enough that their financial values are well formed, and you don't feel that making significant gifts would harm their personal development or motivation.

Whether your estate will be subject to federal estate will depend on the year of your death, and the taxable balance of your estate. I do not like to assume there will be a tax, nor do I want to ignore the possibility that estates that are well under the current Exclusion Amount may be subject to estate tax in the future. I like to make wise choices that work out well for the family, whether there is an estate tax or not. For whatever it is worth, most of my clients hurt themselves and their families by not gifting more until they died, or until their kids were really too old to appreciate the money. (This doesn't include the irrational parents who can't afford to support their ne'er do well children, but do anyway). On to another important type of gift.

The Gift of Education: A Favorite for Grandparents

Economists report that a college education adds many thousands of dollars to a man's lifetime income— which he then spends sending his son to college.

— Bill Vaughan

Most grandparents who can afford it (convincing them they can afford it is a different matter) like the idea of at least partially funding their grandchildren's college education.

Grandparents as well as parents can pay tuition (as well as medical expenses) directly for their children or grandchildren, and, as long as they are paid directly, these payments do not count against the $14,000 annual gift exclusion. These direct payments for tuition as well as direct payment of medical expenses could almost be considered a fourth type of major gift.

Section 529 College Savings Plans are really a variation of a gift. Section 529 plan contributions, which presumably will be used by the beneficiary for college expenses, are unique in that when you die, the proceeds of the gift and the appreciation of the gift are outside your estate. But while you are alive, you retain the power to take the money back if you like. Though I have never seen anyone take back a Section 529 plan contribution, the assurance that the donor has that option appeals to practically every grandparent.

Section 529 plans accomplish the following:

- provide income tax-free growth

- give you the freedom to change beneficiaries within the family, including first cousins

- allow you to divert the fund from the beneficiary back to the contributor and use the proceeds for non-qualifying purposes (subject to a 10 percent penalty)

- are excluded from the estate of the contributor

These four factors make deciding to invest in a Section 529 plan compelling, particularly for wealthy grandparents who want to provide for their grandchildren's education. Joe Hurley's web site, www.savingforcollege.com, is one of the best web sites, if not the best, for Section 529 plans.

Gifts of Life Insurance Premiums

You don't buy life insurance because you are going to die, but because those you love are going to live.

— Unknown Author

Many planners used to recommend Second-to-Die life insurance to pay the estate tax at the second death. I've always liked Second-to-Die life insurance for a different reason – it's so income-tax efficient. True, it was a very effective way for my clients to save estate taxes, but saving income taxes is now the better reason for most readers of this book to consider Second-to-Die life insurance. I cover this topic in detail in Chapter 12. If you can afford the premiums and are looking to pass money to the next generation, Second-to-Die insurance is worthwhile whether there is an estate tax or not. In Chapter 15, we warn of the potential death of the stretch IRA. Of course, there are many types of insurance besides Second-to-Die that are worthwhile variations of a gift. I emphasize Second-to-Die insurance because it is the classic solution, and because in general it has the lowest premium for the highest death benefit. Please note, however, I would only recommend Second-to-Die life insurance if the underlying investment in the insurance policy seemed like a reasonable investment even if it is not used to pay income or estate taxes. Usually it is. Please refer to Chapter 12 for a more detailed discussion regarding Second-to-Die or survivorship life insurance.

Variations on Gifts

There are a number of sophisticated estate planning techniques that are really variations of making a gift. They include:

- Gifts beyond Annual Exclusion gifts that consume the Lifetime Gifting Exclusion (which we discussed above)

- Family Limited Partnerships

- Grantor Retained Annuity Trusts

- Grantor Retained Unitrusts

- Intentionally Defective Grantor Trusts

- Private Annuities

- Qualified Personal Residence Trusts

- Irrevocable Trusts, including Life Insurance Trusts

- Life Insurance without trusts but owned by the heir, not the client

- Generation-Skipping Trusts

I leave discussions of most of these and other legitimate estate planning techniques for another lawyer whose clients are worried about federal estate tax because they have estates that are worth more than the Applicable Exclusion Amount.

Gift Taxes

This section could be skipped by most, but some people really want to understand the gift and estate tax and, frankly, it is tricky. If your gifts exceed the $14,000 annual exclusion amount, the excess is subject to a graduated gift tax with rates ranging up to 40 percent in 2015. To avoid owing gift tax, you may elect to deduct the excess of the gift over and above the $14,000 from your Lifetime Gifting Exclusion. For example, Daddy Donor chooses to give his son a gift of $64,000. Of that money, $14,000 takes advantage of the annual exclusion. The $50,000 is subject to the gift tax. Daddy elects to have the $50,000 deducted from his Lifetime Gifting Exclusion rather than pay the gift tax. In 2015, this leaves him with $5,380,000 that can be used for additional tax-free gifts.

It is important to make this election by filing a gift tax return, Form 709. That tells the IRS that the gift consumed part of your Lifetime Gifting Exclusion. More importantly, filing the gift tax return starts the statute of limitations on the gift. This is particularly important in the event that the value of the gift could be open to interpretation, such as a gift of an interest in a family-limited partnership, a piece of land, a business, or any other asset that by its nature is difficult to value. It is conceivable and common among proactive wealthy clients and readers to use up part or all of their Lifetime Gifting Exclusion during their lifetime, depending on the nature of their lifetime gifts to non-spouse beneficiaries.

The best strategy for wealthy clients who could end up in a taxable estate situation is to take advantage of the annual $14,000 per year per beneficiary exclusion, assuming they can comfortably afford to make those gifts. If the annual gifts of $14,000 per year are not sufficient because there is still too much money left in the estate, further gifts that consume a portion of the entire Lifetime Gifting Exclusion can still be a good idea. Though annual gifts above $14,000 will eat into the Lifetime Gifting Exclusion and reduce what may be inherited at death without tax, it also transfers out of the estate all the appreciation that would have been in the estate had the gift not been made.

MINI CASE STUDY 11.2

Gifts That Use the Total Applicable Exclusion Amount

Jill, a widow with a pension and Social Security that covers her needs, has $8 million and only one beneficiary, her daughter Lucky. Giving away $14,000 per year to Lucky is fine, but it hardly makes a dent in the potential estate tax at Jill's death. Therefore, the annual gifts of $14,000 to her daughter will not be part of this example. Instead, let's compare what happens if Jill gives Lucky $5 million this year vs. making no gift. Also, assume Jill gets 7 percent on her remaining $3 million, and she lives 10 years.

To simplify the math, use the rule of 72s, which roughly holds that Jill's money will double in 10 years. Let's also assume a flat 50 percent estate tax. If Jill gives her daughter $5 million and is left with $3 million, her estate will double to $6 million at her death. Unfortunately we cannot predict what the exclusion amount will be at the time of her death, but let's assume that it's $6 million. If the Applicable Exclusion is $6 million at the time of her mother's death, Lucky will have to pay estate tax on $5 million (total estate of $6 million plus $5 million—*the amount of the Lifetime Gifting Exclusion used*—minus $6 million—*the Applicable Exclusion Amount at Jill's death*). Assume for this example that the estate tax rate at the time of Jill's death is 50 percent. Using the flat 50 percent estate tax rate, Lucky pays $2.5 million in taxes. In the meantime, Lucky also earned 7 percent on her $5 million gift, which is worth $10 million at the time of Jill's death.

Because Jill made the gift before her death, Lucky will have $13.5 million – $6 million inheritance less $2.5 million estate taxes, plus her own $10 million.

If Jill did not make the gift, her estate would have grown to $16 million. Her exclusion amount at the time of her death is $6 million, so Lucky would have to pay tax on $10 million, which would be $5 million in estate tax. Lucky would be left with $11 million. By using the applicable Lifetime Gifting Exclusion in the prior example, Jill managed to increase Lucky's inheritance by $2.5 million.

In the real world, this concept will more likely apply to state inheritance and estate taxes, and the savings will not be as great as shown here. Jill would probably be well advised to make a leveraged gift such as a grantor retained annuity trust (GRAT), a family limited partnership (FLP), a gift of life insurance, or one of the other gifting techniques. Lawrence Katzenstein, an excellent estate attorney with a head for figures and a heart for charity, presented a wonderful original analysis at the Heckerling Institute. He showed that in many cases under the previous law, it was prudent to make a gift so large that it triggered gift taxes while the donor was still alive. The result of the gift and the gift tax paid was a reduction of the overall tax burden at death. The problem with using that analysis today hinges on the uncertainty of future investments and, perhaps more importantly, future changes in the amount of the federal exemption. If a couple who had $6 million had taken that advice earlier, they would have unnecessarily paid gift taxes when there is little likelihood of them having to pay federal estate taxes. I would hate to see you pay gift tax now and then later, through changes in the law and/or in your portfolio, find out that you would not have been subject to estate taxes anyway.

In prior years, the Lifetime Gifting Exclusion was less than the Applicable Exclusion amount. This meant that, if you gave away more than the Lifetime Giving amount, you would have triggered an immediate gift tax problem. This changed with the American Taxpayer Relief Act, which made the Lifetime Giving Amount the same as the Applicable Exclusion amount. Unfortunately, that limit does change. Once your excess lifetime gifts are greater than the Lifetime Gifting Exclusion, the excess cannot be applied to the Applicable Exclusion Amount, but rather you must pay the gift tax.

The Importance of Having After-Tax Dollars to Pay Taxes and Expenses

There is an entire world of literature just on gifting, both simple and sophisticated techniques. I include this brief summary because it is such an important area. It is also particularly important for large estates that are IRA heavy. If clients follow my advice and spend (or give away) their after-tax dollars before their IRA dollars, they will be left with IRA dollars at the end of their lives. Many readers have large IRAs and not much else. The current estate tax thresholds are high enough that few individuals have to worry about estate taxes, but this is worth mentioning for wealthier individuals or if the threshold is reduced in future years. If you die with nothing but IRA dollars, and your heirs need money after you die for expenses, taxes, or even their own personal needs, they will have to go into the inherited IRA. When they go into the inherited IRA, the distribution triggers income tax. In addition to the immediate income tax on the withdrawal from the inherited IRA, beneficiaries lose the opportunity to stretch (defer taxes) on the inherited IRA to the maximum possible. Of course, if the "Death of the Stretch IRA" legislation passes (see Chapter 15), then this problem of accelerated income taxes will become a nightmare for beneficiaries of IRAs and retirement plans.

Worse yet, if a beneficiary has to make withdrawals from the inherited IRA to pay estate costs, he'll end up in a horrendous situation where the withdrawal from the IRA triggers federal and possibly state income tax, and when the only source of paying the income tax is the IRA, then further withdrawals will trigger more taxes—withdrawals and taxes ad nauseam. This is a circular calculation that makes me want to weep. If you know that your estate will be subject to estate settlement costs, it is particularly important to make sure that there are after-tax dollars available to pay them. Preferably, the money available to pay those costs will be in the hands of the heir no later than when the estate is settled. That is, during the life of the IRA owner, he makes gifts (either simple, sophisticated, or through life insurance) to his beneficiary so that the beneficiary will have a stack of after-tax money on hand to pay any estate costs. In the event the IRA owner dies in a situation where, because of the increased Applicable Exclusion Amount, there is no tax, there is nothing lost; in the case of Second-to-Die life insurance, it can be an excellent investment for the family with or without the estate tax.

MINI CASE STUDY 11.3

Using Life Insurance to Pay Estate Taxes

Joe and Carol, both 70 and in good health, have an estate of $6 million consisting mainly of Joe's IRA. In addition to their portfolio, they have a pension and Social Security income. Depending on a number of factors, there is a reasonable chance that their family will never pay estate taxes when Joe and Carol die. On the other hand, legislative changes may be enacted that make it a possibility.

They are interested in passing on a significant amount of money to their heirs. They examine the benefits of a Second-to-Die life insurance policy. They decide they can safely afford the premiums for $500,000 worth of coverage. They know that one of the benefits of the coverage is that upon the second death, their beneficiaries will receive $500,000 free of income and estate taxes. If they have a taxable estate, that $500,000 could go to pay the taxes and expenses, and the beneficiaries would be able to preserve the stretch IRA. This is a classic and effective planning strategy.

Suppose that at the second death, the amount of the survivor's estate is less than the Applicable Exclusion Amount so that the only costs will be the expenses of administering the estate and the state inheritance tax. The $500,000 purchase of the Second-to-Die policy will still have been a good decision because, assuming a good and appropriate choice of policy, it is a good way of passing on wealth even in the absence of the estate tax.

The idea of buying life insurance may not be appealing to some readers, but the fact remains that it can be a very effective way to pass wealth to the next generation. If your estate is "IRA heavy," and you don't have a lot of assets outside of your retirement plan, I encourage you to examine the numbers in the

Second-to-Die analysis before rejecting the idea out of hand. If you can't afford to pay the premiums, your beneficiaries might want to consider doing it for you since it will ultimately protect their inheritance.

Some financial advisors have "pension rescue" programs. Under the right circumstances, these programs are a good idea. They are variants of what is recommended in the gifting section.

The pension rescue involves taking a portion of your IRA, paying tax on the IRA distribution while you are still alive, and giving the proceeds to your beneficiaries. This serves to reduce your estate and to provide your beneficiaries with after-tax dollars to pay any estate taxes. This strategy is often combined with the purchase of life insurance (often a Second-to-Die policy) where the proceeds from the IRA distributions are given as gifts to children (usually through a trust) to purchase life insurance on the parents. When the policy matures (in other words, when both parents die), the insurance proceeds are distributed to the children who can then use the proceeds to pay any estate taxes or other expenses.

Conceptually, pension rescue is similar to a Roth IRA conversion. In both cases, the IRA owner is paying taxes *sooner* to move money into an environment, either the Roth IRA or the insurance policy, where it will grow income tax-free. The advantage of the Roth IRA conversion is that it will benefit the IRA owner as well as his heirs. The benefit of the pension rescue is that unlike a Roth IRA, the proceeds of the policy, if set up correctly, will be outside the estate.

Get Rid of Those Old A/B Trusts

One method of minimizing federal estate taxes in the past had been to draft a trust where upon the death of the first spouse, one Applicable Exclusion Amount was moved into the trust so that the estate was protected from estate taxes on that amount. This traditional estate plan used two separate trusts: the A trust (Marital Trust) and the B trust (Unified Credit Trust). The surviving spouse had the right to use any and all income and principal from the A trust. Typically the spouse's access to the B trust was limited; he or she received the income from the trust, but could only invade the principal for health, education, maintenance, and support. Sometimes there was a "5 and 5" clause, meaning the surviving spouse could also invade the principal of the trust for the greater of $5,000 or 5 percent of the corpus or principal of the trust. If, when the second spouse died, his or her total assets, in combination with the A trust, equaled more than the Applicable Exclusion Amount, the money would be subject to federal estate taxes. On the other hand, because the B trust was not owned by the surviving spouse, the B trust was not considered part of the second spouse's federal estate and was, therefore, not subject to estate tax at his or her death.

This was high-tech planning ten years ago, but the American Taxpayer Relief Act of 2012 introduced a concept called portability that makes it completely unnecessary. Portability means that if the first spouse dies and the value of their estate does not require the use of the deceased spouse's entire Applicable Exclusion Amount (which is $5.43 million in 2015), then the unused amount of their exemption can be transferred to the surviving spouse. This is called the Deceased Spouse's Unused Exclusion Amount (DSUEA). So let's say that your spouse dies in 2015 and leaves $5 million to you, and $3.43 million to your children. There is no federal estate tax due at your spouse's death, because there is no limit to the amount of money that you can leave to your spouse, and the amount that was left to your children is less than his Applicable Exclusion Amount. And, since your spouse didn't use $2 million of the $5.43 million exemption he was entitled to, it is transferred to you. If you also die in 2015, you can leave an estate of up to $7.43 million (your own $5.43 million plus your spouse's unused $2 million), and it will not be subject to federal estate tax either.

> Wow! This can be a confusing chapter but it is very important to complete your estate planning. Take your time and read this chapter twice if you need to. Although it is not pleasant to think about your passing on, it's important to anticipate the needs of your heirs. After all, none of us get out alive. You want to be sure your family will continue to be taken care of after you are gone.

The Cruelest Trap of All

What follows is an analysis of how bad it can be if you have fairly standard wills and trusts that you have not updated within the past five years. The quick analysis: It is nasty. The quick conclusion for clients with traditional documents and estates of less than $5.43 million: It is time to review your wills and trusts.

The problem lies in the use of confusing but commonly included language "the spouse shall receive an amount equal to the maximum marital deduction amount available after taking into account the applicable credit amount." What a mouthful! But if your will and/or trust uses a formula indicating the maximum marital deduction with language like this, chances are that, under current law, the document requires the dreaded mandatory funding of the B (exemption equivalent) trust, even if funding it is no longer a good idea. Unfortunately, many old wills and trusts do contain this language (or similar language), and in light of the higher exemption amounts, it creates a terrible trap for the surviving spouse. With the higher exemption amounts now in place, you must take action and reevaluate your wills, trusts, beneficiary designations, IRAs, etc. Don't let your inertia compromise your spouse's comfort after your death.

The Details of the Nasty Provision

Let's assume the will or revocable trust or beneficiary designation of the IRA or retirement plan creates a trust (B trust, Unified Credit Amount Trust) as described above. Upon the death of the first spouse, the Applicable Exclusion Amount is automatically paid into this trust. Though this isn't mechanically accurate for the purpose of the IRAs or retirement plans, it is conceptually accurate. The trust will pay income to the surviving spouse for his or her life and provide the right to additional money for the health, maintenance, and support of the spouse. The trust may even allow the spouse to invade the principal for $5,000 or 5 percent of the trust, whichever is greater, and may have additional provisions allowing invasion of principal for children or grandchildren, if needed. At the death of the surviving spouse, the trust is usually distributed to the children equally.

Under the old law, this type of trust helped save a lot of money on estate taxes, but unfortunately, under the new law, it creates a trap for the surviving spouse. Most of these trusts are structured so that:

1. The Applicable Exclusion Amount (it was $1 million in 2003, and now is $5.43 million in 2015) is distributed to the trust.

2. The balance of the estate (if any) is distributed to the surviving spouse.

The complication is that as the Applicable Exclusion Amount increased and the concept of portability was introduced, fewer and fewer second estates will be large enough to be subject to federal estate taxes. Thus, if the first spouse leaves everything to the second spouse, at the death of the second spouse the combined estates may still be under the threshold of the amount subject to federal estate tax. The raised exemption amounts mean fewer estates will be subject to estate tax, which means fewer estates will benefit from this trust. The spouse or family may not benefit from this trust, but the trust may be activated anyway because of the language in the will.

If you have the type of documents that will force an amount equivalent to (or less than) the Applicable Exclusion Amount into the B trust, this may mean that your existing documents will put most—if not all—of your assets into the trust, severely constraining the finances of your surviving spouse. There are some circumstances where these old trusts are still preferable even considering the higher exemption amount, but this is obviously a topic that should be reviewed by an attorney who has expertise in this field.

Nastiest trap of all

Unintentionally Disinheriting the Surviving Spouse

Let's assume that we have a husband whose IRA is worth $1.43 million and his wills and trusts haven't been updated for years. The beneficiary of his IRA is his exemption-equivalent-type trust. If he dies in 2015, and his will has the confusing but common language I mentioned above, all of the money would go into the trust at his death. This is because the Applicable Exclusion Amount is $5.43 million in 2015. If the IRA is the couple's main asset, we have just created a financial catastrophe, because all of the wife's money is now controlled by the trust.

Many surviving spouses will be unhappy to find that as a result of the increased exemption amounts, more money is going to a trust for their benefit and less money is going directly to them. There is a strong chance the surviving spouse would prefer to have the money directly rather than in trust, particularly when there is no tax-savings benefit of the trust. In this instance, a simple "I love you" will or beneficiary designation of the IRA or retirement plan would have been sufficient to avoid estate taxes at the second death.

"I love you" wills are quite common and serve an important purpose. The will says, "I leave everything to my spouse, and my spouse leaves everything to me." At the second death the money is divided equally among the children.

In the above example, having a simple "I love you" will would have been sufficient to avoid estate tax. At the first death, the surviving spouse would have received the $1.3 million and used the unlimited marital deduction to avoid estate taxes. At the second death, the surviving spouse's total estate will likely be less than the Applicable Exclusion Amount. Thus, there will be no estate tax and no messing around with an unnecessary trust. Not only was the entire complicated estate plan misguided and unnecessary, it also poses serious problems for the surviving spouse and the rest of the family.

Though it is not overly costly to draft these trusts, living with them after the death of the first spouse until the second death is far more costly in terms of fees (at a minimum, you have to prepare a special annual trust tax return), aggravation, and restrictions on the surviving spouse. Most surviving spouses want control of all the assets of the marriage and don't want to deal with a trustee to get access to their money. Although loss of control is less of an issue when the surviving spouse or family member is the trustee of the B trust, the trust can still pose unnecessary expenses depending on the surviving spouse's circumstances at the time of the first spouse's death. With the rapidly changing estate tax exemption amounts, the vagaries of the stock market, and the big unknowns such as "When will you die?" and "How much money will be in your estate?," you could incur burdensome and unnecessary expenses *and* lose control of your money. Worse yet, there is no benefit at all from the estate plan for that couple. Individuals who have plans similar to the one referenced above are advised to consider the benefits of revising their estate plans.

While there are advantages and disadvantages to the B trust, a good solution to the problem is provided in Chapter 15.

What If Retirement Assets Will Fund the Trust?

What if the assets that fund the trust are retirement assets (IRAs, 401(k)s, 403(b)s, etc.)? Then, after the IRA owner dies, the Required Minimum Distribution from the trust is based on the life expectancy of the surviving spouse. At the death of the surviving spouse, the children are required to maintain distributions at the rate established when the surviving spouse was alive. Under the old rules, the result was an enormous acceleration of distributions from the retirement plan. Does this mean that a trust is a bad thing? Not necessarily, but I'm going to refer you to Chapter 13 for more details about that.

A Key Lesson from This Chapter

Don't get caught with an estate plan that automatically transfers the Applicable Exclusion Amount into a B trust. Sometimes that type of plan is just bad, other times disastrous, although admittedly in some circumstances, it may be okay.

12

||||||||||||||||||||||||||||||||||

Providing Financial Security for Your Children through Life Insurance

Money is one of the most important subjects of your entire life. Some of life's greatest enjoyments and most of life's greatest disappointments stem from your decisions about money. Whether you experience great peace of mind or constant anxiety will depend on getting your finances under control.

— Robert G. Allen

Main Topics

- Who should read this chapter?

- Life insurance is a gift for your heirs

- Understanding the basics of gifting using life insurance

- Advantages and disadvantages of purchasing a life insurance policy

- A quick reminder about the taxes due at death

- What is second-to-die life insurance?

- Mini-case studies

- Ways to make life insurance even more beneficial

KEY IDEA

Survivorship life insurance can be an excellent strategy for transferring wealth to your heirs.

Who Should Read This Chapter?

This chapter will be most relevant for married couples who have more than enough resources to provide for each other during their lifetimes. This chapter is not about using life insurance to ensure the comfort and security of your surviving spouse. If you still have significant worries that you and/or your spouse may run out of money during your lifetimes, this chapter isn't for you.

If you are married, there may be a need for life insurance on one or both of you. This chapter isn't about that either. This chapter assumes that you and your spouse have more than enough money to support the lifestyle you choose for your lifetimes, and you are interested in using what remains to provide for the financial security of your children or grandchildren.

Life Insurance is a Gift to Your Heirs

When evaluated at its most basic level in terms of your heirs, life insurance is a gift. If you don't think you can afford to give your children a gift of any kind, then this analysis is over right now, and you should not consider buying life insurance. That said, if you can afford it and want to make a long-term gift to your children, there is no better and more certain long-term gift than the gift of life insurance.

It is important to put life insurance and gifting in context. Life insurance is only one type of gift, and should not be the only type of gift for your family. In most cases, I usually like a three-pronged gifting strategy.

1. Gifts of cash or securities for whatever purposes your children want (gifts for short-term use) that are consistent with your values.

2. Section 529 plans, or the gift of education for your grandchildren.

3. Life insurance (in particular, Second-to-Die insurance).

Frequently, by combining these three strategies, my clients receive the satisfaction of seeing their heirs enjoy their generosity, while at the same time ensuring their offspring's financial security in the future.

In Mini Case Study 11.3, we discussed in general terms how survivorship life insurance (also known as Second-to-Die life insurance) can benefit the family when the bulk of the estate is in retirement plans. Let's now look at some specifics.

The insurance proceeds (the death benefit) are paid after the death of both the husband and the wife, or in insurance parlance, "when the policy matures." The death benefit, usually paid to a trust for the benefit of the children or to the children directly, can provide easily accessed cash that can be used to pay taxes and expenses without the executor having to sell other assets at fire sale prices to raise money. What remains after paying taxes and expenses, is typically used for the children's benefit. The classic advice for individuals with an estate that is heavy with IRA and retirement plans is to purchase life insurance. Estates with large IRAs and life insurance are both good things, in and of themselves, but the combination of the two often provides the best estate plan available. In my practice, I have found this to be particularly true when exploring options for clients who have large IRAs and who believe that the "death of the stretch IRA" is imminent. Purchasing life insurance, however, can also be a useful wealth-creating, wealth-preserving, and wealth-transferring technique even for estates that are not IRA heavy and that may never be subject to estate tax and high expenses.

Before we get into the nitty-gritty of analyzing life insurance, and particularly the impact of the potential "death of the stretch IRA" legislation as it relates to the use of life insurance, I thought I would tell you about an email I received from Ed Slott, CPA, who is probably the best known IRA expert in the country.

> **The classic advice for individuals with an estate that is heavy with IRA and retirement plans is to purchase life insurance.**

Ed wrote:

> *Eliminating the stretch IRA will wake people up to do the planning they probably should have been doing all along. That means more IRA money will be withdrawn and leveraged to tax-free vehicles like life insurance that are even better than the stretch IRA...(In addition) life insurance is a much easier and more efficient vehicle to fund a trust with, compared to an IRA.*

I've been evaluating the use of life insurance for my own estate planning clients, and I have to agree with Ed. Life insurance can frequently provide favorable alternatives for beneficiaries if the stretch IRA is eliminated. In order to understand why, you need to have basic knowledge of life insurance, and how it is used for gifting.

Understanding the Basics of Gifting using Life Insurance

A life insurance policy is a contract that has three parties to it. You and/or your spouse are generally the insured(s), and it is at your death(s) that the policy will pay the benefit to your beneficiaries. Your beneficiaries might be your children or grandchildren, or trusts that you have established for their benefit. You and/or your spouse are also generally, but not always, the owner(s) of the policy. The owner is the individual who handles the administrative duties of the policy, such as making the premium payments, filling out beneficiary forms, etc. In many cases, you will be both the owner and the insured, but that's not always the case. In the past, the ownership of life insurance policies could sometimes cause concerns because, if you were the owner in addition to being the insured, the policy was considered part of your taxable estate. Since the exemption amounts have increased, owning life insurance is an issue for far fewer people. If estate taxes are a concern for you, though, there are some things you can do to get the policy out of your taxable estate. The rules about this are very complicated, and I strongly recommend that you talk with a knowledgeable advisor about it. The important thing to remember is that, when you are reviewing your own estate plan with your attorney, do not forget to include life insurance contracts when disclosing your assets.

Usually, you and your spouse pay the premiums for the policy, which are viewed as gifts under IRS rules. If you follow the rules, your children will get the death benefit income, inheritance, and estate tax-free. Therefore, the purchase of life insurance should be looked at as a technique to transfer wealth for the long-term benefit of your children in the most tax-efficient method possible.

The Advantages of Life Insurance

Insurance salesmen are often maligned and are frequently the topic of some pretty bad jokes. At the risk of being categorized with those poor men and women, I'll tell you that I don't hesitate to recommend life insurance to many of my own clients after evaluating their estate planning needs. Why? Because when it is structured properly, life insurance has a number of benefits that make it an excellent and sometimes the best possible wealth transfer strategy. This doesn't mean that I recommend life insurance so that your heirs will receive even more money when you die. I frequently recommend

> When it is structured properly, life insurance has a number of benefits that make it an excellent and sometimes the best possible wealth transfer strategy.

life insurance so that one's heirs, and not the government, will receive the money that is already yours.

Here's why I consider life insurance for my clients, assuming that they have more money than they are likely to need during their lifetimes.

1. The proceeds from the insurance are free from income taxes and, assuming it is properly set up outside of the estate, which is easy to do, it is free of state and federal estate, inheritance, or transfer taxes. Because of these tremendous tax-free features (some would say loopholes), life insurance is one of the best legal tax shelters around.

2. Without life insurance, many of our clients are reluctant to enjoy their lives and spend their money freely because they feel like they may be spending their children's inheritance. Life insurance policies guaranteeing a death benefit for your children can give you the peace of mind to freely spend as much money as you want to, while knowing that your children will be still provided for after your death.

3. Income taxes are generally due on April 15, and estate and inheritance taxes are generally due nine months after death. If your assets are not liquid by nature (for example, real estate or a family business) or are invested in stocks that happened to have declined in value at the time of your death, life insurance can provide sufficient cash to pay those taxes. Without it, your heirs may be forced to hold a fire sale and liquidate your assets for far less than what they are worth, just to raise cash to pay taxes. A detailed example of the tax problem follows a little later.

4. On a related note, life insurance can also facilitate equalizing distributions among family members when only one beneficiary is going to inherit the family business and cash is needed to make the other beneficiaries' shares equal.

5. Similarly, you may have real estate such as a vacation home that you would like to keep in the family. After you are gone, there may be a continued need for cash to fund the upkeep of the property. Life insurance policies can provide the needed liquidity to maintain the property in the family for many years. We had a client who had a beautiful second home on a lake that he wanted to keep in the family but didn't know where the money would come from to maintain the property. The solution was a Second-to-Die life insurance policy. Fair warning about estate planning for second homes: we sometimes spend as much time planning for modest cabins or vacation homes as we do in planning for the $1+ million IRA because that is what people want to talk about.

6. Most of your assets are in traditional retirement accounts. At your death, cash will be needed to pay federal income tax, state death taxes and the estate administration costs. If your heirs have to withdraw money from traditional retirement accounts to pay these expenses, income tax will be owed on the withdrawal. Then they will have to withdraw even more money from the IRA to pay those taxes. Life insurance can help keep the IRA in a tax-deferred status for as long as possible, for the surviving family members.

7. Life insurance is a useful asset to have as part of your estate plan if you have some type of trust as a beneficiary. Only the interest and dividends earned on the life insurance proceeds are taxable income to your beneficiary (or to the trust created for the benefit of your beneficiary), whereas distributions from retirement accounts (other than Roth IRAs) are 100 percent taxable. Most individuals pay income taxes at a lower rate than trusts do, and naming a trust as the beneficiary of your taxable retirement account can be a very bad move if it is not done correctly. Sometimes, though, there are considerations other than taxes that are far more important. One example is protecting a disabled beneficiary who is currently receiving public assistance benefits. If the beneficiary is left money outright in your will, he may be disqualified from receiving any more benefits. Distributions from the trust that are made for non-qualifying reasons may also cause him to

The return (or death benefit) from a life insurance policy is guaranteed. If you want to add safety to your estate, life insurance will almost always have a better return than the vast majority of fixed-income investments.

lose public assistance benefits. By having life insurance as part of the plan, the family can minimize taxes for the disabled beneficiary while providing the best income tax deferral possibilities from the retirement benefits to the other beneficiaries.

8. Part of the financial security provided for the family by life insurance is that the return (or death benefit) from a life insurance policy is guaranteed. If you want to add safety to your estate, life insurance will almost always have a better return than the vast majority of fixed-income investments. If your family's investment returns are lower than the guarantee, the insurance will have an even greater advantage because the death benefit is not contingent on a particular rate of return.

The Disadvantages of Life Insurance

If you are considering purchasing life insurance, you must also consider the disadvantages of doing so.

1. First, let's go back to the basics. Life insurance is still a variation of a gift, and if you don't want to or can't afford to make the gift, then life insurance is probably not appropriate for you or your family.

2. Another problem with life insurance is that the heirs, usually your children, are likely to have better uses for money while they are young and you are still alive. Therefore, if you can afford a gift, the strategy of just making simple gifts to your children so they can spend and enjoy it while they are young has a natural appeal.

3. To expand on that thought, if later in your lives you can't afford to continue these gifts (by paying the premiums due), you could potentially regret buying the insurance. This problem is partly tempered by the fact that if that happens, your children will probably want to continue the premium payments themselves in order to receive their inheritance. If that happens, it's not a gift, but potentially a financial burden for them.

4. If you have a Second-to-Die (or survivorship) policy, both spouses must be committed to paying premiums all their lives. If one spouse dies and the survivor does not continuing paying the premiums, then

the policy will lapse. The premium payments that had been made up to that point will have been a waste of money.

Remember, your expenses can increase in your later years because of medical bills and/or the cost of nursing home care. Before you purchase life insurance, it is a good idea to consult with a financial professional who can run the numbers for you and make sure that you will be able to pay the premiums comfortably for the rest of your life.

A Quick Reminder about Taxes that Are Due at Death

Federal and state taxes are often avoided at the death of the first spouse, but there could be a need for easily accessible cash to pay taxes at the death of the second spouse. A life insurance policy can provide the needed funds. Life insurance can be especially helpful if the bulk of the remaining estate is in an IRA or other pre-tax investments that are subject to tax after death. Federal and state inheritances taxes are a problem for fewer people now than in previous years but, if they are due on the second estate, there can be multiple prongs of federal and state income tax, and federal estate and state inheritance taxes, which could cause the marginal tax rate on the retirement funds in the estate to rise well above 50 percent:

Potential income taxes on retirement funds	39.6%
Federal estate taxes	40.0%
State inheritance taxes (PA, for example)	4.5%
Potential marginal tax rate	84.1%

It should be noted that income taxes could be more in states that tax retirement fund withdrawals. State inheritance taxes could also be more or less, depending on the residency of the IRA owner at death. We'll cover more about the reasons why in Chapter 13, but the more likely problem right now for most beneficiaries is not estate tax, but income tax.

In our practice, the Roth IRA conversion and Second-to-Die life insurance are not competing strategies, but complementary strategies.

The solution that goes the farthest to avoid the double tax hit of federal estate tax and income tax is a life insurance policy. This is the classic solution for estates that will be subject to taxes and that are IRA heavy. As a consequence, it is a common strategy for advisors to recommend taking withdrawals from the IRA, paying income tax now on the withdrawals, and using the net proceeds to purchase a Second-to-Die life insurance policy. Conceptually, this is quite similar to making a Roth conversion, where you pay the income tax up front to get income tax-free growth in the future. In a way, the life insurance is better because if it is set up correctly, it is outside the IRA owner's estate, unlike a Roth IRA which is included in the Roth IRA owner's estate. In our practice, the Roth IRA conversion and life insurance are not competing strategies, but complementary strategies.

The strategy of taking IRA dollars, paying taxes now, and using the proceeds to purchase life insurance (with some variations) is commonly known as pension rescue. This strategy was previously described in the Chapter 11. With the pending "death of the stretch IRA" law, pension rescue now makes more sense than ever.

What is Second-to-Die Life Insurance?

There is a special type of policy that I love to use with married couples that is called Second-to-Die (or Survivorship Life). I prefer this type of policy because the premiums are low relative to the face amount or death benefit, even though the annual premium must be paid every year until the death of the second spouse. And, Second-to-Die policies are typically less costly in terms of annual premiums than single-life policies.

Those facts might cause a cynic to ask, "If the premiums are so low and it seems so advantageous for the family, how does the insurance company make any money?" First, the insurance company realizes tremendous tax benefits with the premium funds that are not available to the individual insurance buyer. The insurance company collects and maintains large reserves of premiums, but does not pay any income tax on the investment income earned on that money. If you just invested the money for your premium payment yourself, or if you made gifts to your children and your children invested the money, there would be income tax on dividends, interest, and capital gains.

Furthermore, there is something else that is going on in the pricing of Second-to-Die life insurance that heavily favors the consumer. As with all types of insurance, many policies lapse or lose their guarantee when people stop paying for them. When the owner of a policy stops paying the premium, the insurance company is no longer obligated to honor the guarantee they have in the contract. The insurance companies know that a large percentage of their sold policies will lapse or lose their guarantee, so they take that into consideration when determining their premiums. This allows the rates others pay for insurance to be lower.

But why would so many people let a Second-to-Die insurance policy lapse? Here's my theory. The math on the Second-to-Die policy usually seems extremely favorable and attractive to the more quantitative person in the marriage. Sometimes the other spouse prefers to see their children get the money as gifts now, instead of using it to pay premiums. (Our preference is that parents diversify their gifts to their children so the children will get some money now, even if their parents do opt for the insurance). The money person persists, and the other spouse grudgingly goes along with the decision to purchase the Second-to-Die insurance. The spouse who wanted to purchase the insurance dies first and the surviving spouse, who never liked the idea of the insurance in the first place, then stops paying premiums. The insurance company becomes the big winner. If you decide to go with the Second-to-Die insurance, please be prepared to pay premiums for the rest of both of your lives. If not, don't waste your money by buying this type of insurance policy.

> **If you decide to go with the Second-to-Die insurance, please be prepared to pay premiums for the rest of both of your lives.**

In 2013, the National Association of Insurance Commissioners put into effect new guidelines for insurance companies to maintain certain minimum reserves for the Guaranteed No Lapse provisions used in their policies in the past decade. The Guaranteed No Lapse provision doesn't mean that your policy can never lapse – you still have to pay for it, and it will lapse if you don't. What it means is that your insurance company has set aside sufficient reserves to comply with these new guidelines (called AG 38), and that payment at the second death is guaranteed regardless of age. These new guidelines caused some carriers to re-price their Second-to-Die or survivorship plans, or even stop selling them completely. So if you have looked at a Second-to-Die plan in the past and decided against it, you may find it is no longer available from the company you were dealing with, or that it is more expensive now than when you had considered it before.

Now we get into the nitty-gritty and run the numbers to analyze a survivorship policy. We start with a case study, which compares the advantages of paying the premiums to the insurance company in exchange for the death benefit, to the advantages of investing the premiums and including them as part of the estate.

MINI CASE STUDY 12.1

Quantifying the Advantages of Purchasing a Survivorship Life Insurance Policy

Consider the case of Robert and Mary Jones. Robert has just retired at age 65. Mary is 64. Robert rolled his 401(k) plan balance into an IRA to provide him with more investment flexibility. Robert and Mary have spent their working lives making a comfortable living for their family and funding Robert's 401(k) with the maximum allowable contributions. Robert and Mary have saved additional money outside his retirement plans. Their lifetime of diligent savings has resulted in total accumulations of $1,500,000 in Robert's IRA upon retirement and $200,000 in after-tax money and investments. They receive Social Security income of $28,000 and $22,000, respectively, and Mary has a teacher's pension income of $32,000 per year. They spend $100,000 per year after income taxes, which includes a system of planned gifting for their children and grandchildren. After going over their retirement and estate plan, Robert and Mary investigated the potential advantages of getting a life insurance policy for the benefit of their children and their grandchildren. Robert and his wife are active seniors, but have some medical problems that prevent them from qualifying for preferred rates on a survivorship life insurance policy. After a health examination revealed them to be non-smokers of average health for their ages, their premium is $14,337 per year for a $1,000,000 Second-to-Die policy.

In Mary and Robert's case, their estate is not large enough to be subject to federal estate taxes.

Figure 12.1 on page 248 illustrates that, the longer that Robert and Mary live and continue to pay premiums, the less beneficial the life insurance policy becomes. Assume that Mary survives Robert and dies at the age of 90. The advantage to their children at her death after paying premiums for twenty years is not $1 million – it's $218,588. And at her age 94, the cost of the premiums paid over the decades outweighs the benefit paid to their children at Mary's death.

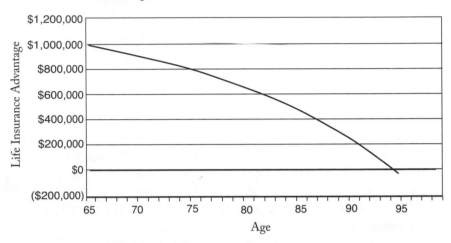

Figure 12.1
Advantage of $1 Million Survivorship Policy
Assuming 6% Return and No Federal Estate Tax

But suppose Congress gets their way and eliminates the Stretch IRA? Figure 12.2 illustrates what happens if a parent leaves a retirement account worth $1 million to a child who is in the 28% tax bracket, and the child is required to withdraw all of the money from the account within five years. Assuming that there are no other assets from which the child can pay the taxes, look at the difference that life insurance can make.

Figure 12.2
Long-Term Value of Life Insurance to Beneficiaries

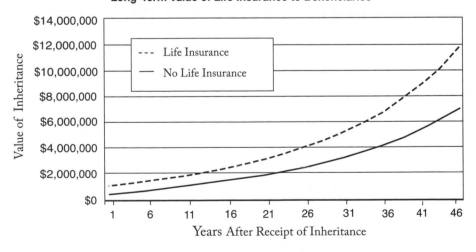

Even if the child tries to spread out the withdrawals at a relatively equal rate of about $225,000 per year, his individual tax rate jumps to 33% during the years of distribution. This is because the child has income of his own and, when the IRA distribution is added to his normal wage income, he is pushed in to a higher tax bracket.

In our practice, we have many retired clients whose adult children are stretched to the limits because the costs of sending their own children to college are greater than they bargained for. Some have little or no savings outside of their own retirement plans and, for them, receiving life insurance in addition to the IRA would provide them with liquid funds to pay the tax due on their inheritance. On the other hand, I have clients who feel that the income tax is their child's problem, and they should be grateful for what they do receive.

Different Amounts of Death Benefits

While many individuals will consider a $1 million policy, there is no rule that the death benefit must be $1 million. In our practice, purchasing $1 million policies is fairly common and most of our clients are older than Robert and Mary. For many clients, we determine the death benefit by working backwards. For example, we might have a situation where the family feels they can afford $10,000 per year in premiums and with that as a starting point, we see how much insurance they can get for that annual premium.

Ways to Make Life Insurance Even More Beneficial

Before wrapping up this chapter, I would like to let you in on some things we do in our own estate planning practice related to life insurance. One strategy that I really like is to combine life insurance with multigenerational planning. As we will discuss in Chapter 13, under current law, an inherited IRA is worth more to a young beneficiary than to an older beneficiary. That law may change, but as we went to press, an inherited IRA is currently worth more to your grandchildren than to your children (the increased benefit is "time-held" related). One of the benefits of the Second-to-Die insurance is that the insurance proceeds can be used to fund or partially fund the needs of your children, and your inherited IRA, or at least a portion of your inherited IRA can go into well-drafted trusts for the benefit of your grandchildren. This is such a technical subject that I could devote an entire book to it, but instead I will give you a brief quantification of life insurance to the third generation even if the children keep the insurance and the IRAs and the grandchildren don't get anything until the children die. Figure 12.3 below shows the difference that a $1 million life insurance policy can make to the third generation of heirs, comparing both the current law and the proposed legislation that requires Inherited IRAs to be liquidated within five years.

Figure 12.3
Benefits of Life Insurance to Second and Third Generations

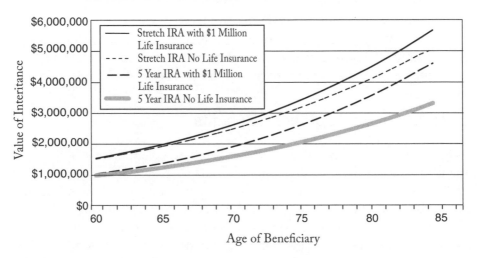

This illustration assumes that your child inherits your estate when she is age 60, and she invests it at an average rate of return of six percent. She dies at age 85, and leaves your estate to her own children. This graph shows that, whatever happens regarding the death of the stretch IRA, your grandchildren can be significantly better off if your own children received life insurance as part of their inheritance from you.

Chapter 15 introduces a concept called disclaiming, which allows your children to decide how much of your IRA should go to them and how much should go directly to your grandchildren after your death. If your children disclaimed part of the inherited IRA to your grandchildren, and we had factored the advantages of a multigenerational strategy into our example above, the benefits of life insurance, especially Second-to-Die insurance, would increase significantly.

Now let's take this one step further. Suppose you do believe that the government is going to do away with the Stretch IRA. Chapter 17 suggests a possible alternative to prolong your distributions, specifically by adding a Charitable Remainder Unitrust (CRUT) to your estate plan. We examine that strategy in detail in Chapter 17, but for now, please review Figure 12.4 below, which shows how life insurance can be used to benefit your children if you do establish a Charitable Remainder Unitrust that provides income to them for as long as they live, and the remainder goes to a charity when they die.

Figure 12.4

Benefits of Life Insurance When IRA Beneficiary is a Charitable Remainder Unitrust

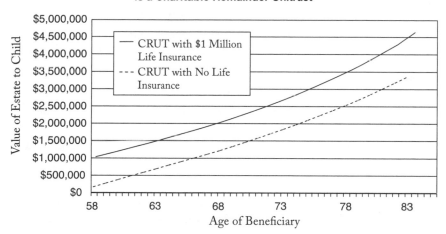

In summary, life insurance can make a tremendous difference in your estate, and you should consider including it in your own. But here is a tip many insurance professionals won't tell you. If you are shopping for life insurance, it is almost always best to go to an independent broker who has access to virtually all the life insurance companies. After you determine what type and how much insurance you want, it is the broker's job to get you the best deal. Obviously, you want the lowest possible premium. To be offered the lowest premium, you (and your spouse) will need a favorable physical exam, and the exam has to be conducted by an examiner approved by the insurance company. Either the insurance company or the broker will pay for the exam, but you cannot substitute this exam with a physical from your personal physician—even if you just had your annual exam. You will also need to give the insurance company permission to ask your doctor (or doctors if you see specialists, too) for your medical records. To get the best possible results from your physical, I have a couple of recommendations. The night before the exam, have your regular evening meal. Then, fast until after your exam—no snacks, no alcohol—water is fine. Personally, I like to get up and eat right away so I would schedule my exam very early, like 7:00 a.m. Whatever time you choose, it is important that there is no food in your stomach. No coffee either. You will get better results and a lower premium!

Disclosure

I am licensed to sell life insurance and that is part of my estate planning practice. When I am working with a client and I think my client would benefit from an insurance policy and the client agrees, I work closely with an ethical broker to help the client get the best deal. I do receive compensation from the broker.

In terms of the integrity of the information, you should also know that I have been a firm advocate of Second-to-Die or survivorship insurance for over 30 years. In 1986 I made a presentation touting the benefits of Second-to-Die insurance for clients with significant IRAs and retirement plans. This was 20 years before I made a nickel selling life insurance.

If you are interested in this type of insurance for your family, please visit www.paytaxeslater.com or go to the back of the book for more information.

A Key Lesson from This Chapter

For many married couples who are interested in protecting their children, survivorship life insurance is a classic, tax-favored, leveraged form of a gift that can be a great, if not the best, tool for creating and preserving wealth.

13

||||||||||||||||||||||||||||||

Laying the Foundation for Estate Planning

Using the Required Minimum Distribution Rules after Death

A man has made at least a start on discovering the meaning of human life when he plants shade trees under which he knows full well he will never sit.

— Elton Trueblood (1900–1994)

Main Topics

- The difference between choosing your spouse and your child as the beneficiary of your IRA

- How choices made by your spousal beneficiary after your death can accelerate income taxes on your IRA

- How do beneficiaries calculate and stretch Required Minimum Distributions?

- Options for giving a younger spouse access to the IRA without premature distribution penalties

- Why beneficiaries should continue to take the least possible amount out of their Inherited IRA, while they can

- When it is appropriate to name a trust as the beneficiary of your IRA

KEY IDEA

Individuals profit from deferring income taxes during their lifetime—so can their heirs.

Most people want to incorporate some planning for their heirs, beyond the needs of their spouse. Providing for the surviving spouse is usually the highest priority, but after the death of the survivor, you might hope to offer a cushion to children and/or grandchildren with the remaining funds. So, how does maintaining money in the IRA environment accomplish those two objectives?

Just as it was advantageous for you to keep money in your IRA, it is best for the beneficiaries of IRAs to retain the money in the tax-deferred environment for as long as possible.

Don't pay taxes now—pay taxes later. Just as it was advantageous for you to keep money in your IRA, it is best for the beneficiaries of IRAs to retain the money in the tax-deferred environment for as long as possible. Starting with that premise, let's examine planning for two types of beneficiaries.

Who Can Inherit an IRA?

For purposes of determining minimum distributions for inherited IRAs, there are two different types of beneficiaries.

- Spousal beneficiary
- Non-spouse beneficiary

Just as at some point you must take minimum distributions from your own IRA, the beneficiaries of your IRA must also take minimum distributions after your death. The distribution rules are different depending on your relationship to your beneficiary.

Spousal Beneficiary

If your surviving spouse is your beneficiary, he or she will have three options at your death:

1. Treat the IRA as his or her own, by doing one of the following:

   - changing the name on the IRA (if not changing financial institutions)

   - executing a trustee-to-trustee transfer to his or her own new or existing IRA

   - executing a spousal IRA rollover to his or her own new or existing IRA

2. Treat himself or herself as the beneficiary of an Inherited IRA from a spouse

3. Disclaim all or part of the inherited IRA to another heir

Normally, the surviving spouse will choose the option of treating the IRA as his or her own. If your surviving spouse is happy with the financial institution holding your IRA, he or she can simply tell them to change the name on the account. If your surviving spouse is unhappy with the institution holding your IRA or with the investment choices available, he or she can complete a trustee-to-trustee transfer and move the IRA to a new custodian. An IRA spousal rollover is also a possibility. I prefer the trustee-to-trustee transfer rather than the spousal IRA rollover for the same reasons that I like the trustee-to-trustee transfer while the IRA owner is alive (see Chapter 6). If your surviving spouse elects this option, he or she can defer minimum distributions until age 70½. Any withdrawals taken prior to your surviving spouse reaching age 59½, however, are included in your beneficiary's taxable income and are subject to a 10 percent premature distribution penalty.

Your surviving spouse also has the option to be treated as the beneficiary of your IRA. The account title will be changed to specify that you are deceased, and the IRA is for your spouse's benefit. It is different from a joint account, because the title will look something like this: "IRA of Bob Jones, Deceased, For the Benefit Of (FBO) Carol Jones." By electing this option, your surviving spouse will not be subject to the 10 percent penalty on any withdrawals he or she needs to make prior to age 59½. It allows flexibility if your survivor is younger than 59½, and might need additional income. As of this writing, there is no time limit restricting the surviving spouse's ability to roll the Inherited IRA into his or her own account. Let's assume that your survivor needs some income until his or her own pension starts at age 62. Your surviving spouse can withdraw income from your IRA prior to age 59½ without penalty until he or she turns 62, and then roll it into his or her own IRA so that he or she can defer further distributions until she or he reaches age 70½.

If your spouse disclaims your IRA, he or she refuses the right to inherit the assets, and they are transferred instead to other eligible beneficiaries. We'll talk about disclaimers in detail in Chapter 14, but sometimes this is the appropriate course of action if your surviving spouse does not need the income from your IRA.

By default, your spouse will be considered to have chosen to treat the IRA as his or her own if they are the sole beneficiary of the IRA and if they make additional contributions to the account, or if they do not take a RMD for a year after inheriting the account. It is generally best for your surviving spouse to treat the IRA as his or her own rather than as an Inherited IRA. There are several reasons why:

- If you (the account owner) have begun taking RMDs from the account, your spouse can defer future distributions until he or she reaches age 70½.

- If your spouse is 70½ or older, he or she can take the lowest possible RMD based on the Uniform Life Table (please refer back to Chapter 5 for an illustration of why that is significant).

- Your spouse can name new beneficiaries on the account. This can give the newly named beneficiaries the ability to stretch the IRA after you and your spouse die (more about stretching your IRA later in this chapter).

If your surviving spouse decides to treat the IRA as his or her own, the tax treatment of the account is similar to what the original owner was experiencing. Only the distributions are taxed. The difference is that the future RMDs will be calculated from the Uniform Life Table based on the surviving spouse's age. As I showed you in Chapter 5, this can be very important, especially if your surviving spouse is younger than you (it leads to a longer distribution period). The one exception occurs during the year the first spouse dies. If there is a RMD for that year, it will be based on the deceased spouse's previous distribution schedule and must be withdrawn by the surviving spouse prior to completing the trustee-to-trustee transfer. That specific RMD becomes the property of the beneficiary, not the estate (that goes for non-spouse beneficiaries also). Finally, by assuming ownership of the IRA, your surviving spouse can name his or her own beneficiaries (usually your children and/or grandchildren who will become eligible to stretch the tax-deferral period over their individual life expectancies).

If the IRA is to be split among multiple beneficiaries, separate accounts should be established for each beneficiary after the first death. If separate accounts are not established, minimum distributions will be required based on the beneficiary who has the shortest life expectancy! Special care should be taken with the titling of the beneficiary accounts. Also, make sure to change Social Security numbers on the account.

Spousal Beneficiary Who Chooses the Spousal Inherited IRA Option

There are situations when the surviving spouse might choose not to be treated as a surviving spouse but instead assume ownership of his or her deceased spouse's IRA using the spousal *Inherited IRA* option. This strategy is usually made by people who don't understand the implications or they would most likely opt to treat the IRA as their own. Choosing this option might make sense if your surviving spouse is at least 10 years younger than you, and he or she needs the money to live on. Treating your IRA as an Inherited IRA allows them to withdraw money without a 10 percent penalty, even if they are younger than 59½. Their future RMDs, however, will be based on a shorter life expectancy.

So let's make sure you understand what this means:

- If your surviving spouse takes over your IRA (meaning, treats it as his or her own) and is younger than 59½, he or she must comply with Section 72(t)—Premature Distribution Exceptions—to avoid the 10 percent penalty on early distributions. Minimum distributions will be required based on your spouse's life expectancy.

- If your surviving spouse treats your IRA as a Spousal Inherited IRA, rather than as his or her own IRA, he or she can take out as much as needed before age 59½, without penalty. Your spouse will be required to take minimum distributions starting in the year you would have turned 70½.

Now that you know what your options are if you inherit an IRA, we need to talk about stretch IRAs.

What is a Stretch IRA?

If you don't really know what a stretch IRA is, don't feel bad. Many readers and even many financial professionals could not give you a simple definition.

A stretch IRA is an IRA that has a beneficiary designation that provides for the possibility of maintaining the tax-deferred status of the IRA after the death of the IRA owner. You might be thinking, "I wish I had a stretch IRA. I only named my spouse as my primary beneficiary and my kids as my successor or contingent beneficiary." Well, guess what? You have a stretch IRA. After your death, your spouse and/or your children could continue to defer income taxes for many years after your death, as long as the right moves are made by your heirs. If someone does something really stupid, without extreme precautions, they may ruin the stretch IRA.

I've talked at length about the importance of IRA beneficiaries, both here and in Chapter 5. Choosing the correct beneficiary for your IRA, and having your beneficiary make the correct choices after your death, are critical to providing your heirs with the ability to stretch your IRA for as long as possible.

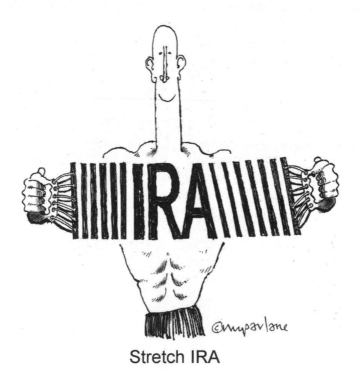

Stretch IRA

Spousal Beneficiary

If your surviving spouse chooses to treat your IRA as a Spousal Inherited IRA, the long stretch for the ultimate beneficiaries, usually the children, will be gone unless your spouse rolls the Inherited IRA into his or her own IRA at a later date (as long as that option is available). When your spouse acts as a beneficiary of an Inherited IRA, as opposed to treating the IRA as his or her own, the RMD will be calculated each year based on their life expectancy using the Single Life Table. That table generates big numbers, both in terms of the RMDs that deplete the account and in terms of the income taxes due on those RMDs. When your spouse dies, the beneficiaries who inherit the account will be locked into taking distributions based on your surviving spouse's remaining life expectancy according to the Single Life Table, and the divisor will be reduced by one for each subsequent year. A full explanation of the rules and regulations for this option can be found below under the heading "Non-spouse Beneficiary."

> A stretch IRA is an IRA that has a beneficiary designation that provides for the possibility of maintaining the tax-deferred status of the IRA after the death of the IRA owner.

Compromise Solution

In my practice, we have come up with a compromise that works well when a surviving spouse is younger than 59½, and he or she needs the proceeds from the IRA for normal living expenses. First, we make a projection of how much money he or she will need until turning 59½. I include in the calculation some growth of the assets. Then we treat only that amount (the combination of his or her needs and the assumed interest and appreciation of those funds) as an Inherited IRA, and for the rest we do a trustee-to-trustee transfer. The advantages are clear:

- The surviving spouse has access to the entire Inherited IRA without penalty.

- There are allowances for immediate distributions.

- The portion that is rolled over into the IRA will continue to grow tax-deferred, stretching the IRA both before he or she is 70 and after he or she is 70½.

Sometimes it is a delicate calculation to figure out how much the surviving spouse will need and what interest rates are likely to do. I would probably prefer to err on the side of overproviding for the surviving spouse until 59 ½, even at the expense of some income tax acceleration.

If you are uncomfortable with that approach because you don't want to pay any extra taxes, you could underestimate and then plan to do a Section 72(t) periodic payment schedule before 59½ for a portion of the IRA that would be rolled over into the surviving spouse's IRA. Section 72(t) payments, also known as Substantially Equal Periodic Payments, allow you to withdraw money from a retirement plan before age 59½, and still avoid the 10 percent premature distribution penalty. The catch is that the distributions have to be calculated so that they will be paid equally, over your life expectancy (or over the joint life expectancy of yourself and the IRA's beneficiary). You are not allowed to take out extra money if you need it. Once you begin Section 72(t) distributions, you must continue taking them for five years, or until you reach age 59½, whichever comes later. Once you've started taking distributions, you're locked in to taking them until you've been taking them for five years and you've reached age 59½. If you think that you'd like to change your mind and discontinue your 72(t) payments early, be prepared to pay substantial penalties and interest. Once you've been taking payments for five years and you've reached age 59½, you are allowed to discontinue the payments.

Spouses younger than 59½ who have a need for considerable money before they turn 59½ should seek professional help from someone who will run the numbers to help determine how to split up the IRA.

What if the Younger Spouse Dies First?

Another example when a spouse might choose to act as a beneficiary rather than assume ownership of the IRA occurs when the younger spouse predeceases the older spouse. The advantage here is that he or she may defer taking distributions until the IRA owner would have turned 70½. However, even though there might be some additional deferral period until the surviving spouse has to take the money out, I generally do not like this election. Unfortunately, when the time arrives to begin taking distributions, the surviving spouse must take out minimum distributions based on his or her sole life expectancy if he or she does not complete a rollover of the IRA.

Non-spouse Beneficiary

If you die and the beneficiary of your IRA is not your spouse, he or she will own that special asset called an Inherited IRA. A non-spouse beneficiary may not roll an Inherited IRA into his or her own IRA, and cannot make additional contributions to the account. Assuming that you have drafted your beneficiary designation correctly (more about that in Chapter 16), and there is proper follow-through after your death, the beneficiary of the Inherited IRA will not have to pay income taxes on the account, at least not all at once. He or she will be able to stretch the Inherited IRA and take his own RMDs based on Table I (Single Life Table) found in IRS Publication 590.

The RMD for the beneficiary of the Inherited IRA is based on the beneficiary's life expectancy as of December 31 of the year following the year the IRA owner died. Please note, however, that the beneficiary must be determined no later than September 30 of the year following the year that the IRA owner died. That might sound like a strange thing to say considering that the account owner has to fill out his beneficiary forms while he's still alive, but what it really refers to is the idea that a beneficiary always has the right to disclaim, or refuse, the inheritance. Disclaimers can be very significant when planning your estate, and we'll cover a lot more about them in Chapter 14. But for now, it's just important to know that the IRS gives your beneficiaries almost two years to complete the process of transferring your IRA to your beneficiaries after your death. The reason for the September 30 deadline is to give the IRA custodian sufficient time to make the RMD before the end of the year.

Let's look at what happens when the beneficiary of your IRA is not your spouse. Assume that Judy (from the Tom and Judy example described in Mini Case Study 11.1) is now a widow and cannot name her spouse as the beneficiary of her IRA. Judy names her six children as equal beneficiaries and then dies at age 88. For this example, assume that Judy had exactly $6 million in her IRA on December 31 of the year that she died. Each beneficiary's share is $1 million, and separate accounts were established for each beneficiary. The RMD for each beneficiary of Judy's Inherited IRA is calculated by dividing the balance in the account as of December 31 of the previous year by the life expectancy of that beneficiary. At the time of her death, her youngest beneficiary is 50, and her oldest beneficiary is 67. Judy's oldest child would have a deemed life expectancy of 18.6 years (the life expectancy for a 68-year-old using the Single Life Table) for the first distribution, which would have to be withdrawn by December 31 of the following year. The RMD for the oldest child would be $1 million divided by 18.6, or $53,763. As the beneficiary (survivor) ages, the factor is reduced by one year, that is, the next year's factor would be 17.6, then 16.6, and so on. Naming a younger beneficiary means a larger life expectancy factor and a lower RMD. The youngest child, who was 50 at the time of Judy's death, has a more favorable outcome. He is still required to take distributions using the Single Life Table, but his deemed life expectancy at the time of Judy's death is 33.3 years. His RMD in the year following Judy's death would be $1 million divided by 33.3 years, or $30,030. His life expectancy is also reduced by one each year after, but his distributions are still spread out over a much longer period than his older siblings. Thus, a younger beneficiary who inherits an IRA will have a greater potential for long-term tax deferral than would an older beneficiary.

> A younger beneficiary who inherits an IRA will have a greater potential for long-term tax deferral than would an older beneficiary.

Stated another way, the present value of the future cash flows to a younger beneficiary is greater than it is for an older beneficiary. Even when the surviving spouse uses a joint life expectancy (his or her life expectancy and a beneficiary 10 years younger) to calculate the RMD, the Inherited IRA has a greater tax-deferral potential for the surviving spouse's child than for the surviving spouse. As the law stands right now, the inherited IRA would have its greatest tax deferral potential in the hands of a grandchild (preferably via a well-drafted trust). A younger beneficiary means a longer life expectancy. A long life expectancy equates to lower annual RMDs; the greater the portion of assets that remains in the tax-deferred environment, the greater the accumulation.

> A long life expectancy equates to lower annual RMDs; the greater the portion of assets that remains in the tax-deferred environment, the greater the accumulation.

This may all change, however, and very soon. For several years, Congress has been looking for ways to reduce the tax benefits of stretch IRAs. They need tax revenue, and are trying to impose a finite term on the tax-deferred benefits of an inherited stretch IRA. In 2013, Senate Finance Committee Chairman Max Baucus proposed limiting the stretch to five years after death for non-spouse beneficiaries. Effectively, this would make the beneficiary pay all of the income taxes on the inherited IRA within five years. Thankfully for many of my clients, that proposal was withdrawn for lack of support. The idea reappeared, however, in April 2013 in President Obama's budget proposals and made a grand entrance that summer when the measure was reintroduced as part of a bill to reduce student loan debt in the future. Killing the multi-generational benefit of the stretch IRA, along with a few other measures, would provide enough revenue to reduce student loan rates for college tuition for one year.

This bill was introduced in June of 2013 and was passed by the Republican House, but died in the Senate by a vote of 51-49 in favor of another bill to reduce student loan rates. President Obama wanted to sign it, but the Senate said no. After checking several sources and speaking with a well-connected colleague, it is becoming increasingly clear to me that this measure, or a similar one, may eventually pass – some say as early as 2015. The President's 2016 budget contains the same proposition, and it will be interesting to see how the recent change in the dynamics of the Senate will affect his ability to get the measure passed.

The bottom line is that Congress, in its infinite wisdom, has decided that forcing your non-spousal heirs to pay income taxes on your entire IRA or retirement plan within five years of your death will provide them with a quick budget fix. Unfortunately, that fix may have dire consequences for your children or grandchildren.

Estate as Beneficiary

Naming an estate as the beneficiary of your IRA is almost always a mistake because the beneficiaries of an estate do not qualify as designated beneficiaries for purposes of the RMD rules. Thousands of misguided souls will cause their beneficiaries massive income tax acceleration unless someone or something intervenes.

- If the current beneficiary of your retirement plan or IRA is your estate, you should revise the beneficiary designation immediately.

- If you have not named a beneficiary and the default beneficiary of your IRA is the estate, then you must name a beneficiary.

In order to achieve the maximum possible stretch for the beneficiary, you must have a designated beneficiary for your IRA. That used to be easier said than done. Now, it is hard to avoid, assuming you fill out the beneficiary form as recommended in Chapter 16. If the estate is named beneficiary of an

IRA, a limited stretch for the remainder of the owner's unused life expectancy is available if the owner dies after the required beginning date without naming a designated beneficiary.

Trust as Beneficiary

There are many situations when a trust will be a good choice for a beneficiary of an IRA. The most common reason is if the beneficiary is a minor child. Even if the beneficiary is an adult child, we like to give the adult child the right to disclaim his or her rights to the account. In that case, having a well drafted trust for the benefit of the grandchild or grandchildren would be appropriate.

If your intended beneficiary is, or potentially will be, receiving public assistance of any kind, including Medicaid, you should consider using a trust. If they receive money outright as a named beneficiary, they may be disqualified from receiving future benefits. Naming a trust as your beneficiary might, under the right circumstances, allow your beneficiaries to continue the tax-deferral benefits of the stretch IRA. (This is very complicated. Please refer to Chapter 17 for more details).

You may want to use a trust if your beneficiary is not responsible with money and you want to make sure that he or she doesn't do anything stupid with your money. This is typically called a spendthrift trust. If you want to ensure that the beneficiaries don't spend all of your money at once, naming a trust as the beneficiary of an IRA will achieve your goal.

Another time you should consider a trust is if your child or children are involved in a marriage where divorce and/or other money issues are an important consideration. If you die leaving a large IRA to a married child and that child later goes through a divorce, it is possible your future ex-son or daughter-in-law could walk away with a portion of your money. In these situations, we have done a lot of trusts that we (tongue-in-cheek) call the "I don't want my no good son-in-law to inherit one red cent of my money trust."

There are a growing number of estate attorneys who routinely draft IRA beneficiary trusts for the benefit of the IRA owner's adult children. They argue that the trust forces the beneficiary to get the stretch effect and the trust protects against creditors. Though I think there is good reason to support their practice, I personally prefer to keep things simple and flexible. Assuming that your adult children are financially responsible and aren't experiencing financial or marital strife, I would prefer the default be to the children outright rather than a trust for the children. That way, you can avoid the trustee fee, and the accounting and tax return preparation fees associated with the trust.

Generally, we assume that a beneficiary will want to continue to defer income taxes after the IRA owner's death. We also know that a drafting error in the trust or a procedural error could prevent this from happening and lead to a massive acceleration of income taxes.

It is important that any trust that will serve as the beneficiary of an IRA or retirement plan be drafted with extreme care to ensure that:

- The retirement plan or IRA beneficiary designations are properly in place.

- The trust qualifies as a designated beneficiary.

If those two qualifications are met, the life expectancies of individual beneficiaries of a trust can be used for purposes of the RMDs.

Technical Requirements for a Trust to Get the Stretch IRA Treatment

For the trust to qualify as a designated beneficiary (and get the stretch treatment), it must meet the following five requirements:

1. The trust must be valid under state law, or would be but for the fact that it is not yet funded.

2. The trust is irrevocable or will become irrevocable at the creator's death.

3. The trust beneficiaries must be identifiable. That is to say, by the last day of the year following the creator's death, it must be possible to identify all the persons who could possibly be beneficiaries of the trust.

4. All the trust beneficiaries must be individuals.

5. Documentation about the trust must be provided to the plan administrator by October 31st of the year following the person's death. This consists of a copy of the trust instrument or a final list of all the beneficiaries.

Depending on the ages of the beneficiaries, the amounts, and the individual's situation, it may be worthwhile to establish a trust as the beneficiary of an IRA. If so, please be sure to comply with all the requirements so the beneficiary can enjoy tax benefits as well as the protection provided by a trust.

This is an area where an attorney's input is advisable. Unfortunately, many attorneys, even estate attorneys, just don't know this stuff. Since it is so easy to botch one of the requirements above, choose your attorney with care, and be sure to ask specifically about their experience with drafting a trust as a beneficiary of an IRA.

A Key Lesson from This Chapter

While you are alive, don't pay taxes now—pay taxes later. The same advice holds true for your beneficiaries. I encourage you to discuss this concept with your beneficiaries so that they are aware of the material advantages of stretching an IRA. Now, we move on to the ultimate solution for estate planning with IRAs and retirement plans.

14

||||||||||||||||||||||||||||||||||

Using Disclaimers in Estate Planning

*If you cannot accurately predict the future, then you must
flexibly be prepared to deal with various possible futures.*

— Edward de Bono

Main Topics

- How disclaimers work

- Mistakes to avoid

- Advantages of disclaimers

- Comparing the disclaimer approach to the traditional approach

- The problem of estate planning in a nutshell

KEY IDEA

An individual who disclaims an inheritance simply steps
aside and the next person in line (the contingent beneficiary
or beneficiaries) inherits. Planning with this option in mind
allows a family to assess and respond to the actual financial
needs of the family after the death of the first spouse.

How Disclaimers Work

In traditional families, the standard procedure is for the IRA owner to name his or her spouse as the primary beneficiary and their children equally as contingent beneficiaries (the same ingredients of the *I Love You* will). But here is the key point: the surviving spouse always has *the option to accept or refuse* the inherited IRA. He or she can *disclaim* the entire IRA or a portion of the inherited IRA. But why on earth would someone not want to accept an inheritance? Because refusing (disclaiming) an inheritance can provide significant tax benefits to the family.

The surviving spouse always has the option to accept or refuse the inherited IRA. He or she can disclaim the entire inherited IRA or a portion of the inherited IRA.

Let's assume that your spouse names you as the beneficiary of his/her $3 million IRA, and your three children as secondary beneficiaries. If, after running the numbers, you conclude you will be completely comfortable financially with your current income plus $2 million of your spouse's IRA, consider disclaiming $1 million to be split among your children. Assuming that your disclaimer meets the federal requirements for a qualified disclaimer and the applicable state law requirements for a valid disclaimer (as described later in this chapter), you can do just that. The IRA can then be divided into as many Inherited IRAs as there are secondary beneficiaries – in this case, three, for your children. No matter how large the IRA, the surviving spouse will not be deemed as having made a gift for gift or estate tax purposes. It is as if the deceased IRA owner left $2 million to their spouse and the remaining $1 million to their children. Then, each child will be required to take minimum distributions from his or her Inherited IRA based on his or her individual life expectancy.

Please do not misunderstand this concept. You cannot *change* the beneficiaries on the account after the original IRA owner dies. If the three children were named equally as the contingent beneficiaries, the surviving spouse cannot pick and choose among the children, nor alter the amounts or percentages they receive. The surviving spouse can only disclaim to all three children in equal shares, if that was what the original owner had specified when he filled out his beneficiary form.

You cannot change beneficiaries after the IRA owner dies. Disclaiming simply means that one beneficiary steps aside in favor of the next beneficiary or beneficiaries.

Disclaiming simply means that one beneficiary steps aside in favor of the next beneficiary or beneficiaries. Should the first beneficiary disclaim, under current law the contingent beneficiary is able to use his or her life expectancy to determine the Required Minimum Distribution (RMD) of the inherited IRA, allowing the IRA to be stretched. Even if the law does change and non-spousal beneficiaries are required to withdraw all of the money from the IRA in five years, it still can make sense in many cases for the primary beneficiary to step aside and disclaim an inheritance, though the extended or "stretch" income tax savings of disclaiming under current law would be gone.

Under most state disclaimer laws, the surviving spouse has nine months to decide whether or not to accept, disclaim, or partially accept and partially disclaim his or her interest in the estate. That time lag can help prevent hasty decisions. You can take the time to evaluate your financial position and the consequences of the disclaimer, before you make a decision. In our practice, I never hurry the surviving spouse to make that critical decision. If anything, I want to make sure that whatever decision is made, it is well thought out and preferably made after "running the numbers" to compare various disclaimer amounts. We have saved many families millions of dollars of income taxes through the proactive use of disclaimers. Of course the primary goal is to protect or over-protect the surviving spouse. That said, disclaimers can offer enormous tax advantages, especially for surviving spouses who are wealthy but not spenders.

The other advantage of disclaimers, which is harder to quantify, is that the children will get access to a portion of the family estate while they are still young enough to enjoy it. I sometimes ask my clients if they would change their lifestyle if they were to inherit $1 million dollars tomorrow. Most of them say no. Most of them say they would not even go out to dinner more frequently! But, if I ask them if they had inherited even $100,000 thirty years ago, they all say it would have been a life-changing event.

Many of my clients are financially comfortable and relatively set in their ways. They aren't going to radically change their spending patterns, even after a death of one spouse. Their children, on the other hand, are usually struggling, even if they have good incomes. When young adults are starting their own families, they frequently face challenging financial pressures. Raising children is more expensive than ever, especially in terms of education (and not just college). Perhaps there are excellent private secondary schools that your grandchildren would benefit from. Does it make sense to sit on millions of dollars that are not about to change your life, but which could have a monumental impact on the lives of your children and grandchildren—and while you are alive to see it?

Even if your children are doing well financially, they have competing pressures on their income including education, housing, their own retirement savings, insurance, lessons, etc. To inherit money earlier in life rather than later could make an enormous difference in the quality of their lives. If you can afford to relieve some of that stress from your children, isn't that a good thing?

People frequently raise the objection that giving money to a child or children too early will reduce their motivation to work hard. That is actually a very legitimate objection that should be considered on a case by case basis. I would never suggest that you give an irresponsible young adult a free pass to self-indulgence. But, for those who have graduated from college, maybe with an advanced degree, and held down a job for a number of years, or those who are on the road to becoming successful entrepreneurs, a boost in finances at an opportune time could make all the difference in the world.

Please note, *these theoretical benefits are in addition* to the potentially enormous tax benefits of disclaiming. And, some of the same arguments can be made for gifting!

The requirements for a qualified disclaimer under federal law (which are generally the same requirements as under state law, although you must always review applicable state law to confirm that the proposed disclaimer meets the requirements) include the following:

1. The disclaimer must be irrevocable, unqualified (unconditional), and in writing.

2. The written disclaimer must be delivered to the custodian of the owner's account or the owner's legal representative (i.e., executor or retirement plan administrator).

3. The disclaimer must be received by the custodian of the owner's account or the owner's legal representative no later than nine months after the date of death or nine months after the disclaimant attains age 21, whichever is later. (Even though the beneficiary is not finally determined until September 30 of the year following the year of the IRA owner's death, to be effective the disclaimer must be filed within nine months).

4. The disclaimant has not accepted the interest (the interest can be either a partial interest or the entire interest) or any of its benefits.

5. The property must pass to the alternate beneficiary without any direction on the part of the disclaimant.

Avoid This Mistake

After a death, if the named beneficiary is even considering a disclaimer, the most important thing to do is nothing!

The death of a spouse is a very emotional time. If you are the survivor, there is no need to immediately take control of or change the titling of your spouse's assets. Do not transfer or roll the assets into your name until you have met with your professional advisors and know whether or not you want to disclaim any portion of the inheritance. Although the IRS has permitted disclaimers in certain situations after the spouse has partially accepted the assets (meaning, changed the name on the account, or rolled it or transferred it), it is more prudent and considerably less expensive to not accept any assets until after consulting with a qualified advisor.

> **It is more prudent and considerably less expensive to not accept any assets until after consulting with a qualified advisor.**

I recently had a situation where the surviving spouse, in an attempt to save money, tried doing some of the estate administration on her own. She figured she could take care of making the trustee-to-trustee transfer of her husband's IRA over to her own name before she came in to see us. She filled out paperwork to complete the trustee-to-trustee transfer; later that month, she informed us of her husband's death and came to see us regarding the rest of the estate administration. I immediately saw the potential for saving hundreds of thousands of dollars for the family by using a disclaimer, something she had forgotten about during this period of stress. Unfortunately, I was too late. Before our office became involved, she took control of the IRA and transferred it into her own name. We could not do a disclaimer on any portion of her husband's IRA, something that would have provided great benefits to the family.

> The death of a spouse is an emotional time. It's easy to make big mistakes when you're in an emotional state. Discuss, plan, and prepare ahead of time, and please make sure you have a flexible plan that will survive changes in both the tax code and how your investments do over time. Then your surviving spouse will have all the options at his or her disposal and will have an entire nine months to make decisions on what to do.

Advantages of Disclaimers

> *Trying to predict the future is like trying to drive down a country*
> *road at night with no lights while looking out the back window.*
>
> — Peter F. Drucker

A disclaimer offers several potential advantages, but they're easier to understand by using an example. When reading the following scenarios, please assume that the surviving spouse, Jean, was named as the primary beneficiary of Mike's IRA and their children were named, equally, as contingent beneficiaries. If Jean disclaims Mike's IRA or a portion of Mike's IRA to her children, rather than accepting the inheritance, it accomplishes three objectives.

1. The IRA is not included in Jean's estate, which could reduce federal estate and state inheritance taxes for the children upon her death. (Federal estate taxes are not a problem for as many people now since the exemption amount has been raised, but if the value of your own estate is high enough, you should consider this. And, for those who live in states with an inheritance tax, such as Pennsylvania, then that adds more reason to consider disclaimers).

2. The second, and perhaps the more important financial advantage, is that the RMDs of the inherited IRA would be based on the life expectancy of the children rather than the shorter statutory joint life expectancy of the surviving spouse (longer life expectancy equals longer tax deferral). Again, the laws allowing this advantage may change. Our government wants to make all non-spouse beneficiaries withdraw all of the money from Inherited IRAs within five years. But at least for now, disclaimers of IRA can save an enormous amount of income taxes.

3. The kids don't have to wait until both parents are gone to realize a financial benefit.

Many of my clients who have disclaimed to their children have told me later that they were gratified to be able to see their children enjoy their inheritance. If the survivor does not have sufficient income to support their needs, disclaiming is not appropriate and he or she should choose to retain the entire IRA. If the surviving spouse has significantly more money than he or she needs, choosing to disclaim the entire IRA could be a powerful course of action. In some cases, the best solution is for the surviving spouse to keep a portion of the IRA and disclaim the remainder.

> **In some cases, the best solution is for the surviving spouse to keep a portion of the IRA and disclaim the remainder.**

The beauty of considering a disclaimer as part of your estate plan is that the decision of whether or how much to disclaim can be made after the death of the first spouse, when a much clearer picture of the surviving spouse's financial situation is available.

In the chapter on Lange's Cascading Beneficiary plan, we discuss the possibility of using disclaimers over one or even two generations—with our plan, children can disclaim into well-drafted trusts for the benefit of a grandchild. Passing on tax-deferred IRA dollars in this manner could dramatically reduce the RMD of the inherited IRA after the first death.

Please note that using disclaimer strategies is not limited to IRAs and retirement plans. You can incorporate the same flexibility with disclaimers on all the assets in the estate. That will allow the surviving spouse (with help from advisors and family) to determine that best plan after the first death.

For example, in today's environment and for some readers, the best asset to disclaim to the children might be part of the IRA. On the other hand, in a different environment and in a different situation, the best asset to disclaim might be the Roth IRA, or some after-tax dollars, or even the life insurance. One of the advantages of setting up flexibility ahead of time through the planned use of disclaimers is that you can better assess the proper course of action in the future than you can right now.

Comparing the Disclaimer Approach to a Traditional Approach

If you have an outdated estate plan that includes an A/B trust, the following information is enormously important and similar to the analysis presented in Chapter 11 under the heading "The Cruelest Trap of All."

The problem with the fixed-in-stone traditional approach used by many attorneys is that no one can predict:

- the future value of the investments.

- which spouse will die first.
- the needs of the surviving spouse.
- the needs of the children.
- the needs of the grandchildren.
- what estate tax laws will be in force at the death of the first spouse and/or the death of the second spouse.

The traditional approach only allows you to guess at what might be an optimal plan for the surviving spouse and family.

The appeal of the traditional approach is that the bequeathing individual exercises control; he or she decides how to leave money at death and sees that the appropriate documents are drafted. This also means that the traditional approach does not allow the surviving spouse to make nearly as many discretionary decisions as the more flexible plan. I cannot emphasize enough the value of structuring your estate planning documents so that they are as flexible as possible.

One problem with a traditional approach is that any plan that is put in place today will likely be far from optimal within one or two years, let alone 10 to 20 years. As the laws change and the balances in the estate and other factors change, the traditional will or beneficiary designation must be redrafted. Then clients, who I am meeting with for the first time, get upset because I have to point out to them why their estate planning documents are not only inefficient, but rather they're downright dangerous.

The traditional answer to justify the fixed-in-stone approach is that if the situation changes, you can always update your documents. Standard advice recommends people review their will every several years. Good luck with that one. Many if not most of my new clients come in with wills that are ten, sometimes 20 and sometimes 30 years old. Those old wills and documents can never respond adequately to current conditions on either the tax front or, in many cases, the family front. Our clients who are using LCBP don't have to worry as much about many factors that will concern others, such as exclusion limits—although they might have to make some changes as families grow and shrink. We believe it is far better and safer to set up flexible estate plans that will survive changing circumstances than to set up a fixed-in-stone type estate plan and pretend you are going to review it every couple of years. And let's face it, situations can change overnight, and you may not have the luxury of a time window to make important changes.

Congress, of course, is responsible for much uncertainty on the tax front. Between 2010 and 2015, they have established Applicable Exclusion Amounts (the amount that you can die with before you incur federal estate tax) that range from zero to over $5 million. The shifting target of the Applicable Exclusion Amount creates chaos for the estate planner. Traditional estate planners who do not use disclaimer-type planning will be forced to revise your will, trust, and beneficiary designations every year if they expect

The shifting Applicable Exclusion Amount could have been called "The Estate Planners' Full Employment Act" because it creates a steady need for redrafting and tinkering with the estate plan.

to achieve optimal results, because the dollar amount they need to worry about changes every year. (Of course, perhaps the traditional planner should not complain. All this revising brings in lots of revenue)! The shifting Applicable Exclusion Amount could have been called "The Estate Planners' Full Employment Act" because it creates a steady need for redrafting and tinkering with the estate plan.

The use of disclaimers in estate plans is controversial. But there is a rapidly growing group of attorneys, with me leading the charge, who love using at least some form of disclaimer in the estate plans of most of their clients. I have been using them in my practice since the early nineties and in the vast majority of my cases, they have worked out very well. We always provide or over provide for the surviving spouse. But if there is money left over after that, why not take advantage of the enormous tax and other life-style benefits mentioned earlier or at a minimum set up your estate to make those decisions later. So I believe in them for the reasons stated here. To be fair, however, the majority of estate attorneys don't use disclaimers in their practice. I could be glib and say that is because many estate attorneys haven't considered the advantages of using disclaimers, which, at least for some attorneys, is unfortunately true. There are, however, a significant number of estate attorneys who fear that the surviving spouse will screw everything up by failing to disclaim the inheritance. These attorneys believe it is better not to give the surviving spouse any choices. I obviously disagree. I think for many families, giving the surviving spouse as many options as possible is a sound course of action.

Full disclosure however, I must report one situation that I handled, where the disclaimer didn't work out. The estate attorneys who don't typically use disclaimers can gloat after reading this story because it validates their fears.

I drafted a cascading beneficiary plan known as Lange's Cascading

Beneficiary Plan™ (LCBP -- more fully discussed in Chapter 15) for clients with $3 million in the husband's IRA. Other than a modest house, that was the only significant asset in the estate. When I heard about my client's death, it saddened me as I generally like my clients. The good thing was the surviving spouse was set up just the way I wanted with LCBP.

This event happened when the Applicable Exclusion Amount was only $1 million. For some odd reason, I often remember the general holdings and configurations of my clients' estate plans. This family, as are many of my clients, was better at saving than spending. They lived a relatively frugal lifestyle and spent less than $60,000 a year. They also received Social Security.

As soon as I learned of his death, I remembered his holdings and knew what the best course of action would be. My plan was to recommend that his spouse disclaim $1 million to the secondary beneficiaries (their children and grandchildren) and keep the rest.

It would have worked out beautifully, but despite my best efforts, the surviving spouse insisted on keeping the entire IRA, but she did not change her frugal spending habits, so now her estate is worth well over $5 million and still growing. The result of her failure to disclaim when she could have will likely cost her children unnecessary estate taxes when she dies, and they may very well be too old to fully enjoy the money when they finally do inherit it.

The moral of the story is that there is a genuine risk of the surviving spouse refusing to disclaim when he or she should.

Personally, I feel the advantages of disclaimers far outweigh the disadvantages, but I believe that my job is to educate my clients about their options and have them decide what is best for them. The majority of my clients, perhaps due in part to my bias, have chosen to use disclaimers as part of a more flexible plan, instead of the traditional plan. I believe that if you have a long-term traditional marriage, the LCBP should be the starting point because adjustments can be made if needed. Disclaimers can also be used quite effectively in planning for non-traditional relationships. No matter what the relationship, however, the spouses/partners involved must trust each other in order to make disclaimers work as planned.

The decision of whether the surviving spouse should keep all the funds or whether the children should receive some portion of them (not to mention other possible options) can be most effectively made if the survivor is in possession of current facts and figures. We continually refer to the importance of "running the numbers" and after the death of the first spouse is definitely a great time to "run the numbers." Properly drafted documents and beneficiary designations using disclaimers can provide the surviving spouse with enormous wealth building options after the death of the first spouse.

The Problem of Estate Planning in a Nutshell

With little fanfare or public discussion, Congress enacted two changes that can make estate planning documents that were created prior to 2010 completely obsolete, or, worse yet, potentially catastrophic for the surviving spouse. When the Applicable Exclusion Amount was less than $1 million, many couples established wills that included A/B trusts. With the enactment of the Taxpayer Relief Act of 2012, an Applicable Exclusion Amount of $5 million (adjusted annually for inflation) per person was made permanent. In 2012, you and your spouse could each leave $5 million without being subject to federal estate tax. In addition, the executors of estates of decedents dying on or after January 1, 2011 could elect to transfer any unused estate tax exclusion (called the Deceased Spouse's Unused Exclusion Amount, or DSUEA), to the surviving spouse. This concept, known as portability, meant that a married couple could pass up to $10 million to their heirs without having to worry about federal estate tax. In 2015, that inflation-adjusted number is $5.43 million per person, or $10.86 million per married couple.

So what is the problem? The problem is that most married couples are not likely to have to worry about estate taxes any more, and their A/B trusts are unnecessary. And if your own estate planning documents contain certain language that is commonly used in wills, the executor of your estate could be forced to transfer an amount up to the Applicable Exclusion Amount – in 2015, that's $5.43 million – in to your B trust. That might not be a problem if you are leaving an estate of $15 million, but if you are leaving an estate of $2 million, that means that all of your money will go into the trust and your spouse's access to the money will be controlled entirely by the terms of the trust. And the terms of the trust, if written at a time when it was expected to shelter far less money than it would today, may be far too restrictive to meet your surviving spouse's income and "fun" needs.

Another problem can exist if your beneficiaries have financial problems that cause them to file bankruptcy. In 2014, the Supreme Court ruled that Inherited IRAs are not a protected asset in bankruptcy proceedings. In the past, parents generally did not have to worry about their children's creditors before naming them as the beneficiaries of their retirement plans. This new ruling means that retirement money left outright to children is now considered fair game to a creditor, and in the absence of alternate planning, some children may never see a dime of their parent's legacies.

And what if Congress does eliminate the stretch IRA? As I demonstrated in earlier chapters, the ability to allow your IRA or retirement account to continue to grow by limiting withdrawals to the required minimums makes a tremendous difference in what will serve your family best. There are some possible alternatives to the Stretch IRA, but if the provisions for those alternatives do not exist in your estate planning documents, then your family can lose some of the options to fund the additional income taxes that will be due on the IRA.

The problem, of course, is that there are many variables, and we cannot predict which ones will be relevant at the time of death. How much money will there be at the first death? Who will die first? What tax laws will be operative in the year of the first death? What will the needs of the surviving spouse be? Are you adding to the problem by hanging on to estate planning documents that are no longer relevant? Now that we understand the problem, what is the solution? The answer lies in the next chapter even though we have mentioned a few hints along the way.

A Key Lesson from This Chapter

It is extremely difficult to make a plan that will survive all foreseeable and unforeseeable events, but it is to your heirs' benefit to set up your plan so that it is as flexible as possible.

15

||||||||||||||||||||||||||||

The Ideal Beneficiary Designation of Your Retirement Plan

Stretching and Disclaiming: Lange's Cascading Beneficiary Plan

The circumstances of the world are so variable that an irrevocable purpose or opinion is almost synonymous with a foolish one.

— W. H. Seward

Main Topics

- How Lange's Cascading Beneficiary Plan works

- Who should use the strategy

- Who shouldn't use this strategy

KEY IDEA

Lange's Cascading Beneficiary Plan's disclaimer strategy preserves the safety net for the natural heir of the IRA owner (i.e., the surviving spouse) by allowing complete discretion for the surviving spouse to keep funds for him/herself, or to disclaim to the children, or to trusts for grandchildren. The decision of whether and how much to disclaim can be made after the death of the IRA owner.

Critical Information: A Will or Living Trust Does Not Control the Distribution of an IRA or Retirement Plan

In my practice, clients often come in with sophisticated and lengthy wills or revocable trusts covering every contingency, including a variety of trusts or subtrusts. When I ask them where most of their money is they often reply, "in my IRA" or "in my retirement plan." Then, when I ask about the beneficiaries of their IRAs and retirement plans I find that, despite their long and complex wills, the beneficiary designation that controls the vast majority of their wealth is often two lines long:

- Surviving spouse

- Children equally

What follows in this paragraph is one of, if not the most, important concepts in this book. *Your will and trust documents do not control the distribution of your IRA or retirement plan. Any account that has a specific beneficiary designation will be distributed to the individuals listed on that beneficiary form, regardless of what your will or trust says.* And for many of the people I meet for the first time, all of the time and expense that went into creating their wills or revocable trusts turns out to be of limited and sometimes no use at all. This is especially true for clients whose estates include large retirement accounts, and it is because the beneficiary designations they have listed on their retirement accounts contradict the instructions in their wills or revocable trusts.

Your will and trust documents do not control the distribution of your IRA or retirement plan.

Unfortunately, this mistake is deadly and all too common. In my experience, effective planning for the retirement plan and/or IRA is the exception, not the rule. In the area of estate planning for IRAs and retirement plans, the difference between effective and ineffective planning can mean hundreds of thousands, sometimes millions of dollars.

Why do *The Wall Street Journal, Newsweek, Financial Planning* magazine, *Kiplinger's, The Tax Adviser* (AICPA), and a host of other national periodicals sing the praises of Lange's Cascading Beneficiary Plan?

It's simple. It's a secure way for you to easily, safely, and with maximum flexibility, plan your estate and provide for your heirs before one of you dies. It's a plan that has stood the test of time! Read on and take notes. You'll want to implement this with the help of your attorney.

For discussion's sake, I am going to assume that you are married and that you are willing to answer the following question with an unequivocal "yes." Are you ready for this? I love this. I ask this in my practice all the time. "Do you trust your spouse? Seriously, do you *trust* your spouse?"

Let's assume the answer is yes, that you trust your spouse. For discussion's sake, let's say that you have a traditional marriage, you and your spouse have only been married to each other and you have the same children and grandchildren. When it comes down to it, you will likely have four natural choices for your beneficiaries.

The first will be your surviving spouse. We love our spouse. We want to provide for the comfort and security of our spouse after we die. I'm happy to report to you that in 35 years of practice nobody ever came in and said, "My goal for my estate is to have my grandchildren so stinking rich that they'll never have to work a day in their life." Nobody ever said that. I'll tell you what people say. "I want to take care of my spouse." That even comes before saving taxes. That comes before everything. I want to take care of my spouse. Let's leave that as the number one option. In prior years, some estate planners named the B trust for the spouse as the primary beneficiary of the IRA, and then the children as contingent beneficiaries. As we discussed in Chapter 14, though, in the current tax environment, estate taxes are less of a concern for most people, and naming the B trust as the primary beneficiary could severely limit your surviving spouse's access to the money.

The second beneficiary choice could be your children. They might be a good choice as secondary beneficiaries, given that:

- The children may need the money now, rather than many years from now when both you and your spouse will be gone.

- Your estate is large enough that you could possibly have an estate tax if you leave everything to your spouse and she then dies with more than the applicable exclusion amount.

But the children may not need the money, in which case you'd want to give it to your grandchildren and let them stretch the inherited IRA for as long as possible. Or perhaps one child doesn't need the money and has children, yet another one of your children does need the money. Suppose one child is suffering from health problems that you are afraid might lead to his permanent disability.

What are you going to do? How can you decide between these four choices?

1. Surviving spouse

2. Children

3. Grandchildren

4. A trust

Maybe do a little bit of each? Maybe try to figure it out? I know. Let's do a projection! Let's project how much money we are going to have when we die! Oh, come on! We don't know when we are going to die. I know, let's make a projection based on how much money we are going to have and what the tax laws are going to be! Oh . . . we don't know what the tax laws are going to be. Well, I'll tell you this, in 35 years I've done a lot of projections, and one thing is common to every single one of them. They have all been wrong. Every time I've been wrong! People had more money than I thought. People had less money than I thought. The tax laws changed. The wrong person died first. So how can we handle this? How can we make this decision now if you don't want to come back and redo your will every year or two. I have an idea. Let's not decide. We just won't decide. I refuse to decide.

Well, how do you refuse to decide? It's surprisingly easy. You draft the appropriate wills and trusts, and add specific beneficiary designations to your IRAs and retirement plans that allow your surviving spouse to make these decisions. The decisions have to be made within nine months after the date of your death, but at that point, your surviving spouse will have answers to all of these questions. Your surviving spouse will know what his or her needs are. He or she will know exactly how much money there is after you die. Your surviving spouse will know what tax laws were in effect at the time of your death, and can make a decision at that time that meets the needs of your survivors.

If you were to look at my will or my IRA beneficiary designation, with the exception of money going to charity, if my wife wants it, she can have it all. End of story. But suppose she doesn't want it? If the professional who is helping her handle my estate tells her that income or estate taxes might be a problem at the time of my death, she could direct that the money go into a trust that she can draw income from. At her death, the remainder will go to our daughter. If my wife doesn't need the income from a trust, she can choose to direct the proceeds into a trust for our daughter. And if our daughter is grown up with kids of her own and she doesn't want it, my wife can specify that it go into a trust for our grandchildren. Perhaps best of all, my wife can choose to have the money directed in some combination of options.

I'm not going to decide now, because I trust my wife. She can do whatever she wants. I'm going to suggest that if you trust your spouse, don't decide now. Let your spouse decide. If you survive your spouse, then you decide.

I've been drafting these types of flexible documents for Pennsylvania residents since the early 1990s. Even though most of my clients are alive and kicking, we have had a sufficient number of clients who have died to know for certain that the plan works beautifully. It's always tragic when a client dies. But if they die with this plan in place, we almost always get a good financial result for the family. If you use a more traditional plan, decisions are fixed and set in advance. Many traditional plans were drafted when the exemption amounts were $600,000, and they've never been updated. This means that, at the first death, too much money goes into a trust and the surviving spouse is underprovided for. It happens all the time, and it is going to get worse as the exemption amounts continue to go up.

By the way, I have a little story for you. When they changed the law in 2001, I knew within days of Congress changing the law that this flexible estate plan was going to be the best estate plan there was. I was very excited. I had an e-mail newsletter, which at that time was going out to 5,000 readers. I wrote this little article called "The Ideal Beneficiary of Your IRA." I sent it out into e-mail land. I was surprised by a call I received two days later when I heard, "Hi. This is Jane Bryant Quinn." I talked to her at length, and she put my plan in her column. Then *Financial Planning* magazine asked me to write about this plan. I did, and they published my article. The American Institute of Certified Public Accountants (AICPA) published my peer-reviewed article and sent it to 60,000 CPA subscribers with this plan as part of the article. *The Wall Street Journal* also got hold of this. They loved the idea, and have written four articles on it. *Kiplinger's* also chimed in several times. I call it Lange's Cascading Beneficiary Plan, but it is also cited as a Cascading Beneficiary Plan in the professional literature. The concept of cascading beneficiaries appears widely in print and on the Internet. So this isn't just some crazy, fluky idea. This is something you should seriously think about putting in place for yourself.

How the Plan Works

First, a bit of background on terminology. To the best of my knowledge, I am the first person to have used the term Cascading Beneficiary Plan to describe the layering of beneficiaries through the use of disclaimers. Furthermore, Lange's Cascading Beneficiary Plan takes the technique to a new level of sophistication and flexibility. It is not uncommon currently to see references to cascading beneficiary plans in estate planning literature. Journals and magazines that originally published my articles on Lange's Cascading Beneficiary Plan continue to promote the concept, although some have dropped my name and simply refer to a cascading beneficiary plan. Using the cascade or disclaimer technique is a sound and excellent solution for many estate planning problems. I cannot attest, however, to how other financial professionals use the concepts and would not know if all the advantages to my particular plan are incorporated in the work of others. So, for the sake of clarity and because I have a vested interest in maintaining the integrity of my plan, I will refer to it as Lange's Cascading Beneficiary Plan, or LCBP for short.

LCBP recognizes the importance of providing for the surviving spouse and also the advantage of keeping options open after the death of the first spouse. LCBP accommodates the surviving spouse's need to take stock of his or her financial situation before deciding whether or not to disclaim. If he or she does decide to disclaim, the next question is how much and to whom? Relevant facts to consider include the family's finances at the time of the first death, tax laws at the date of the first death, family needs, and perhaps most importantly, the needs of the surviving spouse. LCBP gives the spouse both the time to make decisions, and the power to act on them. Many traditional families—that is, families without the complications of second marriages and stepchildren—would be wise to consider incorporating LCBP with disclaimer options into their estate plans. Please note that LCBP, when appropriate, can and should be used for wills and living trusts as well as IRAs or retirement plans.

> **LCBP gives the spouse both the time to make decisions, and the power to act on them.**

Typically, to take full advantage of LCBP, the IRA owner should name primary and contingent beneficiaries to their IRAs according to the following hierarchy:

1. The spouse

2. A child (or the children equally)

3. An adult grandchild (or grandchildren)

4. A trust, possibly for the benefit of a minor grandchild

By naming your surviving spouse as the primary beneficiary on your retirement plan, you give him or her ability to be flexible when settling your estate. I do want to mention one point here for readers who may have had wills and trusts prepared in the past, or perhaps were executors of their parents' estates and saw the B trust strategy used in practice. When federal estate tax was a concern for far more people than it is today, we used to establish a B trust so that the surviving spouse could elect to disclaim to the trust. By disclaiming to the B trust, the survivor could save the children hundreds of thousands, and possibly millions of dollars in federal estate taxes. While this is still an option, disclaiming to the B trust only makes sense for individuals who have estates that exceed the exemption amount. Assuming that the estate is under the exemption amount, it is perfectly acceptable for the surviving spouse to disclaim directly to the children, and there is no difference in the estate tax.

Currently, the LCBP contains provisions for your surviving spouse to disclaim some or all of his or her interest directly to the contingent beneficiary, which would most likely be a child, or if there is more than one child, to the children equally. Then that child would be deemed a primary beneficiary, and the Required Minimum Distribution (RMD) of the inherited IRA would be based on the child's life expectancy.

I like to give my clients as many options as possible. The language within the IRA beneficiary designation that I generally recommend also allows an adult child to disclaim his or her interest in what had been disclaimed from his parent (the surviving spouse). If your adult child doesn't need the inheritance, then why not have him disclaim to a trust for the benefit of his or her own child or children (your grandchildren)? If he does so, the trust for your grandchild would be deemed a primary beneficiary of your retirement account and, under the rules in effect at the time this book was written, could use his or her own life expectancy for RMD purposes (the ultimate stretch).

The Ultimate Cascade of a Very Flexible Plan

The best news is, your surviving spouse is not limited to using just one choice. In a perfect cascade, your surviving spouse:

- could retain some of your IRA, roll it over into his or her own name, and appoint his or her own beneficiaries to the account.

- would have the option to disclaim a portion to a trust, most likely for the benefit of your children or grandchildren.

- could disclaim a portion to an adult child or children, who would be the deemed primary beneficiary for that portion, which would allow the beneficiary to use his or her own life expectancy for RMD purposes.

At which point, each adult child:

- could retain some of your IRA and take RMDs based on his or her life expectancy.

- disclaim a portion to a trust for his or her own child, who would become the primary beneficiary for that portion and could then use his or her own life expectancy for RMD purposes.

If your surviving spouse chooses to roll the entire IRA into his or her own IRA, then the path of distributions is fairly straightforward (see column one of Figure 15.1). Your surviving spouse must begin taking RMDs based on his or her joint life expectancy with a beneficiary deemed to be 10 years younger, by April 1 of the year following the year that he or she turns 70½. He or she would use Table III of the Uniform Lifetime Table, which is presented in the appendix of this book. Using this table, your surviving spouse's life expectancy is recalculated each year, which means he or she can never outlive the IRA.

Your surviving spouse will also be able to name his or her own primary and contingent beneficiaries. At your spouse's death, the remaining IRA is included in his or her estate for estate tax purposes. Most people don't have to worry about estate taxes any longer because the exemption amounts have been increased, but if your own estate exceeds the exemption amount then this could be a concern for you. The RMD for the ultimate beneficiary of your inherited IRA—in traditional families, usually the children equally, assuming none of the children further disclaims—is calculated based on each of the different life expectancies of as many children as there are using the life expectancy of each beneficiary as of December 31 following the year of the death of your spouse. The beneficiaries of the IRA would then use Table I of the Single Life Table, which is presented in the appendix. Unlike your surviving spouse, the spouse's beneficiary may exhaust his or her IRA even if only withdrawing RMDs because his or her life expectancy is determined based on his or her age at the surviving spouse's death. Each year after your spouse's death, the life expectancy is reduced by one.

LCBP protects or overprotects your surviving spouse. It allows the greatest flexibility to stretch your IRA and allows decisions to be made after your death. However, this flexibility is a two-edged sword. By giving your surviving spouse that much power, the estate planner takes the risk that your surviving spouse will make inappropriately conservative decisions, such as failing to disclaim when he or she probably should. If that happens, your family could end up with less-than-optimal results.

You can see why this plan might not work well in families with the complications of second marriages and stepchildren. The potential exists that your spouse will have no motivation to pass the money on to your children from your first marriage. Rather than disclaim any of the money to your children, your surviving spouse might be more inclined to keep all of the money and eventually leave it to his or her own children and grandchildren. Or, your surviving spouse might be very trustworthy, but become mentally incapacitated after your death.

Perhaps the best short explanation of LCBP comes from Jane Bryant Quinn in *Newsweek*:

> *For moneyed families, where the heirs won't need the IRA right away: When you die, your spouse could refuse to accept ("disclaim") all or part of the IRA. That money could go to a trust that pays your spouse a lifetime income and then passes to the children. Alternatively, your spouse could disclaim the IRA proceeds directly to your children, who could either take the money or disclaim to your grandchildren. They'd still have to take their minimum distributions, but the bulk of the IRA could be tax-deferred for generations.*

Figure 15.1
Lange's Cascading Beneficiary Plan

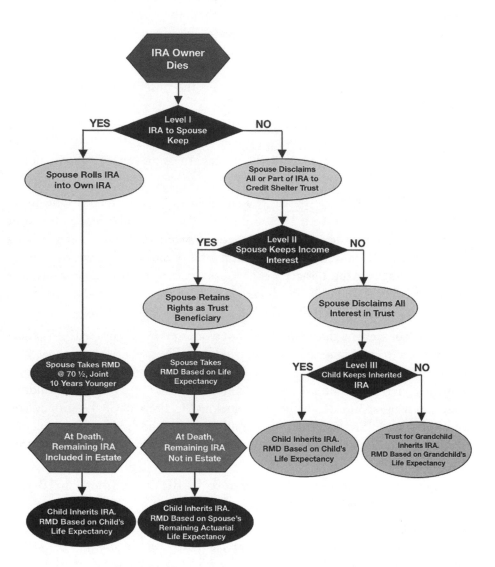

Kiplinger's Retirement Reports writes:

> *If you're looking to stretch out your IRA's life but want to make sure your spouse is provided for when you die, you can use what Pittsburgh attorney and CPA James Lange calls a "cascading beneficiary" strategy.*
>
> *Lange paints this scene: You are married with children and grandchildren. You name your wife as the primary beneficiary and a bypass trust as first contingent beneficiary. The second contingent beneficiary is the children equally. The third is a trust for the grandchildren. At your death, your spouse could roll over all or part of the IRA into her IRA and could also disclaim a portion into the bypass trust.*
>
> *The advantage of disclaiming to the bypass trust is that upon your wife's death, the proceeds of the trust are not included in her estate. She could also disclaim all or part to the children, who could then take withdrawals based on their longer life expectancy. Finally, if neither your spouse nor your children need all the money, they could disclaim all or a portion to a trust for the grand-children.*

Another interesting feature of LCBP is that it is also suitable and recommended for wills and revocable trusts. If you want the entire spectrum of options open for your surviving spouse, then drafting LCBP for the will (and/or revocable trust) and the IRAs and retirement plans is an excellent, probably the best, estate plan.

Are People Happy with Lange's Cascading Beneficiary Plan?

I developed and employed an early version of the cascade in the early 1990s. It has been tested and proven worthy. After determining that the fundamentals of the cascade were sound, I added the full Cascading Beneficiary Plan in January 2001, immediately after the overhaul of the IRA and retirement plan distribution rules, which increased the options for a stretch IRA. Most of my clients are still kicking. We have, however, been writing these plans long enough to have had quite a few deaths. The surviving spouses have appreciated the flexibility of our plan, and most of them who made decisions based on their personal circumstances at the time of their spouse's death were able to make better decisions—that is, more advantageous to them and their families— than the decisions that would have been forced upon them with the traditional estate planning. People always say hindsight is 20/20. This plan offers a unique opportunity to actually use hindsight in deciding the best way to divide up the estate.

If you are interested in exploring the benefits of Lange's Cascading Beneficiary Plan for your own family, please feel free to contact me at www.paytaxeslater.com.

> I have written this chapter from the standpoint of the IRA or retirement plan owner who is planning his or her estate. What if you are the beneficiary of an inherited IRA or retirement plan? What should you do? At first, do nothing. I mean it. Don't do something quickly that you may later regret. If you inherit an IRA or retirement plan, it is absolutely critical to review your options with a qualified expert in IRAs and retirement plans. You might even need to take a couple of months to think over all your options and plan accordingly. Not only is this an area where thousands of people make mistakes, but the scope of the mistakes can often be measured in hundreds of thousands or even a million dollars or more.
>
> When you are planning to leave your IRA and/or retirement plan to your heirs, you must impress upon them how important it is they get appropriate advice after your death.

What if the Federal Estate Tax Laws Are Changed?

Even if Congress is successful in its attempts to kill the stretch IRA, the LCBP is still fundamentally sound because of the flexibility it offers to your heirs. My advice regarding what type of will, revocable trust, or even beneficiary designation you should have for your IRA and retirement plan would be the same. That is to say, even in the event there are major changes in the exemption amounts or in the RMD rules for IRA beneficiaries, at this time, I would still advocate LCBP for most readers. The financial benefits of the plan will not be as significant as in previous years if Congress successfully eliminates the stretch IRA, but I believe it will still provide the best possible outcome for most of my clients. And since A/B trusts are not required for smaller estates any longer, many people can now implement the plan using only their family members as beneficiaries.

One point that we have not discussed much in this chapter is the effect of state death taxes, which vary greatly. You may live in a state that has separated its state death taxes from the federal estate tax and calculates the tax based on older rates. In those states, the LCBP can be especially relevant because of the flexibility it provides for the beneficiary to disclaim the ideal amount calculated based on that state's law rather than having a more traditional estate plan leaving all of the assets to one beneficiary.

If you have the LCBP and they change the law, you can shrug and say, "I don't have to redo my documents." If they change the tax laws again after the first set of changes, you can shrug again and say, "I still don't have to redo my documents." If you don't have the LCBP but rather have a traditional estate plan and want to keep traditional fixed-in-stone estate planning documents (the old outdated A/B trust format), you should make changes to your documents if they change the law, and you should make changes again when they change it again. You should make changes again if there is a change in your own personal financial circumstances.

In conclusion, I recommend Lange's Cascading Beneficiary Plan for wills and trusts. For very large estates, I would still include the B trust possibility, even for IRAs and retirement plans, even knowing that it might never be used. For estates of $5,000,000 or less, you can consider using LCBP without the B trust. The overriding thought, however, is that the LCBP is the best and most flexible estate plan, and you should not have to continually change your documents every time there is a federal estate tax law change or if there are changes in your circumstances.

A Key Lesson from This Chapter

Having a flexible estate plan offers several advantages including providing the surviving spouse with multiple options for distributing the inheritance based on the family's circumstances at the time of the first death. By incorporating the cascade into an estate plan, you give yourself the best chance to stretch an IRA and pay taxes later.

16

||||||||||||||||||||||||||||

Changing Beneficiaries for Retirement Plans and IRAs

When at last we are sure,
You've been properly pilled,
Then a few paper forms,
Must be properly filled.

— Dr. Seuss

Main Topics

- Filling out the beneficiary form

- Complex beneficiary designations

- Trusts as beneficiaries

- Hazards of naming different beneficiaries to different accounts

---

KEY IDEA

Even the simplest beneficiary designation requires more than a cursory review.

A Caution

Even though I have a disclaimer at the beginning of the book, I want to reemphasize that you should not rely on the information that follows when filling out the beneficiary designation of your IRA or retirement plan. Many forms are unique and each requires attention to details that I cannot anticipate.

I wince when I see books and computer programs that help people draft wills and fill out beneficiary change forms by themselves. In my opinion, they are accidents waiting to happen. Yes, in some simple cases (if there really is such a thing), you might be able to draft your own will or fill out your own beneficiary designation of your IRA on your own without professional help. You might also be able to stuff your own parachute. But I wouldn't recommend it.

Some things I think are best left to competent professionals. In many situations, a considerable amount of judgment and even some legal background is required when filling out IRA beneficiary change forms and/or a will, and a generic book or software program simply cannot supply that judgment. Some of these do-it-yourself resources may be a good thing for people who can't afford an attorney and who just want a very simple will. Even under those circumstances, however, it is very easy to make a mistake. So, if you have enough money at stake that proper planning concerns you, I highly recommend professional guidance from an attorney whose area of expertise is estate planning.

Why am I so concerned about making sure that you hire a professional to help you with your beneficiary designations? It is because over the course of my career, I have seen plenty of people fill out beneficiary forms incorrectly and their family suffered terrible financial consequences. Let's say you have a really simple beneficiary designation: I leave the money to my two sons, Jack and Tom. My secondary (contingent) beneficiaries are my twin grandsons, Bob and John, who are Jack's boys. Bob and John are the apples of my eye, and I've told their father that I would like him to use the money I plan to leave him to send those two boys to college. Unfortunately, something happens to Jack, and he dies before I do. With the beneficiary designation as it stands, where does the money intended for Jack go? Will it go to the grandsons, Bob and John? No, under the default language of most forms, all of the money is going to go to Tom (Jack's brother). I know it wasn't your intent to disinherit your grandsons, but that's what will happen in most instances. Poor Bob and John don't have a father, and now they don't have any money, either.

Most people don't realize the implications of what they put on their beneficiary forms, and the results can be disastrous. By the way, it's not just consumers who fill out their own beneficiary forms who make mistakes. Financial professionals, attorneys, and CPAs who are not knowledgeable in this area also make costly

Even the simplest beneficiary designation requires more than a cursory review.

mistakes. I consider it so significantly important that I don't let my clients fill out their own beneficiary forms. Of course, I talk with my clients on a very personal level about what their wishes are, and years of experience always prompt me to ask "what if" about certain scenarios that, in many cases, my clients had never thought about or imagined could happen. So as part of our estate planning engagement, we not only draft wills, trusts, etc., we also manually fill out the beneficiary designation for every IRA and retirement plan our clients own. I'm not going to do a wonderful plan for people and then let them ruin my masterpiece by filling out the beneficiary form incorrectly. The whole thing could just blow up.

Filling Out the Forms

Even the simplest beneficiary designation requires more than a cursory review. An individual who wants to name adult individuals in his or her beneficiary designations needs to know the names, birth dates, and Social Security numbers of each beneficiary. But it goes beyond that. The account owner must also decide where the money should go if a beneficiary dies before they do or doesn't need or want all the proceeds.

- If there is one primary beneficiary and one contingent beneficiary and the primary beneficiary dies first (or disclaims his or her interest), the contingent beneficiary inherits all.

- If the account owner outlives his primary and contingent beneficiaries, and if no successor beneficiaries are named on the form, two things can happen. The proceeds could be paid to the estate of the account owner, or even to an intestate heir (the person who would have received the money had you died without a will). In this situation, it is entirely possible that a relative that you never liked, or even a spouse from who you are estranged but not yet divorced, could inherit your estate if they are determined to be the intestate heir. In addition to the possibility of the wrong person getting the money, the account could be subject to probate costs and delays, and an income tax nightmare could also result.

- If the children of the first-named beneficiary are designated to inherit their parent's share in the event of their parent's death, then the account will be paid to those children—a much better plan. But even the children need to be evaluated, especially if they are young or can't handle money. You should probably have a trust for those children if they are young or can't handle money, and the trust, not the children, needs to be named as the second beneficiary. Another fear is the no good son-in-law that requires special consideration when drafting your IRA beneficiary designation.

> It is critical to carefully read the form and instructions and develop, with the assistance of a qualified advisor, a strategy that is specific to your situation.

Clearly there are too many combinations for me to outline all possible scenarios. Furthermore, no two beneficiary forms and/or change forms that are issued by different financial institutions are alike. It is critical to carefully read the form and instructions and develop, with the assistance of a qualified advisor, a strategy that is specific to your situation.

MINI CASE STUDY 16.1

Filling Out the Forms—Simple Designation

Abe Account Owner is filling out his beneficiary forms. His first priority is to provide for his wife, Wanda, and, after her, his children, Charlie and Charra. He also wants to ensure that, if either of his children should predecease him, their individual shares will pass on to their own children (his grandchildren). If the deceased child had no children, then the share would pass to his or her sibling.

1. He designates his wife, Wanda, as the 100 percent primary beneficiary, inserting her Social Security number, date of birth, and where requested, her address. By designating her as 100 percent primary beneficiary, no other primary beneficiaries can be listed, and he will now move on to the contingent beneficiary section of the form.

2. He then designates his two children as the contingent beneficiaries, allocating 50 percent to each of them. He inserts their Social Security numbers, dates of birth, and, where indicated,

their addresses. As contingent beneficiaries, they will receive the money if Wanda is not living at the time of his death or if she disclaims in part or in whole.

3. He must now go one step further. Some beneficiary forms (TIAA-CREF, for example) have a box that, when checked, directs that the money going to a child who predeceases the account owner should be paid to his or her children (the account owner's grandchildren) in equal shares. What happens if the form doesn't have such a box? If it doesn't, then Abe has to write the words "per stirpes" after each of his children's individual names. By using this term, the financial institution will know to pay the share of that deceased child to the predeceased children's children in equal shares. This is true whether there is one beneficiary or two, and will ensure that the retirement account passes to the next generation. So if Charra dies before her father, and her father is perhaps too distraught to even think about changing his beneficiary designation, things will still work about the way he wanted after his death. Charlie will still get his share, and the share that Charra would have inherited had she lived, will go directly to her children. Without those words "per stirpes" after Charra and Charlie's names, all of the money may go directly to Charlie, or if Charlie is also deceased, to Abe's estate.

4. Finally, Abe must sign and date the form where indicated, and submit it to his plan administrator for processing. Within a couple of weeks, Abe should receive confirmation from the plan administrator that the changes he requested have been put in place.

There is one extra step that must be taken if the account owner wants to name someone other than his or her spouse as beneficiary to their qualified plan account. If the account in question is an ERISA type plans [a 401(k) or a 403(b), for example, but not an IRA], the spouse must provide written consent to any beneficiary designation that does not leave all the proceeds to the surviving spouse. The spouse must sign a consent form agreeing that they are not the beneficiary of the account, and their signature on the form must be notarized. This section of the beneficiary form is usually below where the account owner is required to sign. The spouse's notarized consent must be completed before the plan administrator will accept the form. Most qualified plans are subject to this spousal consent rule (with exceptions that are beyond the scope of this book) whereas IRAs and Roth IRAs are not subject to the rule.

Complex Designations: Incorporating the Perfect Cascade

The simple beneficiary designations outlined in Abe's case might work effectively. The problem is that, if the money passes to a minor or someone who is not financially prudent, that person can use it to buy a fast car or host the party of the century as soon as he or she reaches 21 (or even 18 in some states).

Now we have to consider more complex situations. For the purposes of this chapter, we assume that the account owner has designated his or her spouse as the primary beneficiary but wants to designate a trust as the contingent beneficiary. (See Chapter 17 for a discussion of the ramifications of designating a trust as the primary versus contingent beneficiary of a retirement plan). This scenario is likely under four circumstances:

1. Where we want to provide for a spendthrift child and ensure that he or she receives smaller amounts of money over the longest period of time possible.

2. Where an individual wants to allow for grandchildren or other young beneficiaries to receive retirement monies, but not before they reach a specific age. This can be accomplished through a subtrust under a standalone trust or a revocable trust, or a trust within a will called a testamentary trust.

3. There is another purpose for a trust, such as when a beneficiary is disabled and you are trying to protect their inheritance from the government.

4. When the "I don't want my no good son-in-law to inherit one red cent of my money trust" is appropriate (more and more common these days).

If the client wants to use a standalone trust (our office uses what is called a Revocable Trust) to control the distribution of his or her retirement benefits, the beneficiary designation is relatively simple: The spouse is designated as the primary beneficiary, and the Revocable Trust is designated as the contingent beneficiary. The Revocable Trust incorporates the perfect cascade to provide the option of the children equally and the option of various trusts for grandchildren.

In some cases, a client can accomplish all of the distribution options of a Revocable Trust through a simple and well-drafted beneficiary designation that includes all of the options stated in the trust. The beneficiary designation of the IRA or retirement plan should then refer to the proper Article of the will, or to the Revocable Trust. Regardless of the mechanics, the key is that the money be directed where the IRA owner wants.

In some situations an account owner might want his or her spouse to be the primary beneficiary and their children the contingent beneficiaries, but the account owner can add an additional element of control by giving his or her children the right to disclaim some part or all of their shares to their own children (the account owner's grandchildren). Rather than using the per stirpes designation discussed above, which would pay the money directly to the grandchild if the child disclaims (though subject to a guardian's control until the grandchild becomes 18), the account owner may want to designate separate trusts for the grandchildren as the beneficiaries. We generally prefer to set up separate trusts for each grandchild. Please read on.

One Consolidated Group Trust versus Individual Trusts for Grandchildren

If one group trust is used, then all beneficiaries are stuck taking distributions according to the life expectancy of the oldest beneficiary—undermining the stretch for the younger beneficiaries. Some clients, however, want to have one trust with several beneficiaries believing that there is no need for equalization, and prefer having the flexibility to make unequal distributions.

For example, assume you are leaving money to three grandchildren, all children of your only child. You could leave the money in three separate trusts, or you could leave the money in one trust. If you choose three separate trusts, you would get the longest stretch for the youngest beneficiary. In addition, you would make sure or nearly sure that each grandchild would be treated equally. If one grandchild went to college, his or her trust could be used for college. If another grandchild didn't go to college, eventually he or she would get the money for other purposes.

On the other hand, if you weren't worried so much about equality and just wanted to emulate real life where you spend money on your children and grandchildren without keeping track of each dollar and equalizing at the end, the single trust may work well for your needs even though you are slightly accelerating distributions from the IRA. Many families prefer the flexibility of one trust if one of their primary estate planning goals is to educate their grandchildren. If separate trusts are established for the grandchildren, it is possible that one grandchild's education costs may not be fully covered because he or she was accepted to a very expensive school, while another grandchild takes his inheritance and drinks beer and buys a fast car. In our practice, our clients are about evenly divided as to whether they prefer a separate trust for each grandchild to maximize IRA deferral or a single trust for all the grandchildren to permit unequal distributions.

Finally, you want to think about how you want your retirement plan to be distributed in the event that neither your spouse nor your descendants survive you. Under these circumstances, you might want to do something for charity or give the assets to your siblings, or possibly your siblings with the right to disclaim to your nieces and nephews. All of these considerations must be spelled out in your documents, or else the assets might pass to someone you don't intend to receive the inheritance.

Since no beneficiary change form allows for this kind of stepped plan, an attachment should be drafted that clearly spells out how the beneficiary designations should work. Most plan administrators are willing to accommodate such sophisticated planning when it is presented in a clear and concise manner.

The Hazards of Naming Different Beneficiaries for Different Accounts

It is quite common in my practice for clients to say they want one particular account to go to one beneficiary and a different account to another beneficiary. The accounts might reflect the relative proportionate value that the client wants each of the different beneficiaries to receive, but I think this can turn into a nightmare.

- You will have a terrible time trying to keep track of the different distribution schedules.

- As the different investments go up or down, the amount going to the different heirs would also go up and down, which is probably not the intent.

- A beneficiary designation may say, "I leave my Vanguard account to beneficiary B and my Schwab account to beneficiary A." If during your lifetime you switch or transfer money from Vanguard to Schwab, you have, in effect, changed who is going to get what, and that may not be your intention.

- Suppose that you become ill, and you (or the person to whom you gave a Power of Attorney) need to spend money for medical bills and/or nursing home care. You might not even have the mental capacity to understand that, by spending one account instead of spending all accounts equally, you are reducing (or maybe even completely eliminating) the inheritance intended for one beneficiary.

In general, I prefer one master beneficiary designation for all IRAs, retirement plans, 403(b)s, 401(k)s, and the like. In it, I describe distributions as I would in a will or irrevocable or revocable trust. For example, I might say 50 percent to my son Bob and 50 percent to my daughter Cindy, per stirpes – and use that beneficiary designation on every single account. That way, we can avoid mistakes and simplify estate administration after the retirement plan owner dies.

I recognize that, for investment purposes, people use different accounts for different beneficiaries. For example, you might treat the investments of a grandchild beneficiary differently from those of a child or spouse. Under those circumstances, I would be willing to bend and accept different beneficiaries for different accounts. This is especially true if the account is a Roth.

The one area where it might make sense to direct certain money to particular beneficiaries is FDIC insured deposits. FDIC currently protects accounts up to $250,000 per individual. Assuming the money is outside the IRA (there are different protections for IRAs), one way to get more FDIC insurance is to have different beneficiaries by using different Paid On Death (POD) designations. If you are a parent with four kids and you have four $250,000 CDs, you can do a POD account for each child and have the entire $1 million federally guaranteed. It is important to know that this is not a gift – your children have no access to the money until after you die. If the money was in an IRA, you are also insured up to $250,000, but you can't get additional coverage by naming additional beneficiaries.

Submitting the Forms

For any trust that is a beneficiary of an IRA, the IRS requires that, by October 31 of the year following the year of the account owner's death, the plan administrator must be provided with either a copy of any trust designated as a beneficiary or a certified list of all the beneficiaries. A testamentary trust, where the contingent beneficiary is a trust contained in the account owners' will, is treated differently from a standalone trust. Then, a copy of the will should be provided to the plan administrator just as a standalone trust would be.

Where the trust is a tertiary beneficiary—that is, where the children are the contingent beneficiaries and the trusts for grandchildren receive money only at the death of the children or via the children disclaiming, then a copy of the will is generally not provided until it is determined that the trust will actually become a beneficiary.

In the past, when taxpayers made a mistake, they would ask the IRS to let them slide with a private letter ruling. Now, between the IRS fee and the professional fee to prepare the ruling, the cost could be $18,000 or more. Moral of the story: Prepare your beneficiary form carefully, or better yet, have a competent attorney prepare the forms and submit them as early as you can.

A Key Lesson from This Chapter

Do not underestimate the attention to detail that is required to fill out a beneficiary designation form. For many people, their IRA or retirement plans constitute the bulk of their wealth, and the beneficiary designation, not the will, controls the disbursement of those funds.

17

||||||||||||||||||||

Trusts as Beneficiaries of Retirement Plans

Put not your trust in money, but put your money in trust.

— Oliver Wendell Holmes

Main Topics

- Whether to consider a trust as a beneficiary to your IRA
- The proper beneficiary designation when using a trust
- Young beneficiaries
- Spendthrift trusts (or the "I don't want my no good son-in-law to get one red cent of my money" trust)
- Unified Credit Shelter Trust
- Qualified Terminal Interest Property Trust (QTIP)
- Charitable Remainder Unit Trusts (CRUT)

KEY IDEA

Setting up a trust for the beneficiary of a retirement plan and/or IRA can be an excellent method of protecting the beneficiary. Creating trusts for minors, for spendthrifts, and for spouses can be appropriate under certain circumstances.

A General Observation about Trusts

There are many types of trusts, and each one serves a particular purpose. As I mentioned earlier, many good estate attorneys routinely create trusts for adult children. Though I think this practice has merit, for responsible older adult children without marital problems, I believe the simplicity of leaving money outright outweighs some of the risks that the trust protects against. Remember, though, you should never name your estate as your beneficiary because that makes it subject to probate, which is a time consuming and expensive process, and which accelerates the income tax that would have been due on the retirement account.

The Proper Beneficiary Designation When Using a Trust

Please remember the basics. Your beneficiary designation, not your will, controls the distribution of your IRA at your death. Therefore, you need to make sure that the beneficiary designation of your retirement plan is completed correctly.

You can either submit a correctly worded beneficiary designation form, or name as the beneficiary a qualifying trust that complies with the five conditions listed in Chapter 13. Assuming that it is done correctly, you will have the same result using either option. If the beneficiary form is completed incorrectly or if the terms of the trust do not meet the five conditions described in Chapter 13, then we have enormous problems. Please refer back to Chapter 16 for details on actually filling out the beneficiary forms.

I do not allow my clients to fill out beneficiary change forms for their IRAs or retirement plans. Granted, it takes additional time for us to do it, and requires even more work if there are many IRAs and retirement plans in different investment companies, all of which are likely to have their own beneficiary change form. I have seen enough instances where the client and/or his attorney were cavalier about the IRA beneficiary form, and the form was filled out incorrectly. I have also seen situations where the attorney's directions to the client were not clear or, worse yet, the client didn't follow the attorney's instructions. With large IRAs or retirement plans, there is too much at stake to allow errors.

In my office, we draft a special document to be used as the retirement plan or IRA beneficiary designation. Within that long document (see Lange's

Cascading Beneficiary Plan), we draft a special trust or, more often, a series of trusts to be used as the beneficiary of the IRA. Currently, we typically refer to the will or a revocable trust that contains all the details. The trust within the will or revocable trust, however, always meets the five conditions required for the trust or beneficiary to stretch the IRA.

> **With large IRAs or retirement plans, there is too much at stake for inadvertent errors; get help from a competent attorney who understands how to draft IRA beneficiary designations.**

My original intention was to include detailed sample language with this book, but after thinking it through, realized that with large IRAs or retirement plans, there is too much at stake for inadvertent errors; get help from a competent attorney who understands how to draft IRA beneficiary designations.

The attorney should understand your entire financial situation and have the requisite technical knowledge of the law and the forms before being asked to properly fill out the forms. This is one instance when I think paying an attorney is money well spent. Other financial professionals may be competent to perform this task, but please make sure that filling out a beneficiary form is not incidental to a sale but rather a task taken seriously by whoever is performing it.

Mechanics of a Trust as the Beneficiary of the IRA

Let's start with these basic assumptions. An IRA or a 403(b) or 401(a) participant owner dies. A trust is the primary beneficiary, or it becomes the beneficiary because the surviving spouse, who had been named as the primary beneficiary, disclaims and the trust is the secondary beneficiary.

We have discussed the Required Minimum Distribution (RMD) rules for the inherited IRA owned by the trust both during the life of the surviving spouse and after the surviving spouse dies. What perhaps is not clear is the mechanics of how the account should be handled after death in order to avoid a massive acceleration of income taxes—which would happen if all the money in the IRA were disbursed to the beneficiary.

After death, the inherited IRA will be retitled to something like "Bob Jones, deceased, for the benefit of Sam Jones, Trustee of the Bob Jones Plan Benefits Trust." However, the money is not actually transferred to the trust at that point. The *name of the account is retitled*, but that is not an income taxable event.

The money sits in this newly named account held by the plan administrator. The RMD rules for a spouse who inherits an IRA are based on his or her life expectancy. If, for example, the surviving spouse has a 20-year life expectancy, we would divide 20 into the account balance as of December 31 of the year the IRA owner died in order to calculate the RMD. In subsequent years, the life expectancy factor would be 19, then 18, and so on. Even after the death of the surviving spouse, children would still have to take withdrawals based on the surviving spouse's remaining life expectancy according to the tables, if any money remains.

When any trust is the beneficiary of an inherited IRA, whether the end beneficiary is a trust for children or the spouse, income taxation generally occurs when the money is transferred from the inherited IRA to the trustee of the trust. To minimize the taxes, I generally recommend that the transfers happen only on a RMD basis. The trustee will receive the check from the plan administrator and deposit it into a checking account in the name of the trust. If the money is kept in the trust, the trust must pay income taxes on the distribution at trust income tax rates. More commonly, the trust will pay out 100 percent of the RMD it receives to the trust beneficiary, the surviving spouse. The reason for paying the RMD (or whatever amount is withdrawn) to the beneficiary, rather than keeping the money in the trust, is to avoid the higher income taxes imposed on the trust (which are usually higher than an individual's income tax rate).

Here is an example of how it happens in our office. We calculate the annual RMD early in January. We have a monthly automatic transfer of one-twelfth of the RMD from the inherited IRA to a separate trust checking account. Then we have an automatic transfer from this trust account to the bank account of the surviving spouse. At the end of the year, the plan administrator issues a Form 1099 (or multiple 1099s) to the trust. The trustee files a tax return called a Form 1041 reporting the distribution it received as income, and deducts the amount it paid to the surviving spouse as a distribution deduction, via a Schedule K-1. Since the deductions equal the income exactly, the trust pays no tax. The surviving spouse includes the Schedule K-1 income (which is the amount distributed from the inherited IRA) on her own Form 1040 for the year and pays the income tax accordingly.

Therefore, what you may have heard in the past—that when the money goes to a trust it becomes taxable—is accurate. However, it is important to understand that after the death of the IRA owner, the money is transferred into an inherited IRA account and *not* the trust account until minimum distributions or other distributions are *deposited* into the trust account. Simply renaming the account to the name of the trust is not a withdrawal of the entire IRA (which would generate a huge tax bill).

MINI CASE STUDY 17.1

The Perils of Inaccurate Beneficiary Designations

Tom fills out his beneficiary form with wording provided by the Human Resources Department where he works: "My grandchild Junior, in trust." Tom does have a will that includes a trust for Junior, but there is no specific reference to that will in this beneficiary designation. The result is that Junior may not be able to reach this money when he is 21 because, in effect, there is no trust as a beneficiary specific to the beneficiary designation. Less technically, that means that the words Tom used on his beneficiary form were too vague, and the IRA custodian will delay releasing the funds while they try to figure out which trust Tom was talking about. And while Junior's parents (or their lawyers) may eventually be able to argue that the trust mentioned in Tom's beneficiary designation is definitely the same one as the trust mentioned for Junior's benefit under Tom's will, considerable time and expense could have been saved if Tom had had good advice and knowledgeable help to complete the beneficiary designation properly.

Perils of a Trust That Doesn't Meet the Five Conditions

Let's consider another example. Tom fills out the beneficiary form with "The Tom Family Trust for Grandchildren, found in my will." Assuming the trust in the will meets all five requirements, the money will pass as intended, in trust. Let's review the five requirements again:

1. The trust must be valid under state law, or would be but for the fact that it is not yet funded.

2. The trust is irrevocable or will become irrevocable at the creator's death.

3. The trust beneficiaries must be identifiable. That is to say, by the last day of the year following the creator's death, it must be possible to identify all the persons who could possibly be beneficiaries of the trust.

4. All the trust beneficiaries must be individuals.

5. Documentation about the trust must be provided to the plan administrator by October 31 of the year following the person's death. This consists of a copy of the trust instrument or a final list of all the beneficiaries.

If, on the other hand, the trust in the will violates one of these five conditions, then we do not have a qualifying trust as a beneficiary. If that is the case, the income from the IRA is accelerated and Junior loses the ability to stretch the proceeds of the IRA for as long as possible.

Therefore, it is critical that the five conditions are met for all trusts with the potential to become beneficiaries of IRAs and/or retirement plans.

Trusts to Protect Young Beneficiaries

> **The most prudent way to leave money to a young beneficiary is through a trust.**

The most prudent way to leave money to a young beneficiary is through a trust.

Typically I draft trusts for young beneficiaries with the following provisions:

- The trustee is given the discretion to make distributions for health, maintenance, support, education, postgraduate education, a down payment for a house, seed money for a business, and if the parent or grandparent is a real sport, one summer in Europe.

- Then, at the age of 25 (not 21), the beneficiary is entitled to withdraw one third of the principal of the trust.

- At age 30, the beneficiary is entitled to make a withdrawal of up to one-half of the remaining balance.

- At age 35, the beneficiary has unlimited access to the principal.

This example provides a reasonable starting point, but is not the only way to draft a trust for young beneficiaries.

It is easy to vary the terms of the trust according to your personal preferences. The type of trust I described works well when the beneficiaries are young, usually for grandchildren when it is unclear how they will turn out as young adults. If the beneficiary is already in his or her late teens or early twenties, you can alter the terms as seems prudent to you. Some 25-year-olds are perfectly capable of handling money without the need for a trust, but I've also met 35-year-olds who were nowhere near ready for that type of responsibility. If your beneficiaries are old enough for you to assess their level of responsibility, and you have confidence in their judgment, then you don't have to rely on the general language recommended above.

Most of the trusts for minors that we draft are for the benefit of a grandchild (or grandchildren). The trust takes effect when the IRA owner dies and the first beneficiary (often the IRA owner's child) has either predeceased the grandchild or chooses to disclaim to his or her children.

MINI CASE STUDY 17.2
Protecting Junior

Tom Smith, a retired IRA owner, has one son, Joe, and one grandson, Junior, age 3. He fills out his beneficiary form as follows:

1. My son, Joe Smith (as primary beneficiary)

2. My grandson, Junior Smith (as contingent beneficiary)

Tom dies. Joe doesn't want or need the money and, as his father had asked him to, he disclaims his right to the IRA. The money will then go to Junior, who is the contingent beneficiary. Since his grandfather did not establish a trust for his benefit, Junior will have complete access to the IRA money when he reaches 21 (younger in some states). Tom's legacy might be a Corvette and a year of drunken partying for Junior.

Assume, instead, that Tom names his beneficiaries as follows:

1. My son, Joe Smith

2. The Tom Smith Family Trust for Grandchildren under Articles V & VI of the Last Will and Testament of Tom Smith dated March 1, 2015

As Tom's will states, he has already drafted a trust for Junior. With this structure, his son, Joe, can be much more comfortable. Joe can disclaim his inheritance to the trust that he knows has reasonable restrictions for Junior, rather than disclaiming the assets outright to him. Now Junior will not have access to all of the money at 21, but if he has legitimate needs—education, for example—they can be met by the trust. Joe could even be named trustee. By going to the trouble of drafting the trust, Tom protected the money from premature taxation and frivolous spending. The trust also protects Junior's inheritance from his creditors, who may range from a bank or credit card company, to someone suing him for damages in an automobile accident, and even to his future spouse if their marriage goes sour.

Spendthrift Trusts

This type of trust may also be referred to as a *forced prudence trust,* or, and this is my personal favorite, the "I don't want my no good son-in-law getting one red cent of my money" trust.

The basic spendthrift trust is usually drafted because not every child, even those beyond 35 years old, will have developed sufficient maturity or sense of fiscal responsibility to make wise choices after the death of his or her parent or parents. It is also possible that parents may feel their children will never be financially responsible so the parents want to control from the grave for the remainder of their child's life. Since the greatest value of an inherited IRA is to stretch the benefits for as long as possible, it would be a financial disaster to have an inappropriate and premature withdrawal of these funds.

A spendthrift trust will put a trusted relative, friend, or financial institution in control of the beneficiary's money and will ensure that the inherited IRA is used as a lifetime fund rather than an "I want a brand new Porsche fund." In more severe cases, where drug addiction or alcohol abuse comes into play, I often recommend additional special provisions. Spendthrift trusts typically also include creditor protection language, and even though such language does not offer the beneficiary perfect protection, it does go a long way toward protecting the beneficiaries not only from themselves but also from their creditors or potential creditors. One set of potential creditors for your children that you may not have thought about are your children's spouses in the event that they divorce. Other times, even without a divorce, a child's spouse may be pushing the child to act irresponsibly with the inherited funds. In some cases, a trust can be used to protect a child from his or her spouse's irresponsibility.

Our law firm is experiencing an ever-growing number of clients who love their kids, but who don't trust their kids' spouses.

True Story Ensuring the No Good Son-in-Law Gets Nothing

One of life's greatest mysteries is how the boy who wasn't
good enough to marry your daughter can be the father of
the smartest grandchild in the world.
— Proverb

A couple came into my office, and the first thing the husband said was, "I don't want my no good son-in-law to get one dime of my money." Only after discussing this issue could we proceed with providing for his wife, his other children, his grandchildren, and saving taxes. What we ended up with was, basically, leaving any money that his daughter might inherit to a trust for the benefit of the daughter. We named an independent trustee whose job is to make sure the money is protected from the son-in-law, even if the daughter wants to give her husband money. In terms of actual drafting, the language is similar to a traditional spendthrift trust.

Although I have no qualms in drafting a trust when the client thinks there is a significant need to protect the beneficiary, other practitioners go much farther in the direction of controlling from the grave. For some children, spendthrift trusts are certainly justified, and it is far more prudent to leave money to a child in trust. Some practitioners see leaving money for adult children in trust as the norm rather than the exception. Personally, I am a cheapskate, and I like to keep things simple if I can. Therefore, my default is not to draft a trust for an adult beneficiary.

One noted expert who recommends using a trust for an adult child as the rule instead of the exception advocates putting virtually all of an adult child's interest from an inherited IRA into a trust. As he correctly points out, this forces the child to stretch the benefits over his or her lifetime and protects the child from creditors. He claims that the adult children are happy with this arrangement. Many financial firms offer boilerplate trusts as beneficiaries of the IRA. I generally do not like this approach.

I prefer the simplicity of trusting the adult child's judgment unless there is a reason not to. The idea of forcing the adult child to stretch the IRA for as long as possible and not permitting anything other than mandatory withdrawals is a reasonable idea under some circumstances, especially if the child needs the maximum protection possible from creditors. If you do use a trust (even in a spendthrift situation), the trust should have a provision allowing for distributions beyond the Required Minimum Distribution (RMD) from the IRA. It should also have a provision for distributions for health, maintenance, support, education, and so on.

A relevant issue when naming a trust as a beneficiary of an IRA is whether the drafter wishes to treat the RMD as income, or part income and part principal for the trust's accounting purposes. Pennsylvania and some other states in accordance with the Uniform Principal and Income Act of 1997 (UPAIA) have adopted tracing rules which require the trustee to allocate a portion of the RMD as income and the remainder of the RMD as principal. If the income portion of the RMD cannot be traced, the UPAIA states that a RMD payable to a trust will be treated as 90 percent principal and 10 percent income for trust accounting purposes. Accordingly, if the objective is for the income beneficiary of the trust to pay the income tax due on the RMD (my usual preference because the income tax rates for individuals are lower than the rates for trusts), drafters should opt out of the UPAIA by mandating that RMDs payable to the trust be treated as income and paid out to the income beneficiary.

Unified Credit Shelter Trust, or B Trust, as Beneficiary

In years past, it was common to see the B trust, or the Unified Credit Shelter Trust, named as the contingent beneficiary of the retirement plan. This type of trust gave the surviving spouse all of the trust income and the trustee the flexibility to distribute principal for the health, maintenance, and support of the surviving spouse. The surviving spouse was also often given a "5 and 5 power," meaning that each year the surviving spouse could withdraw the greater of an additional five percent of the corpus (assets excluding profit and interest) of the trust, or $5,000. At the death of the surviving spouse, the trust proceeds generally went to the children equally. The main purpose of this type of trust was to ensure that, for federal estate tax purposes, the proceeds of the trust would not be included in the estate of the second spouse to die.

Currently, federal estate taxes are not a concern for most taxpayers, and so avoiding estate taxes should not be the reason for establishing (or keeping) this type of trust. The Applicable Exclusion Amount has been increased to a level ($5.43 million in 2015) that far exceeds the estates of most couples. In addition, the estate of the first spouse to die can now elect to transfer any unused Applicable Exclusion Amount, to the estate of the surviving spouse. This concept, known as portability, brings the amount of a married couple's assets that are completely exempt from federal estate tax to well over $10 million.

Married couples whose estates are not likely to ever exceed $10 million, who still have this type of trust as part of their estate plan, should have their documents reviewed by a competent estate planning attorney immediately. Please read "The Cruelest Trap of All" in Chapter 11 to find out why.

The QTIP (The A Trust of the A/B Trust)

I hate to see QTIP trusts (Qualified Terminal Interest Property) and/or B trusts as beneficiaries of retirement plans and IRAs and, in my practice, use them only as a last resort. But since it is not unusual to see QTIP trusts in second marriages, I will give you a brief overview of how they work. Basically, the trust says to pay the surviving spouse an income for life, but at the second spouse's death, have the principal revert to the children of the first marriage.

The terms of the QTIP trust have provisions for the surviving spouse that are similar to the provisions for the surviving spouse in a B trust. Like a B trust, it provides income to the surviving spouse and the assets revert to the children at the surviving spouse's death. The purpose of the QTIP trust, however, is not to avoid estate taxes at the second death. Rather the purposes are to provide an income to the surviving spouse, to preserve a marital deduction at the death of the first spouse, and to preserve the assets for the children from the decedent's first marriage. The marital deduction allows the first estate to escape federal estate taxation on the assets transferred to the QTIP trust. But unlike the B trust, the balance of the QTIP trust is included in the estate of the second spouse to die. As a result, there are no estate tax savings with the QTIP trust.

It is natural to want to protect your second spouse and then have the money revert to children from your first marriage. For after-tax assets, QTIP trusts, though not a perfect solution, are often the best solution. In reality, for IRA owners using this type of plan, the biggest question in my mind is who will be most unhappy: the surviving spouse, the children of the first marriage, or the poor trustee.

This type of trust accelerates income taxes by forcing both the surviving spouse and the children of the first marriage (generally the ones who inherit the remainder of the trust at the second death) to take RMDs based on the surviving spouse's age. Because QTIP trusts are usually the primary beneficiaries and the interests of both spouses are usually different because frequently they each have their own set of children, there are few disclaimer opportunities providing alternative ways to reduce income taxes.

As a result, during the surviving spouse's life, minimum distributions are accelerated faster than if the surviving spouse had been named outright. When the surviving spouse dies (assuming the surviving spouse predeceases the children), the children of the first marriage will also have an accelerated RMD schedule based on the life expectancy of their stepparent, not their own life expectancy (the same situation as the RMD of a Unified Credit Shelter Trust). (See Mini Case Study 14.1).

An Alternative Solution to the QTIP

Instead of setting up a QTIP trust, provide:

- X percent of your IRA to your surviving spouse

- 100 – X percent of your IRA to the children of your first marriage

For example, if the value of an income stream for a 65-year-old surviving spouse based on a six percent rate of return is worth roughly 58 percent of the principal of the IRA (based on the life expectancy of the surviving spouse and depending on what tables you use), then it is simpler and preferable in the vast majority of cases to leave the surviving spouse 58 percent of the IRA and the children 42 percent of the IRA.

Upon the death of the IRA owner, the surviving spouse takes his or her share and rolls it into an IRA. Until the surviving spouse reaches 70½, there is no RMD. When he or she reaches 70½, he or she will take RMDs based on the Uniform Life Table (see the appendix). The children take their shares as an inherited IRA and stretch distributions based on their own life expectancies. Clean. Simple. Cheap. No trusts, no fuss, no muss.

This solution may not fit with the IRA owner's goal of making sure the surviving spouse always has an income. In some circumstances, particularly for an older and less sophisticated beneficiary spouse, it may be prudent to direct the executor to buy an annuity that will guarantee the second spouse an income for life (see Chapter 8).

Another solution is to buy life insurance. But please, no QTIPs for IRAs.

Charitable Remainder Unitrusts

With more frequency, we are using Charitable Remainder Unitrusts (or CRUT) as contingent beneficiaries of IRAs. If a CRUT is established and is named as the beneficiary, the descendant's IRA is paid as a lump sum into the CRUT. Distributions can be paid to income beneficiaries of the trust (usually the children) for years, possibly even for the duration of their lifetimes, but there is a specific amount that eventually must be turned over to the charity that is named as the final beneficiary. The amount that can be paid to the income beneficiaries is calculated yearly, using a complex formula required by the IRS. There are no taxes due at the time the IRA is moved to the CRUT because the final distribution is to a charitable entity, and the trust can take a tax deduction for the charitable contribution even though the contribution doesn't get paid until the trust is dissolved. However, the annual distributions made to income beneficiaries are subject to income tax.

Even if they have generously donated to charity over the course of their lifetimes, many of my clients have done a double take when I've brought up the idea of leaving their large IRA to a charitable trust. Understandably, they're concerned about how their children will react when they find out that they aren't the beneficiary. But once they understand how the CRUT works, then the idea begins to make sense. Often the benefit of the deferred incoming growing inside the CRUT exceeds the amount of the final payout to the charity.

MINI CASE STUDY 17.3

Using a Charitable Remainder Unitrust

Margaret, a retired IRA owner, has no children of her own. She wants to leave her IRA, valued at $1 million, to her sister's only child, Thomas, who is 57 years old. As you know from reading Chapter 5, in the absence of proper planning, Thomas will be required to withdraw all of the money from his aunt's IRA within five years, causing a maximum acceleration of income taxes. Is there anything that Margaret can do to minimize Thomas' tax bill, while at the same time maximizing the amount he receives from her IRA?

The answer is yes. Margaret can establish a Charitable Remainder Unitrust that names her nephew as the income beneficiary, and her favorite charity (or charities) as the final beneficiary. Because the beneficiary form on her IRA was completed correctly, the account will be transferred to the trust at her death. Thomas reinvests all of the distributions he receives into a brokerage account, until his death at age 84. The value of his account at his death if he received the distributions from the IRA is $3,299,558. The value of his account at his death if he had received the distributions from the CRUT is $3,798,384 – and her favorite charity also receives $179,717. Please refer to Figure 17.1 below.

Figure 17.1
CRUT vs. Inherited IRA with 5 Year Stretch

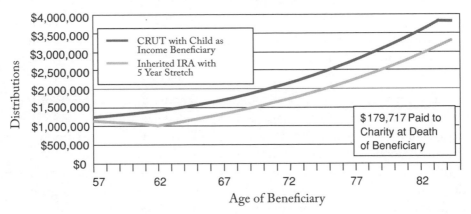

The income tax consequence of removing all of the money from the tax shelter of the IRA within five years is significant. If Congress does limit the number of years that a beneficiary can make withdrawals from an inherited IRA, the CRUT can serve as an alternative method to "stretch" the proceeds of the IRA for longer than five years, possibly for the lifetime of the beneficiary. In addition, naming the spouse as the primary beneficiary of the IRA and the CRUT as the contingent beneficiary allows maximum flexibility, because the spouse can access the money if she needs it, and disclaim to the trust if she doesn't.

A Key Lesson from This Chapter

Establishing a trust as a beneficiary is most successful for protecting minors and spendthrifts. B trusts and QTIP trusts, though sometimes an interesting option, are usually not best for IRA and retirement plan beneficiary designations. Charitable Remainder Unitrusts should be considered if the IRA owner is charitably inclined.

18

‖‖‖‖‖‖‖‖‖‖‖‖‖‖‖‖‖‖‖‖‖‖‖‖‖‖‖

How Donors Can Do Well by Doing Good

As I started getting rich, I started thinking, "What the hell am I going to do with all this money?". . . You have to learn to give.

— Ted Turner

Main Topics

- Charitable estate planning with IRA and retirement assets

- Charitable trusts in general

- Lifetime charitable remainder trusts

- Alternatives to charitable trusts

- Testamentary charitable trusts

KEY IDEA

By understanding a few concepts, you can do far more for charity than you may have expected, while still providing for your family.

Charitable Lifetime Planning with IRAs

The Pension Protection Act of 2006 included the first charitable rollover provision for IRAs. They were renewed on October 3, 2008, when Congress passed and President Bush signed into law the *Emergency Economic Stabilization Act of 2008*. It was extended in 2009 and this provision of the Act has been extended every year since then. The provision allows taxpayers who are age 70½ or older to directly donate up to $100,000 from their IRAs to charity. A direct donation means that, since you never take possession of the money, the IRA distribution can be excluded from your taxable income. Having the distribution completely excluded from your income is far superior to including the donation as an itemized deduction, because itemized deductions are often limited and lower income often provides other tax savings.

To be eligible to benefit from this provision, you must have an IRA (versus a qualified plan), be 70½ or older, and the distribution must be to a public charity (not to a private foundation or a donor advised fund). All of my clients are asking me if they can make a qualified charitable distribution for 2015, and, as of this writing, the answer is "I don't know." The extension allowing 2014 distributions was not granted until December 16, 2014. My feeling is that, if you don't need the income from your Required Minimum Distribution (RMD), and are going to donate money to charity anyway, you might as well instruct your custodian to send the money to the charity directly regardless of the current status of the law. If Congress decides at the last minute to extend this provision, then the IRA distribution that you sent to the charity will not be included in your taxable income and your tax situation will be significantly improved. If they don't extend the provision, then the worst that will happen is that the IRA distribution will be included in your taxable income, and you can deduct the charitable contribution if you itemize.

The charitable IRA rollover provision is a welcome addition to charitable lifetime planning. Frequently, my clients take RMDs from IRAs not because they need them but because they are required to take them. This provision gives these taxpayers a convenient and tax-savvy way to benefit charity. Many people have asked why is it better to donate your RMD directly to charity rather than withdraw your RMD and then donate it to charity? The primary reason is that donating your RMD directly to charity provides you with greater income tax benefits.

The first benefit to your family is that the charitable deduction for the direct IRA donation will be, effectively, 100 percent deductible. Writing a check for a charitable donation of the same amount may not be fully deductible, especially for high income taxpayers who at tax time are subject to adjusted gross income limitations as well as phase outs of their itemized deductions. Donating IRA distributions directly to charity may minimize the amount of taxable Social Security benefits because you are excluding that money from your income. A lower income can reduce your Medicare premium. Also, the charitable IRA rollover provision gives non-itemizers a way to deduct their charitable contributions.

Converting your RMD to a direct donation can make a lot of sense, but there is an additional benefit that most people, including financial advisors, rarely think about. A donation of this type frequently results in substantial income tax savings – so why not take advantage of those savings and convert part of your traditional IRA to a Roth? For example, a $100,000 direct donation from an IRA may save $25,000 in federal income taxes, which is enough to cover the taxes you would owe from a $100,000 Roth IRA conversion. (Please have a qualified tax advisor run the numbers for you before doing a conversion, because there are many factors that could affect your tax scenario). My point is, I think that donating your RMD from your IRA (cannot exceed $100,000) to charity is a great way both to benefit charity *and* help your family when you use the income tax savings to do a Roth IRA conversion into a tax-free Roth account. (See Chapter 7, "Roth IRA Advantage to the Beneficiary" on the benefits of inheriting a Roth IRA).

Charitable Estate Planning with IRA and Retirement Assets

Some people have charitable intentions, and regardless of any tax benefits, they plan on giving large amounts of money during their lives and at their deaths to worthy charities. Some people are not charitable at all and make neither lifetime gifts nor death transfers to charity. Then, there are the rest of us, including me, whom I will label, tongue-in-cheek, as greedy givers.

The greedy giver's primary concern is providing for his or her inner circle. We do, however, have some charity in our soul and want to make some provision for charities both while we are alive and at our death. If we can make a large impact with our charitable dollars, particularly if we get Uncle Sam to significantly subsidize our charitable intentions, we are that much happier. To this group, we address this chapter.

Sometimes simple planning goes a long way toward providing great value to the charity, great value to your heirs, and eliminates, or at least reduces, the amount going to the IRS.

A Simple Example of Which Dollars to Leave to Charity

Assume you have an estate consisting of $500,000 in an IRA and $500,000 in after-tax money. Assume further that you want half to go to charity, and the other half to your heirs. Many planners, in an attempt to keep things simple, would prepare wills and beneficiary designations leaving one-half of the IRA and one-half of the after-tax funds to the charity and the rest to the heirs. Or worse, they would leave the entire IRA to the heirs and make a bequest of the after-tax money to charity.

Charities don't care in what form (IRA, after-tax, highly appreciated dollars, Roth IRA, etc.) they get their money, because they do not pay income taxes. Individuals do care because of the different tax implications of the different types of inherited funds.

Under most circumstances, it makes sense to give the IRA to charity. In the past, if the beneficiary of the IRA was age 40 or younger, the advantages of the stretch IRA usually outweighed the fact that income taxes will be due on the distributions. So to clarify, for a 50⁺-year-old beneficiary, I used to recommend that he or she inherit the after-tax funds and that the charity receive the IRA. For a 30-year-old who planned to stretch the IRA by limiting distributions to the minimum, I used to recommend that he or she

Charities don't care in what form (IRA, after-tax, highly appreciated dollars, Roth IRA, etc.) they get their money, because they do not pay income taxes. Individuals do care because of the different tax implications of the different types of inherited funds.

get the inherited IRA and the charity the after-tax funds. In either case, the charity doesn't care because it is all the same to them. However, with the death of the stretch IRA seeming imminent, planning for family members becomes more complicated. Ultimately, it may make more sense to always leave IRAs and retirement accounts to charity, since they will be of less value to family members if the stretch is eliminated. If the IRA is the biggest asset in the estate and there is no other money to leave to family members, it might also make sense to consider leaving the IRA to a charitable trust benefitting the family.

Charitable Trusts in General

Split-interest gifts are gifts where the donor or his family maintains some interest in the property and a charity (or charities) also receives an interest. They are often found in some form of a charitable trust. These trusts can be established and funded either during your life or at your death. The living or inter vivos trust involves a transfer of assets to a charitable trust while you are alive. Testamentary charitable trusts take effect at death and are created in a will, a revocable trust, or even the beneficiary designation of an IRA and/or a retirement plan.

With a charitable trust, the people or charity receiving distributions while the donor is alive receive what is commonly referred to as an income interest. This means that recurring payments are paid to the non-charitable beneficiary. The charitable trust can be set up so that the payments can last a specified number of years, or for the life of the donor or spouse or other non-charitable beneficiary, or the joint lives of the donor and spouse or other non-charitable beneficiary. The remainder interest is what is left in the trust at the end of the term or at the end of the life (lives) of the donor (donors). If the charity gets the remainder interest (which is most common), it is called a charitable remainder trust. If the charity gets the regular payments but the donor's family gets the remainder, it is called a charitable lead trust.

The term *unitrust* is used when the annuity amount is calculated as a percentage of the value of the trust assets, so unitrust payments typically vary in amount as the investment values change (hopefully, they grow), and distributions to the income beneficiary increase. If the value of the trust goes down in a unitrust, the payments to the individuals will decrease. This unitrust is properly called a *charitable remainder unitrust,* or CRUT. If the payments to the income beneficiary are constant, then you have a *charitable remainder annuity trust,* or CRAT.

If the donor creates a trust where the charity gets the regular payments and at a certain time in the future, the principal is returned to the family, it is called a *charitable lead annuity trust,* or CLAT. If the payments to the charity vary based on the value of the investments held by the trust, it is called a *charitable lead unitrust,* or CLUT.

A donor is entitled to a charitable income tax deduction based on the value of the income or remainder interest irrevocably pledged to the charity. In these trusts, the donor is taxed only on distributions from the trust as he receives payments from the trust. This can create income tax-deferral advantages as shown in the following mini case studies.

MINI CASE STUDY 18.1

When a Donor Should Consider a Charitable Remainder Annuity Trust

Paul and Mary, a married couple, both age 62, want to receive a regular income during their upcoming retirement which they anticipate will occur when they reach age 65. They have $500,000 worth of GE stock that has a basis of $100,000. (This is not IRA or retirement plan money, and they have other assets besides this stock). They have been worrying about the lack of diversification in their portfolio for years, but did not want to sell the stock and incur a large capital gains tax. Neither has defined benefit pensions where they work, and the idea of guaranteed income in retirement is appealing to them.

They are also charitably inclined. They have been approached by their local charity and told if they make a gift of the $500,000 of stock using a charitable remainder annuity trust, they could receive an immediate income tax deduction of $53,988 on the value of the remainder interest and a fixed income of $25,000 per year for the rest of their lives. At their death, their heirs would not receive any of that money; it would go to the charity.

Paul and Mary figure if they sold the stock without the charitable trust, they would have $420,000 left. (Sale proceeds of $500,000 - $100,000 cost basis = $400,000 capital gain x 20% = $80,000 tax. $500,000 - $80,000 = $420,000). If the $420,000 is invested at six percent, their annual income would be $25,200, but they have no guarantee the money will earn six percent.

With the charitable remainder annuity trust, however, they will:

- Avoid $80,000 in capital gains tax from selling the stock, while receiving an upfront income tax deduction of $53,988. (They could even take advantage of the tax savings from the charitable deduction and make a Roth IRA conversion)!

- Receive a fixed stream of income equal to five percent of the donated assets, which will continue even if the trust value declines. This gives them a guaranteed annual income of $25,000 (5% of $500,000). The income received from the trust is taxable, but the tax rules are very complicated and careful planning is advisable.

- While they are still working and in a high ordinary income tax bracket, they can invest the CRAT portfolio for growth, so that the trust generates as low an income as possible. After they retire, when they plan to be in a lower tax bracket, they can sell the appreciated securities and invest the portfolio for income.

MINI CASE STUDY 18.2

When a Donor Should Consider a CRUT

Peter is Paul's identical twin. He also has $500,000 of GE stock with a cost basis of $100,000. Peter and his wife, Linda, are more optimistic about potential investment returns, and want a higher annual income when they retire at age 65. They are willing to risk lower monthly income in the future if the investments in the trust decline in value, but they also want to get larger payments if the investments do well. They can choose a CRUT that will pay them 9.818 percent of the annual value of the trust each year, which yields $49,700 in the first year. This is the maximum percentage of the CRUT payment permitted in their case, based on their ages and a Section 7520 interest rate of 2.0 percent. This results in the minimum charitable deduction of $50,000 or 10 percent of the initial trust value. Every year, the trust is revalued. The future payments will increase in amount if the CRUT earns more, and will also decrease in amount if it earns less.

For people with charity in their heart, the CRAT and CRUT approaches are good deals. After the transfer of the stock to the charitable trust, the stock is sold. The donor owes no capital gains tax on the sale, and there is no federal income tax owed by the charity or the trust. (In states like Pennsylvania, which does not recognize charitable trusts as tax-exempt, there can be state income taxes on the trust earnings). Then, with the proceeds of the stock, the trustee of the charitable trust purchases a well-diversified portfolio that generates income for the donors. That income is taxed when it is received. The charitable remainder interest's value is a good current tax deduction, and the annuities provide a great retirement income benefit.

MINI CASE STUDY 18.3

Using a NIMCRUT—a Variation of a CRUT

A *Net Income with Makeup CRUT* (NIMCRUT) is a CRUT that stipulates that the annual payments are only to be paid to the extent of the current year's realized income. If the income is less than the payout percentage, the deficiency is withdrawn in addition to the annual percentage amount in future years when there is sufficient income. From Mini Case Study 18.1, assume Paul and Mary funded their trust with cash instead of highly appreciated GE stock. If their trust was a NIMCRUT, they could defer any annual income while they are both still working and are in a high marginal tax rate. They can do this by investing the trust's assets only in growth stocks, and completely avoiding investments that produce income. After they retire, but before they are again in higher tax rates due to RMDs on their retirement income, they can sell the appreciated securities in the NIMCRUT. Assuming that they've invested the trust assets well and it has grown in value, the annual payments will be higher. In addition, they get retroactive payments for amounts not collected in prior years. Since they will be in a lower tax bracket during the interval between retirement and beginning RMDs, this strategy, though more complicated than a regular CRUT, is an interesting variation that should be considered. If there are remaining deficiencies at their deaths (i.e., the actual returns were lower than the stated amount on the CRUT, and they would have been entitled to take more money from the trust in future years), the heirs of Paul and Mary are entitled to the deficiency amounts with the remainder of the trust value going to charity.

Here is a summary of possible scenarios for Paul and Mary and the charity (or charities) by using a CRAT, CRUT, or NIMCRUT.

- If Paul and Mary live long enough, they would be much better off by donating the stock to the charitable trust, than if they had sold the stock and tried to live off of the proceeds. There may be little remaining for the charity, though.

- If Paul and Mary don't live long, the charity will do well.

- If Paul and Mary live to their normal life expectancies, both they and the charity will do well, but Paul and Mary will still do better than the charity.

Given a normal life expectancy, will Paul and Mary do better than if they had invested the money and left the proceeds to their children with no charity involved? Probably not, but I don't encourage charitable trusts for people who are not at all charitably inclined.

Charitable remainder trusts work out so well in terms of taxes and what the family receives that, even if the donor has only made minimal donations to charity over his or her lifetime, the benefits can make the idea of becoming a philanthropist appealing to just about everyone. Some CRUTs are designed to retain 90 percent of the benefits (the projected value of the annual payments) for the family, and the charity receives only 10 percent of the benefits (the projected value of the remainder interest). Not bad for donors who want to provide for themselves and their family, but also want to provide for charity. The donor:

- Receives a current charitable deduction for the percentage of the transfer to the CRUT allocated to the charity's remainder interest (10 percent, in this case)

- Avoids a large capital gains tax on the sale of the appreciated assets used to fund the trust

- Receives a regular income for life, some or all of which may be taxable at capital gains or ordinary rates. And, the income to the donor can be much higher than many people realize.

At the donor's death (or, if there is more than one income beneficiary, at the death of the last income beneficiary), the remaining proceeds go to a charity. The NIMCRUT election can also be used for CRUTs to provide additional tax-deferral opportunities by careful investment planning.

Less commonly used are CLATs and CLUTs, where remainder interests are transferred to heirs. These trusts move future appreciation out of the taxable estate, and can result in lower estate taxes. Since federal estate taxes are less common now, these are less frequently used. CLATs and CLUTs, however, also provide larger initial charitable deductions at formation, so they can become useful when current tax deferral is appropriate.

Charitable trusts are often packaged together with life insurance. One strategy involves using the insurance proceeds, often a Second-to-Die policy, to replace what the children would have received had the donor not established the charitable trust. In many situations, the premiums for the life insurance can be paid for with the income generated from the trust. Life insurance and charitable giving go well together in a variety of circumstances.

Alternatives to Charitable Trusts

Charitable trusts do have some negatives. They are irrevocable, so you can't change your mind years down the road. They come with inherent administrative burdens which include setting up the trust, preparing annual income tax returns for the trust, annual calculations of the withdrawal amount, and investment management. Although CRTs have advantages for large transfers of money, simpler alternatives are available for those who would rather avoid these burdens. These include charitable gift annuities, pooled income funds, and life insurance owned by charities under certain circumstances.

Charitable Gift Annuities

Charitably motivated individuals may enter into a charitable gift annuity contract with charitable organizations that offer the option—a common practice for many universities. This is an agreement contract between the charity and the donor.

It is similar to a CRT in that:

- The donor transfers a sum of money to the charity.
- The donor gets a regular (often annual) annuity income from the charity.
- The donor gets a partial income tax deduction for the gift.
- The charity gets the remainder interest.
- The agreement is irrevocable.

The charitable gift annuity differs from a CRT in that:

- Smaller amounts can be contributed. Minimums can be as little as $10,000 or $25,000, whereas a CRT is usually only done with hundreds of thousands of dollars or more.
- No annual tax returns have to be filed.
- No investment management by the donor is necessary.

The annuity income to the donor must be a fixed amount and does not vary from year to year. This is similar to the CRAT, but unlike the CRUT where the income could change with a change in the value of the trust. The annuity payouts are often determined using guidelines set up by the American Council of Gift Annuities. For example, a 65-year-old individual transferring $25,000 could receive a $1,175 per year annuity (4.7 percent of the initial amount), which is partially taxable. They would also get an up-front charitable deduction. The amount of the deduction is equal to the amount of the contribution less the present value of the payments that will be made to the donor and/or the donor's beneficiary during their lifetime. So if you live a long and healthy life, you can do very well by making a donation using a charitable gift annuity.

Charitable gift annuities are great for people who like the idea of a CRT but want to participate on a smaller scale. Charitable gift annuities are typically more generous to the charity than a CRT, which are often more generous to the family.

Pooled Income Funds

Pooled income fund giving is similar to charitable gift annuities, except the annual income paid to the donor is variable and consists of the interest and dividends earned in a pooled investment account. The payout does not include capital gains income, so the payout is typically smaller, but the up-front charitable deduction is larger. Therefore, more money eventually goes to the charity. For example, a 65-year-old individual transferring $25,000 may receive a smaller annuity, (in this case, $875 per year or 3.5 percent of the donation amount), and an up-front charitable deduction of $14,200.

Many people want to continue their pattern of charitable giving after their deaths, but do not want to deprive their family of an inheritance or want to minimize the impact of their charitable gift on their family's inheritance. The following two examples will illustrate two strategies that include the use of life insurance in charitable planning.

Charitable Life Insurance

Suppose that Joe and Mary feel they can afford to give $10,000 to their favorite charity, every year. Joe and Mary, however, would prefer to make a major impact with their gifts, and they would also like to continue supporting the charity after their deaths. Their trusted advisor suggests that they restructure their annual charitable gift by giving $5,000 directly to the charity of their choice to use as they please, and giving another $5,000 to the charity to use for a specific purpose. The second $5,000 is given so that the charity can purchase in its own name a $500,000 survivorship life insurance policy on the lives of Joe and Mary, on which they will name themselves as beneficiary. Joe and Mary would still get the same annual charitable income tax deduction as they were getting when they were just giving the $10,000 to charity each year. Therefore, Joe and Mary do not lose any tax benefits by considering this approach. Joe and Mary can even specify the purpose for the $500,000 death benefit that will go to the charity after they both die. They may set up a fund within the charity that must be used for the purpose they specify, such as a scholarship, and that fund could continue into perpetuity.

Charitable life insurance is also a wonderful way to fund a large endowment or scholarship for a charity of your choice.

Charitable life insurance is also a wonderful way to fund a large endowment or scholarship for a charity of your choice. A number of years ago, I worked with a couple whose family was very financially comfortable and who really wanted to make a significant charitable gift at their death to endow a university chair in their names. The only way it worked for the client and the university was through the use of life insurance.

The couple realized the following benefits:

- They received a tax deduction for all the gifts to the university.

- They met their goal of providing sufficient money to the university to endow a chair.

- They received a flood of kudos from their peers and the university for making this gift during their lifetimes, which reinforced their positive feelings about the gift.

In conclusion, charitable life insurance can be a wonderful way to continue a pattern of charitable giving beyond your lifetime and/or to make a significant charitable gift with often fewer dollars than having to contribute the entire principal at the death of the donor or donors.

If you are interested in using life insurance for charitable purposes, please see the back of the book for information on requesting a free consultation, or visit **www.paytaxeslater.com** and request a free consultation.

MINI CASE STUDY 18.4
Testamentary Charitable Trusts

May your charity increase as much as your wealth.

— Proverb

Now the fun really begins. Let's assume the parents of a 40-year-old child have a large estate including a substantial amount of money in their IRA.

Freddy and Frieda have given a lot of money to their child already. They think Frank is too carefree with his money, and they are worried that he may blow his inheritance. At the same time, they don't want Frank to end up living under a bridge when he is 70 years old.

Freddy and Frieda are charitably inclined. When Frank was young, they made sure he did volunteer work because they consider charitable involvement a blessing. They are not blind to estate planning nor do they scorn effective tax planning. They want all the tax benefits they can get. Though they ultimately want a significant amount of their money to go to charity, they also want Frank to have access to a regular income during his lifetime. In addition, they want to encourage Frank to have the option to direct some of their money to the charity or charities of his choice at his death.

After a lengthy conversation with their advisor, they establish a charitable trust and name it as the secondary beneficiary of their IRAs. (They are each other's primary beneficiary). Their action has the following benefits:

- During their lives, it is still their money, and they can do whatever they want with it.

- If they ever need to reconsider their decision, they can change the beneficiary to Frank; they can choose to give all the money to the charity; or they can devise something completely different.

- At their deaths, assuming they don't change the beneficiary, the money would go to the trust. If they die this year when Frank is 40, Frank will get an income of 7.29 percent of the principal every year for the rest of his life.

- At Frank's death, whatever is left can go to a charity of Frank's choosing.

The numbers work out pretty favorably, and Freddy and Frieda's wishes are respected. The charity must wait to get their money, but they will get it. The loser is the IRS, because they were unable to get deferred tax revenue from Freddy and Frieda's large estate after their deaths.

This chapter provides only a small glimpse into the window of charitable giving. It is one of my goals to present objective information and encourage individuals who would not have otherwise considered charity or charitable trusts to do so after realizing all the tax and other benefits.

If you haven't any charity in your heart, you have the worst kind of heart trouble.

—Bob Hope

A Key Lesson from This Chapter

I believe there are many donors who have charity in their hearts but whose interest in themselves and their families comes first. If after reading this book, you have some incentive to explore some charitable options, even if the charity has to wait, then there will be charitable value as well as commercial and educational value to this book.

19

A Point-by-Point
Summary of
the Whole Process

*Money isn't everything, but it sure keeps you
in touch with your children.*

— J. Paul Getty

If you are still working, please:

1. Contribute at least the amount to your retirement plan that your employer is willing to match or partially match.

2. If you can afford to, contribute the maximum allowed to your retirement plan even if your employer does not match.

3. Once you have maximized contributions to your plan at work, contribute the maximum you can to an IRA, even if you cannot take a tax deduction for it.

4. Consider your personal tax bracket when trying to decide if you should contribute to a Roth or a traditional IRA/retirement plan.

5. Do not take loans against your retirement plan. Allow the tax-deferred or tax-free status of the account to maximize the growth of your money.

6. If you don't need the income, don't take distributions from your retirement plan until you are required to.

At retirement, when you need money:

7. Understand the advantages and disadvantages of moving your old company retirement plan. If you do move it, consider using a trustee-to-trustee transfer to move it to an IRA or a one-person 401(k). Look for opportunities to make tax-free transfers of after-tax contributions to a Roth IRA. If you have company stock in your retirement plan, look for opportunities to transfer it while avoiding capital gains tax on the appreciation.

8. When you need to spend money, spend non-retirement assets (money you already paid income tax on) first.

9. Then, when your after-tax assets run down, spend your traditional retirement plans and Roth plans strategically, to minimize the impact the withdrawals will have on your income taxes.

10. Plan for needed or Required Minimum Distributions from retirement plans during your lifetime.

11. Keep distributions from retirement plans to a minimum.

12. If you don't need the income from the minimum distributions, consider improving your tax situation by directing that all or part of the distribution be sent to a qualified charity.

13. Take advantage of the years after you retire, but before you are required to take minimum distributions, to convert some of your traditional retirement assets to Roth accounts.

14. Consider using annuities if you want a guaranteed lifetime income.

When planning for your heirs:

15. If you have not had your wills and/or trusts reviewed in the past five years, do so as soon as possible. Changes in the laws have made many older documents obsolete.

16. These legislative changes also make it necessary that you review your beneficiary designations. If the Stretch IRA is eliminated, you should consider alternatives that allow your beneficiaries to minimize the income taxes that will be due on your retirement assets.

17. Make your estate plan as flexible as possible by incorporating the use of disclaimers.

18. Consider implementing a formal gifting strategy to benefit your children, grandchildren and favorite charities.

Part Four

|||||||||||||||||||||||||||||||||||||||||||||||||||||||||||||||||||||||||||||||||||||||||||||||||||||||

VALUABLE RESOURCES

Everyone Needs a Good Financial Game Plan to Retire Secure.

Appendix:
Life Expectancy Tables

Table I
Single Life Expectancy Tables (For Use by Beneficiaries)

Age	Life Expectancy	Age	Life Expectancy	Age	Life Expectancy	Age	Life Expectancy
0	82.4	28	55.3	56	28.7	84	8.1
1	81.6	29	54.3	57	27.9	85	7.6
2	80.6	30	53.3	58	27	86	7.1
3	79.7	31	52.4	59	26.1	87	6.7
4	78.7	32	51.4	60	25.2	88	6.3
5	77.7	33	50.4	61	24.4	89	5.9
6	76.7	34	49.4	62	23.5	90	5.5
7	75.8	35	48.5	63	22.7	91	5.2
8	74.8	36	47.5	64	21.8	92	4.9
9	73.8	37	46.5	65	21	93	4.6
10	72.8	38	45.6	66	20.2	94	4.3
11	71.8	39	44.6	67	19.4	95	4.1
12	70.8	40	43.6	68	18.6	96	3.8
13	69.9	41	42.7	69	17.8	97	3.6
14	68.9	42	41.7	70	17	98	3.4
15	67.9	43	40.7	71	16.3	99	3.1
16	66.9	44	39.8	72	15.5	100	2.9
17	66	45	38.8	73	14.8	101	2.7
18	65	46	37.9	74	14.1	102	2.5
19	64	47	37	75	13.4	103	2.3
20	63	48	36	76	12.7	104	2.1
21	62.1	49	35.1	77	12.1	105	1.9
22	61.1	50	34.2	78	11.4	106	1.7
23	60.1	51	33.3	79	10.8	107	1.5
24	59.1	52	32.3	80	10.2	108	1.4
25	58.2	53	31.4	81	9.7	109	1.2
26	57.2	54	30.5	82	9.1	110	1.1
27	56.2	55	29.6	83	8.6	111 and over	1.0

Table II
Joint Life and Last Survivor Expectancy Table
(See IRS Publication 590)

Table III
Uniform Lifetime Table (For Use by Unmarried Owners, Married Owners Whose Spouses Are Not More Than 10 Years Younger, and Married Owners Whose Spouses Are Not the Sole Beneficiaries of Their IRAs)

Age	Distribution Period	Age	Distribution Period
70	27.4	93	9.6
71	26.5	94	9.1
72	25.6	95	8.6
73	24.7	96	8.1
74	23.8	97	7.6
75	22.9	98	7.1
76	22	99	6.7
77	21.2	100	6.3
78	20.3	101	5.9
79	19.5	102	5.5
80	18.7	103	5.2
81	17.9	104	4.9
82	17.1	105	4.5
83	16.3	106	4.2
84	15.5	107	3.9
85	14.8	108	3.7
86	14.1	109	3.4
87	13.4	110	3.1
88	12.7	111	2.9
89	12	112	2.6
90	11.4	113	2.4
91	10.8	114	2.1
92	10.2	115 and over	1.9

About the Author

James Lange, CPA, Attorney, and registered investment advisor is a nationally recognized IRA, 401(k), and retirement plan distribution expert. With 32 years of experience, Jim offers unbeatable recommendations when he tackles the #1 fear facing most retirees: running out of money. Jim has also developed Lange's Cascading Beneficiary Plan, which is widely regarded as the gold standard of estate planning for many IRA and retirement plan owners.

Jane Bryant Quinn introduced the country to Jim's mantra, "Pay taxes later," in *Newsweek*. Jim's recommendations have appeared 33 times in *The Wall Street Journal*, and his articles have appeared in *Journal of Retirement Planning, Financial Planning, The Tax Adviser (AICPA), The Bottom Line*, and other top financial, legal, and tax journals. In the fall of 2014 alone, Jim had two peer-reviewed articles published in the prestigious *Trusts & Estates* magazine.

In 1998, Jim wrote the definitive article on Roth IRA conversions for *The Tax Adviser*, the peer-reviewed journal of the American Institute of Certified Public Accountants. Much of that analysis is updated and included in *Retire Secure!*

Jim is the principal member of Lange Legal Group, LLC, Lange Accounting Group, LLC and Lange Financial Group, LLC. Jim's companies serve over 1,600 clients. Jim has presented hundreds of workshops for taxpayers and financial professionals throughout the country, and his workshops consistently get the highest ratings. Please see **www.paytaxeslater.com** for additional information about Jim's workshops, or www.jameslange.com to register for reminders and sign up for the next workshop.

Jim lives in Pittsburgh, in the home he grew up in, with his wife, Cindy, and their daughter, Erica. When Jim is not devising new strategies for retirees to save taxes and accumulate wealth (which is most of the time), he enjoys bicycling, hiking, skiing, and traveling with his family. Jim also plays chess and bridge both online and with his friends.

Looking For More Proven Wealth-Building Strategies from Lange Financial Group, LLC?

Check out these online resources…yours *FREE!*

The Lange Letter

With 5,000+ subscribers, our e-mail newsletter, *The Lange Letter*, is a popular resource with our friends and clients. In this bi-weekly e-mail, you get a never ending stream of news as well as a review of classic tax-cutting and estate-building ideas.

Please visit **www.paytaxeslater.com** and sign up for your free subscription to *The Lange Letter* today and download a FREE Bonus Report which will be a valuable supplement to this book.

The Lange Money Hour Online Archive

In 2010, we started **The Lange Money Hour: Where Smart Money Talks,** a financial radio show that we think provides the best audio information on the topics of IRAs and retirement plans available anywhere. We have had some of the top financial, legal, and IRA experts as guests over the years. These luminaries include such industry greats as John Bogle (the founder of Vanguard), Jane Bryant Quinn, Ed Slott, Natalie Choate, Bob Keebler, Roger Ibbotson, Jonathan Clements, and dozens more.

We have transcribed the shows as well as added subtitles of topics covered during the shows. We are in the never ending process of attempting to help you find the information you want as quickly as possible.

With over 150 hours of solid content, these audio files and transcriptions are a great resource and are available for free at **www.paytaxeslater.com**.

Want to Learn More from Jim Lange, Attorney and CPA?

Introducing

Personal Financial Growth Products from Retire Secure Press, LLC

We are committed to helping grow your wealth.

—Jim Lange

2-Hour General Audience DVDs

- **Cut Taxes on Your IRA Withdrawals: More Money for You and for Your Heirs** – *Updated for 2015*

  My classic IRA workshop reveals the most important things you need to know about IRAs, Social Security, Roth IRA conversions, and the best estate plan for married couples. $97

- **Enhanced Social Security Planning: Getting the Most Out of Your Social Security Benefits** – *Updated for 2015*

  This DVD, partly based on a peer-reviewed Social Security article I wrote for *Trusts & Estates* magazine, "runs the numbers" on different

Social Security strategies for married couples. Getting Roth IRA conversions and Social Security right can literally make a difference of hundreds of thousands of dollars. $97

- **What Every IRA Owner Should Know About Roth IRAs and Roth IRA Conversions** – *Updated for 2015*

  This is my classic Roth IRA workshop. If you have an IRA or retirement plan, you and your family could benefit significantly by using the techniques in this DVD. In fact, I used to charge $10,000 to present this same information to financial advisors. $97

- **Who Says You Can't Control from the Grave? The Appropriate Use of Trusts to Protect Your Family** – *Updated for 2015*

  Get the full picture on the appropriate use of trusts. This DVD covers how and when to avoid probate, plus trusts for minors, spendthrifts, and beneficiaries with special needs. Also discussed is the increasingly popular, "I don't want my no-good son/daughter-in-law to inherit one red cent trust." $97

Special: Want the Best Deal of All? (Shown on page 345)

Get all **4 updated DVDs for $197** and as our way of thanking you, we will include the following 3 CDs as bonuses:

1. **The Best of The Lange Money Hour: Where Smart Money Talks**

   This is a compilation of some of the highlights of 130 radio shows. Guests: John Bogle, Jane Bryant Quinn, Ed Slott, Robert Cass, P.J. DiNuzzo, Joe Hurley, Paul Merriman, Grant Oliphant, Natalie Choate, and Roger Ibbotson (CD 60 minutes)

2. **Using Nobel Prize Research to Maximize Your Investment Return**

   Guest: Paul Merriman, author, journalist, and nationally recognized expert on index funds, asset allocation, and financial management strategies. (CD 50 minutes)

3. **Following an Efficient Strategy Produces Dividends**

   Guest: P.J. DiNuzzo, a nationally recognized expert in investment management and our partner in passive index investment management. P.J. and his firm rank in the top 1% of America's more than 800,000 investment advisors. (CD 50 minutes)

Please go to **www.jameslange.com** for product details and order forms.

2-Hour Niche Market DVDs

For Professors and University Faculty:

- **Cut Taxes on Your TIAA-CREF, Vanguard and IRA Withdrawals: More Money for University Faculty and Their Heirs**

   This DVD covers the most important financial issues for current and retired faculty members. Get unique recommendations for one of life's great mysteries: "How do I get money out of TIAA when I retire?" It also provides strategies that are in your best interest, not your financial advisor's best interest. $97.

For Same-Sex Couples:

- **Live Gay, Retire Rich: New Financial Planning Strategies for Same-Sex Couples**

   Same-sex couples have great opportunities to provide for the financially weaker partner by getting married. This DVD guides you and your partner through the complexities of taking advantage of the financial prospects now available. In particular, the issues of inheriting IRAs and collecting spousal benefits for Social Security are examined in detail. $97

- **New Estate Planning Strategies for Same-Sex Couples with IRA and Retirement Plans**

   New thinking about estate planning after a series of changes in federal and state laws is essential to protect and provide for yourself and your partner. Learn what you need to know in this highly specialized DVD. $97

Books

- *Retire Secure!: A Guide to Getting the Most out of What You've Got* ($24.95)

   Now more than ever, Americans approaching or already in retirement are asking, "Will my money last as long as I do and what can I do to make sure I get the most from what I've got?" In this updated Third Edition of *Retire*

Secure!, Jim provides new examples and strategies developed from his 32 years as a practicing estate attorney and CPA.

The Third Edition shows how to use IRAs, retirement plans, Roth IRAs and Roth 401(k)s, Roth IRA conversions, as well as other tax-favored strategies to let Uncle Sam subsidize your retirement and your family's lifestyle for the remainder of your life, your spouse's life, and long beyond that.

Jim has a history of seeing ahead of the curve and in this edition, he analyzes the possible repercussions if Congress kills the "Stretch IRA" or seriously truncates its stretch. But, he also provides new avenues to reach the best outcomes if the laws are changed. For example he shows how using a Charitable Remainder Unitrust (CRUT) as a beneficiary of your IRA will potentially be more favorable for many families than just leaving an IRA to your children.

Every chapter of **Retire Secure!** contains recommendations, analysis, and case studies based on a deep understanding of tax law, estate planning, investing, and running the numbers. Most importantly, they are time tested and proven to work.

• *The Roth Revolution: Pay Taxes Once and Never Again* ($19.44)

In essence, a Roth IRA conversion requires paying taxes on the portion of your IRA or 401(k) that you convert, but then that money can grow income tax-free for the rest of your, your spouse's, your children's and grandchildren's lives. The advantage of a tax-savvy long-term Roth IRA conversion is often measured in the millions. The real eye-opener, however, is that Roth IRA conversions are great for older IRA owners, regardless of the benefits to future generations.

The Roth Revolution addresses the following topics clearly and objectively:

1. Whether, how much, and when to convert

2. Costs and benefits of a Roth IRA conversion

3. Advice for taxpayers in each income tax bracket

4. The impact of future tax increases

5. Synergy of delaying (or returning) Social Security and Roth IRA conversions

6. Combining charitable gifts and Roth IRA conversions

7. Tax-free conversions of after-tax dollars in IRAs and retirement plans

8. Converting and recharacterizing strategies

You may be asking, "Who in their right mind would pay taxes before they have to?" The answer is James Lange and thousands of his readers and clients, all the top IRA experts, and after reading *The Roth Revolution,* hopefully you will too.

- *Live Gay, Retire Rich* ($19.95)

There were two gay couples with identical financial resources. They each had the same amount of money, identical investments, identical taxes, and identical earnings history for Social Security purposes.

The first couple did no planning. The second gay couple followed the advice offered in *Live Gay, Retire Rich!* Doing reasonable projections, the first couple runs out of money in 28 years while the second couple has $1.4 million dollars and their portfolio continues to increase.

What was the difference? The first couple never got married, started Social Security at 62, didn't make any Roth IRA conversions, and didn't use key IRA, retirement plan and estate planning strategies. The second gay couple did get married, used our recommended apply and suspend technique for Social Security, did a series of Roth IRA conversions, and used key IRA, retirement plan and estate planning strategies.

Live Gay, Retire Rich! gives same-sex couples the knowledge they need to get their retirement right!

Please go to **www.jameslange.com** for product details and order forms.

Free Informational DVDs and Audio CDs

- **Index vs. Active Investing: Nobel Prize Winning Research Sheds Light on Investing**

Learn the distinctions between the two philosophies of investing and also why we are huge fans of Dimensional Fund Advisors (DVD 30 minutes)

- **How We Sabotage our Retirement Planning and Why Index Investing Offers the Best Solution**

This is the longer version of our investing DVD with more background and details on the advantages of index investing. (DVD 110 minutes)

For more videos, recommended reading lists, and an audio archive of all of our radio shows be sure to visit **www.jameslange.com**.

Here is a detailed overview of just one of Jim's classic workshops captured on DVD for IRA owners:

- **Cut Taxes on Your IRA Withdrawals: More Money for You and for Your Heirs**

Many people underestimate the value of coordinating multiple strategies that, in concert, form a cohesive financial plan designed to yield the best results over time.

Among those decisions which require coordination are: timing your IRA distributions, your Roth IRA strategy, and your Social Security distributions. Comprehensive planning, when done properly, can preserve your IRAs, retirement plan, and Roth IRAs long after you are gone.

James Lange has devoted a lot of energy to educating financial advisors and consumers about the strategies he has been using with his clients for decades. He founded **The Roth IRA Institute**™ to provide financial professionals with the tools they need to educate their clients. For consumers, his two-hour workshop titled *Cut Taxes on Your IRA Withdrawals: More Money for You and Your Heirs* has been drawing record crowds for years.

Now, Jim wants to get this important information into the hands of all taxpayers. He realizes that people across the country are searching for these answers but are unable to travel to one of his workshops. They may want to see and hear, rather than just read about these strategies in *Retire Secure!* With that in mind, Jim is making his current live workshops available to everyone in a package that contains a DVD plus transcript. With this DVD of the live workshop, you can learn from participant's questions and Jim's answers.

Now You Can Experience Jim Lange's Workshops from the Comfort of Your Own Home!

Even if you've already read Jim's books—you'll gain valuable insights from Jim's *Cut Taxes on Your IRA Withdrawals* workshop. This workshop covers optimal distribution planning for IRA and retirement plan owners, Roth IRA conversions, and tax-savvy methods of preserving IRA and Roth IRA to pass to your heirs. It is geared toward investors between the ages of 60 and 75 with $250,000 or more in their retirement plans, but the information is of benefit to people of all ages and financial situations. Here's what you'll discover:

- The tax-savvy way to spend different classes of assets in retirement.
- The "secret" of the Roth IRA and why it's such a powerful retirement planning tool.
- How you can enjoy tax-free growth with a Roth IRA conversion.
- Coordinating the timing between Roth IRA conversions and Social Security distributions.
- A little-known technique for making a Roth IRA conversion while legally avoiding certain taxes.
- Accumulation strategies if you're still working.
- Peer-reviewed articles discussing the benefits of a Roth IRA conversion.
- And much, much more!

We invite you to visit our website **www.jameslange.com** for a full list of resources including books, DVDs, CDs, and easy access to our radio show—**The Lange Money Hour**—archives. Some products are for sale, but many are free or available for streaming.

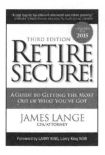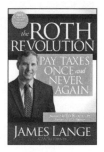

Visit www.jameslange.com for more details.

Everyone Needs a Good Financial Game Plan to Retire Secure.

Let's Run the Numbers and Find Yours...

Okay. Let's say you want to follow the proven strategies for retirement investing presented in this book. *We can help.*

Our team of CPAs, estate attorneys and money managers apply the concepts of this book to help our client's cut taxes and retire securely. Then, we help them strategically pass on whatever is left.

The CPA firm, the law firm, and the investment advisory firm are all owned by me, Jim Lange, and operate under the same roof in Pittsburgh, PA. Clients benefit by having professionals with different backgrounds and disciplines work together, always keeping in mind the client's best interest. Preparation of wills, trusts, and IRA beneficiary designations is performed through the law firm, is separate from our financial advisory firm, and is only available for Pennsylvania residents. Our Investment Advisory services are available to clients in Pennsylvania, New York, Ohio, Virginia, Florida, and California.

Our team of CPAs "run the numbers" to help determine the best strategies for our clients' IRA and retirement plans, converting IRAs to Roth IRAs, and developing a tax-savvy estate plan. They also run the numbers for other areas not covered in *Retire Secure!* such as how to maximize Social Security benefits, and gifting strategies that can include subsidizing the education of your grandchildren with 529 plans. Beyond running the numbers, we provide something else: a big-picture perspective. For instance, we may discover that a client who assumed they had to work an additional five years actually has sufficient funds to retire tomorrow. Or, they can continue to work, but on their own terms. Observations like these can be life-changing and liberating.

We also address other pressing retirement concerns such as how much money can you afford to spend and never run out of money? This information could help you make difficult decisions that require both "running the numbers" and perspective. Let's say you want to move to Florida but your wife wants to stay in the family home. Is it financially feasible to become snowbirds and get the best of both?

Because managing money is more than a full-time job (as is keeping up with the "ins and outs" of the legal and tax system), we do not manage investments internally at Lange Financial Group, LLC. Instead, we looked at the universe of possibilities and determined what the best options would be for our clients.

Happily, we found our primary collaborator, DiNuzzo Index Advisors, Inc., right in our backyard. They are a first class organization, use what we believe are the best low-cost index funds on the planet as the underlying investments, and have become our main go-to resource when it comes to professionally managed portfolios for our new clients. For clients who prefer an active money management style, we utilize Fort Pitt Capital Group, Inc.

When you become a client of Lange Financial Group, LLC, you will benefit from the integrated experience of our financial professionals all of whom have different but complementary expertise. In essence, you are getting what we think are the best retirement and estate planning strategies along with the best money management services that I am aware of for a combined fee of between 50 basis points (one-half of one percent of the money we actually manage) and 1% depending on how much money is invested.

Your Single Source for Planning, Tax and Investment Advice

There is much to be gained from a coordinated strategy. We believe that your CPA, your attorney, and your investment advisor should be working together to provide you with the best strategies for retirement and estate planning using a well-diversified portfolio of low-cost index funds as the underlying investment.

Frequently, individuals will have a lawyer, an investment advisor, a CPA, and maybe even an insurance broker. But communication among the professionals may be the missing component. The result is a collection of professionals presumably all working with the client's best interest at heart, but there is no comprehensive strategy and sometimes lax or missing communication.

With our "one-stop-shop" approach, you can benefit from the best integrated strategies for your IRA and retirement plans, Social Security strategy, investments, as well as wills, trusts, and estate planning needs. We believe that having experts in different fields all under the same roof is the most effective model for integrated retirement and estate planning. We do offer clients a choice of money managers, but these days, we advise most of our new clients to have their money managed using the best low-cost index advisory firm we know, DiNuzzo Index Advisors, Inc. DiNuzzo Index Advisors, Inc. invests money for clients using what we believe is the best set of low-cost index funds on the planet: Dimensional Fund Advisors or "DFA."

With our "one-stop-shop" approach, you can benefit from the best integrated strategies for your IRA and retirement plans, Social Security strategy, investments, as well as wills, trusts, and estate planning needs.

We think this multidiscipline approach is a win/win/win. It is a win for us because we get to do what we do best: implement our tax and estate planning strategies and help people retire securely and wisely pass it on. It is a win for DiNuzzo Index Advisors, Inc. because they get to do what they do best: manage money, but always keeping the big picture into account. Assuming a client gives us permission (which they always do), we provide DiNuzzo Index Advisors, Inc. with our recommendations which they often implement.

The biggest win, however, is for the client. You get our statistical advice that came as a result of our running the numbers as well as comprehensive retirement and estate planning, and integrated money management using low-cost index funds *all for one low fee of between 50 basis points and 1%.*

The biggest win, however, is for the client. You get our statistical advice that came as a result of our running the numbers as well as comprehensive retirement and estate planning, and integrated money management using low-cost index funds all for one low fee.

We enjoy a 99% client retention rate with the mutual Lange/DiNuzzo clients. We are proud of this success and would be happy to tell you more in person, should you qualify for a free consultation.

Our association with DiNuzzo Index Advisors, Inc., is growing at roughly $50 million per year of assets-under-management. We are expecting to grow even faster in the future. At press time, we have roughly $180 million under management with DiNuzzo Index Advisors, Inc. What follows is a firm history. If that doesn't interest you, please skip to the next section, **Lange Financial Group Today**.

How Lange Financial Group Got Started

Frankly, it was only recently that I pinpointed what I wanted to be when I grew up. That might sound funny coming from a middle-aged man and a long-time business professional, but I find that re-thinking my mission in life, from time to time, keeps important distinctions fresh and top-of-mind. So here goes: I want to be the best, most trusted financial advisor leading the best team of CPAs, estate attorneys, and money managers you can find anywhere.

But my aspirations didn't start out that high.

When I started out after college in 1978, I worked at a small CPA firm and did some moonlighting preparing tax returns. As my side business grew, I opened my first office in my mother's house. Many of my long-time clients remember that walk up to the third floor.

I changed my "day job" to working in the Tax Department of Arthur Andersen (formerly a big 8 CPA firm) and later Buchanan Ingersoll (a big Pittsburgh corporate law firm) and continued to grow my side business while I attended Duquesne University School of Law at night. It was a busy time. When I finished law school in 1984, I gave up corporate America and hung out shingles for both a CPA firm and a law firm. My practice concentrated exclusively on taxes, wills, trusts and estates.

I started (and continue) to work with clients who were "IRA heavy," meaning they had more money in their IRAs and retirement plans than outside their IRAs and retirement plans. How did they get that way? Generally speaking, the IRA and retirement plan owners I work with today are and were prudent savers.

While they were working, it was hard to save money because of bills, taxes, groceries, a mortgage, the car payments, the children's braces, college tuition costs, etc. But, despite the expenses, they didn't take their future for granted. They generally contributed money into their retirement plans at work, and took advantage of employer matching programs if they were available.

Upon retirement, they often have between $500,000 and $3 million in their retirement plans, two modestly priced cars, a house that is paid for, kids who are finally out of the house, and not much else. So, to best serve their needs, I knew I had to become an IRA and retirement plan strategy expert.

As part of my journey, I studied IRA literature extensively, especially "the bible" on IRAs and retirement plans, *Life and Death Planning for Retirement*

Benefits, by Natalie Choate, Esq. This is a 500+ page book basically written in IRS code, but full of gems.

What Natalie doesn't do, however, is run the numbers to quantify and compare the results of the different IRA and estate planning strategies she presents in her book. So I ran the numbers, and I was thrilled when I realized how many cool strategies IRA owners could take advantage of. A client's financial outcome can be dramatically different depending on the strategy he or she uses.

> Someone who uses the best strategies, as determined by *running the numbers*, generally has much better results than the individual who *wings it*. And the individual who wings it usually never realizes they missed the best strategies because no analysis was done to figure out what the best strategies were for his or her personal situation!

Let's "run the numbers" became our mantra. Then and now we offer our assets under management clients immediate and long-term advice backed up with solid quantitative analysis and excellent statistics—this, in particular, appeals to our discerning clientele.

We offer our assets under management clients immediate and long-term advice backed up with solid quantitative analysis and excellent statistics.

Over the years, I put together a crackerjack team of estate attorneys and CPAs, including several "number crunching" extraordinaires. Together we expanded the scope of running the numbers to include testing different levels of spending in retirement, maximizing Roth IRA conversions, Social Security optimization, different methods and amounts of gifting including 529 plans for grandchildren's education, sophisticated estate planning strategies, and other relevant issues.

Add Roth IRA Conversions into the Mix

In 1997, a whole new type of retirement plan called a Roth IRA was proposed by Congress. I knew this was going to be a great thing for most IRA and retirement plan owners, but especially my IRA heavy clients. Even before the law took effect, I ran more numbers that specifically tested the advantages of Roth IRAs and Roth IRA conversions.

> **I knew that making the appropriate Roth IRA conversion recommendations for the right people at the right time could mean hundreds of thousands of dollars in reduced taxes and additional tax-free wealth for them.**

Again, I was astounded by the results. I knew that making the appropriate Roth IRA conversion recommendations for the right people at the right time could mean hundreds of thousands of dollars in reduced taxes and additional tax-free wealth for them. And when I continued the analysis to the next generation, I saw that taking my advice could mean millions of additional dollars for their children and grandchildren.

I wrote the first peer-reviewed article on Roth IRAs and Roth IRA conversions for the American Institute of CPAs Tax Division journal, *The Tax Adviser*. That article catapulted me into national standing as a Roth IRA expert, author and speaker. But more importantly, my clients benefitted when we began to apply the principles of my tested and peer-reviewed Roth IRA and Roth IRA conversion analysis and "ran the numbers" for their individual situations.

Articles, Radio Shows and Books

I continued writing articles for many financial journals including *The Journal of Retirement Planning*, *The Tax Adviser*, and *Bottom Line* and many more. As recently as 2014, we published two peer-reviewed articles in *Trusts & Estates* magazine: one on Social Security and the other on IRA and retirement plans. Our strategies have been featured in *The Wall Street Journal* 35 times.

In 2010, we started **The Lange Money Hour: Where Smart Money Talks**; a financial radio show that we think provides the best audio information on IRAs and retirement plans available anywhere. We have done over 150 shows, many with the top financial, legal, and IRA experts as guests–industry giants such as John Bogle (the founder of Vanguard), Jane Bryant Quinn, Jonathan Clements, Ed Slott, Natalie Choate, Bob Keebler, Roger Ibbotson (all on multiple times), and dozens more. Our guests have written some of the top financial books of our time. In preparation for the shows, I read most of the books and prepare the questions. Having this much access to the top financial minds of our time is thrilling and has been a true education for me and my listeners.

But I also wanted to write an encompassing retirement and estate planning book with solid recommendations backed by concrete proof. Furthermore, I wanted to provide a detailed explanation of what I still consider the best estate plan for traditional married couples. I call it **Lange's Cascading Beneficiary Plan**. I wrote *Retire Secure!* (Wiley 2006 & 2009), and I was pleased to get glowing reviews from some of the top people in the field, including Charles Schwab, Jane Bryant Quinn, Larry King, Ed Slott, Roger Ibbotson and virtually all the nationally known IRA experts. This book, the one you are reading now, is the Third Edition of *Retire Secure!*

Although I included Roth IRA and Roth IRA conversion analysis in all editions of *Retire Secure!*, I also knew the entire Roth IRA conversion subject required a dedicated book, so I wrote and published *The Roth Revolution, Pay Taxes Once and Never Again* (Morgan James, 2010) to fill the gap.

The publication of these books led to prestigious speaking engagements around the country. I was hired to educate financial professionals throughout the United States. It became very clear to me, after speaking to and with thousands of financial advisors, that very few retirees were receiving great proactive retirement and estate planning advice *combined* with good investment advice.

History of Collaborating with Money Managers

Since I wanted to do the work described above but not the actual money management component, I knew I had to collaborate with the top money management firms I could find. My first collaboration was with Fort Pitt Capital Group, Inc., an excellent money management firm using an active management approach (see page 361 for details). Then, I started working with DiNuzzo Index Advisors, Inc.

The History of Working with DiNuzzo Index Advisors, Inc.

A significant turning point for my company was when I learned about low-cost index investing and what I believe to be the best set of index funds on the planet, Dimensional Funds (offered through Dimensional Fund Advisors, also known as DFA). After learning of their great philosophy and strong performance results, I wanted to represent DFA myself.

But DFA is very fussy about the advisors they will allow to represent their funds, and my application was rejected. They declined to approve me because they knew of my collaboration with Fort Pitt Capital Group, Inc., an excellent active money management firm that we also work with. DFA told me they only appoint advisors who work exclusively with index funds.

I explained that I wanted to give my clients a choice between active money management and low-cost index money management or even a combination of some money with an active manager and some money with an index manager. I failed to convince them and they maintained that the only way I could become a DFA provider was by dropping my association with Fort Pitt Capital Group, Inc., which I was not willing to do. Accordingly, DFA and I went our separate ways.

Years later, I was talking with a colleague from California, and he told me how happy his clients were with DFA. He had a hard time believing that they rejected me as, by this time, I was a fairly well-known IRA expert with three best-selling books. He recommended I contact a friend of his who works for DFA. His friend asked me to send him my books and he would at least consider making an exception to their rule. As it turned out, the DFA contact liked my books enough to approve my firm as a DFA provider.

That was great, but I still faced a dilemma. I am not really qualified—nor do I have the time to become qualified—to provide expert money management services. Then I had another idea. I asked Dimensional Fund Advisors and other industry experts who they believed was the best DFA provider in western Pennsylvania. And that is how I met P. J. DiNuzzo.

I contacted P.J. DiNuzzo, and we came to an arrangement. He and his firm, DiNuzzo Index Advisors, Inc. would handle the money management responsibilities for our clients, and our firm would continue to "run the numbers" and provide advice on Roth IRA conversions, estate planning, Social Security planning, safe withdrawal rates, and other financial strategies. The arrangement is quite similar to the one I have with Fort Pitt Capital Group, Inc. Having these associations with Fort Pitt Capital Group, Inc. and DiNuzzo Index Advisors, Inc. leaves me open to focus on what I and my team love—financial calculations and strategizing—rather than money management.

Lange Financial Group Today

The arrangement described above is also utilized with several other money management firms. The two most important firms, and the ones I will discuss in this book, are Fort Pitt Capital Group, Inc. and DiNuzzo Index Advisors, Inc.

Fort Pitt Capital Group, Inc.

For more than a decade, I've had a working relationship with Fort Pitt Capital Group, Inc., an independent Registered Investment Advisor (RIA) with an impressive track record. Clients who are interested in "active" investment management (as opposed to an index approach) are referred to them for portfolio management. Clients pay an annual management fee of 1% or less, depending on how much is invested. For this fee, clients get the benefit of our tax planning strategies and other financial advice listed above, as well as Fort Pitt Capital Group, Inc.'s money management expertise and services. This collaboration continues to work very well.

Fort Pitt Capital Group, Inc. has their own processes that they go through before they accept an individual as a client. For example, they produce a written investment plan for all prospects. Services for ongoing clients include quarterly performance reporting, periodic investment plan updates and regular meetings to discuss life events or changes that might affect portfolio goals or risk tolerance. The bottom line our firms combine to provide a powerful blend of planning and money management that we believe is unequaled in the Pittsburgh marketplace for active money management.

DiNuzzo Index Advisors, Inc.

P.J. DiNuzzo and his firm, DiNuzzo Index Advisors, Inc. (DIA) is the best financial planning firm I know. They use Dimensional Fund Advisor funds which I believe are the best set of low-cost index funds on the planet. P.J. DiNuzzo has put together a superb team of CFPs, ChFCs, CPAs, MBAs and financial advisors, and they have been serving their clients brilliantly since 1989. P.J. and his team are truly the hardest working group of financial advisors I know.

DIA conducts an extensive financial analysis, including constructing a personal balance sheet and a personal income statement and a lot more. They focus on investment decisions, asset allocation, and diversification.

Their process is in-depth and impressively client focused. It includes two to three meetings before they even agree to manage a client's money. An example of one of the strategies P.J. and his team use with our mutual clients is the **DiNuzzo Money Bucket Stack Analysis**™ (DMBSA). With this strategy, P.J. separates the client's investible assets into different accounts or "buckets" based on the time periods and purposes in which the client anticipates using those assets.

For instance, the client may have an account or "bucket" for current expenses and funds needed within the next two years for necessities, which would be invested conservatively. They may also have a "legacy bucket" with money that they never intend to touch in their lifetimes; this bucket may be invested with a longer horizon. We would likely fund the "legacy bucket" with Roth IRAs, another way our tax strategies and their investment planning combine in an effort to produce the best results for our clients.

Many clients have four or five different "money buckets" with various allocations, allowing them to enjoy a higher level of comfort in the market and to avoid unnecessary risks with funds they are counting on for support and retirement. The ultimate goal: to combine our strategies and to optimize the client's return potential within a risk category that suits their preferences and volatility/loss tolerance.

Then, after both P.J. and his team develop an investment plan, and we develop a comprehensive retirement and estate plan, we help our mutual client implement the plan. But our involvement doesn't end there.

All good plans need to be modified and adjusted due to changing circumstances—portfolios increase and decrease because of market conditions, children marry, grandchildren are born, and divorces happen. That's why clients meet with someone from our firm at least once on an annual basis to update their numbers, and with P.J.'s team on a semi-annual or annual basis to review portfolio performance. The DiNuzzo team also manages a client's portfolio using a "best practice" in the industry called "regular rebalancing."

> **Our clients see the value in our combined services. And as I said, we have a 99% retention rate for all the clients we share.**

Suffice it to say, the arrangement has been a win-win-win. Our clients see the value in our combined services. And as I said, we have a 99% retention rate for all the clients we share. It has been an interesting and rewarding journey, but I am far from complacent.

Our Team

I firmly believe that a lot of our success and client retention has to do with our team. I have an extremely loyal team of accomplished professionals who all chip in to bring our clients the best service possible. They include:

Glenn Venturino, CPA	27 years
Sandy Proto, Office Manager	23 years
Steve Kohman, CPA, CSEP, CSRP	19 years
Donna Master, Bookkeeper	16 years
Daryl Ross, Legal Assistant	15 years
Diane Markel, CPA	15 years
Alice Davis, Client Service Coordinator	12 years
Matt Schwartz, Attorney	12 years
Karen Mathias, Attorney	6 years
Curt Borowski, Office Assistant	5 years
Carol Palmer, Writer	4 years
Amanda Cassady-Schweinsberg, Marketing Director	3 years
Eric Emerson, Internet Marketing Director	1 year
Shirl Trefelner, CPA	1 year
Tanya Chiu, Administrative Assistant	4 mos.

With this outstanding team and the expertise of Fort Pitt Capital Group, Inc. and DiNuzzo Index Advisors, Inc., we have a formidable knowledge base to offer our clients.

Helping People with the Best Strategies

I love helping people live happier lives by helping them cut taxes, save money, and plan for retirement. Of course having more money doesn't necessarily mean you will be happy, but it sure helps. Many times, the feeling of financial security and the absence of worry about money is as important as the money we save clients.

There are all kinds of money saving strategies that professionals who *quantitatively as well as qualitatively* understand IRAs and retirement plans can recommend and implement. In fact, we have helped our clients for years by implementing many of the plans mentioned in this book, saving them tens of thousands of dollars, and sometimes even hundreds of thousands of dollars, on their taxes. If you consider the benefit that our planning has on future generations, some of those savings can be counted in millions of dollars.

We have also developed what we think is the best estate plan on the planet—**Lange's Cascading Beneficiary Plan** which is described in detail in *Retire Secure!* We incorporated that planning in the early nineties before anyone even heard of it. That plan was first published in a peer-reviewed journal in 1998 and has since been featured in *The Wall Street Journal* twice, *Newsweek,* and literally hundreds of other publications.

Over the years, we have drafted thousands of wills that include some variation of **Lange's Cascading Beneficiary Plan**. Unfortunately, as with any estate practice, some of our clients have died. Fortunately, however, our estate plans have performed exactly as we envisioned, providing enormous benefits to the survivors.

So there it is. After many years of trying to figure out what was best for my clients, I inadvertently found out what was best for me and who I truly wanted to be: A trusted advisor who, with my team, supplies the best tax-saving, Roth IRA conversion, Social Security, retirement and estate planning advice that you can find.

The Client Experience: What You Can Expect When You Work With Lange Financial Group, LLC

Running the Numbers

Once a client signs up for the combined services of Lange Financial Group, LLC and one of our investment advisors, they are entitled to multiple "running the numbers" sessions with Lange Financial Group, LLC.

The first session usually concentrates on determining the best tax and financial strategies for the client; when and how much of a Roth IRA conversion would be advisable; how much money can safely be spent in retirement; determining if gifts are appropriate and, if so, what type of gifts, and how much and when.

Frequently, the client asks questions like: "Can I afford a second house and if so, how much house can I afford?"; "Should I take a lump sum or a monthly pension?"; "If I take a pension, what terms should I choose?"; and "What is the best way to address my grandchildren's education?" These "running the numbers" consultation services are provided by my team at Lange Financial Group, LLC.

Our veteran "number runner" is Steve Kohman, a CPA with 30+ years of experience. Steve did the original "number running" for the first two editions of *Retire Secure!,* and has also done the projection analysis for many of our publications and many of our assets-under-management clients. We also have on board Shirl Trefelner, CPA, who did much of the updated analysis for the third edition and also runs the numbers for our clients.

We also run the numbers so that we can calculate how to maximize a client's Social Security benefits (not covered in this book, but something we do in our practice). Karen Mathias, one of our estate attorneys/tax preparers made an extensive study of Social Security strategies, and we have learned to use excellent Social Security optimization software. Obviously, we do the analysis based on the client's individual situation including their earnings record, current age and health, and both current and former marital status.

Sometimes the financial issues that we address can be resolved in one meeting, though more commonly we schedule two meetings to make sure that all of the client's concerns are satisfied. We have run numbers for hundreds of clients, including many engineers, scientists, and CPAs, including two of my old bosses, and many others. These sessions often lead to proactive strategies that significantly improve the financial future of our clients and their descendants.

We prefer to have the client in the room while we are doing our calculations. That way, clients see where we are getting our numbers from, and we can explain why we are making the recommendations that we make. It isn't simply a matter of sticking numbers into a spread sheet; there is a great deal of critical thinking that goes into picking the *right* numbers and hypothesizing realistic scenarios.

Furthermore, clients can pose their own "what if" scenarios on the spot. Our team members have the skill to adapt the numbers for virtually any scenario. If you have a particular concern, we can address it. As with all projections, we have to make some assumptions, but no one can predict with certainty what will happen in the future. Projections that include reasonable assumptions, or even a range of projections with different assumptions, can help determine the best strategies possible.

Another unique feature of the way we run the numbers is that we use multiple professional software programs to arrive at our conclusions, including our customized in-house adaption of an Excel spreadsheet. At this point, there is no one software program that allows users to enter a lot of data, hit the "optimize" button, and have it provide the definitive answer.

The skill and experience of the "number runner" is far more important than the choice of software that we employ. When we think we have the best strategy, we test it – not only with the "number running" software, but also with sophisticated tax preparation software.

We input the data from a client's entire tax return, plus our proposed solution just to make sure there are no surprises. Sometimes we are surprised. For example, sometimes we encounter an unexpected tax increase or decrease that may be a consequence of the alternative minimum tax, the phase-out of itemized deductions, taxes on Social Security and/or Medicare Part B, etc.

> **The beauty of running the numbers and testing them before we implement anything is that adjustments that need to be made are done well in advance. That way *we* catch the issues, *not* the IRS.**

When this happens, we adjust our recommendations. The beauty of running the numbers and testing them before we implement anything is that adjustments that need to be made are done well in advance. That way *we* catch the issues, *not* the IRS.

Finally, when we arrive at what we and the client thinks is the best long-term strategy, we work with DiNuzzo Index Advisors, Inc. or Fort Pitt Capital Group, Inc. (depending on which management style the client is most comfortable with); we also help implement the investment part of that strategy.

Experience and Perspective

Another dimension our firm adds is experience and perspective. We often get involved in areas where the "solution" is obvious to us without running the numbers. Here are some examples where our experience and perspective has made a difference to clients and the way they live their lives.

We've told people:

- You have enough money to retire and the decision to work or retire should be based on what you want to do, not on money. (One professor client commented, "I am not going to quit tomorrow, but I am not going to take any **** from the chair anymore.

- You have enough money to become "snowbirds," and you can enjoy that lifestyle without running out of money.

- You need to think about pre- and post-nuptial agreements for your children (a difficult subject at the best of times and an outsider's perspective can be a great help). Or, if you rejected the pre-nup/post-nup boat because you didn't want to start a family fight, you might want to think about the "I don't want my no good son-in-law to inherit one red cent of my money trust."

- You might want to think about the timing and the best types of gifts for your children and grandchildren.

- You want to move to a state that has a higher tax rate? With your $5 million, you can. You should live where you want to live, even if taxes are higher.

In Conclusion

Business models change over time (as mine has), and I imagine there will be additional changes ahead. I feel like I am well on my way to achieving my dream of being the best and most trusted advisor I can be. I have done this by always putting my client's interests above my own.

Many of the strategies I advocate (maxing out retirement plans, doing Roth IRA conversions, waiting for as long as possible to collect Social Security, using existing assets and retirement plans if appropriate) actually reduce my compensation. But, ultimately that doesn't matter. I want to be on the same side as my clients, not have competing interests!

After all, isn't that what we all want from our service providers? Are the plumbers and mechanics of the world acting in their clients' best interests? I hope so. Would they offer the same advice and charge the same fee to trusting consumers as they would to savvy retired plumbers or mechanics? That's what I do—I give the same quality honest advice to all my clients, no matter who they are.

I run my business the way that I do because I believe that advisors who act with their clients' best interests at heart feel better about what they are doing. Call it karma if you like but, in the long run, trusted advisors acting in their clients' best interests lead happier lives.

When you care and do the right thing for the client it shows. I walk around my community with confidence knowing that I can look everyone I meet in the eye with no fear of being seen as "that lousy advisor who took advantage of me." I have known many of my clients for decades. I have been with them through marriages and divorces, triumphs and tragedies, births and deaths. Being their trusted advisor gives me a profound sense of satisfaction and purpose. We are growing old together, and I really like that.

Thank you for investing the time to read my book. I hope it helps you on the way to becoming who and where you want to be—personally and financially.

Are You Interested in Working with Lange Financial Group, LLC?

To find out if the combination of our services and our "one-stop-shop" business model works for you, I am offering a limited number of FREE initial consultations for those who qualify.* During every initial consultation, we will go over your current estate planning documents, your tax returns, your investments, and discuss your primary goals.

If it seems like we can have a compatible relationship, then we analyze your portfolio using an objective reporting service. As a part of this initial consultation, we will also prepare extensive recommendations designed to help you achieve your ideal retirement and estate plan, and we will supplement our recommendations by providing you with all the books, CDs, DVDs that we think are relevant for your situation (we will even prioritize the most important ones to read, listen to, or watch).

If you like our initial recommendations, then you will meet with appropriate members of our teams to further refine your plan (i.e., our legal or tax team; or P.J. DiNuzzo and his investment team; or a Fort Pitt Capital Group, Inc. representative).

If all the relationships seem compatible, and you feel that the planning is right for you, then we will do the paperwork and you will officially become a client (although you may already feel like one by then)! It can be a lengthy process to become a client, as we aren't the right fit for everyone, and we want to make sure you will enjoy working with us, but the results and relationships are truly worth it. We believe the thorough process is one of the reasons we enjoy a 99% retainage rate with the mutual Lange/DiNuzzo clients.

To inquire about a *Free Second Opinion** please:

Call 1-800-387-1129

or go to www.retirementpittsburgh.com/bookoffer

* FREE Second Opinion meetings are reserved for those with a minimum of $500,000 in investible assets.